# THE MEASUREMENT OF CAPITAL

# THE MEASUREMENT OF CAPITAL

## Theory and Practice

Edited by

K. D. Patterson and Kerry Schott

*First published 1979 by*
THE MACMILLAN PRESS LTD
*London and Basingstoke*
*Associated companies in Delhi*
*Dublin Hong Kong Johannesburg Lagos*
*Melbourne New York Singapore Tokyo*

*Typeset in Great Britain by*
PREFACE LTD
*Salisbury, Wilts*
*and printed in Great Britain by*
*Billing & Sons Limited*
*Guildford, London and Worcester*

**British Library Cataloguing in Publication Data**

The measurement of capital
1. Capital – Measurement
I. Patterson, K D    II. Schott, Kerry
332′.041    HB501

ISBN 0-333-24637-3

# Contents

# List of Figures

# List of Tables

# Acknowledgements

The Conference on Capital Measurement held at Southampton University in the summer of 1976 was planned and organised by David Heathfield. His efforts along with those of the contributors have made this volume possible. The index was cheerfully compiled by John Bone, and Anne Batchelor and Fiona Savory provided secretarial expertise that proved essential in getting the final manuscript together. To all these people, and other colleagues who advised, we give our thanks.

K.D.P.
K.E.S.

# Notes on the Contributors

*I. F. Pearce* is Professor of Economic Theory at the University of Southampton.

*Ian Steedman* is Professor of Economics at the University of Manchester.

*John Craven* is Senior Lecturer in Economics at the University of Kent at Canterbury.

*Tom Griffin* is a statistician at the Central Statistical Office.

*A. G. Armstrong* is Senior Lecturer in Economics at the University of Bristol.

*D. E. L. Thomas* is Lecturer in Economics at the University College, Swansea.

*E. R. Chang* is Senior Lecturer in Econometrics at the University of Southampton.

*K. Hilton* is Professor of Financial and Managerial Control at the University of Southampton.

*H. A. Yaseen* is Lecturer in Accountancy at the University of Zagazig, Egypt.

*William Peterson* is a Research Officer in the Department of Applied Economics at the University of Cambridge.

*David F. Heathfield* is Senior Lecturer in Economics at the University of Southampton.

*Derek L. Bosworth* is Lecturer in Economics at the University of Loughborough.

*K. D. Patterson* is Lecturer in Economics at the University of Reading.

*Kerry Schott* is Lecturer in Economics at University College, London.

# Introduction

Nine of the papers presented here originate from a conference on the measurement of capital held at the University of Southampton in the summer of 1976. These papers were subsequently revised for publication in this volume. Two further papers, one by Alan Armstrong and the other by William Peterson (on total factor productivity), which are germane to the conference theme but were not available at the time, are also included. The conference was convened and organised by David Heathfield whose chief concern was to promote discussion between theorists, statisticians and applied economists. This aim seems particularly relevant in the case of capital measurement. Here we have all theorists agreed that an aggregate measure of the stock of physical assets is impossible except under extremely stringent conditions[1]. In addition the theorists have reached a consensus that the particular aggregation conditions required for the specification of capital within an aggregate production function will not be met in reality; any parameter estimates based on such an exercise may be misleading except under certain circumstances. Furthermore, the measure of capital usually used in this function is not strictly independent of prices and distribution[2]. Meanwhile, back at the Central Statistical Office, and elsewhere, statisticians provide measures of something they call capital stock and applied economists continue to use these aggregate measures in econometric models based on either strict neoclassical parables about aggregate production functions or stories of another ilk.

One of the reasons for this apparent conflict between theory and practice arises because of the way applied economists must go about their work. As John Helliwell explains it:

> The primary issue in applied econometrics involves decisions about what to assume and what to estimate . . . The more complete the set of prior assumptions, the less is left to be estimated from the data sample. In terms of the realism of the final equation, there may be either gains or losses from the use of additional prior assumptions. The gains may come because the assumptions reduce the number of parameters to be estimated. Since relevant aggregate data samples are inevitably few and small, any reduction in the number of coefficients to estimate increases

the likely accuracy of estimation. In addition, the use of a more *a priori* information also increases the precision of the estimating equation, as long as the prior information is correct. On the other hand, if the additional restrictions used are not correct, then the resulting equation may be less accurate in terms of either structure or prediction[3].

Hence, at least to some economists, the important question is whether the capital measure used in regression equations represents a gain or a loss in terms of the accuracy of the parameters that are estimated. A loss in accuracy comes from the fact that the stringent conditions required for a rigorous aggregate capital measure are violated. But is this loss in accuracy quantitatively important? Judging from current practice many economists consider that the gains in the use of a capital stock measure outweigh the loss. This viewpoint, which will accept some inaccuracy in the data, should also consider the use of an appropriate econometric framework, for example, the errors in variables or unobservable variables approach.

Even more fundamental than this judgment, however, is the prior choice of model specification and, in particular, whether capital can be regarded as a factor of production, which, at least for the purposes of empirical work, is independent of prices and distribution. If independence is incorrectly assumed do the estimated parameters of the model tell us anything about the way the economic world really works or are these parameter estimates simply nonsense?

At the moment most empirical work which investigates the determinants of investment, factor productivity and growth, does rest implicitly on the assumption that capital can be measured independently of prices and distribution so this latter question is certainly important.

Applied economists choose their model specification on the basis of some theoretical framework which enables them to impose restrictions and thus reduce the parameters to be estimated. The art of econometric work therefore lies in choosing those restrictions which will give precise estimates which are not misleading and they look to economic theory to provide such restrictions. This demand upon theory is difficult and challenging and is not always met.

Theorists tend to tackle their work by abstracting away from certain problems that they do not wish to consider at that moment. Thus the problem of measuring capital can simply be solved by assuming that all the conditions needed for aggregation are upheld. Thus, we have models that treat capital as jelly, Meccano sets or treacle and such capital is theoretically measurable and independent of prices.

This research strategy can often be useful as it turns attention to other aspects of the theoretical model but it can also be dangerously seductive.

Insufficient attention may be paid to the abstractions that have been made and in addition it is difficult to assess how much the results that emerge are useful in the real world.

General equilibrium models, based on different abstractions, avoid the assumption of independence between capital and prices and distribution but the actual estimation of such systems requires some level of aggregation to make the task manageable. What degree of model aggregation is it best to work with and how much do the assumptions needed for general equilibrium specifications matter? It is obvious that whatever model is chosen assumptions will be violated at some point. How quantitatively important will this turn out to be? These issues are important and immediate ones for all economists if only for the obvious reason that policy decisions are derived from economic models (estimated or otherwise) and these policy decisions affect masses of quite innocent bystanders.

An example of the different approaches of theorists and practitioners is provided by Solow. Wearing his theorist hat he has described in Solow (1956) the strict conditions which allow the aggregation of heterogeneous capital goods into a single number. On the other hand, in his empirical hat, he asks us (Solow, 1957) to 'suspend disbelief' and uses an aggregate capital measure. The time has indeed come, as Fisher (1969) suggests, for the suspension of disbelief to stop while we attempt to assess the consequences of our assumptions. Fisher's (1971) paper is a step in this right direction and shows how difficult the task will be. The questions we must proceed to answer are how much does it matter empirically to assume measures of aggregate capital, and indeed, other inputs and outputs, when we know such measures do not strictly exist? What aggregate theoretical specifications might serve best at the empirical level and under what conditions?

A preliminary step in these directions requires some knowledge of what the theorists, statisticians and econometricians are all doing. The papers presented here are in some sense a sample of work from the theoretical and practical worlds of capital measurement. Each paper can stand on its own merits as a piece of independent research but taken together they illustrate the need for more communication between theorists and practitioners. If this volume stimulates some thoughts and ideas which bring theory and practice closer together, it will have achieved its purpose.

## 1 DIFFERENT CONCEPTS OF CAPITAL

The particular concept of capital which is used in both theory and practice depends on what is being done with it. The first paper, by Ivor Pearce, postulates a method of measuring money capital along classical lines and within a general equilibrium context. This concept of capital is not the most familiar one, although John Hicks (1974) suggests it is coming back into favour. We attempt an explanation of money capital here as an aid in understanding the Pearce paper. The way the classical economists (Smith, Marx, Jevons, Bohm-Bawerk and Taussig for example) regarded capital was as a fund of money (or financial) capital which enabled some process of production to occur. Wage labour was employed on land to produce output and this production process was made possible by the provision of a fund of money capital. Labour inputs were necessarily paid wages before the revenue from sales was realised. Thus money capital was needed because production took time. Physical equipment was an asset and its value duly appeared on the asset side of the entrepreneur's balance sheet; money capital appeared on the liability side of the balance sheet and was a fund that was embodied in all assets. An aggregate measure of money capital for the whole economy was obtained by consolidating all the individual balance sheets of the single businesses. In the consolidation the liabilities of one entrepreneur would cancel against the assets of another. Thus when all debts and paper claims had been cancelled we would be left with the total value of actual goods (and external claims) on the assets side and a stock of money capital on the liabilities side.

This approach is easily managed if all entrepreneurs are simply merchants who use virtually no land and virtually no physical equipment. Their real assets are mainly stocks of finished goods which are valued at prevailing prices. If entrepreneurs are farmers the rent paid on land must be deducted from gross profit to obtain net profit and then the classical economists argued that the rate of net profit on the money capital would tend to be equalised by competition. If entrepreneurs own machines or fixed capital the big problem arises as to how this asset is to be valued. Physical equipment, unlike land, does not continue indefinitely but its use is typically longer than the accounting period. Thus, only some proportion of the cost of physical capital must be offset against the value of sales in any given accountancy period. The choice of the proportion to offset is usually some fairly conservative rule of thumb chosen by accountants with an eye on legal tax commitments and the rate of price changes. As the importance of physical equipment in entrepreneur's balance sheets increased after the Industrial Revolution many economists shifted away from this valuation problem and began to deal with measures of physical capital which were not value measures but volume measures. In the latter sense physical equipment is valued at its replacement cost and not in terms of its contribution to the value of output.

In returning to the classical procedure Ivor Pearce begins with company balance sheets and his main focus of attention is on the process of production and the time elements involved in such a process. Money capital is required because products cannot be made and sold instantaneously. It is defined as money obtained from shareholders plus profit, less the amount of profit distributed to shareholders. The main idea is that companies wish to keep the money raised from shareholders down to some minimum amount required for production. At the same time the money capital requirement fluctuates because input costs can occur at discrete and irregular intervals. Companies attempt, however, to keep their money capital requirement steady on average. This behaviour is crucial to Ivor Pearce's argument and in the real world it is analagous to the attention companies pay to their cash flows. Large fluctuations in these can easily cause bankruptcy. The argument is discussed in some length in the appendix to the Pearce paper and it is pointed out that there is only one profit rate consistent with the aim of maintaining a steady money capital requirement. Thus, it is postulated that entrepreneurs choose this profit rate. This argument is important.

Now, in a stationary state this money capital requirement must hold along with a set of technically given production functions and a set of equilibrium conditions defining the equality of total revenue and total cost. Various behavioural equations are then added to complete the general equilibrium system. Total cost is minimised subject to the prices of inputs; input prices are determined by all total quantities and aggregate income; and finally rates of return on all inputs are equalised. This fully defines the whole system in a stationary state. In addition, given the rate of profit consistent with a steady money capital requirement over time, the stock of plant and equipment can be valued using its known original cost and the chosen profit rate. It is obvious in this system that the value of physical capital is not independent of the profit rate. Further, it is clear that once any variable changes the effects will flow throughout the whole model. This development of the classical ideas within a general equilibrium context is a stimulating contribution although it does not escape from various theoretical criticisms which have been levelled at the neoclassical general equilibrium approach. These are discussed in section 2.

The concept of capital as a stock of physical assets is more common although we have already pointed out that an aggregate measure of it is not strictly possible in reality. However, in empirical work a volume measure of aggregate capital is frequently used where physical capital is valued at replacement cost. This measure is then often used as a proxy for physical capital services in a production function. Samuelson (1962) noted the difference in approach between theorists and practitioners and attempted to show that a construct, which he labelled the surrogate production function, could provide some rationalistation for the validity of the use of neoclassical parables in empirical work. If the actual capital measure used in practice behaved 'as if' it were his surrogate capital measure and if the aggregate production function specified behaved 'as if' it were his surrogate function then the practitioners could be saved from embarrassment by the theorists and in particular from those theorists in Cambridge, England who were staging a vehement protest[4].

It turns out, however, that the actual assumptions required for the 'as if' relations to hold are extremely restrictive and this gets us back to the problem of worrying about how much it matters to violate the assumptions. Samuelson himself listed various conditions necessary for the surrogate capital measure and the surrogate production function to hold. A necessary condition is that each type of machine or capital employs the same amount of labour whether it is used in making consumer goods or in making machines of the same kind. This implies that the wage rate and the interest rate must be related by a linear function and that relative prices are constant for all combinations of the wage rate and the interest rate[5].

This condition is obviously very restrictive and in his paper Ian Steedman points out a further restrictive requirement. The surrogate capital measure will hold only when the depreciation rate used to calculate the value of old capital goods is independent of the wage rate and of the interest rate or when capital goods can be expected to last for ever. We know that physical assets do not last forever and Sraffa (1960) has shown that the value of old capital goods is not independent of the wage rate and the interest rate[6]. Thus, it is apparent that the surrogate construct is not going to save the practitioners from embarrassment. Indeed, work by Feldstein and Foot (1971), Eisner (1972), Feldstein and Rothschild (1974), and Griffin this volume, suggests that the replacement proportion of gross investment is large (and hence quantitatively important) and that the depreciation rate cannot be assumed to be exponential, and hence independent of price effects, without causing the empirical parameter estimates to be seriously biased. The surrogate measure of capital and its related production function are not the required answer to our problems because the required 'as if' assumptions are very restrictive and when these are violated the empirical results are likely to be substantially biased, if not meaningless.

This situation is all good cause for scholarly headaches but not a lot of help if we want to explain such matters as the determinants of investment, economic growth and relative factor shares. In an attempt to overcome these difficulties various theoretical approaches have been explored.

## 2 CURRENT THEORETICAL APPROACHES

To begin with, it seemed sensible to restrain analysis to an apparently easy world where we have a steady state[7]. One tool which has proved theoretically popular in this imaginary world is the price efficiency curve or the factor price frontier. This curve, which is not necessarily linear, as in Samuelson's (1962) paper, relates the wage rate, $w$, to the profit rate, $r$, for some particular technique of production. Once the price efficiency curve for a technique is permitted to be non-linear reswitching between different techniques becomes possible. The problems this poses for capital theory and measurement are by now well known and are reviewed in Harcourt (1972). The price efficiency curve has a dual relation, the quantity efficiency curve, which relates the consumption output per unit of labour, $h$, to the growth rate, $g$. If both the price and quantity efficiency curve exist (which is not necessarily true) they are coincident.

John Craven's contribution carefully explains the conditions under which these price and quantity efficiency curves exist and shows how such curves can be used both to provide a measure of capital intensity and an explanation of the distribution of income between capital and labour measured either in market prices or in labour value terms. The dual nature of the price and quantity efficiency curves is used in obtaining these results. If the efficiency curves exist within certain ranges it also follows that steady state competitive equilibria exist and that the Marxian rate of exploitation is positive if the profit rate is positive.

Work is also in progress on the extension of general neoclassical and Keynesian equilibrium models where economic variables are fundamentally interdependent and mutually determining. Values, market prices and distributive shares are determined simultaneously. This approach, however, raises many problems and various issues of contention can be singled out. These issues are often based on disagreements about the microeconomic behaviour underlying the general equilibrium model. First, there is concern over the extent to which orthodox neoclassical economics can explain the distribution of income independently of political and social power and the nature of existing institutions. Second, the behaviour of general equilibrium models depends critically on the time period in which they are specified to be operating. If the model is in equilibrium is it permanent or temporary? Has there been sufficient time for markets to clear or not? Third, are the equalities implied in general equilibrium simply tautological? In any case perfect capital markets are required for the equality of the interest rate, the rate of return on investment and the rate of time preference, and in the real world perfect future markets (let alone perfect present markets) do not exist. Fourth, there is the tricky matter of how technology should be represented, and finally the way the model adjusts when it is in disequilibrium is crucial[8].

It is thus clear that the general equilibrium model based on orthodox theory is not without problems and particularly once it departs from the steady state. There are, of course, alternative theories based, for example, on the work of Kaldor and Kalecki but these approaches have also been criticised[9]. Prices in these types of models are often determined by a cost mark-up equation which it is suggested does not always explain actual pricing behaviour. Another main behavioural element assumes that the propensity to save out of profits is greater than the propensity to save out of wages and this crucial assumption may not always hold.

Exploring the empirical results of these various models requires aggregate measures of the relevant economic variables, including capital. The particular measure of capital used clearly depends on the task in hand and while this may seem self-evident few textbooks in the area of capital or growth theory relate their concepts to the available statistics and their limitations. Hicks, once again, throws a great deal of light on this aspect of the relationship between theory and practice, e.g. Hicks (1973); and there is a good discussion of some of the problems in Hacche (1979). We turn now to a consideration of the various capital measures developed by the statisticians.

## 3 MEASURES OF CAPITAL

The concepts of capital in economic theory are intimately related, in one way or another, to the idea of income creation. This is so whether one adopts, to use the terms suggested in Hicks (1974), the 'Fundists' or value, or 'Materialists' or volume, view of capital. This distinction is, as we noted in introducing the paper by Ivor Pearce, related to the two sides of a balance sheet; the 'Fundists' concentrating on the liabilities side and the 'Materialists' on the tangible part of the assets side. Thus the ability to create income may alternatively be viewed as embodied in a fund of money capital or in a bundle of assets. As the idea of a balance sheet may be extended from the firm to the industry, then to the sector and nation a fairly comprehensive set of statistics would be demanded for economic analysis. To accord with the idea of income creation these statistics should encompass tangible and intangible assets whether socially or privately owned and there should be a consistent set of national income accounts.

Although the most comprehensive statistical coverage exists for the 'Materialists' view of capital there have been several recent developments of interest. In the United States, Kendrick (1976) has provided estimates of total investment and capital stocks; these estimates cover human, non-human, tangible, and intangible assets, and he has provided a consistent set of estimates of national and sector incomes. It is only with such a set of estimates that we will be able to consider such questions as the importance of total capital growth in explaining growth in output.

In the United Kingdom there have been some important developments by the CSO in compiling national and sectoral balance sheets. Details of these are given in *Statistical News* (HMSO, 1976), *Economic Trends* (1978) and Bank of England (1978). An important spur to the development of this work was the setting up of a Royal Commission on the Distribution of Income and Wealth which, clearly, would be severely hampered without, at the least, estimates of the personal sector balance sheet. This work by the CSO and other statistical agencies will considerably extend the available statistics, and thus the scope for economic analysis particularly along the lines suggested by Ivor Pearce. Earlier work by Revell (1967) and Roe (1971) is also of interest.

As might be expected, the distinction between the two views of capital is reflected in the debate on the appropriate revaluation of tangible assets for an inflation-adjusted company sector balance sheet. The distinction is, essentially, between the revaluation of assets based either on their (written down) replacement cost or on the potential stream of earnings to be derived from them. That is, between current cost accounting, CCA and constant purchasing power valuation, CPP; for CCA price indices are required for a fairly complete disaggregation of the assets, e.g. CSO (1977), whereas for CPP a general price index is required; revaluation by these alternative methods is therefore likely to lead to different results. For a comparison of these approaches see Baxter (1977).

## ESTIMATES OF FIXED TANGIBLE ASSETS

The papers in this volume by Armstrong and Thomas present estimates of tangible assets not available in the official statistics; and Griffin, of the CSO, considers the appropriate use of the statistics of the capital stock. As estimates of the stocks of tangible assets have been produced primarily for neoclassical analysis it may be as well to consider the underlying conceptual framework.

According to the neoclassical theory of capital, goods designated as capital are defined with respect to particular production processes. A capital good, in this sense, is one which has successive uses. Thus, whether a particular item is capital will depend crucially on the nature of the blueprint relating inputs to outputs. A versatile product, such as timber, may, in one process of production, be completely embodied or, in another, it may survive to provide further service.

This conceptual framework suggests that the measure of capital to be used in analyses of production and productivity growth should:

(i) be measured with reference to the use of various commodities and not on the basis of the commodities themselves (for example, not all timber is raw material);
(ii) include all assets which contribute to the gross product; and
(iii) the measure should relate to 'periods of production' and not accounting time periods.

The distinction in (i) is recognised by the CSO and other statistical agencies in that the two main methods of collecting the data are respectively: (a) expenditure based, (b) commodity flow. (See, e.g. Maurice (1968), p. 367.)

In practice the most comprehensive data coverage exists for *tangible reproducible* assets of the company sector, though some attention is now being given to estimates of non-reproducible and intangible assets in the construction of sectoral and national balance sheets, and there are unofficial estimates of the stock of human capital. (See Chang, Hilton and Yaseen in this volume.)

A distinction of the third kind is, in practice, too difficult to make and in most systems of national accounts capital goods are defined as such if their lifetime of use exceeds a given time period usually related to accounting conventions.

The United Nations, in its *System of National Accounts* (SNA, 1968), suggests that this time period should, in general, be one year. This practice however, is not, uniform across nations which suggests that a great deal of care should be taken in making international comparisons using capital stocks which purport to measure the same concept.

Some examples may serve to illustrate the pitfalls awaiting such comparisons. In the Swedish system of accounts a three year durability criteria is adopted for most capital goods, whereas the SNA guideling is adhered to in the United Kingdom. In the West German accounts residential buildings are fully allocated to the 'enterprise' sector, no matter whether the owner is a corporate enterprise, a private person or a public agency (Lutzel 1976, p. 70); and livestock, for example breeding stocks and dairy cattle (which generally have a life exceeding one year), is allocated to the stock of inventories, contrary to the SNA guidelines (SNA 1968 p. 112).

Primed with the task of providing a measure, or measures, of the capital stock for use in analyses of production the statisticians have typically used one or a combination of three main methods:

(i) The perpetual inventory method (PIM);
(ii) Census, usually partial when it may be referred to as a survey, of assets;
(iii) Insurance values.
(One may add a fourth method, that of proxies, which has been suggested and used by economists, see, for example, Heathfield and Bosworth in this volume.)

These are ordered in terms of their present day importance. The perpetual inventory method is used in most western countries, perhaps in combination with surveys to provide benchmarks. Survey methods are quite often used in less developed countries as the main requirement of the perpetual inventory method, for a long and consistent series of gross investment, is unlikely to be met.

Although the third method mentioned above is now little used it has played an important part in the development of statistics on the capital stock; see Barna (1959). Ward (1976A) gives a comprehensive survey of the methods used in the OECD countries; and (Ward 1976) indicates some of the problems facing less developed countries.

As the perpetual inventory method is widely used we may concentrate here on some of the problems involved in its application. Ward (1976A), Hibbert *et al.* (1977), Griffin (1975) and in this volume also discuss some of the issues. The method is actually quite simple; its basis is the following identity:

$$K_t^G = K_{t-1}^G + I_t^G - R_t$$
$$= \sum_{i=0}^{m} (I_{t-i}^G - R_{t-i}) + K_{t-i-1} \qquad \text{(i)}$$

when $m = L, K_{t-L-1} = 0$

where $K_t^G$: the gross capital stock
$I_t^G$: gross investment
$R_t$: retired or scrapped assets in period $t$
$L$: length of life of the longest-lived asset.

Substituting $C_t$ and $R_t$, where $C_t$ is capital consumption (depreciation), would give net capital stock. We can see from (i) that unless a benchmark estimate is available gross investment is cumulated from as far back as the life of the longest-lived asset and, as in the case of buildings, data may be required for 80 or more years. (Thomas discusses some of the ways of estimating capital stocks when data is available only from $m$ periods where $m$ is less than $L$). It is also necessary to obtain a set of price deflators consistent with the classification of assets in the gross investment series[10].

A likely source of error or approximation is usually involved in the estimate of retired or scrapped assets If asset lives are constant then:

$$R_t = I^G_{t-\ell}$$

for each class of asset distinguished. Then retirements in year $t$ are just gross investment $\ell$ years ago. Until recently this was the assumption used by the CSO based on work by Redfern (1955) in estimating asset lives. However, asset lives are not constant and are likely to be related to intensity of use which itself will vary with the phase of the cycle; asset lives are more likely to be choice variables than parameters to economic agents; on the utilisation rate as a choice variable see Taubman and Wilkinson (1970). Unfortunately, there is not much empirical work to hand on this subject. Bacon and Eltis (NEDO; 1974) have examined the evidence for machine tools and attention is now being paid to the scrapping rates for vehicles, Parks (1977), Groes (1976).

The official estimates of retired assets are not always accepted; for example, Armstrong in this volume, uses data on newly-licensed vehicles to determine retirements in his estimates of vehicles for the disaggregated manufacturing sector.

There have recently been changes to the CSO practice which are described in Griffin (1975). Assets are now retired uniformly over the mean life $l \pm s$ years, where $s$ is determined as a percentage of the assumed mean life. This avoids the bunching or echo effect which was a consequence of the fixed life assumption.

Griffin's paper, in this volume, is a timely reminder to think carefully about the use to which the official statistics should be put For example, he suggests that the gross stock is superior to the net stock in studies of the potential rates of gross output To understand the reason for this we have to look at official estimates of capital consumption Following the SNA guidelines, capital consumption is calculated on a straight line basis with reference to the expected lifetime of an asset. Thus, if an asset is assumed to last $l$ years the services assumed to be obtainable decline (or expire) at the rate of $1/\ell$ per year[11]. Clearly this may be an extreme estimate of the decline in the ability of the asset to contribute to output.

Griffin illustrates the distinction between the assumed pattern of retirements and the straight line depreciation assumption with the aid of some simple numerical examples and Groes (1976) and Ward (1976A) consider a number of alternative 'survival' and retirement functions.

If one is willing to suspend disbelief and estimate an aggregate production function a considerable degree of disaggregation across assets would seem desirable; and it should be the services of these asset stocks and not the stocks which are the explanatory variables[12]. Consider two assets each costing the same but with one asset very short lived, say three years, and the other lasting a lot longer, say 20 years, then if their contribution to output is measured by the stock it would seem unlikely that substitutability is such that each would make an equal contribution. This consideration suggest that assets should be aggregated only if they are considered perfect substitutes in the provision of their services. If this is not the case and, for example, buildings, plant and machinery, and vehicles are aggregated, by units of money measuring constant replacement costs, and used in a production function then the resulting coefficient estimates are unlikely to make sense. Griffin provides more discussion of this issue, and the Heathfield and Bosworth papers examine the possibility of measuring the input to the production process by proxy measures, primarily based on estimates of fuel inputs, which have a flow dimension.

Thomas, in a paper which is a *tour de force* of the practical problems facing the statistician, presents estimates of the capital stock of Welsh manufacturing disaggregated by buildings, and plant and machinery. His paper is both salutary and impressive. He confronts many problems not least of which is that to use the perpetual inventory method data is required on gross investment for the assumed lives of the assets; where the data run is too short for this proviso to be satisfied the statistician has to estimate the capital stock in existence at the beginning of the period for which he has data on gross investment. It is to be hoped that, despite the inevitable simplifying assumptions, these estimates will form the basis of studies evaluating the performance of regional economies.

The value of data disaggregated either by region or industry, or both is illustrated by the complementary studies of Armstrong and Peterson (on factor productivity). Armstrong updates and considerably extends data which, in an earlier version, provided the basis for Peterson's disaggregated study which extends the seminal work of Solow (1957) and Jorgenson and Griliches (1967). The data made available here relates to a disaggregation of manufacturing industry into 23 groups. It has been used by Panić (1978), who studied capital utilisation in manufacturing industry, and other researchers should find it of great value.

## 4 APPLICATIONS

The particular measure of capital used in applied work can affect parameter estimates in a startling way. Capital measures used in early models which attempted to explain the determinants of economic growth caused a practical worry when it appeared, contrary to *a priori* notions, that capital growth played only a minor role in explaining total economic growth. An early paper by Solow (1957) illustrates the problem. The existence of an aggregate production function is assumed along with neutral disembodied technical progress which is represented by a residual factor. The growth in output per worker then equals the rate of growth of technical progress plus the rate of growth of capital per worker times the relative share of capital. Estimates of the contributions to economic growth suggested that technical progress accounted for up to 90 per cent of growth and that the effect on growth of capital deepening was therefore quite small.

One of the reasons suggested for this surprising result was that the residual factor was not really a measure of technical progress but more a measure of our ignorance. It represented all factors omitted from the production function as well as the measurement errors included in the factors that were represented. The factors that may have been omitted included embodied technical progress, learning and education. Education, which contributes to human capital stock, was subsequently incorporated in a study of economic growth by Bowman (1964) and Denison (1962) who found that the contribution of education to growth was about 25 per cent.

The particular methods and measures used in this work are subject to debate and are reviewed in Kennedy and Thirlwall (1972). Nevertheless it is unquestionably true that human capital is an important element in the total capital stock. Empirical work on the importance of human capital in British growth has been hampered by lack of data and the paper in this volume by Chang, Hilton and Yaseen gives an estimate of the stock of human capital in the United Kingdom. They suggest that the value of human capital is now quantitatively as large as the value of non-human capital which is a similar type of finding to that of Kendrick (1971) using United States data. Chang, Hilton and Yaseen discuss two alternative approaches that can be used in arriving at the estimates of human capital stock and ultimately use a cost approach in their work. They are careful to spell out the steps they make in arriving at their conclusions and whatever degree of scepticism we may share with them about the accuracy of their final measure the inherent problems that are faced in getting them are quite apparent.

Jorgenson and Griliches (1967) turned their attention to Solow's

(1957) surprising results and argued that the capital concept used was not properly measured. They advanced alternative measures of the services of inputs, including capital services, and found in their well-known analysis of factor productivity that the growth in factor inputs, now appropriately measured, accounted for 96.7 per cent of the growth of final output. Many studies have been done on factor productivity and the literature is surveyed by Nadiri (1970, 1972). This body of work has been criticised by Rymes (1971) who points out that capital is treated as a primary input and hence any efficiency change in the method of production of capital goods can be taken into account only by corrections for quality changes. These quality change corrections, if attempted at all, are also likely to underestimate the rate and contribution of technical progress because the full effects of interdependence between industries are ignored. Rymes proposes that a Harrodian measure of capital should be used where capital is an intermediate product and is the sum of dated labour, cumulated using the current profit rate that would be required to reproduce the existing stock of plant using currently available technology.

William Peterson in his factor productivity study uses disaggregated UK data for 35 industries and compares the factor productivity results that emerge from the neoclassical approach of Jorgenson and Griliches with the Harrodian approach. This paper is a fine piece of work and it demonstrates that the Harrodian approach gives higher estimates of the growth in total factor productivity as one would expect. More importantly, it enables those industries to be identified which are suffering from technical stagnation or where small improvements in productivity would lead to substantial gains for the economy because of industrial interdependence. These Harrodian measures appear to be more useful than the neoclassical measures of total factor productivity because each industry's contribution to the rate of technical advance of the whole economy is apparent and the interdependence between industries is not ignored. Capital should not be treated as a primary input on an equal footing with labour when total factor productivity and the contribution of technical advance are being assessed.

As we have already pointed out, and as Griliches (1963) has argued, the 'best' definition of the stock of capital depends on the use which will be made of the numbers. In production relations the capital stock measure ought to be defined in terms of capital services provided per time period and these units need to be homogenous with respect to marginal productivity and the possible degree of factor substitution. The stringent conditions required for the aggregation of fixed inputs are discussed in Gorman (1968).

It is often assumed that the existing stock of capital is fully utilised and this convenient simplification avoids the need to consider questions about optimal productive capacity for the capital stock. However, such an assumption can be misleading as Jorgenson and Griliches (1967) have shown. One of the modifications they made in redefining the capital measure within their model was to adjust the stock of capital equipment to take account of relative utilisation rates over time and it turned out that the effect of this adjustment was significant. They assumed that each type of equipment was used at the same utilisation rate but that the uniform rate varied over time. As a measure of relative utilisation they used data for the relative utilisation of power and these fuel proxy variables are now frequently used as measures of capital utilisation.

One advantage of such a procedure is that capital services can, at least conceptually, be treated as comparable to labour services; the stock of capital and the number of persons employed are stock inputs and the rate of utilisation of the capital stock corresponds to the number of hours worked per person. In the study by David Heathfield the relations between output, capital and labour are explored when capital utilisation is explicitly allowed for. He uses electricity consumption data to derive a measure for capital utilisation and not surprisingly finds that the introduction of capital utilisation into production function estimates alters the implied elasticities. He also argues that the usual assumption of a uniform rate of utilisation across machines of all types and vintages may not be unreasonable.

The paper by Derek Bosworth complements the Heathfield work on capital utilisation. Bosworth argues that the use of fuel proxies for utilisation rate measures is a very suspect procedure. Different types of fuels are used and must all be considered. Furthermore, aggregating these different fuels together requires weights that should reflect both the marginal productivity of the particular type of capital as well as the technical relation between the capital and the fuel consumed. It certainly seems that fuel proxy measures of capital utilisation should be treated with some scepticism.

A common requirement in the estimation of investment functions is that of data on the capital stock or, more correctly, capital services. This results, usually, from the specification that firms are adjusting the services to be derived from the actual capital stock to a desired level. In the second of the papers by Peterson factor demand functions are estimated which do not call for data on capital services. He argues that we have data on the flow of intermediate inputs but not, without unrealistic simplifying assumptions, on the services yielded by the stock of capital goods.

Peterson's approach is to use the hypothesis of cost minimisation to derive a system of input demand equations; in so doing he makes explicit the restrictions imposed by this particular hypothesis and the additional restrictions imposed if the production function is assumed to be homothetic. Within such a framework various hypotheses, for example about substitution possibilities and the separability of technology, may be tested for conformity with the data. It seems appropriate to end the volume with this paper which combines an awareness of data limitations with the derivation of hypotheses embodying restrictions which are subsequently tested.

## NOTES

1 The aggregation of other factors of production and output also requires stringent assumptions. The theory of aggregation is surveyed by Green (1964). The particular problem of the capital aggregate is dealt with extensively in the literature. For example see Solow (1956), Gorman (1968), Fisher (1965).
2 This area of the literature is surveyed by Harcourt (1969, 1972). The works of Robinson (1953–54), Champernowne (1953–54) and Sraffa (1960) are most important.
3 Helliwell (1976), p. 13.
4 Harcourt (1969, 1972) writes the debate up in terms of a prize fight. His surveys are a valuable summary of this field.
5 Kregel (1976), Chapter 3.
6 Sraffa (1960) also suggested that for an industry producing a single product the substitution of capital for labour assumed to result from a lower rate of interest could just as easily occur when the interest rate was higher. Robinson (1956) also developed a similar result for the economy as a whole but considered it a 'curiosum'. Levhari (1965) attempted to show that the result did not hold for the economy as a whole but his results have been proved incorrect by four writers in a symposium reported in the *Quarterly Journal of Economics*, November 1966.
7 On the concept of the steady state in growth theory see Hahn (1971).
8 These matters are dealt with in more depth in Brown, Sato and Zarembka (eds.) (1976). See also Hahn (1977).
9 A recent example of a Kaleckian model is Asimakopulos (1977).
10 Some of the difficulties involved in obtaining appropriate price deflators are discussed in more detail in Griffin's paper, and in Hibbert *et al.* (1977).
11 An alternative to straight line depreciation, that of declining balance, may well be applied to the official estimates of the stock of consumer durables.
12 Even this statement is a considerable simplification of what is involved; for a thorough discussion of the time element which has been so

abused in a lot of the literature on production functions see Georgescu-Roegen (1971).

## REFERENCES


Armstrong, A. G. (1974), *Structural Change in the British Economy 1948–1968* vol. 12, in Stone, R. (ed.), *A Programme for Growth* (London: Chapman and Hall).

Arrow, K. J., Chenery, H. B., Minhas, B. S. and Solow, R. M., (1961), 'Capital-Labour Substitution and Economic Efficiency', *Review of Economics and Statistics*, vol. 43.

Asimakopulos, A. (1977). 'Profits and Investment: a Kaleckian Approach', in G. C. Harcourt (ed.), *The Microeconomic Foundations of Macro-economics* (London: Macmillan).

Bank of England (1978), *Statistics Users Conference on Financial Statistics* (London: Bank of England).

Barna, T. (1959), 'Alternative Methods of Measuring Capital', in Goldsmith, R. and Saunders, C. (eds.), *Income and Wealth*, Series VIII (London: Bowes and Bowes).

Barna, T. (1957), 'The Replacement Cost of Fixed Assets – British Manufacturing Industry in 1955', *Journal of the Royal Statistical Society*, series A, vol. 120.

Baxter, W. T. (1977), 'Accountants and Inflation', *Lloyds Bank Review*, October no. 126.

Bliss, C. J. (1975), *Capital Theory and the Distribution of Income* (Amsterdam: North Holland).

Bowman, M. J. (1964), 'Shultz, Denison and the Contribution of "Eds" to National Income Growth', *Journal of Political Economy*, October.

Brown, M., Sato, K. and Zarembka, P. (eds.) (1976), *Essays in Modern Capital Theory* (Amsterdam: North Holland).

Campbell, C. (1977), *Capacity Capital Formation in New Zealand Manufacturing Industries*, Victoria University of Wellington Occasional Paper, no. 31.

Champernowne, D. G. (1953–54), 'The Production Function and the Theory of Capital: A Comment', *Review of Economic Studies*, vol. 21.

Central Statistical Office (1978), *Economic Trends*, no. 291 (London: HMSO).

Central Statistical Office (1977), *Price Index Numbers for Current Cost Accounting* (London: HMSO).

Denison, E. F. (1962), *The Sources of Economic Growth in the US and the Alternatives Before Us*, Committee for Economic Development (New York: Library of Congress).

Eisner, R. (1972), 'Components of Capital Expenditures: Replacement and Modernisation versus Expansion'. *Review of Economics and Statistics*, vol. 54.

Feldstein, M. S. and Foot, D. K. (1971), 'The Other Half of Gross Investment: Replacement and Modernisation Expenditures', *Review of Economics and Statistics*, vol. 53.

Feldstein M. S. and Rothschild, M. (1974), 'Towards an Economic Theory of Replacement Investment', *Econometrica*, vol. 42.

Fisher, F. M. (1965), 'Embodied Technical Change and the Existence of an Aggregate Capital Stock', *Review of Economic Studies*, vol. 39.

Fisher, F. M. (1969), 'The Existence of Aggregate Production Functions', *Econometrica*, vol. 37.

Fisher, F. M. (1971), 'Aggregate Production Functions and the Explanation of Wages: A Simulation Experiment', *Review of Economics and Statistics*, vol. 53.

Georgescu-Roegen, N. (1971), *The Entropy Law and the Economic Process* (Harvard University Press).

Goldsmith, R. W. (1975), 'A Synthetic Estimate of the National Wealth of Japan 1885–1973', *Review of Income and Wealth*, series 21, no. 3.

Goldsmith, R. W. (1976), 'A Correction: Japan is Different', *Review of Income and Wealth*, series 22, no. 3.

Gorman, W. M. (1968), 'Measuring the Quantities of Fixed Factors' in Wolfe, J. N. (ed.), *Value, Capital and Growth* (Edinburgh University Press).

Green, H. A. J. (1964), *Aggregation in Economic Analysis: An Introductory Survey* (Princeton University Press).

Griffin, T. (1975), 'Revised Estimates of the Consumption and Stock of Fixed Capital', *Economic Trends*, no. 264, October, HMSO, London.

Griliches, Z. (1963), 'Capital Stock in Investment Functions: Some Problems of Concept and Measurement', in Christ, C. F. *et al.* (eds.), *Measurement in Economics* (Stanford University Press).

Groes, N., (1976), 'The Measurement of Capital in Denmark', *Review of Income and Wealth*, series 22, no. 3.

Haache, G. (1979), *The Theory of Economic Growth: An Introduction* (London: Macmillan).

Hahn, F. H. (1977), 'Keynesian Economic and General Equilibrium Theory: Reflections on Some Current Debates', in Harcourt, G. C. (ed.) *The Microeconomic Foundations of Macroeconomics* (London: Macmillan).

Hahn, F. (1971), *Readings: Theory of Growth* (London: Macmillan).

Harcourt, G. C. (1969), 'Some Cambridge Controversies in the Theory of Capital', *Journal of Economic Literature*, vol. 7.

Harcourt, G. C. (1972), *Some Cambridge Controversies in the Theory of Capital* (Cambridge University Press).

Harcourt, G. C. (ed.) (1977), *The Microeconomic Foundations of Macroeconomics* (London: Macmillan).

Harcourt, G. C. and Laing, N. F. (eds.) (1971), *Capital and Growth* (Penguin).

Helliwell, J. F. (1976), 'Aggregate Investment Equations: A Survey of the Issues', in J. F. Helliwell (ed.) *Aggregate Investment* (Harmondsworth: Penguin).

Hibbert, J., Griffin, T. J. and Walker, R. L. (1977), 'Development of

Estimates of the Stock of Fixed Capital in the United Kingdom', *Review of Income and Wealth*, series 23, no. 2.

Hicks, John (1974), 'Capital Controversies: Ancient and Modern', *American Economic Review*, May.

Hicks, John (1973), *Capital and Time* (Oxford University Press).

Jorgenson, D. W. and Griliches, Z. (1967), 'The Explanation of Productivity change', *Review of Economic Studies*, vol. 34.

Kendrick, J. W. (1971), 'The Accounting Treatment of Human Investment and Capital', *Review of Income and Wealth*, series 20, no. 4.

Kendrick, J. W. and Lee, K. S. (1976), 'Quarterly Estimates of Capital Stocks in the US Private Domestic Economy, by Major Industry Groups', *Review of Income and Wealth*, series 22, no. 4.

Kendrick, J. W. (1976), *The Formation and Stocks of Total Capital* (New York: NBER).

Kennedy, C. and Thirlwall, A. P. (1972), 'Technical Progress: A Survey', *Economic Journal*, March.

Kregel, J. A. (1976), *Theory of Capital* (London: Macmillan).

Levhari, D. (1965), 'A Nonsubstitution Theorem and the Switching of Techniques', *Quarterly Journal of Economics*, February.

Lutzel, H. (1977), 'Estimates of Capital Stock by Industries in the Federal Republic of Germany', *Review of Income and Wealth*, series 23, no. 2.

Maurice, R. (ed.) (1968), *National Accounts Statistics: Sources and Methods* (London: HMSO).

Nadiri, M. I. (1970), 'Some Approaches to the Theory and Measurement of Total Factor Productivity: A Survey', *Journal of Economic Literature*, December.

Nadiri, M. I. (1972), 'International Studies of Factor Inputs and Total Productivity: A Brief Survey', *Review of Income and Wealth*, June.

National Economic Development Office (1974), *The Age of US and UK Machinery* (London: HMSO).

Panić, M. (1978), *Capacity Utilisation in Manufacturing Industry*, NEDO monograph no. 6, HMSO, London.

Parks, R. W. (1977), 'Determinants of Scrapping Rates for Post War Vintage Automobiles', *Econometrica*, vol. 45.

Redfern, P. (1955), 'Net Investment in Fixed Assets in the United Kingdom', *Journal of the Royal Statistical Society*, series A, vol. 118.

Reid, D. J. (1976), *Statistical News*, November (London: HMSO).

Revell, J. (1967), *The Wealth of the Nation* (Cambridge University Press).

Robinson, Joan (1953–54), 'The Production Function and the Theory of Capital'. *Review of Economic Studies*, vol. 21.

Robinson, Joan (1965), *The Accumulation of Capital* (London: Macmillan).

Roe, A. R. (1971), *The Financial Interdependence of the Economy, 1957–1966* (London: Chapman and Hall).

Rymes, T. K. (1971), *On Concepts of Capital and Technical Change* (Cambridge University Press).

Samuelson, P. A. (1962), 'Parable and Realism in Capital Theory: the Surrogate Production Function', *Review of Economic Studies*, vol. 29.

Sen, A. (ed.) (1970), *Growth Theory* (Harmondsworth: Penguin).

Solow, R. M. (1956), 'The Production Function and the Theory of Capital', *Review of Economic Studies*, vol. 23.

Solow, R. M. (1957), 'Technical Change and the Aggregate Production Function', *Review of Economics and Statistics*, vol. 39.

Sraffa, Piero (1960), *Production of Commodities by Means of Commodities: Prelude to a Critique of Economic Theory* (Cambridge University Press).

Taubman, P., and Wilkinson, M. (1970), 'User Cost, Capital Utilisation and Investment Theory', *International Economic Review*, vol. 11.

Tengblad, A. and Westerlund. N. (1976), 'Capital Stock and Capital Consumption Estimates by Industries in the Swedish National Accounts', *Review of Income and Wealth*, series 22, no. 4.

United Nations (1968), *A System of National Accounts*, series F, no. 2, Review 3 (New York: United Nations).

Ward, M. (1976), 'Problems of Measuring Capital in Less Developed Countries', *Review of Income and Wealth*, series 22, no. 3.

Ward, M. (1976a), *The Measurement of Capital: The Methodology of Capital Stock Estimates in the OECD*, OECD, Paris.

# Part I

# Theory

# 1 A Theory of Money Capital, General Equilibrium and Income Distribution

I. F. PEARCE

*University of Southampton*

## THE PROBLEM

Since the appearance of Professor Joan Robinson's *The Production Function and the Theory of Capital*[1] and probably long before that, there has been no observable consensus among economists upon what is, or ought to be, meant by the word capital, or upon the way in which capital might be measured and incorporated into the theory of production. There are on the one hand those who claim that everyone understands the 'rough kernel of meaning' underlying the concept of capital even though there may be some difficulty in finding a number which sums it all up. At the same time models have been presented to show how in special cases capital might be measured so as to demonstrate the equivalence of the marginal product of capital and the rate of interest. Against this there exists an active and vociferous 'school' which asserts that, except along certain 'golden age' growth paths, no meaning can be attributed to the marginal product of capital, the rate of interest or profit being quite indeterminate except in an historical sense.

The problem is important both in its relevance to the theory of entrepreneurial behaviour and in its implications for the theory of income distribution. Those who believe that the 'capitalist' distribution of wealth and income is unfair have consistently sought to use conceptual problems associated with the notion of capital to demonstrate that the prices of factors of production, are even in the long run, determined not by supply and demand but by some arbitrary process of exploitation or political expedient.

The purpose of this paper is to show that there really is no problem. Capital is easily defined in the most general way both in and out of equilibrium. Supply and demand do determine the rewards of all factors in the long run sense that a unique distribution of income must emerge whenever supply equals demand and, conversely, that if some other distribution is imposed supply can *not* equal demand. In the long run factor prices can be raised above their natural level only by some monopolistic restriction of supply.

## THE EQUATIONS OF GENERAL EQUILIBRIUM

We proceed by listing the equations of the system, asking in turn why each must hold at least in the stationary state where there is no incentive to change, at the same time defining precisely the meaning of the symbols used.

There are *m* factors of production other than 'capital' and *n* commodities produced in quantities $S_i$.

$$S_i = S_i(A_{i1} \cdots A_{im}) \qquad \text{(i)}$$

is the production function for the $i^{\text{th}}$ output. The inputs $A_{ij}$ of the $j^{\text{th}}$ factor into the $i^{\text{th}}$ use do *not* include money capital. They consist of the objects, machines, raw materials, labour etc. which are in use at any moment of time, that is, which are part of the productive process. They must be items which can be bought in the market at a given price and hence by implication be available in measurable quantities. For any productive process, $S_i$ defines the maximum output which can be attained with the given inputs. Hence (i) must hold if the entrepreneur is not to be seeking change. If (i) does not hold there is technical inefficiency.

## THE MONEY CAPITAL REQUIREMENT EQUATION

Now notice that to set up in business it is not enough that inputs should be freely available at a given price $p_j$ and that there should be a market for the product. Money capital also is needed so that inputs may be paid for at some date before the flow of revenue from sales begins. *Money capital is necessary because production takes time not because time, or even money, is productive.*

In addition to (i) therefore we have a *money capital requirement* function for each commodity, $i$, which takes the form

$$C_i = \sum_j \sum_k p_j A_{ij}^k \left[ \frac{(1 + r_i)^{t_k - 1}}{1 - (1 + r_i)^{-l_j}} - \frac{1}{r_i l_j} \right] \tag{ii}$$

This identity is not easy to derive although it is of extraordinary interest. An appendix has been included below to show how it is calculated and how precisely it accords with common accounting practice, see appendix equation (viii). In this section we need only define terms and emphasise that (ii) must hold identically *whether or not the productive process is optimal and whatever the values of the variables*. It is a statement of fact. For a productive process with certain timed inputs the amount of money capital needed is absolutely determined by prices, profits and the varying life of equipment. $r_i$ is the rate of profit paid by the $i^{\text{th}}$ industry so as to exhaust the revenue from sales in the manner explained in the appendix below. The problem of calculating $r_i$ has again been the subject of much debate between lawyers and accountants. A general solution consistent with economic theory is given in the appendix.

The variables $t_k$ measure the timing of the inputs $A_{ij}^k$. The index $k$ is added because the same physical $j^{\text{th}}$ input may have different timing structures; see appendix for the precise meaning of $k$. In the appendix the $j^{\text{th}}$ input is defined as $x_j$. This less complex notation is satisfactory there since the production only of a single commodity is considered. The subscript $j$ in the appendix refers to the $j^{\text{th}}$ factor with a given time structure, that is, labour with a time period four would be allocated a subscript $j$ say when the same physical factor, labour, with a time period three would be allocated a different subscript, say $k$. This notation is not possible in the general equilibrium equation system since we need to sum the same physical factors over different commodity usages and different time structures.

$l_j$ is the life of the $j^{\text{th}}$ physical input. Throughout this note we take $l_j$ to be given constant but there is no particular reason why we should. $l_j$ could be a variable, chosen so as to minimise cost when used with each time structure or commodity. In this case we should have to distinguish $l_{ij}^k$, the life of the $j^{\text{th}}$ factor used in the production of the $i^{\text{th}}$ commodity with the $k^{\text{th}}$ time structure. The choice of minimum cost introduces a new optimal condition and hence a new equation for each $l_{ij}^k$ considered to be a variable under the control of management. If therefore the number of equations and unknowns is the same where any or all $l_{ij}^k$ are fixed the same must be true where any or all $l_{ij}^k$ are considered to be economic variables. We add nothing of present interest by supposing equipment life to be variable. Naturally of course if lives were to be considered variable it would be necessary to accept the idea of loss of efficiency with age, or alternatively to choose a model with technological change. No more need be said at this time about equation (ii) except to emphasise once again that $C_i$ is not a variable input into the productive process which has a product of its own. It is determined completely by factor prices, the rate of profit and the chosen technology. There is no way in which more money could be used without changing the technology and no way, for a given technology, of getting by with less money.

## TOTAL REVENUE EQUALS TOTAL COST

We now come to $n$ equations which show that all revenue is distributed to some factor of production or becomes profit. The logic of equation (iii) is set out in the appendix – see appendix equation (v). $mF$ in the appendix equals $S_iq_i$ in this section, and $x_j$ equals $A_{ij}$.
Thus

$$S_iq_i = \sum_k \sum_j p_jA_{ij}^k \frac{r_i(1+r_i)^{t_k-1}}{1-(1+r_i)^{-l_j}} \tag{iii}$$

Notice especially that (iii) may be written in the form

$$S_iq_i = \sum_k \sum_j \frac{p_jA_{ij}^k}{l_j} + r_i \sum_k \sum_j p_jA_{ij}^k \left[\frac{(1+r_i)^{t_k-1}}{1-(1+r_i)^{-l_j}} - \frac{1}{r_il_j}\right] \tag{iii)a}$$

which says that the revenue $S_iq_i$ received in each time period just pays (i) the across-the-counter cost of each item in use divided by its life measured in the same time units plus the rate of profit times the money capital tied up in the productive process.

## THE BEHAVIOURAL EQUATIONS

So far the identities set out have not been behavioural. They reflect the facts of life, the physical constraints under which any economy must operate. The laws of physics determine the production functions, existing payment conventions determine the money capital requirement of producers and the requirement that purchases of inputs and rent of money capital must come out of revenue. Similarly all revenue belongs to someone. We now turn to behavioural equations.

It is reasonable to suppose that whatever the political system and whatever may be the aims of producers no-one will think it sensible to produce and sell a given output at less than the lowest possible cost. If the same output could be produced at lower cost using a different technique the same revenue could be earned and hence a residual could be secured which could be used to raise the reward of any factor, in particular to raise profit.

Thus minimising total cost, i.e. the right hand side of (iii), subject to the constraint $S_i$ = constant, we have equations (iv)

$$p_j \frac{r_i(1+r_i)^{t_k-1}}{1-(1+r_i)^{-l_j}} - \lambda_i \frac{\partial S_i}{\partial A_{ij}^k} = 0 \qquad \text{(iv)}$$

Notice that in this exercise we take the cost of money capital $r_i$ as fixed. An alternative way of looking at the problem is to suppose that each business is choosing a production technique which will maximise the rate of profit $r_i$ for a given output. In this case we think of (iii) as an implicit function which can be used to solve for $r_i$ given $p_j$. To maximise $r_i$ we require that all possible sets of changes $dA_{ij}^k$ in inputs (subject only to the constraint $\Sigma_j \Sigma_k (\partial S_i / \partial A_{ij}^k)\, dA_{ij}^k = 0$) should leave $dr_i$ unchanged whilst preserving the identity (iii). Thus we have as a necessary condition,

$$\sum_k \sum_j p_j \frac{r_i(1+r_i)^{t_k-1}}{1-(1+r_i)^{-l_j}} dA_{ij}^k = 0$$

for all $dA_{ij}^k$ satisfying the constraint. This will hold if and only if (iv) above holds.

The same would obviously be true if the objective of the business were to maximise *any* factor reward $p_j$ for any given output. This is of course only to be expected for, as observed above, the only technique which does not permit an increase in any factor reward is that which minimises cost given factor prices and the rate of profit.

The point is an important one. For any and every likely objective of the firm, whether under capitalism or socialism or worker participation or any other political regime someone will be seeking change if (iv) is not satisfied. (iv) is a natural condition for equilibrium under almost any system.

## CONSUMER BEHAVIOUR

Two other purely behavioural sets of equations must now be discussed. First, it is supposed that goods produced are sold in a market and that consumers seek to maximise utility subject to an income constraint. More simply it would seem to be a behavioural rule that the aggregate sales of each commodity must depend upon all prices and upon aggregate expenditure. Thus we have

$$q_i = q_i(S_1 \ldots S_n Y) \tag{v}$$

where $q_i$ is the market price of the $i^{\text{th}}$ commodity and $Y$ is aggregate spending. The equations (v) could be the inverse of the ordinary equations of demand theory. $Y$ must of course be the sum of the payment to all factors $\Sigma_i r_i C_i$ plus $\Sigma_i \Sigma_j \Sigma_k p_j A_{ij}^k$ but we use the symbol $Y$ and assume $Y$ to be given as *numeraire* to avoid a system of equations homogeneous in prices $p$ and $q$.

## EQUALISATION OF PROFIT RATES

The next and last behavioural equation is crucial. We assume that no manager will be content if he can at any time see some other production unit earning a greater rate of return on capital than he is able to earn. Implicitly of course we are assuming the same thing for all other factors of production. We have set $p_j$ the same whatever the current use. Homogeneous labour earns the same reward whatever commodity it is producing. If it did not, we assume it would wish to move to another firm where the wage rate for its own particular skill was higher. Similarly capital is supposed to seek its highest return.

It should be noted especially that we nowhere assume that all businesses take the market price of their product as given. There is no implication of perfect competition or constant returns to scale. It does not matter that manfacturers are aware that they can affect the price of their product by changing the level of sales. We simply cannot imagine any management resting content with a lower rate of profit when it consistently observes some other firm whose technique or sales policy could be copied to earn a higher return, just as we cannot imagine any individual resting content when he observes a person with the same skills earning a higher wage in another industry.

We therefore introduce

$$r = r_j \quad \text{for all } j \tag{vi}$$

where $r$ is the common profit rate.

If the reader believes that businessmen might after all rest content with different rates of return on capital, perhaps because of some imagined or actual barrier to imitation, then it is open to him to believe instead that the level of his output will be chosen so as to maximise the rate of return on capital employed,[2] or for that matter the rate of reward paid to any factor of production. In either case it would be necessary to believe also that the manufacturer is aware of some 'perceived' elasticity of demand for his product. Maximisation of the rate of return, or any other price $p_j$, yields a set of equations derived at once by differentiating equations (iii) with respect to each $A_{ij}^k$ taking all $p_j$ and $r_i$ as given. (iii) is regarded as an implicit function of the price to be maximised and the only difference in the procedure from that leading to (iv) is that $S_i$ is no longer constrained to be constant so the $\lambda_i$ does not appear. Instead we have to allow both $S_i$ and $q_i$ to change in accordance with the assumed elasticity of demand for the product.

To replace equations (iv) we should have

$$p_j \frac{r_i(1+r_i)^{t_k-1}}{1-(1+r_i)^{-l_j}} = q_i \frac{\partial S_i}{\partial A_{ij}^k} + S_i \frac{dq_i}{dS_i} \frac{\partial S_i}{\partial A_{ij}^k}$$

$$= q_i \frac{\partial S_i}{\partial A_{ij}^k}\left[1 + \frac{S_i}{q_i}\frac{dq_i}{dS_i}\right]$$

$$= q_i \frac{\partial S_i}{\partial A_{ij}^k}\left[1 + \frac{1}{E_i}\right] \qquad \text{(vi)a}$$

where $E_i$ is the known or discovered elasticity of demand for the product. (vi)A may be interpreted as marginal cost equals marginal revenue if both sides are divided by $(\partial S_i/\partial A_{ij}^k)$.

In fact the author takes the view that (vi)a is not really a viable alternative since there is no way in which $E_i$ can be defined much less discovered; but the result is nonetheless included since it accords with current conventional wisdom and, as it happens, for present purposes we neither gain nor lose by taking either view.

If we substitute equations (vi)a for (iv) and leave out the condition (vi) we have $n$ fewer equations (vi) but at the same time we have $n$ fewer unknowns $\lambda_i$.[2] If the system involving equations (vi) is determinate then so is the system involving (vi)A and *vice versa*. If either is not determinate then neither is the other. We continue therefore with the system including (vi).

It should be noted in passing however that the two actual equilibria would be quite different in general if the numbers $E_i$ were known and the second system could be solved. Equal profit rates is not consistent with marginal cost equals marginal revenue.

## THE EXOGENOUS FUNCTIONAL IDENTITIES

Consider now the total capital stock of the community. We note that this is

$$C = \sum_i C_i = \sum_i \sum_j \sum_k p_j A_{ij}^k \left[ \frac{(1 + r_i)^{t_k - i}}{1 - (1 + r_i)^{-l_j}} - \frac{1}{r_i l_j} \right]$$

which may be broadly defined as the value of work in progress. Clearly it is possible to move a unit of the $j^{\text{th}}$ factor from one use to another or from one time structure to another. If we cease to apply a factor to use $i$ with time structure $t_k$ then after $t_k$ unit of time the flow of product attributed to it will cease; but if the new use also has time structure $t_k$ then the flow of new product will begin at the same moment that the flow of old product ceases. Capital *can* be shifted between uses without altering the total capital stock; but in many cases, where the time structure is changed an act of saving or dis-saving is involved.

We should naturally not expect equilibrium prices to remain unchanged when the aggregate capital stock changes so we introduce the restriction

$$C = \bar{C} = \sum_i C_i \tag{vii}$$

which simply recognises that the total supply of capital $\bar{C}$ is a factor determining the price structure.

Finally, we should not expect to find all prices the same at different levels of employment of factors. Thus we have full employment equations

$$\sum_k \sum_i A_{ij}^k = \bar{A}_j \tag{viii}$$

or, to put it another way the aggregate supplies $\bar{A}_j$ of the various factors also determine the structure of prices. Factor rewards may be changed by changing factor supplies.

We could of course make the quantities $\bar{A}_j$ depend upon the vector of factor prices $p$; but this would add nothing since the determinacy of a system is undisturbed by adding $m$ more equations and $m$ more unknowns.

## DETERMINACY OF SYSTEMS

We are now ready to compare equations and unknowns. We assume that there are $t$ possible time structures $k$. Some $A_{ij}^k$ may of course be zero in equilibrium.

| *Equations* | *Number of equations* | *Unknowns* | *Number of unknowns* |
|---|---|---|---|
| (i) | $n$ | $S_i$ | $n$ |
| (ii) | $n$ | $C_i$ | $n$ |
| (iii) | $n$ | $q_i$ | $n$ |
| (iv) | $m \times n \times t$ | $A_{ij}^k$ | $m \times n \times t$ |
| (v) | $n$ | $\lambda_i$ | $n$ |
| (vi) | $n$ | $r_j$ | $n$ |
| (vii) | 1 | $r$ | 1 |
| (viii) | $m$ | $p_j$ | $m$ |

We recall that $Y$, $\bar{C}$ and $\bar{A}_j$ are exogenous, $Y$ being a *numeraire* and $\bar{C}$ and $\bar{A}_j$ price determining factor supplies.

PRODUCTION OF COMMODITIES BY COMMODITIES

The results above are not affected by recognition of the fact that some commodities might also be inputs into productive processes. Suppose, for example, that the input with price $p_t$ was known to be the output of the $i^{\text{th}}$ industry. We should then have

$$q_i = p_t \qquad \text{(a)}$$

On the other hand we should not be able to write

$$\sum_k \sum_i A_{ij}^k = \bar{A}_j$$

as in equation (viii). Instead it would be necessary to break up the output $S_j$ into output $S_j^p$ for further input and output $S_j^c$ for consumption with

$$S_j = S_j^p + S_j^c \qquad \text{(b)}$$

The market clearing functions (v) contain $S_j^c$ rather than $S_j$ and in place of the full employment equation (viii) we have

$$\sum_k \sum_i A_{ij}^k = S_j^p$$

In sum therefore we have two additional equations (a) and (b) and two additional unknowns $S_j^p$ and $S_j^c$. The system remains determinate.

## CONCLUSIONS

We conclude that 'capital' is quite easily defined and is a strictly operational concept. Factor prices, commodity prices and the rate of profit are simultaneously determined by the forces of supply and demand. There is no difficulty with capital in the definition of the production function or anywhere else. We do not claim that trade union activity does not affect factor prices in the short run or that historical events do not affect the supply of factors, particularly capital accumulation. What is claimed however is that as long as prices are *not* the equilibrium prices defined by the system because of trade union activity or government decree then change is inevitable. An overdetermined world is an unpredictable world and an unpredictable world is bound to be unhappy.

## NOTES

1 In *Review of Economic Studies*, vol. 21, 1953/4, pp. 81–106.

2 It may appear also that the system involving (vi)A can do without a market rate of interest $r$ and is therefore overdetermined, but this is not so. It does not make sense to suppose that just exactly the right number of shareholders own monopoly rights in each company so that the rate of return is maximised on all shares. There must be a market for money capital. In practice $C_i$ will be made up of $\alpha C_i$ of shares paid fixed interest at the market rate and $(1 - \alpha)C_i$ receiving a monopoly rate $r_i^*$. Evidently $r_i$, the profit rate in (vi)A, is

$$r_i = \frac{\alpha C_i r + (1 - \alpha)C_i r_i^*}{C_i} = \alpha r + (1 - \alpha)r_i^*$$

There exist $n + 1$ profit rates in the system involving (vi)A just as there are in the system making use of (vi).

## APPENDIX: The concept of capital and conventional accounting procedures

As a matter of interest and because it is essential to a proper understanding of the main paper this appendix is included exactly as it was written in 1957 with the addition only of some clarifying footnotes. This appendix was intended to be a chapter in a book the publication of which has in fact awaited the solution of a number of other problems associated with the theory of production, not least that in the main paper. Attention has been drawn to the date when the appendix was written partly to excuse certain anachronisms.

## THE NEED FOR MONEY CAPITAL – THE COMPANY BALANCE SHEET

It is important to note the very special role of money capital as a factor of production. This point will now be further developed with particular reference to the balance sheet of the enterprise. An example will be quoted to show how the balance sheet records simultaneously the amount of money necessarily tied up in the process at a given date and the amount of money actually contributed by shareholders either directly or by way of undistributed profit. The difference between the two sums is the amount free for the payment of dividend. Thus, it is by analysis of the balance sheet that we derive the basic formula for capital upon which all later work is based.

The first requirement for the setting up of any business enterprise is money capital. It is our purpose to enquire precisely how much money is needed, given the prices and quantities of all other inputs and the expected revenue from the sale of the product. This question is not as easily answered as might appear at first sight; timing is all important. If the product could be created and sold instantaneously at the moment of payment for inputs and if all of the inputs purchased were immediately embodied in the product sold then no money capital would be required at all. In practice neither of these requirements is met.

First, in order to create a flow of output, some inputs must be paid for before the moment when the output flow first appears. Second, some inputs are durable items, which have to be paid for at discrete intervals of time as and when they wear out or when repairs become necessary. The product which they help to create however appears as a continuous flow. The full value of the product of any durable input is not realised until the end of its life. To bridge these time gaps money capital is required. Moreover, as the lives of different pieces of equipment differ, the age composition of the elements making up the whole plant will vary over time. This means, as we shall see, that the money capital requirement varies over time.

The fact that the money capital requirement varies over time, theoretically for ever, poses problems for the accountant as well as the management of the firm. Obviously, the ideal is to keep the actual money put up by shareholders down to a minimum; that is, down to the exact capital requirement at each moment of time. But this would involve a continuous series of adjustments of shareholders' capital subscriptions. Besides paying profit to shareholders the firm would be required to refund any capital temporarily not required and to call it again each time it became necessary to renew plant or buildings. The administrative costs involved in such a procedure would almost certainly be prohibitive.

Accordingly, the usual practice is to require shareholders to subscribe a fixed sum referred to as 'issued' capital and to invest independently any excess cash which may from time to time become available. The firm in fact administers temporarily free capital on the shareholders' behalf. This may be lent at interest or invested in some enterprise other than that for which it was originally subscribed. In other words, the difference between the fixed issued capital and the money capital requirement which varies over time is retained to form a fluctuating depreciation fund available for the replacement of durable equipment as necessary.[1] Issued capital can therefore be taken to the maximum expected capital requirement as estimated. Fluctuations in the depreciation fund are equal and opposite to the fluctuations in the money capital requirement. The aim will usually be to keep the depreciation fund at a minimum, consistent with the purpose of having cash available when it is needed without calling upon shareholders.

## THE DEPRECIATION FUND AND THE MONEY CAPITAL REQUIREMENT

It follows that the accountant's interest in the question what is the appropriate sum of money to set aside for depreciation is no more than an indirect interest in the money capital requirement[2]. The amount put to depreciation is chosen so that, having in view the current value of all assets, the total 'wealth' retained within the business is equal to the maximum expected money capital requirement, namely, 'issued capital'. Any wealth held over and above issued capital is profit and is available for distribution. Consideration of the main items of a typical company balance sheet will make these points clear.

The accountant will notice only one unusual feature about this balance sheet. He will point out that the balance of profit available for distribution need not be exactly equal to cash and usually is not. This means, if the balance sheet is to balance, that, contrary to the principle enunciated above, the total value of all assets except cash need not be equal to issued capital. That is, the total wealth retained within the business need not be equal to the maximum expected capital requirement. There are two possible reasons for this apparent contradiction.

First, the depreciation fund may not be entirely invested. Some part of it may be held in cash and the accountant does not distinguish between cash held against depreciation and other. Thus a part of what is strictly

TABLE 1.A1 XYZ Co. balance sheet, 31 December 1959

| *Liabilities* | | *Assets* | |
|---|---|---|---|
| | 3 | Durable plant & buildings | (Valued at cost less depreciation) |
| 1 Issued Capital (remains fixed) | 4 | Raw material stocks | |
| | 5 | Work in progress | (At cost) |
| | 6 | Finished stocks | |
| | 7 | Trade debtors less trade actual creditors | |
| | 8 | Outside investments against depreciation | (Equal to depreciation deducted from cost of plant) |
| 2 Balance of profit available for distribution | 9 | Cash | (Actual) |

item 8 may appear in item 9. Second, when the general price level is changing or when the firm has grown in size by making use of non-distributed profit the figure for issued capital no longer represents the maximum expected money capital requirement. In this case, it is usual to show the cash withheld as a reserve fund. An extra entry 'reserves' appears on the liability side of the balance sheet and item 8 will now include some investments held against the reserve fund as well as those held against depreciation. All that this means is that the expected future money capital requirement has grown by the amount of the reserve either because of price inflation or because the scale of production has changed. The new money capital requirement is issued capital plus reserves. In short, both the accountant's objections turn out to be solely matters of presentation. The balance sheet should balance twice as shown. Item 1 should equal items 3 to 8 and item 2 should equal item 9.

Indeed, in setting out our balance sheet in this way we have done no more than make explicit a common sense rule which accountants intuitively follow though perhaps inexactly. Provided there is no wish to change the scale of the productive activity under review, businessmen will aim to adjust the depreciation fund and if necessary to create a reserve so as to be able to maintain the process just but only just intact, or, as it is sometimes put, to maintain *real* capital intact. We have interpreted this to mean that outside investments are bought and sold so that the money value to the firm of all assets (including outside investments) is just equal to the maximum expected money capital requirement.

Put this way we see that choice of the correct amount of depreciation requires first the valuation of assets and second the determination of maximum expected money capital requirement. In practice the valuation of part worn assets and work in progress, is far from easy. Nor have accountants any precise rule for determining money capital requirement. Without any established theory and faced with an uncertain future they tend to fall back upon ultra conservative rules of thumb. The problem is still further complicated by taxation law which often prescribes maximum rates of depreciation based on the initial cost of the items to be depreciated. This encourages accountants to set depreciation at the legal maximum and cover the remainder of the expected maximum money requirement by setting up a general reserve.

## PROFIT OR ILLEGAL PAYMENT OUT OF CAPITAL?

The absence of a precise rule has led to a great many legal wrangles. It is often a matter of great importance to distinguish between a payment of profit and repayment of capital. If the value of assets is set too low and depreciation accordingly too high obviously profits are understated. The view might be taken that there has been an unwarranted addition to capital (outside investment in our balance sheet) at the expense of profits. If on the other hand assets are overvalued, investments against depreciation will be correspondingly low. In this case it might be held that profits are being paid out of capital. The real value of the undertaking is being run down in order to pay profits. In practice, lawyers and accountants have nothing more precise than common sense to guide them in their attempts to define which is which. We shall proceed now to show that at least some progress can be made towards the ideal precision even if we begin only from the accountant's common sense. And, what is perhaps more important in the present context, it will be found that the formal solution to what is apparently an accountancy problem turns out to be a useful tool of economic analysis.

## THE CALCULATION OF THE MONEY CAPITAL REQUIREMENT

Let us suppose that it is intended to set up an enterprise designed to produce a continuous even flow of some product. Suppose in fact that the plant will produce $F$ units of the product per unit of time. Assume further that in order to maintain this product flow $n$ inputs $x_1, x_2$ etc. to $x_n$ have to be *in use* in each period of time. We emphasise 'in use' because it should be understood that inputs need not be *used up* in the period. For example, if $x_2$ means five machines of type two, every machine will be constantly in use throughout each time period but may have a 'life' lasting many time periods.

The inputs $x_1$, $x_2$ etc. do not include money capital which will be separately treated. They are simply the raw materials, machines and labour which the firm must buy from time to time. They have unambiguous prices $p_1, p_2$ etc. to $p_n$ and entries recording their purchase can be found in the accountant's books. They do not include items like organisation, or risk. In addition to prices and quantities inputs must be thought of as having a time dimension which is all important.

## THE MATURITY TIME

In order to set up a flow in output commencing at a given date it is necessary to purchase inputs at various times before that date. The time elapsing between payment for the first batch of each input and the sale of the first batch of the product is the time dimension of the input. Each input will be said to have a maturity time $t_K$.

It is important that there should be no misunderstanding about what is meant by maturity time as all that follows depends upon it. In attaching a maturity time to each input we do not imply that it is possible to relate any particular unit of output to particular units of input; for in general this cannot be done. On the contrary, each unit of the product will usually embody many units of say labour, applied at many different points of time and conversely one particular machine bought at one moment of time will be embodied in many units of output appearing at different times.

The maturity time is best thought of as associated only with the original build-up period required to set up the process. Once the flow of output is set up we notice that, at any moment of time, $n$ inputs of quantities $x_1, x_2 \ldots x_n$ are *in use*. In order to attach a maturity time to each input we go back to the moment when the very first batch of $x_1$ units of input one were purchased. We observe also the moment when the very first unit of product was sold. The difference between these two times is the maturity time $t_1$ of factor one. Notice that if factor one is a machine there is no suggestion that the whole input is embodied in the product which appears when the maturity time has elapsed. Notice also that if, as is likely, the first batches of $x_2$ and $x_3$ units of inputs two and three were purchased at a later date than the first batch of $x_1$, these will have shorter maturity times; and the first unit of sales will have embodied in it at least some part of the shorter dated input.

Two other important points have to be made. First, inputs, say $x_1$ and $x_2$, need not be different in a qualitative sense but we may have to distinguish between them because they have different maturity times. Thus we may have, say, $x_1$ units of labour with maturity time three and $x_2$ units of labour with maturity time two. This means that, in setting up the process, $x_1$ labourers must be paid at three time units before the commencement of the flow of product sales and $x_1$ labourers must be paid for at two time units before the commencement of the flow of sales. There is no difficulty about this. When we write

$$F = F(x_1 \ldots x_n)$$

meaning that the flow of output $F$ per unit of time is dependent upon (i.e. a function of) the use for one period of $x_1$ units of factor one with maturity time one and $x_2$ units of factor two with maturity time two etc. we have simply numbered our inputs by their maturity times. Factors 1 and 2 may in fact both be labour.

The second point to notice is that negative maturity times are not ruled out. Input with negative maturity times will usually represent repairs to fixed equipment. In this way we are able to admit the possibility that equipment may not be of the 'one hoss shay' type[3]. At the moment when sales of product commence all machines will be relatively new and not in need of repair. Later, however, it may be necessary to employ staff to undertake repairs, numbers gradually being built up as time progresses. Inputs for repairs will therefore have negative maturity times.

## THE LIFE OF DURABLE INPUTS

We shall use the symbol $\ell_i$ to represent the life of the $i^{\text{th}}$ input. The life of any input is the time which elapses between the moment of purchase of the first unit and the moment when it becomes necessary to pay for a replacement. Single-use goods such as raw materials or labour/hours, which are used up in one time period, have a life of one. As already noted the existence of a definite life for a durable asset does not exclude the possibility that it may need to be repaired many times during the course of that life.

THE MONEY CAPITAL REQUIREMENT AT ANY TIME $T$

We are now in a position to dervie the money capital requirement for the enterprise at time $T$ measured from the commencement of the product flow. The product flow is of course assumed to be a continuous flow at a constant rate. Any change in the rate of flow at a later date must be treated as the creation of a new flow equal to the amount of the change. Money capital tied up time $T$ is simply money actually raised from shareholders plus profits due to shareholders less amounts paid to shareholders. We count this up from the earliest beginnings of the enterprise in two states. First, we pretend that the firm has no revenue. Shareholders' capital would then consist of every single payment ever made to contracting factors plus profits due to shareholders on capital so accumulated. Then we imagine that *all* revenue is paid to shareholders as it becomes available and that interest on this is charged by the firm against the shareholders from the time of payment to them. It is, in fact, as if the firms were accumulating capital invested in the shareholders in precisely the same way as the shareholders accumulate capital in the firms. The difference between the two capital sums at any time is the money capital requirement we are seeking. The exact method will become obvious as we proceed.

Consider first the notional capital accumulated by shareholders in the firm. We assume that from the beginning money is demanded from shareholders only as required to make payments to contracting factors. In practice, this is achieved by a system of share allotment and call. A person applying for shares does not pay for them at once in full. Payments are made only on 'call' by the enterprise. Profit therefore is charged from the actual date of the purchase of input and not from the date when shares were allotted.

The total expenditure, excluding profits, on the full set of first batches of all imputs is evidently

$$\sum_{i=1}^{n} p_i x_i$$

This is the total bill for all first purchases of all inputs 1 to $n$. Notice that all bills were not paid at the same moment of time. If the time is now $T$ from the commencement of product sales the bill for the first $x_i$ units of the $i^{\text{th}}$ input will have been paid $T + t_i$ time units ago by the definition of maturity time. If we include profit due to shareholders, therefore,

$$\sum_{i=1}^{n} p_i x_i (1+r)^{T+t_i}$$

represents shareholders' capital accumulation on account of the first batch of inputs 1 to $n$. $r$ is the percentage rate of profit payable. The fact that we have not yet determined what is the appropriate rate of profit does not matter for the moment. We shall show later how this is discovered.

At the end of the life $\ell_i$ of the first batch of $x_i$ units of input $i$ a second batch must be bought. Profits will have been payable on the cost of the second batch for a period of $T + t_i - \ell_i$ time units. Hence total expenditure plus profits to date on the second batch of all inputs is

$$\sum_{i=1}^{n} p_i x_i (1+r)^{T+t_i-\ell_i}$$

For the third batch of all inputs it will be

$$\sum_{i=1}^{n} p_i x_i (1+r)^{T+t_i-2\ell_i}$$

and so on.

We now enquire how many batches of the $i^{\text{th}}$ factor will have been purchased up to the time $T$. Clearly, this will be the number of lives in $T + t_i$ units of time plus one since the input is paid for at the beginning of its life not at the end. It is therefore convenient to introduce temporarily another variable $S_i$ defined by the identity

$$S_i + 1 \equiv \frac{T + t_i - h_i}{\ell_i} + 1$$

where $h_i$ is that fraction of $\ell_i$ by which $(T + t_i)/\ell_i$ exceeds its nearest whole number. This simply says that $S_i$ is the number of *whole* lives in $T + t_i$ with the fraction left over neglected.

Consider the meaning of the expression

$$\sum_{S=0}^{S_i} p_i x_i (1+r)^{T+t_i-S\ell_i} \qquad \text{(i)}$$

This is no more than a way of writing the sum of the total expenditure plus profits payable on the 1st, 2nd, 3rd etc. up to the $(S_i + 1)$th batch of units of the $i^{\text{th}}$ input. In other words $S$ takes all $(S_i + 1)$ values from 0 to $S_i$ and the whole is summed.

The grand total for all expenditure and profits payable up to time $T$ is therefore

$$\sum_{i=1}^{n} \sum_{S=0}^{S_i} p_i x_i (1+r)^{T+t_i-S\ell_i} \tag{ii}$$

which means simply the sum of expressions like (i) for all inputs 1 to $n$.

We now have to find the notional capital invested by the firm in the shareholders as explained above. This may be written down at once. The revenue per period of time is $mF$ where $m$ is the product price and $F$ is the flow of output. We imagine that this has been paid over to shareholders each period from time $O$ to time $T$. The total, including notional profit, therefore is

$$\sum_{t=0}^{T} mF(1+r)^t \tag{iii}$$

where $t$ takes all values from $O$ to $T$.

Thr difference between (ii) and (iii) is the net money capital requirement of the enterprise at time $T$. i.e.

$$C_T = \sum_{i=1}^{n} \sum_{S=0}^{S_i} p_i x_i (1+r)^{T+t_i-S\ell_i} - \sum_{t=0}^{T} mF(1+r)^t \tag{iv}$$

There is another way of interpreting this expression for capital tied up which some readers may prefer: (iv) can be thought of as the difference between total payments made by the firm up to time $T$ including profit payments, less receipts by the firm up to time $T$. Any excess of payments over receipts must have been made out of funds supplied by shareholders. Profits are charged on all expenditure in term one of (iv) which implies that all expenditure is out of capital. As the firm is not of course required to pay profit on any expenditure out of revenue we deduct from term one not only revenue but revenue compounded at the profit rate.

## CALCULATION OF 'TRUE' PROFIT

Armed with our formula (iv) we can now look again at the legal/accounting problem we set out to consider. So far we have begged the question what is the proper value of $r$? It is a remarkable fact that a very weak condition which will command ready acceptance everywhere is quite sufficient to enable us to define $r$ precisely in terms of revenue, inputs and input prices. We have already hinted at this condition above. Attention has been drawn to the fact that if assets are undervalued profits will be set too low and investment against depreciation too high. This is another way of saying that if the profit rate is set too low this must be because assets are correspondingly undervalued, and investments against depreciation must be growing too fast. Consider what would happen to our balance sheet if this same too low profit rate were paid each period indefinitely. Outside investments against depreciation would become indefinitely large and to make the balance sheet balance it would theoretically be necessary to put a negative value on assets (items 3–7 in the balance sheet). Of course, in practice this never occurs though individual items are sometimes entered at no value. The fact, however, that in practice the profit rate would be changed before it became necessary to put a negative value on assets does not prevent us from asking the question, *would* it be necessary to value assets negatively *if* the present profit rate were continued indefinitely? In fact we could ask, would it be necessary to value assets at an infinite negative amount if the proposed profit rate were continued for an infinite period of time?

This may seem a silly question, but it is not. For we shall discover that putting this question and the converse–'would it be necessary to value assets at an infinite positive price if the proposed profit rate were continued for an infinite period?'–enables us to set here and now the theoretically correct profit rate we seek. We have already seen that the value of assets at time $T$ (items 3–7 in balance sheet) is the money capital requirement $C_T$ at time $T$. In terms of our formula (iv), therefore, our ridiculous question can be framed, does $C_T$ become infinitely large and positive or infinitely large and negative, as $T$ tends to infinity. If the answer is yes, $r$ is too large or too small. If the answer is no, $r$ is theoretically correct. In this case and in this case only the money capital requirement $C_T$ fluctuates indefinitely around some kind of average as long as there is no change in the technical process carried on. Let us now manipulate the expression (iv) to see all this implies.

First we find

$$\sum_{S=0}^{S_i} p_i x_i (1+r)^{T+t_i-S\ell_i}$$

Using the well known formula for the sum of a geometric series[4] we can write this in the form

$$p_i x_i \left[ (1+r)^{T+t_i} - (1+r)^{T+t_i-(S_i+1)\ell_i} \right] / (1-(1+r)^{-\ell_i})$$

which, remembering that $S_i + 1 = (T + t_i - h_i)/(\ell_i + 1)$ becomes

$$P_i x_i \, [(1 + r)^{T + t_i} - (1 + r)^{h_i - \ell_i}] \, / \, (1 - (1 + r)^{-\ell_i}).$$

Again summing a geometric series we have

$$\sum_{t=0}^{T} mF(1 + r)^t = mF[1 - (1 + r)^{T+1}]/r$$

Substituting these results in formula (iv) for capital we obtain

$$C_T = \sum_{i=1}^{n} p_i x_i [(1 + r)^{T + t_i} - (1 + r)^{-Z_i}]/(1 - (1 + r)^{-\ell_i})$$
$$+ mF[1 - (1 + r)^{T+1}]/r$$

where for convenience we have introduced a new variable $Z_i = \ell_i - h_i$. This equation can be put in the form

$$\left[ \sum_{i=1}^{n} p_i x_i \frac{(1 + r)^{t_i}}{1 - (1 + r)^{-\ell_i}} - \frac{mF(1 + r)}{r} \right] (1 + r)^T$$

$$= C_T - \frac{mF}{r} + \sum_{i=1}^{n} \frac{p_i x_i (1 + r)^{-Z_i}}{1 - (1 + r)^{-\ell_i}}$$

$$\text{or } A(1 + r)^T = B$$

where the definitions of $A$ and $B$ are obvious.

We now prove that $B$ is bounded, i.e. that it can never be greater than some given number and never be less than some finite number whatever the value of $T$.

First, we note that

$$-\frac{mF}{r} + \sum_{i=1}^{n} \frac{p_i x_i (1 + r)^{-Z_i}}{1 - (1 + r)^{-\ell_i}}$$

must be bounded; for over time $Z_i$ takes values $\ell_i, (\ell_i - 1) \ldots . \; 2, 1, \ell_i$ etc. Thus $Z_i$ can never be less than unity or greater than $\ell_i$ and all other elements of our expression are constants which do not vary with time.

We may now introduce our basic assumption namely that $r$ is chosen so that $C_T$ is bounded; that is, so that $C_T$ fluctuates indefinitely around some fixed average. It follows at once that all terms in $B$ are bounded, therefore $B$ itself is bounded.

Consider again the equation

$$A(1 + r)T = B$$

$A$ is clearly independent of $T$ for it is a fixed number determined by prices, inputs, maturity times, equipment lives and the chosen rate of profit. It follows that $A(1 + r)^T$ cannot be bounded unless $A = 0$; for if $A$ were any number other than zero and $r$ is not zero then $A(1 + r)^T$ must tend to $+\infty$ or $-\infty$ as $T$ tends to $\infty$. That is $A(1 + r)^T$ gets indefinitely larger or smaller as $T$ gets larger and larger. But if $B$ is bounded as we have proved, our equation cannot hold for all time unless $A(1 + r)^T$ is also bounded; therefore $A$ must be zero. And if $A$ is zero $B$ also must be zero. To choose $r$ so that $C_T$ is bounded is exactly equivalent to choosing $r$ so that both $A$ and $B$ are zero. This gives two equations of great interest, namely

$$mF = r \sum_{i=1}^{n} p_i x_i \frac{(1 + r)^{t_i - 1}}{1 - (1 + r)^{-\ell_i}} \tag{v}$$

and

$$C_T = \frac{mF}{r} - \sum_{i=1}^{n} p_i x_i \frac{(1 + r)^{-Z_i}}{1 - (1 + r)^{-\ell_i}} \tag{vi}$$

## THE CRUCIAL IMPORTANCE TO ACCOUNTANCY, LAW AND ECONOMICS OF EQUATIONS (v) and (vi)

It would be difficult to exaggerate the importance of these two results. We shall show that together they provide us with a foundation for a great deal of economic theory as well as a solution to the balance sheet problem from which we began[5].

Consider a problem which has consistently bedevilled economists' attempts to generalise the theory of investment. It is a simple matter to write down what rate of profit is yielded by a single investment say $Q$ which gives rise to a set of revenue, say $p$, at times $t_1, t_2, t_3 \ldots$ to $t_n$. Economists have long understood that the profit rate for such an investment must be that which will equate the value of the investment with the present value of the future revenues it creates. All that is necessary to find $r$ is to solve the equation

$$Q = p \sum_{t=t_i}^{t_n} (1 + r)^{-t}$$

Similarly it is easy to determine the profit rate appropriate to any combination of dated inputs leading to known dated outputs provided the process comes to an end. To put it another way there is no difficulty as long as we can match up inputs with outputs and write some equation similar to that above.

Unfortunately in practice production processes are very seldom of this simple kind. At any moment of time, the businessman who attempts to draw up a profit and loss account for some previous period will find that he has made some investments in the period which have not yet yielded revenue and has received some revenue properly attributable to investments made at a much earlier date. No matter how long the period of the account is extended in either direction it is impossible to disentangle the inputs and outputs belonging to any period of the accounts from those which do not. In short the profit rate cannot be determined by equating the present values of inputs and outputs because it is impossible to write down for any finite period what the inputs and outputs appropriate to that period are. To do so requires a foreknowledge of the very profit rate it is desired to determine.

All of this simply recognises the fact from which we began, namely that the 'proper' profit rate payable in any period depends in an important way upon a 'proper' valuation of work in progress and part worn assets. The accountant meets the difficulty by adopting rules of thumb. In the main, economists have tended to solve the accountants' problem by assuming it away. It will be noticed that theories of investment which purport to show how the profit rate is determined are usually based on very simple examples where there is no work in progress left and no part used equipment to value at some one point of time at least. In some cases part used equipment is valued at some 'scrap' value without any explanation of how such a value is determined or why the investor should be willing to part with his asset at such a price. When the problem appears explicitly as one of valuing part worn assets rather than setting a profit rate economists tend to evade it by assuming some known normal or market rate of profit at which the future earnings of the asset to be valued can be discounted. This procedure is appropriate in some contexts but may be incorrect when the valuation is required to fix the profit rate in a going concern where the 'true' profit rate is different from the market rate.

The device suggested above leading to equations (v) and (vi) is the only logical way of breaking the vicious circle: (v) is in fact a definition of the profit rate in terms of revenue inputs and prices in the most general case. Moreover it is derived by formulating explicitly a definition of profit which in the present writer's experience comes close to that intuitively recognised by lawyers and accountants.

It is important to understand that the claim that profit is 'that rate which could be paid indefinitely if the productive process were to continue indefinitely with no change in revenue or input prices' does not in any way depend upon whether the process is in fact continued or not: (v) yields a rate which it is appropriate to pay today given today's prices and revenue. We shall consider later what is 'correct' if prices change or have change at some time between the founding of the enterprise and the present.

## THE MONEY CAPITAL REQUIREMENT IN TERMS OF FACTOR PRICES, PROFITS AND PRODUCTION TECHNIQUE ALONE

Formula (vi) defines money capital in terms of revenue, input prices and the profit rate determined by (v): (v) and (vi) together give money capital at time $T$ in terms of prices of inputs and the profit rate. Thus

$$C_T = \sum_{i=1}^{n} p_i x_i \frac{(1+r)^{t_i - 1} - (1+r)^{-Z_i}}{1-(1+r)^{-\ell_i}} \qquad \text{(vii)}$$

Profit payable in any period is $rC_T$ plus any revenue derived from outside investments against depreciation. As $C_T$ fluctuates over time and as $r$ is constant given revenue and prices, $rC_T$ must fluctuate over time. Against this, revenue from investment will fluctuate as the size of the depreciation fund varies. If the rate of return on external investments happens to be the same as the internal rate $r$, the two fluctuations will exactly compensate one another. Total profits payable will be constant over time being $r$ per cent of the fixed issued capital.

## VALUATION OF BALANCE SHEET ASSETS

Formula (vii) gives also the clue to the proper valuation of balance sheet assets. Before turning to this however it is convenient to consider for a moment the relation between (vii) and various formulae for capital devised by economists interested in the theory of investment.

Consider the average value around which $C_T$ fluctuates. We observe first that $C_T$ is in fact the sum of a series of expressions, one for each input, all of which fluctuate indefinitely. The average value of this sum is therefore the sum of the means of its separate components, that is, the sum of the means of all terms like

$$p_i x_i \frac{(1+r)^{t_i-1} - (1+r)^{-Z_i}}{1-(1+r)^{-\ell_i}}$$

which contain only one variable over time, namely $Z_i$. Evidently we need only to find the mean of $(1 + r)^{-Z_i}$ which may be written down at once

$$\frac{1}{\ell_i} \sum_{Z=1}^{\ell_i} (1+r)^{-Z_i} = \frac{1-(1+r)^{-\ell_i}}{r\ell_i}$$

Putting this in (vii) yields

$$\bar{C} = \sum_{i=1}^{n} p_i x_i \left[\frac{(1+r)^{t_i-1}}{1-(1+r)^{-\ell_i}} - \frac{1}{r\ell_i}\right] \qquad \text{(viii)}$$

where $\bar{C}$ is the mean $C_T$ we are seeking.

Economists will recognise (viii) as a generalised form of various formulae for capital devised by the various creators of investment theory. For example if we assume with Wicksell that all goods are single use goods (all $\ell_i = 1$) (viii) reduces that writer's formula for the value of social capital as set out in his celebrated account of the economics of maturing wine[6]. If on the other hand all maturity times are unity (viii) can be seen to be equivalent to Wicksell's alternative formula for the value of capital equipment[7].

We have in fact established the interesting conclusion that the formula for the value of capital derived from the analysis of simple cases where a finite number of inputs and outputs can be directly linked turns out to be the mean of the more general formula which hold when inputs and outputs cannot be linked. Again we notice that (viii) cannot help the accountant. For if $C$ is always constant as given by (viii) then the depreciation fund is always zero (or constant) and hence no problem of revaluation of assets can ever arise. We must bear in mind also that (vii) holds quite generally whether the enterprise is in economic equilibrium or not, $r$ being the internal rate of profit not necessarily equal to the 'normal' market rate. This is a point crucial to later work. We are now in a position to reconsider our company balance sheet.

## THE BREAKDOWN OF CAPITAL INTO STOCKS, FIXED ASSETS AND WORK IN PROGRESS

It has already been argued that once profits are known assets are valued and vice versa. Formulae (v) and (vi) confirm this for they lead directly to

(vii) which is no more or less than the sum of the value of all items in the balance sheet excluding outside investments and cash. Indeed (vii) divides neatly into two parts, fixed assets and work in progress, as we shall proceed to prove.

Since we now know the correct value of $r$ we beg no questions by using $r$ to determine what proportion of the total cost of the $i$th input (including profit) should be regarded as having become embodied in the product during each time period. It is natural to assign an equal share of total cost to each time period although of course there is an arbitrary element in such a procedure which must be justified later. We find the required proportion $E$ by imagining that some shareholder who has contributed a sum of money $p_i\, x_i$ is to be repaid in equal instalments $E$, at each time period up to $\ell_i$, the life of the $i$th input. Profit is always paid on the balance due to the shareholder. The last payment must just exhaust the balance owing at the end of the last time period.

Thus

$$E_i(1+r)^{-1} + \ldots + E_i(1+r)^{-\ell_i} = p_i x_i$$

or what amounts to the same thing

$$E_i(1+r)^{\ell_i - 1} + \ldots + E_i = p_i x_i (1+r)^{\ell_i}.$$

Summing, we note that

$$E_i = p_i x_i \frac{r}{1-(1+r)^{-\ell_i}}$$

It may help the reader to assume for a moment that all maturity times are unity so that revenue always appears at the end of the time period in which $E$ is embodied. In this case it is obvious that a payment to shareholders equal to the sum of all $E_i$ at each period of time will fully discharge the obligation of the enterprise to its shareholders. The sum of all $E_i$ must therefore equal total revenue $mF$. Remembering our definition of $E$ we see at once that equation (v) express this fact for ($t_i = 1$).

Now if all maturity times are unity there can be no work in progress. Raw materials pass through every phase of production and are sold in one time period only. In this case $C_T$ reduces to

$$C_T = \sum_{i=1}^{n} p_i x_i \frac{1-(1+r)^{-Z_i}}{1-(1+r)^{-\ell_i}}$$

Furthermore it is easily confirmed

$$p_i x_i \frac{1-(1+r)^{-Z_i}}{1-(1+r)^{-\ell_i}} = \sum_{Z=1}^{Z=Z_i} E_i(1+r)^{-Z}$$

Remembering that $Z_i$ is the balance of life remaining in the $i^{\text{th}}$ asset at any moment of time we recognise $C_T$ as the present value of notional cost payments belonging to existing assets which have not yet at time $T$ been embodied in the product. This is precisely what is meant by fixed capital.

Let us now write $C_T$ in the general case in a form obviously equivalent to (vii)

$$C_T = \sum_{i=1}^{n} p_i x_i \frac{(1+r)^{t_i-1}-1}{1-(1+r)^{-\ell_i}} + \sum_{i=1}^{n} p_i x_i \frac{1-(1+r)^{-Z_i}}{1-(1+r)^{-\ell_i}}$$

From the argument above it is clear that the second term in this expression is fixed capital. This suggests that the first term must be work in progress and this is evidently so. For

$$p_i x_i \frac{(1+r)^{t_i-1}-1}{1-(1+r)^{-\ell_i}} = \sum_{t=0}^{t=t_i-2} E_i(1+r)^t$$

that is, it is the sum of notional costs already embodied in the product (but not yet sold), at time $T$, compounded at the profit rate from the time the input was actually embodied to time $T$. In other words work in progress is valued at notional cost $E$ as work is carried out, but, in addition, profit is charged on notional cost for the time elapsing between the moment work is carried out and the moment of sale of the final product.

Readers who may wonder why the summation is made from $E$ to $E(1+r)^{t-2}$ and not $E(1+r)$ to $E(1+r)^{t-1}$ are reminded that the notional cost $E$ is not regarded as embodied in the product until the end of the period in which work is carried out and that the product is sold $t_i - 1$ periods after the $i^{\text{th}}$ input is embodied.

Raw materials *not* embodied in work in progress at time $T$ are included in the fixed capital item – for this contains a number of elements $p_j x_j$, $p_k x_k$ where $j$ and $k$ are single use inputs with unit life. The objection that raw material stocks are not usually treated as fixed capital by accountants can easily be met by separating the second terms of (viii) into two parts, those inputs with unit life (single use goods) and those with a life of more than one time unit.

## A BALANCE SHEET 'PROPERLY' VALUED

Our balance sheet at time $T$ can now be rewritten with general formulae in place of values.

In our balance sheet, $r^*$ is the rate of return on outside investments. If $r = r^*$ then the balance due to shareholders reduces to $rC_I$. Items 4 and 5 are shown as adjusted for amounts owing and due because maturity times are measured from the moment of payment for inputs to the moment when cash is received for the product and not from the moment of receipt of the input to the moment of delivery of the product. If it is desired to follow accounting conventions more closely we could add back creditors to item 4 and show the item again separately. Similarly with item 5.

The accountant may object to some of our valuations. In particular he is likely to object most violently to the profit taking on work in progress which is implied by the formula for item 5. It is often argued that profit is not 'earned' until the product is actually sold.

We on the other hand have *proved* that if work in progress is valued at anything less than the sum implied by formula (v) then two things must have occurred. First, in at least one past period by the standard we have set too little profit must have been paid out. Second, and this is a consequence of the first, more money has been retained in the enterprise than is necessary to sustain the process. The depreciation fund has been set too high. It is important to recognise that this is not a value judgement about which differences of opinion are admissible. It is a question of fact about which there can be no disagreement. If issued capital has been chosen correctly so that at some time in the cycle of asset replacement the depreciation fund is zero than the accountant's under-valuation of work in progress will create a situation where the depreciation fund is never zero. This is in contradiction with our desire to minimise the depreciation.

Next the accountant may consider that we have overvalued item 3 on at least three counts. First, it is common practice to value fixed equipment at original cost less a proportion of the original cost equal to the expired fraction of the asset's life. That is, the balance sheet item 3 would be valued $p_i x_i (Z_i/\ell_i)$. And it is easy to show that this will be less than our valuation for reasonable values of $r$[8]. The discrepancy will be greater the greater is $r$. Second, anticipating the next few paragraphs, accountants might concede the principle that equipment should be priced at the discounted value of its future earnings but argue that, if $r$ is greater than the normal market rate, we have over-valued by setting $r$ too high. Finally, the assumption that an equal proportion of the cost of any machine is embodied in the product in each time period might be questioned. Ac-

TABLE 1.A2 XYZ Co. balance sheet, at time $T$

| *Liabilities* | | *Assets* | |
|---|---|---|---|
| 1 Issued capital | $C_I$ | 3 Plant and buildings | $\Sigma p_i x_i \dfrac{1-(1+r)^{-Z_i(T)}}{1-(1+r)^{-\ell_i}}$ for all $l_i \neq 1$ |
| | | 4 Raw material stocks less creditors | $\Sigma p_i x_i$ (for all $\ell_i = 1$) & $t_i = 0$ |
| | | 5 Work in progress and finished stocks less creditors plus debtors | $\sum_{i=1}^{n} p_i x_i \dfrac{(1+r)^{t_i-1}-1}{1-(1+r)^{-\ell_i}}$ |
| | | 6 Investments against depreciation | $C_I - C_T$ |
| 2 Balance of profit due to shareholders | $rC_{T-1} + r^*(C_I - C_{T-1})$ | 7 Cash at bank | $rC_{T-1} + r^*(C_I - C_{T-1})$ |
| Total | $C_I$ + Cash | | $C_I$ + Cash |

countants sometimes depreciate an asset heavily in the early years of its life implying that the rate at which it is embodied diminishes over time. It is easy to see that our method reverses this, depreciating least in the early years of life. This is logical because as time passes the remaining future earnings become less and less heavily discounted.

Against all this we set the same argument used in the case of work in progress. If plant and machinery are not valued as in the balance sheet entry number 3 then at some time or other a 'wrong' profit payment must have been made. And too low a profit rate involves the temporary or permanent retention in the enterprise of more cash than the minimum sufficient to carry on the productive process. If the wrong profit rate is paid once only, depreciation investments are permanently too high. If two offsetting wrong profit payments are made, that is, if there is a time delay in paying profit then depreciation investments are too high temporarily. The depreciation of assets at a greater rate than that implied by our valuation in the early years of life and at a slower rate later could be arranged so that correct profits are paid on the average but is bound to result in the temporary retention of unnecessary cash.

## DURABLE ASSETS – VALUE-IN-USE OR MARKET PRICE?

It should be pointed out also that there is a certain logic about our choice of asset value quite independent of the profit rate argument. As already indicated most of our difficulties arise out of the fact that it is impossible to associate inputs at particular times with outputs at some other time. Having derived our basic equation (v) namely

$$mF = r \, \Sigma \, p_i x_i \, \frac{(1+r)^{t_i - 1}}{1-(1+r)^{-\ell_i}}$$

it is tempting to regard

$$rp_i \frac{(1+r)^{t_i - 1}}{1-(1+r)^{-\ell_i}} = L_i$$

as the revenue due to the use of one unit of the $i^{\text{th}}$ input for one time period. Indeed it will be shown later that *provided inputs are used in proportions and scales such that r is the maximum profit rate possible* $L_i$ is the change in revenue flow which would result from the addition to the input flow of one more unit of $i$ per period.

In view of this it is natural to set the future expected earnings of any part worn asset with a life remaining of $Z_i$ and $L_i$, $t_i$ periods of time hence, $L_i$ at $(t_i + 1)$ periods and so on to $(t_i + Z_i)$. The present value of this stream of earnings discounting at the rate $r$ is

$$\sum_{-t_i}^{-(t_i + Z_i)} L_i(1 + r)^t = L_i \frac{(1 + r)^{-(t_i - 1)}(1 - (1 + r)^{-Z_i})}{r}$$

which is precisely the same as our balance sheet valuation.

This last argument does not hold in the general case where the production process is not optimal and where $r$ is not the normal market rate. This however is not surprising for in any situation not an economic equilibrium, cost price and value cease to have the same measure. The value in use to the owner of a piece of equipment is no longer measured either by its market price (if any) or by its replacement cost. The whole notion of valuing part worn equipment in such circumstances becomes ambiguous. This does not mean that our formula against entry 3 in the balance sheet is in any sense incorrect, for it is the only formula which gives rise to the correct rate of profit. On the contrary it is now clear that the only way to make a proper entry in 3 is by the use of our formula. It is impossible to decide what it should be by setting some 'value' upon the assets in circumstances where the meaning of the word value is ambiguous.

## THE TREATMENT OF PRICE CHANGES IN ACCOUNTS

At this point the reader may feel rightly that the accountant's problem is a great deal more difficult than we have so far made it appear. It is true that accounting could be carried on entirely on the basis of our proposed formulae provided prices, inputs, maturity times and revenue conveniently remained constant for an indefinite period. In practice they do not. How should the accountant face both changes which actually have occurred and changes which he expects to occur in the future? As a preliminary to an investigation of this problem consider the Profit and Loss Account for a single period in the simple case we have been considering so far.

Wages and salaries appear as item 1 along with raw materials. As no maturity times have changed there will be no change in any stocks. Item 2 is evidently no more that the difference $C_T - C_{T-1}$ between the 'value' of fixed equipment at time $T$ and 'value' at time $T - 1$ where $Z_j$ is appropriate to time $T - 1$. That is:

$$\Sigma p_j x_j \frac{(1 + r)^{-Z_j+1} - (1 + r)^{-Z_j}}{1 - (1 + r)^{-\ell_j}} = \Sigma p_j x_j \frac{r(1 + r)^{-Z_j}}{1 - (1 + r)^{-\ell_j}} \quad \ell_j \neq 1$$

TABLE 1.A3 XYZ Co. profit and loss account, period (*T*-1)

| | | | |
|---|---|---|---|
| 1 Initial raw materials stock plus purchases and wages less current stock | $\sum_i p_i x_i$ ($\ell_i = 1$) | 4 Sales | $mF$ |
| (N.B. initial and current stock same) | | 5 Revenue from investments | $r^*(C_I - C_{T-1})$ |
| 2 To additions to depreciation | $\sum_{j=1}^{n} p_j x_j - \dfrac{r(1+r)^{-Z_j(T-1)}}{1-(1+r)^{-\ell_j}}$ ($l_j \neq 1$) | | |
| 3 Profit to shareholders | $rC_{T-1} + r^*(C_I - C_{T-1})$ | | |
| Total | $rC_{T-1} + \Sigma p_i x_i \dfrac{r(1+r)^{-Z_i(T-1)}}{1-(1+r)^{-\ell_i}} + r^*(C_I - C_{T-1})$ | Total | $mF + r^*(C_I - C_{T-1})$ |

Evidently also both sides of the profit and loss account are equal by our basic equation (vi). All that is meant is that revenue in the period is just sufficient to meet current outgoings, profit payment and adjustment of depreciation fund. New fixed equipment will of course be paid for out of the depreciation fund itself.

To illustrate what happens when parameter changes take place consider a simple example. Suppose that at time $T^0$ input prices change from $p$ to $p^1$ leading to a change in the profit rate from $r^0$ to $r^1$. To find $r^1$ we can follow precisely the same procedures that have already been developed except that the computation is now more complex. Evidently, capital tied up is the difference between all payments to date compounded up to time $T$, less revenue similarly compounded. The new profit rate $r^1$ is that which, if it is paid out from time $T^0$ onwards, leaves capital fluctuating about a finite mean. To compute this it is quicker to use the old formula for capital at time $T^0$ and to add to this payments and receipts from time $T^0 + 1$. Profit must of course be calculated at the new rate for all subsequent payments. Thus

$$C_T^1 = C_{T^0}(1 + r^1)^{T-T^0} + \sum_{i=1}^{n} \sum_{S=0}^{S_i} p_i^1 \, x_i(1 + r^1)^{T-T^0-Z_i^0-S\ell_i}$$

$$- \sum_{t=T^0}^{T-T^0} mF(1 + r^1)^t \tag{ix}$$

where $Z_i^0$ is the value of $Z_i$ at time $T^0$ and where we recall that the maturity time of the $i^{\text{th}}$ input for the process with revenue beginning at $T^0$ is $-Z_i^0$, since the first payment will be made at $T^0 + Z_i$. Accordingly, summing and rearranging (ix) we have

$$C_T^1 = (1 + r^1)^{T-T^0} \left( C_{T^0} - \frac{mF}{r^1} + \Sigma p_i^1 x_i \frac{(1 + r^1)^{-Z_i^0}}{1 - (1 + r^1)^{-\ell_i}} \right.$$

$$\left. + \frac{mF}{r^1} - \Sigma p_i^1 x_i \frac{(1 + r^1)^{-Z_i}}{1 - (1 + r^1)^{-\ell_i}} \right) \tag{x}$$

For $C_T^1$ to remain finite the first term in the expression above must be zero. Hence the new capital at time $T$, ($C_T^1$), is given by

$$C_T^1 = \frac{mF}{r^1} - \Sigma p_i^1 x_i \frac{(1 + r^1)^{-Z_i}}{1 - (1 + r^1)^{-\ell_i}} \tag{xi}$$

## VALIDITY OF THE CAPITAL FORMULA EVEN UNDER PRICE CHANGES

This, of course, is the old formula (vi) with the parameters $p^1$ and $r^1$ substituted. A general rule emerges. Whatever parameter changes take place formula (vi) *always* holds provided the *current* parameters are inserted. We have not proved this assertion for all possible cases but it is a matter of common sense that it should be true; for if we take the average over time of both sides of (vi) and multiply by $r^1$ we obtain

$$r^1 \bar{C} = mF - \frac{\Sigma p_i^1 x_i}{\ell_i}$$

or, profits paid out on the average per period must equal revenue less average outgoings per period. It is surely obvious that however $r$ and $C$ are defined $r$ multiplied by $C$ can never be greater or less than revenue less average outgoings if profit payments are to be maintained indefinitely.

## CALCULATING THE NEW PROFIT RATE

On the other hand it will also be seen from the work above that our fundamental equations (v), and consequently (vii), do *not* hold in the case under review. For if (vi) is true at all times it must be true at time $T^0$ for both the old parameters and the new. Thus one of the equations

$$C_{T^0} = \frac{mF}{r} - \Sigma p_i x_i \frac{(1+r)^{-z_i^0}}{1-(1+r)^{-\ell_i}} = \frac{mF}{r^1} - \Sigma p_i^1 x_i \frac{(1+r^1)^{-z_i^0}}{1-(1+r^1)^{-\ell_i}} \qquad \text{(xii)}$$

must be used to determine $r^1$ and not simply formula (v) with new parameters. In words the new rate of profit is chosen in such a way that the quantity of capital at time $T^0$ is not affected by the fact that inputs have changed in price. This is in line with our notion of capital as money tied up in the process; for obviously a change in any input price does not affect the money tied up until it actually becomes necessary to purchase additional units of input at the increased price.

It is not worthwhile actually to work the new formula for capital in the form (vii). It will already be obvious to the reader that it cannot be the same as (vii). The reason for the difference is simply that the money tied up in a process set up before the date of any input price change is different in general from that which would be tied up in the same productive process set up after the date of the price change. And our two formulae tell us what money is actually tied up. They do not measure either the value in use of part worn equipment, the market price of assets or cost less depreciation all of which might be different from one another and from money tied up.

## AMBIGUITY OF THE IDEA OF PROFIT RATE

This raises an interesting point. So far we have defined capital as money tied up in the process and have claimed that this is unambiguously known. There would have been ambiguity however were it not for the fact that a particular notion of profit is implied in our method. Profit has been expressed throughout as a rate $r$ on actual money capital tied up which, it is assumed, should properly be constant over time for any given process as long as there is no change in input price or revenue. But we need not have assumed this. We could, if we chose, think of profit as a rate (say $\pi$) payable per unit of time to be kept constant irrespective of fluctuations in capital tied up (excluding depreciation fund investments). This would yield a very different formula for capital tied up. In fact we find that in this case

$$C_T = \Sigma p_i x_i \frac{t_i - Z_i}{\ell_i} \qquad \text{(xiii)}$$

The profit paid out in each period being

$$= mF - \frac{\Sigma p_i x_i}{\ell_i} \qquad \text{(xiv)}$$

which is the same as $r\bar{C}$ computed according to our earlier definitions.

Clearly, such a formula gives correct profit *on the average* but it is equally clear that capital tied up would not, even in economic equilibrium. be equal to the present value of the future earnings of assets. There is an implication here that although, on the average, profit payments are right, from time to time too much or too little has been paid out in particular periods.

In short our work so far rests on an implicit definition of profit as a *price* for the *use* of actual money capital subscribed in contrast to the rate of earnings per unit of time of a productive enterprise. We have accepted this notion of profit partly because it reflects the ways of thinking of economists, accountants and lawyers and partly because it is consistent with our treatment of other inputs all of which have prices per unit. Indeed, our choice is so obviously a correct one that the point would not have been raised here at all were it not for the fact that we now wish to modify it.

## PROFIT TO INCLUDE 'WINDFALL' PROFIT – AN ALTERNATIVE DEFINITION OF PROFIT RATE

In common parlance, profit is not only the price for the use of capital in a productive process; windfall 'profit' may also accrue as a result of a rise in the price of the assets held. Although usually expressed as a percentage of the initial money investments windfall profits of this kind cannot be thought of as a continuous rate over time. They are none the less profits, and if they occur as a by-product of a productive process they are amounts due to shareholders. Unfortunately (in the short run) for the shareholder, capital gains are of necessity associated with an increased capital requirement so that what is received with one hand must be given back with the other. For this reason we hear a great deal about 'paper' profits which are not really profits. A more accurate decription will be illiquid profits and even this, as will later become clear, may not be strictly correct. Some proportion may be liquid. On the other hand it could be that the increase on capital requirement is greater than the 'paper' profit, in which case more capital must be put up by the shareholder.

In the light of this we have to reconsider our definition of the profit of a productive enterprise and rework our 'correct' profit rate. Profit is not simply the rate $r$. It includes also any capital gains or losses due to parameter changes. It does not matter that not all of these 'profits' are in fact to be paid out. They *could* be paid out in principle if the whole of the new increased capital requirement were raised by new issues of capital. If profits are retained to avoid the necessity of making new issues, then they automatically become capital and profit at the rate $r$ is payable on them thereafter.

## A MORE LOGICAL TREATMENT – REINSTATEMENT OF EQUATIONS (v) and (vi)

We have to include the effect of this modification upon our earlier computation (p. 43). First, we include an unknown capital gain or loss $C^1_{T^0} - C_{T^0}$ into formula (ix) as an addition to money tied up upon which profit is to be paid, i.e.

$$C_T^1 = C_{T^0}(1+r^1)^{T-T^0} + (C_{T^0}^1 - C_{T^0})(1+r^1)^{T-T^0} + \sum_{i=1}^{n}\sum_{S=0}^{S_i} p_i^1 x_i (1+r^1)^{T-T^0-Z_i^0-S\ell_i} - \sum_{t=T^0}^{T-T^0} mF(1+r^1)^t \quad \text{(xv)}$$

or

$$C_T^1 = \left(C_{T^0}^1 - \frac{mF}{r^1} + \Sigma p_i^1 x_i \frac{(1+r^1)^{-Z_i^0}}{1-(1+r^1)^{-\ell_i}}\right)(1+r^1)^{T-T^0} + \left(\frac{mF}{r^1} - \Sigma p_i^1 x_i \frac{(1+r^1)^{-Z_i}}{1-(1+r^1)^{-\ell_i}}\right)$$

Evidently, we have now lost equation (xii) which determines $r^1$, for (xii) simply reduces to (xi) at time $T^0$ and the known $C_{T^0}$ and $r$ disappear. The reason for this is obvious. We have put into (ix) a payment $(C_{T^0}^1 - C_{T^0})$ the magnitude of which is not known until $C_{T^0}^1$ itself is known. It is impossible to proceed until we are able to measure the capital gain according to some acceptable principle, or what amounts to the same thing until we have determined $r^1$.

Fortunately our work so far suggests an obvious principle. The rate of profit in a going concern ought not to depend upon the date it was originally set up. Identical processes operating identically at the same moment in time should show the *same* rate of profit even if one happened to be in being at some earlier date when input prices were different while the other was not.

The method for determining $r^1$ should be the straightforward solution of equations (v) and (vi) with the new parameter $p^1$ which is the same thing as the solution of (v) and (xi). Once we have $r^1$ we have $C_{T^0}^1$ and hence the capital gain.

We now have a set of principles to guide our accounting procedure which applies when prices change, which is independent of any notion of 'valuation' and which is equally valid whether the enterprise is in equilibrium or not.

## THE PROFIT AND LOSS ACCOUNT WITH CHANGING PRICES

To illustrate the working of the principles we now present the profit and loss account for the period $T^0$ during which input prices changed from $p_i$ to $p_i^1$. This may be compared with the profit and loss account for the constant prices case.

TABLE 1.A4 XYZ Co. Profit and Loss Account period ($T^0$)

| | | | | | |
|---|---|---|---|---|---|
| 1 | Initial stock of work in progress | $\sum_{1}^{n} p_i x_i \frac{(1+r)^{t_i-1}-1}{1-(1+r)^{-\ell_i}}$ | | 9 Sales | mF |
| 2 | plus wages and raw material purchases | $\sum_{i} p_i^1 x_i$ <br> $\ell_i = 1$ | | 10 Revaluation of plant and buildings | $\sum_{1}^{n} p_i x_i \frac{1-(1+r^1)^{-Z_i^0}}{1-(1+r^1)^{-\ell_i}}$ |
| 3 | less closing stock | $\sum_{1}^{n} p_i^1 x_i + p_i^1 x_i \frac{(1+r^1)^{t_i-1}-1}{1-(1+r^1)^{-\ell_i}}$ <br> $\ell_i \neq 1$ | | | $-\sum_{1}^{n} p_i x_i \frac{1-(1+r)^{-Z_i^0}}{1-(1+r)^{-\ell_i}}$ |
| | | Sub total | = (Current purchases plus stock and WIP revaluation) | | |
| 4 | Depreciation charge | | $\sum_{i}^{n} p_i x_i \frac{r^1(1+r^1)^{-Z_i^0+1}}{1-(1+r^1)^{-\ell_i}}$ <br> $\ell_i \neq 1$ | 11 Revenue from depreciation fund investments | $r_0(C_i - C_{T^0})$ |
| 5 | Illiquid profit to Capital A/C | | $C_i^1 - C_i$ | | |
| 6 | Profit | $r^1 C_{T^0}^1 + C_{T^0}^1 - C_{T^0}$ | | | |
| 7 | less retained | $C_I^1 - C_I$ | | | |
| 8 | plus | $r^*(C_I - C_{T^0})$ | | | |
| | | | Sub-total | | |
| | | | *Total* | | *Total* |

Evidently, both sides of this account balance by equation (xi). The cost of sales (items 1, 2 and 3) sums to purchase of all single use inputs at old prices plus work in progress revaluation. Gross profit ($= mf -$ cost of sales) includes therefore, the profit or loss on revaluation of work in progress plus the gain due to single use input stock appreciation. Item 10 includes the profit or loss due to revaluation of inputs not yet embodied in product less stock of single use goods. Ordinary profit ($r^1 C^1_{T^0}$) must therefore be adjusted by the gain or loss due to the revaluation of capital as a whole to make the account balance (item 6). As maximum possible capital requirement is affected by the parameter changes some part of profit is not liquid and must be withheld from distribution (item 5). This transaction must be thought of as paying out profit to shareholders which is then used by them to take up new shares in the company. Issued capital is therefore written up to an amount $C^1_I - C_I$. Since by equation (xi)

$mF = r^1 C^1_T -$ depreciation charge (item 4) $-$ expenditure on wages & raw materials cash available after adjustment of depreciation fund investment will be $r^1 C^1_{T^0}$. Accordingly, shareholders dividends can be paid leaving a cash balance of

$$C^1_I - C_I - C^1_{T^0} + C_{T^0}.$$

This money must be used to buy further investments against depreciation so that the total fund becomes

$$(C_I - C_{T^0}) + (C^1_I - C_I - C^1_{T^0} + C_{T^0}) + (\text{Item 4}) = C^1_I - C^1_{(T^0+1)}$$

The enterprise, so far as its balance sheet is concerned, is now in precisely the same situation as it would have been if it had been set up during a period in which current prices were obtained. We are now in a position to use formulae (v) and (vi) to consider the choice of optimal scale and technique of the enterprise and to study the economy as a whole.

## APPENDIX NOTES

1 This simply avoids the tedious alternative which would be to pay back to the shareholders all temporarily uncommitted cash recalling it again as soon as it is needed. Nowadays of course with the almost complete loss of shareholders' control almost all profits are 'retained'.

2 That is, 'true' depreciation not the rules of thumb commonly used in the absence of an acceptable theory or those imposed by tax authorities.

3 Or even the type that is supposed to depreciate at a constant rate.

4 $\sum_{S=0}^{S_i} r^S = \dfrac{1 - r^{n+1}}{1 - r}$ cf. C. V. Durell, *Advanced Algebra*, vol. I, pp. 35ff.

5 That is, how to determine 'true' profit, or what amounts to the same thing, 'true' depreciation.

6 Cf. K. Wicksell, *Lectures on Political Economy* (London: Routledge & Kegan Paul, 1934) p. 176, equation (4).

7 *Op. cit.* p. 283, equation (15) with (4) p. 276 appropriately substituted.

8 It is easy to show this by expanding the formula, item 3 in W. Taylor's series.

# 2 Fixed Capital and the Surrogate Production Function

IAN STEEDMAN

*University of Manchester*

In much macro statistical and econometric work – most notably in the estimation of 'aggregate production functions' – the 'amount of capital' is represented by a single magnitude, the aggregate value of the vast set of heterogeneous objects which constitute the capital stock. The implicit claim is thus that the value of capital is the measure of capital which adequately represents capital's various economically relevant properties. In a well-known paper Samuelson (1962) sought to show that certain properties of some economic systems, involving heterogeneous capital goods, could indeed be approximated, to any desired degree of approximation, by the properties of a 'surrogate production function', in which the amount of capital is represented by its value.

In Samuelson's model of the economy, any technique for the production of the consumption commodity consists of two distinct productive processes. In one of them, labour works with a particular kind of machine to produce the consumption commodity, while in the other process labour works with that same kind of machine to produce further machines of that kind. (A given technique thus involves only one type of machine but capital goods are nevertheless heterogeneous, in the economy, since each technique involves a qualitatively different kind of machine.) Now, as was noted by Samuelson and subsequently shown definitively by Garegnani (1970) Samuelson could not have demonstrated the existence of a surrogate production function had he not made the very special assumption of 'equal proportions'; the assumption, that is, that each type of machine employed the same amount of labour whether used in making the consumption commodity or in making more machines of the same kind. It is shown below that the 'equal proportions' assumption was not, however, a *sufficient* condition for the validity of Samuelson's demonstration of the existence of a surrogate production function. The source of the difficulty is to be found in the fact that Samuelson, unlike Garegnani, did not restrict his analysis to the case of circulating capital but quite explicitly allowed for the existence of fixed capital, which he assumed to be subject to radioactive depreciation.[1] Now the assumption of radioactive depreciation, whilst simple, is hardly a plausible one, as has been pointed out by, for example, Morishima (1969, p. 89) and it will be shown below to have been just as essential to Samuelson's argument as was the 'equal proportions' assumption. Since anyone interested in the measurement of capital in practice will inevitably be concerned with fixed capital, this result will perhaps be of some interest.

To prove that the existence of fixed capital undermines Samuelson's surrogate production function, if radioactive depreciation is not assumed, it will suffice to consider a very simple case in which the machine (the fixed capital) lasts for just two years, working with constant efficiency throughout its life. It will, of course, be appropriate to make the 'equal proportions' assumption throughout, in order to emphasise that we are concerned here with an objection to the surrogate production function which is additional to that discussed by Garegnani.

## A SINGLE TECHNIQUE

Consider a single technique for the production of the consumption commodity, which we shall call 'corn', by means of a machine and labour. The machine, which can be used by labour to produce further machines of the same type, lasts for two periods of production (two 'years'), working with constant efficiency. As is shown in the first two rows of Table 2.1, one new machine can produce, when operated by one unit of labour, either $m$ new machines or $q$ units of corn, one *old* machine being produced in either case as an inevitable by-product. The third and fourth rows show that one old machine and one unit of labour can produce either $m$ new machines or $q$ units of corn. (There is, of course, no by-product in these rows, since the machine lasts only two years.)

TABLE 2.1 A single technique

| *New machine* | *Old machine* | *Labour* | | *New machine* | *Old machine* | *Corn* |
|---|---|---|---|---|---|---|
| 1 | – | 1 | → | $m$ | 1 | – |
| 1 | – | 1 | → | – | 1 | $q$ |
| – | 1 | 1 | → | $m$ | – | – |
| – | 1 | 1 | → | – | – | $q$ |

It is to be noted that Table 2.1 embodies the assumption of 'equal proportions' – one unit of labour always works with one machine, whatever is being produced; and that of constant efficiency – whether working with a new or with an old machine, one unit of labour can produce $m$ new machines or $q$ units of corn. It is naturally assumed that $q$ is positive; as will emerge below, it must also be assumed that $m > 0.5$.

Taking corn as the standard of value, let $p_n$ and $p_o$ be the values of new and old machines respectively [2] and let $w$ be the real, corn wage rate. If the 'annual' rate of profit is $r$ and wages are paid at the end of the 'year', then the following four relations (obtained from the rows of Table 2.1) must hold, stating that, in each process, the gross revenue (including the value of any by-product) is equal to the capital advanced, *plus* profits on that capital, at rate $r$, *plus* wages.

$$(1 + r)p_n + w = mp_n + p_o, \tag{1}$$

$$(1 + r)p_n + w = p_o + q, \tag{2}$$

$$(1 + r)p_o + w = mp_n, \tag{3}$$

$$(1 + r)p_o + w = q. \tag{4}$$

It follows from (1) and (2) (or from (3) and (4)) that

$$p_n = (q/m). \tag{5}$$

On subtracting (3) from (1) (or (4) from (2)) we see that

$$p_o = \left(\frac{1 + r}{2 + r}\right)p_n \tag{6}$$

$$= \left(\frac{1 + r}{2 + r}\right)(q/m), \tag{7}$$

from (5). While the 'equal proportions' assumption suffices to make the value of a *new* machine independent of $r$ and $w$ (equation (5)), it does not affect the standard accounting result, expressed here in equation (6), that, in general, the value of an old machine in terms of new machines does depend on $r$ and $w$. Consequently the corn value of an *old* machine is not distribution-free[3]. Since the essential force of Samuelson's equal proportions assumption was precisely that of making relative prices independent of distribution, this result immediately suggests – without yet proving – that fixed capital can undermine the existence of a surrogate production function.

If relative prices are independent of distribution, then the relationship between the real wage rate and the rate of profit, $w$ and $r$, must be linear for each technique; and this was indeed the case in Samuelson's analysis based on the radioactive depreciation assumption. It follows from (4) and (7), however, that

$$w = q\left[1 - \frac{(1+r)^2}{m(2+r)}\right]. \tag{8}$$

It will be clear that the wage-profit frontier (8) is *not* linear. In fact, as can easily be shown, $dw/dr < 0$ and $d^2w/dr^2 < 0$ so that the frontier is bowed outwards, or concave to the origin. In a stationary economy, which will be assumed here[4], national income per unit of labour, in terms of corn, $y$, is found by setting $r = 0$ in (8); thus

$$y = q\left[1 - \frac{1}{2m}\right]. \tag{9}$$

The wage is zero when $r = R$ where, from (8),

$$(1+R)^2 = m(2+R). \tag{10}$$

By superimposing the graphs of $(1+R)^2$ and $m(2+R)$ it is easy to see that (10) has a unique positive solution for $m > 0.5$ (and that that solution increases monotonically with $m$). The wage-profit frontier defined by (8) is shown in Fig. 2.1.

As is well-known, in a stationary economy the 'corn' value of capital per unit of labour, $k$, is defined by the national accounting identity 'income *equals* wages plus profits' or, expressed per unit of labour,

$$y \equiv w + rk$$

or

$$k \equiv \frac{y - w}{r} \tag{11}$$

which, from (8) and (9), yields

$$k \equiv (q/2m)\left[\frac{3+2r}{2+r}\right] \tag{12}$$

As can be seen by differentiating (12) with respect to $r$ or, more simply, by considering together Fig. 2.1 and equation (11), $k$ is an increasing function of $r$. Even though 'equal proportions' in the production of corn and of the new machine have been assumed, $k$ rises with $r$ and the wage-profit frontier is necessarily concave from below, simply because $p_o$ rises as $r$ rises. With fixed, rather than circulating, capital, the 'equal

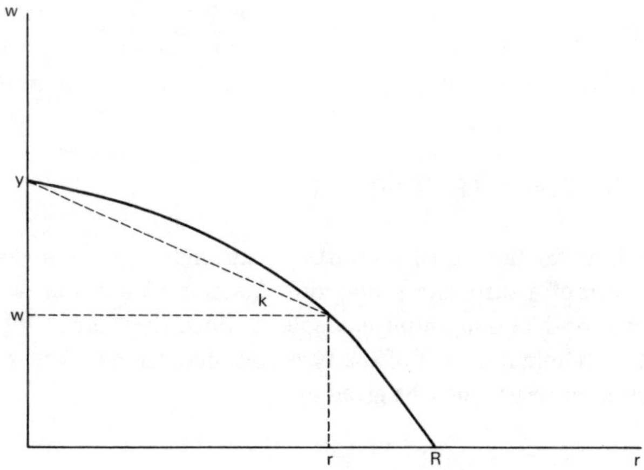


FIG. 2.1 The wage-profit frontier

proportions' assumption does not suffice to make the wage-profit frontier linear[5].

## TWO TECHNIQUES

Suppose now that there are two techniques of the kind described above, each with its own kind of machine which works for two years with constant efficiency. Let the two techniques be described by the parameters $(q_1, m_1)$ and $(q_2, m_2)$. It follows from (8) that the wage-profit frontiers of the two techniques will intersect at the wage rate $\overline{w}$, given by

$$\overline{w} = \left[\frac{(m_1 - m_2)q_1q_2}{m_1q_2 - m_2q_1}\right]. \tag{13}$$

It will be clear from (13) that the two frontiers have at most one intersection for $(w > 0, r > 0)$. Thus there is no possibility of reswitching, i.e. of one technique being the preferred technique at both low and high rates of profit, while the other technique is preferred at intermediate levels of the profit rate[6]. (It should be noted, however, that the 'equal proportions' assumption alone is not sufficient to rule out reswitching, which can still occur if the life of machines *differs* as between techniques. See the appendix to this paper for further discussion of this point).

Considering two techniques between which there is an economically significant switch, while for each of them the 'price' Wicksell effect is negative, the 'real' Wicksell effect must be positive. In the next section we show how $k$ may vary with $r$ when techniques change continuously with $r$.

## INFINITELY MANY TECHNIQUES

To show how far the 'equal proportions' assumption is from guaranteeing the existence of a surrogate production function in the presence of fixed capital, we consider one simple example in which there are infinitely many alternative techniques, each of the type considered above. Let the $q$ and $m$ coefficients for technique $t$ be given by

$$q_t = (7 + 5t - 0.25t^2) \tag{14}$$

and

$$m_t = q_t/(11 + t), \tag{15}$$

and let $t$ vary continuously between 6.69 and 9.00. The wage-profit frontier for technique $t$ will be given by

$$w_t = (7 + 5t - 0.25t^2) - (11 + t)\left[\frac{(1 + r)^2}{2 + r}\right]. \tag{16}$$

As the reader may easily check from (16), for any given value of $r$, $w_t$ is maximised when

$$t = 2\left\{5 - \left[\frac{(1 + r)^2}{2 + r}\right]\right\} \tag{17}$$

By using (17), to eliminate $t$ from (14) and (15), the parameters of the technique used at profit rate $r$ are found and hence, from (8), (9) and (12), the corresponding values of $w$, $y$ and $k$ are obtained. The results of these calculations are given in Table 2.2 and Figs. 2.2 and 2.3.

It will be seen from Fig. 2.2 that as $r$ rises (in logical time) $k$ at first *rises*; only for $r > 62$ per cent are $k$ and $r$ inversely related in the traditional neoclassical manner. This 'capital reversing' occurs, it should be remembered, in a system in which 'reswitching' is quite impossible. (It is an error to think that reswitching is a necessary condition for capital reversing, even when fixed capital is not present.) As $r$ rises from zero to its maximum value of say, $R^*$ (which lies between 1.35 and 1.36), $y$ and $k$ trace out the path shown in Fig. 2.3 in which the arrow shows the direction of movement as $r$ rises. Fig. 2.3 shows, sharply enough perhaps,

TABLE 2.2 Values of $w$, $y$ and $k$

| $r$ | $w$ | $y$ | $k$ |
|---|---|---|---|
| 0.00 | 21.75 | 21.75 | 15.00 |
| 0.20 | 18.67 | 21.73 | 15.22 |
| 0.40 | 15.51 | 21.65 | 15.33 |
| 0.60 | 12.29 | 21.52 | 15.37 |
| 0.80 | 9.04 | 21.32 | 15.35 |
| 1.00 | 5.78 | 21.06 | 15.28 |
| 1.20 | 2.52 | 20.72 | 15.17 |
| 1.35 | 0.09 | 20.43 | 15.06 |
| 1.36 | −0.07 | 20.41 | 15.05 |

that the 'equal proportions' assumption does not suffice for the existence of a surrogate production function.

It will be clear from Fig. 2.3 at least for $r < 62$ per cent, that $r \neq (dy/dk)$. Returning to Fig. 2.1 it will be seen that, for any individual technique frontier $k < (-dw/dr)$. Since each point on the economy wage-profit frontier is tangential to the individual frontier for the technique in use at that point, it follows that $k < (-dw/dr)$ on the economy frontier

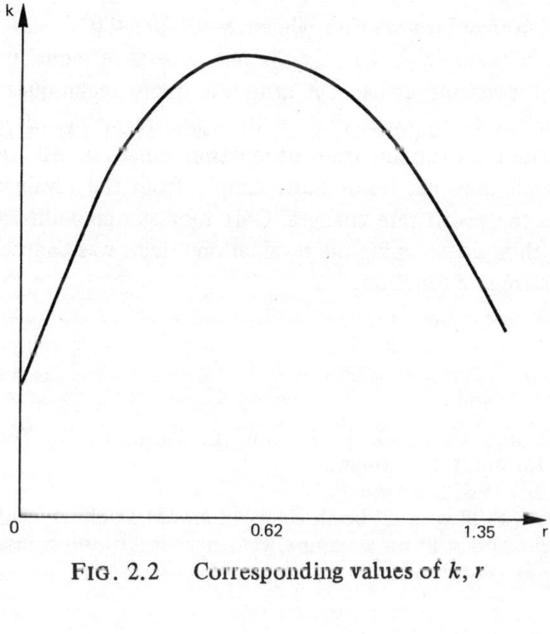


FIG. 2.2 Corresponding values of $k$, $r$

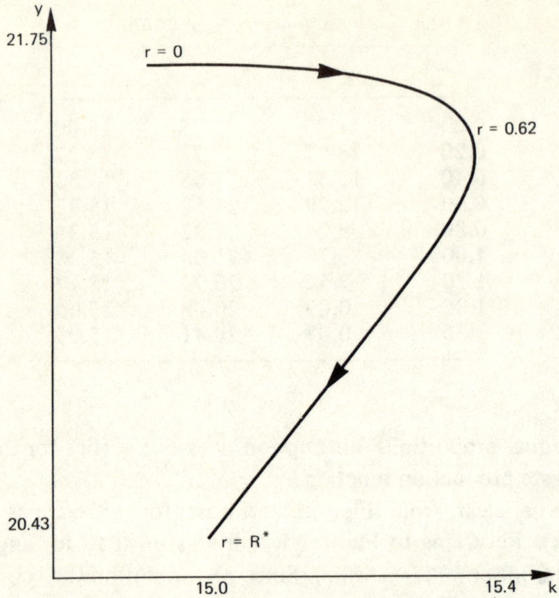


FIG. 2.3 Corresponding values of $y$, $k$

also. Thus, since $(dy/dk) \equiv r + (dr/dk)\ [k + (dw/dr)]$, $(dy/dk) < r$ whenever $(dk/dr) > 0$ and $(dy/dk) > r$ whenever $(dk/dr) < 0$[7].

The above example shows that the phenomena of 'equal proportions', machines of constant efficiency, infinitely many techniques and no re-switching are perfectly compatible with capital reversing, $(dy/dk) \neq r$ and the non-existence of a surrogate production function. All these 'perversities', if such they be, result quite simply from the revaluation of old machines as the profit rate changes. Only by assuming radioactive depreciation, and thus sidestepping the revaluation effect, was Samuelson able to obtain his surrogate function.

## NOTES

I should like to thank P. Leeson, L. Pasinetti, W. Peters and M. Sumner for helpful comments.

1. Samuelson (1962), *passim*.
2 $p_o$ is always the correct 'book-value' of an old machine; *if* old machines are bought and sold on a competitive market with no transaction costs, it will be at price $p_o$.

3 Cf. Joan Robinson's remark in Robinson (1963, p. 409, n.1).
4 Let the proportion of the labour force devoted to the operation of the process shown in the first row of Table 2.1 be $x_i$. A stationary state will obtain provided that $m(x_1 + x_3) = (x_1 + x_2) = (x_3 + x_4) = 0.5$; note that the $x_i$ are not uniquely determined. There will, however, be just one set of such $x_i$ also satisfying the condition that $x_1 = x_3$ and $x_2 = x_4$ (i.e., the condition that no machine need be transferred from one use to another on becoming one year old) namely, $x_1 = x_3 = (1/4m)$ and $x_2 = x_4$ $(2m - 1)/4m$.
5 The assumptions of circulating capital or radioactive depreciation are not the only ones which, in conjunction with that of 'equal proportions', will yield a linear wage-profit frontier. Thus, at the other extreme from circulating capital, the frontier will be linear if machines are *everlasting*, with constant efficiency; such an assumption does not fit in well, of course, with the analysis of a stationary economy. Again, if old machines are *more* efficient than new ones, by a factor of $(1 + m^{-1})$, in each line of production, then the wage-profit frontier will be linear, with $p_o = p_n$ for all $r$.
6 Each technique has a wage-profit frontier of the form shown by (8). Now while $w$ is not a linear function of $r$, it *is* a linear function of $[(1 + r)^2/(2 + r)]$. Since this function of $r$ is monotonic and common to the two technique wage-profit frontiers, it follows that these latter have at most one intersection in the positive $(w, r)$ quadrant.
7 The propositions in this paragraph apply only when $r > 0$; at $r = 0$, $k = (- dw/dr)$.

## APPENDIX: RESWITCHING WITH 'EQUAL PROPORTIONS'

Consider two techniques, each satisfying the 'equal proportions' assumption. One of them has a machine lasting two years just as in the text; its wage-profit frontier will be concave to the origin. The other has a machine lasting only one year; its wage-profit frontier will, of course, be a straight line. There is no reason why these two frontiers should not intersect twice, with the circulating capital technique being used both at low and high rates of profit, while the fixed capital technique is used at intermediate rates of profit. There will thus be reswitching in a system containing only techniques with the 'equal proportions' property.

To illustrate the above, suppose that in the circulating capital technique (technique 1), one machine operated by one unit of labour can produce either 4 new machines or 22 units of corn, while the fixed capital technique (technique 2) has parameters $q_2 = 19$, $m_2 = 19/6$. It is easy to show that the corresponding wage-profit frontiers intersect at both ($r = 100\%$, $w = 11$) and ($r = 200\%$, $w = 5.5$).

It may be of some interest to consider the isoquant diagram for this example. Simple calculations show that for the production of 528 units of corn, the labour and 'capital' used with technique 1 will be given by $L_1 = 32$, $K_1 = 176$, while the corresponding quantities for technique 2 will be given by $L_2 = 33$, $K_2 = 99\ [(3 + 2r)/(2 + r)]$. While $L_1$, $K_1$ and $L_2$ are defined purely by technical conditions, $K_2$ depends on $r$ (and $w$), varying from 148.5 when $r = 0$ to 178.0 when $w = 0$. The 'isoquant' diagram then is as in Fig. 2.A1; point $X$ represents the 'inputs' with technique 1, while all the points on $YZ$ represent the 'inputs', for some $r$, with technique 2.

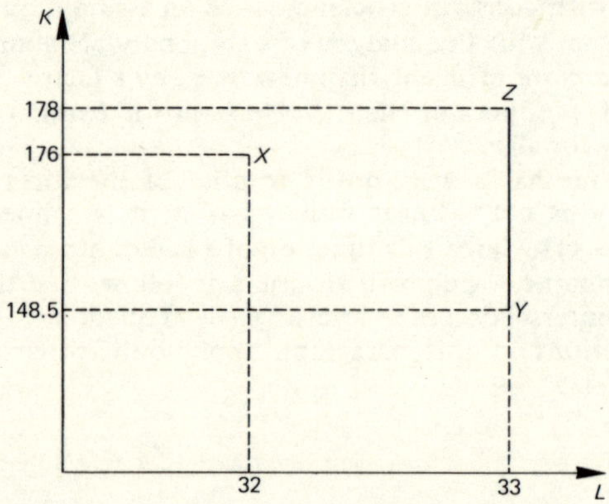


FIG. 2.A1 The isoquant diagram

The variation of technique choice as $r$ and $w$ change cannot be represented quite as easily in Fig. 2.A1 as in the conventional isoquant diagram – simply because the position of $(L_2, K_2)$ itself depends on the slope of the iso-cost line (i.e. on $w/r$) – but it can be done. It is obvious that for low $r$ the iso-cost line through point $X$ passes *below* point $Y$, so that technique 1 is used. As $r$ rises ($w$ falls) the slope of the iso-cost line through $X$ falls and $K_2$ moves up $YZ$. When $r = 100\%$ ($w = 11$) the iso-cost line through $X$ passes through the point $(L_2, K_2)$ and thus we are at a switch-point between the two techniques. For $100\% < r < 200\%$, the iso-cost line through $X$ passes *above the point* $(L_2, K_2)$ so that technique 2 is used. However, at $r = 200\%$ ($w = 5.5$) the iso-cost line through $X$ again passes through $(L_2, K_2)$ and technique 1 is again used. Reswitching has occurred between two 'equal proportions' techniques, simply because of the 'revaluation of old machines' effect.

## REFERENCES

Garegnani, P. (1970), 'Heterogeneous Capital, the Production Function and the Theory of Distribution', *Review of Economic Studies*, pp. 407–36.

Morishima, M. (1969), *Theory of Economic Growth*, (Oxford: Clarendon Press).

Robinson, J. V. (1963), 'Findlay's Robinsonian Model of Accumulation: A Comment', *Economica*, pp. 408–11.

Samuelson, P. A. (1962), 'Parable and Realism in Capital Theory : the Surrogate Production Function', *Review of Economic Studies*, pp. 193–206.

# 3 Efficiency Curves in the Theory of Capital: A Synthesis

JOHN CRAVEN

*University of Kent at Canterbury*

In *Capital and Time* Hicks (1973) introduced the 'efficiency curve' to capital theory. This was not new, except in name, for many authors had written previously of 'factor price frontiers' (Samuelson (1962)), 'optimal transformation frontiers' (Bruno (1969)), 'wage frontiers' (an earlier vintage of Hicks (1965)) and '*w-r* relationships' (Harcourt (1972)). None of these earlier names captured the important dual nature of these curves, which relate not only the real wage to the profit rate, but also the level of consumption output per labour unit to the growth rate. This duality has been demonstrated by Hicks (1973), by Bruno (1969) and in its most general form by Burmeister and Kuga (1970), but none of these authors has exploited the expository powers of efficiency curves to the full. In this paper we shall discuss the role of these curves in many parts of steady state capital theory, including the debates on the measurement of capital and on Marxian theorems. Their usefulness is heightened by the fact that, even in the most complicated models involving joint production, an efficiency curve can be represented in two dimensions without the problems of aggregation which prevent the use of plane geometry so often in multi-sectoral models.

We shall be concerned with models of activity analysis in which there is a finite number of independent constant returns to scale activities. In the first section we shall define the price and quantity efficiency curves for a technique and show that they are coincident whenever both of them exist. In the second section we shall discuss golden rule equilibria in which consumption output per labour unit is maximised – for which a sufficient condition is that the profit rate is equal to the growth rate. We shall establish various comparative properties of golden rule equilibria. In the third section we shall discuss the unrestricted and restricted efficiency curves which Hicks (1973) defines for the neoAustrian model, but which can be defined sensibly in a wider class of models. We shall see that the non-substitution theorem plays an important role in discussions of the existence of restricted efficiency curves. Our two following sections show some of the applications of efficiency curve analysis in capital theory: in section IV we show (following Bruno (1969)) how to illustrate the national accounts; in section V we examine the relation between efficiency curves and the Marxian theorems of Morishima (1973), (1975), and the problems raised by Steedman (1975). The last substantive section shows how the existence of several primary factors (labour and land, or several types of labour) may affect some of the analysis, but not the method of measuring capital.

## I QUANTITY AND PRICE EFFICIENCY CURVES

We need first of all some notation: we define the matrices

$A$ where $a_{ij}$ is the input of good $i$ per unit scale of activity $j$;
$B$ where $b_{ij}$ is the output of good $i$ per unit scale of activity $j$;
$C$ where $c_{kj}$ is the input of primary factor $k$ per unit scale of activity $j$;

and the vectors

$p$ where $p_i$ is the money price of good $i$ (row vector);
$q$ where $q_k$ is the money price of primary factor $k$ (row vector);
$x$ where $x_j$ is the scale of activity $j$ (column vector);
$z$ where $z_i$ is the quantity of good $i$ in the unit consumption basket (column vector);
$b$ where $b_k$ is the supply of primary factor $k$ (column vector).

We assume that there is a uniform time lag in each activity of production, but this causes no loss of generality since longer processes can be subdivided. Constant returns implies that the choice of the unit scale of an activity is arbitrary, and since we shall always use the consumption basket $z$ as *numeraire*, the use of money prices is temporary and unimportant.

Until the last section of the paper we assume that labour is the only primary factor, and its real wage is $w$ in terms of the *numeraire* $z$. The matrix $C$ becomes a row vector $c$, and we shall assume that only one unit of labour is available (this again is an unimportant assumption because of constant returns). Although we use this classical two class analysis, we do not restrict the wage to subsistence.

In this first section we shall define the price and quantity efficiency curves for a *technique*, which consists of some of the activities of production in the economy together with a set of goods which may be overproduced and disposed, and which must be free in competitive equilibrium. We can therefore define a technique by specifying two sets: $H$ is the set of activities to be included in the technique (so that, when that technique is used $x_j = 0$ for $j \notin H$), and $J$ is the set of goods which cannot be overproduced.

The quantity efficiency curve for the technique defined by the sets $H$ and $J$ then relates the consumption output per labour unit ($h$) to the growth rate ($g$): the following conditions must be satisfied for the quantity efficiency curve to exist[1]:

$$\left.\begin{array}{l} \exists x \geqslant 0, h \geqslant 0 \text{ such that } (B-(1+g)A)x \geqslant hz,\ cx = 1 \\ [(B-(1+g)A)x]_i = hz_i \forall\ i \in J \text{ and } x_j = 0\ \forall j \notin H. \end{array}\right\} \qquad [Q1]$$

The *quantity efficiency curve* is then the graph of the value of $h$ against $g$ for those values of $g$ for which $x$ and $h$ are non-negative subject to the conditions of Q1. In order that the economy can both grow and produce consumption output, we require that there is some technique for which the quantity efficiency curve exists with $h > 0$ for some $g > 0$. The following assumptions ensure that this is so:

A1: $\exists x > 0$ such that $Bx \geqslant Ax$ and $(Bx)_i = (Ax)_i$ implies $z_i = 0$ and $(Ax)_i = 0$.

A2: $\nexists x > 0$ *s.t.* $Bx \geqslant Ax$ and $cx = 0$.

If A1 holds for every $z > 0$ the economy is *productive*: if A1 holds for some but not all $z > 0$ the economy is *semiproductive* (Gale (1960)). A2 is 'Lucretian'[2]: labour is always required in production. A1 implies that $\exists \bar{x} \geqslant 0$ s.t. $(B-A)\bar{x} > hz + gA\bar{x}$ for some $h > 0$ and some $g > 0$. A2 implies that $c\bar{x}$ is positive so that $\bar{x}$ and $h$ can be scaled so that $c\bar{x} = 1$. Then a suitable choice of the sets $J$ and $H$ will define a technique whose quantity efficiency curve lies in the positive quadrant in $(g, h)$ space.

The *price efficiency curve* for a technique relates the real wage ($w$) to the profit rate ($r$) under the conditions that non-negative prices exist at which the activities in $H$ earn the profit rate $r$, and that the price of any good not in $J$ is zero. The price efficiency curve is the graph of $w$ against $r$

subject to the conditions:

$$\left.\begin{array}{l}\exists p \geqslant 0, w \geqslant 0 \text{ s.t. } [p(B-(1+r)A]_j = wc_j \ \forall j \in H, \\ pz = 1 \text{ and } p_i = 0 \ \forall i \notin J.\end{array}\right\} \qquad [\text{P1}]$$

The numeraire condition that $pz = 1$ merely scales the prices and ensures that $w$ is the real wage in terms of the consumption basket. We note that no 'competitive' condition has been imposed on the rate of return on the activities not included in $H$: they are not constrained to make no more than the profit rate $r$. A competitive equilibrium using the technique defined by the sets $J$ and $H$ would require also the condition

$$p[B-(1+r)A] \leqslant wc \qquad [\text{C1}]$$

which ensures that no activity makes more than the profit rate $r$[3].

The two efficiency curves summarise the outputs and incomes which can be generated by a particular technique. The most useful property of these curves is that, when both of them exist, they are coincident. More formally, if for some value of $g$ and an equal value of $r$ non-negative $x, h, p$ and $w$ exist satisfying P1 and Q1, then $h = w$. This is easily demonstrated, since whenever $[(B-(1+g)A)x]_i$ exceeds $hz_i$, the corresponding price $p_i$ must be zero.

The possibility that only one of the two curves may exist over certain ranges of $g$ and $r$ can be seen from an example in which $B = \begin{pmatrix} 2 & 1 \\ 4 & 18 \end{pmatrix}$, $A = \begin{pmatrix} 1 & 0 \\ 0 & 6 \end{pmatrix}$, $c = (2 \ 4)$ and $z = \begin{pmatrix} 1 \\ 9 \end{pmatrix}$. Then, if, for example, $H$ = [activity 1] and $J$ = [good 1] the conditions of Q1 tell us that $x = \begin{pmatrix} 1/2 \\ 0 \end{pmatrix}$ and that $1 - g = 2h$, $4 \geqslant 18h$. So, for $g$ and $h$ to be non-negative, $g$ must not be less than 5/9 nor greater than 1. The quantity curve exists for $5/9 \leqslant g \leqslant 1$. The conditions P1 give us that $p = (1 \ 0)$ and that $1 - r = 2w$. The real wage and profit rate will both be positive, and the price efficiency curve exists for $0 \leqslant r \leqslant 1$. Thus the price curve exists over a greater range of values of $r$ than the range of values of $g$ for which the quantity curve exists. Second, for the technique in which $H$ consists of both activities and $J$ of both goods, the conditions of Q1 yield $x_1 = (3-6g)/(26-48g)$, $x_2 = (5-9g)/(26-48g)$ and $h = (4-9g+3g^2)/(13-24g)$. All of the variables are non-negative provided that $g$ is either less than 1/2 or between 5/9 and 2.457. Conditions P1 give $p_1 = (4-6r)/(13-24r)$, $p_2 = (1-2r)/(13-24r)$ and $w = (4-9r+3r^2)/(13-24r)$. All of the price variables are non-negative for values of $r$ less than 1/2 and between 2/3 and 2.457. The quantity curve exists in a range (5/9, 2/3) in which the price curve does not exist.

We have so far said nothing about the shape of the quantity and price efficiency curves, and where only one of them exists there is nothing that can be said of a general nature. But where both of them exist, we can use the following theorem to show that $w$ cannot increase as $r$ increases. The theorem that we prove is somewhat more general, as we show that if the price curve exists for some value of $r$, and the quantity curve at some value of $g$, then $h - w$ cannot have the opposite sign to $r - g$. The conclusion on the shape of the curve is a corollary of this theorem.

*Theorem 1* If the conditions Q1 are satisfied at some value of $g$, and if the conditions P1 are satisfied at some value of $r \neq g$, then $(h - w)/(r - g) \geqslant 0$.

*Proof* From Q1 and P1 we have

$$p(B - (1 + g)A)x \geqslant hpz = h \tag{1}$$

$$\sum_{j \in H} [p(B - (1 + r)A)]_j x_j = w \sum_{j \in H} c_j x_j. \tag{2}$$

Since $x_j = 0$ for $j \notin H$ equation (2) can be written as

$$p(B - (1 + r)A)x = wcx = w \tag{3}$$

and from (1) and (3) we have

$$h - w = (r - g)pAx$$

and since $p_i$, $a_{ij}$ and $x_j$ are non-negative $\forall i$ and $j$, $pAx \geqslant 0$. Q.E.D.

*Corollary* If the price efficiency curve exists in some neighbourhood $(\bar{r} - \delta, \bar{r} + \delta)$ of $\bar{r}$, and the quantity curve exists in the same neighbourhood of $\bar{g} = \bar{r}$, then $w$ cannot be an increasing function of $r$ at $\bar{r}$, and $h$ cannot be an increasing function of $g$ at $\bar{g}$. (Note that, since all the relations in P1 are linear, the price curve is continuous at $\bar{r}$ if it exists in some neighbourhood of $\bar{r}$. Thus if the quantity curve exists also, it is also continuous at $\bar{g} = \bar{r}$.) The proof of this corollary follows from theorem 1.

The conclusion of theorem 1 and its corollary can be strengthened if the value of inputs $pAx$ is positive. For then we can conclude that, if $r \neq g$, $(h - w)/(r - g)$ is positive rather than just non-negative.

## II THE GOLDEN RULE EFFICIENCY CURVE

In the previous section we defined the efficiency curves for the various techniques of the economy. In this section we are concerned to find the maximum level of consumption output per labour unit consistent with a certain growth rate when we can choose from all of the techniques of the economy. We seek in fact to solve the problem

$$\max h \text{ s.t. } [B-(1+g)A]x \geqslant hz, cx \leqslant 1, x \geqslant 0, h \geqslant 0 \qquad \text{[Q2]}$$

When we solve this linear programme, some of the activities will be used at positive levels (defining the set $H$), and some goods will not be overproduced (defining the set $J$), and so we can find the technique which maximises the consumable output $hz$ which can be produced by not more than one unit of labour.

The programme Q2 has a dual, which is best written with $r$ replacing $g$ as

$$\min w \text{ s.t. } p[B-(1+r)A] \leqslant wc, pz \geqslant 1, p \geqslant 0, w \geqslant 0 \qquad \text{[P2]}$$

The solution to the programme P2 yields prices and a real wage at which no activity earns more than the profit rate $r$. With $r = g$, complementary slackness ensures that[4] $w^o = h^o$, and that $p^o z = 1$ whenever $h^o$ and $w^o$ are positive. Hence if $p^o z > 1$, $w^o = 0$, and so the replacement of the *numeraire* condition $p^o z = 1$ by the inequality $p^o z \geqslant 1$ does not affect the use of $z$ as *numeraire* for measuring a positive real wage. Complementary slackness also implies that when $r = g$ the dual programme P2 will choose the technique which maximises consumption output in the sense that the activities of $H$ will earn the profit rate $r$, and the overproduced goods will be free ($p_i^o = 0$ for $i \notin J$). This is the familiar 'golden rule', that a sufficient condition for the choice of the consumption maximising technique at a given growth rate is that the profit rate should equal that growth rate. If we solve Q2 and P2 for a variety of values of $g$ and $r$ we generate the *golden rule efficiency curve* which is the graph of $h^o$ against $g$ and of $w^o$ against $r$. The only assumption required for the curve to exist for all non-negative $g$ and $r$ is A2 which prevents unbounded production from a single unit of labour.

*Theorem 2* Under A2, $\forall\ g \geqslant 0$, $r \geqslant 0$, $\exists\ x$, $h$, $p$ and $w$ satisfying the constraints of Q2 and P2.

*Proof* A2 implies that $\nexists\ x \geqslant 0, h \geqslant 0$ such that

$$\begin{bmatrix} B-A & -z \\ -c & 0 \end{bmatrix} \begin{pmatrix} x \\ h \end{pmatrix} \geqslant \begin{pmatrix} 0 \\ 0 \end{pmatrix} \quad \text{and} \quad (0 \quad 1)\begin{pmatrix} x \\ h \end{pmatrix} > 0.$$

By a well known theorem of linear inequalities (Lancaster (1968) Review 3), this implies that $\exists\ p \geqslant 0$, $w \geqslant 0$ s.t. $p(B-A) \leqslant wc$ and $pz \geqslant 1$. Since $rpA \geqslant 0$, $p[B-(1+r)A] \leqslant wc$ and so the constraints of P2 are satisfied for any $r$. The constraints of Q2 are satisfied for any $g$ when $x = 0$

and $h = 0$. Q.E.D. Since both P2 and Q2 have feasible solutions when $r = g$, they both have optimal solutions, and so the golden rule curve exists for all $g$ and $r \geqslant 0$.

We have already seen that A1 and A2 imply that there is some technique for which $h > 0$ for some $g > 0$, and hence $h^o > 0$ for some $g > 0$. Theorem 2 then tells us that $w^o > 0$ for some $r > 0$, and so A1 and A2 are sufficient for some price efficiency curve to lie in the positive quadrant in $(r, w)$ space. Theorem 2 also tells us that, for any value of $g(= r)$ on the golden rule efficiency curve, both price and quantity efficiency curves exist for the techniques chosen by Q2 and P2. Hence, by theorem 1 and its corollary, the golden rule curve is not upward sloping: $h^o$ is a non-increasing function of $g$[5].

If we further assume that some non-primary input is needed in production, we can show that $h^o(g)$ is positive only for values of $g$ up to a finite limit which measures the maximum feasible growth rate for the economy:

$$\text{A3}: \forall\ x \geqslant 0\ \textit{s.t.}\ (B - A)x \geqslant 0, Ax \geqslant 0.$$

This yields

*Theorem 3* Under A1, A2, A3 $\exists$ finite $g^+ > 0$ *s.t.* $\forall\ g > g^+, h^o(g) = 0$ and $\forall\, g < g^+, h^o(g) > 0$.

*Proof*: A3 implies that $\forall\ x > 0, \exists\ i, g > 0$ *s.t.* $[(1 + g)Ax]_i > (Bx)_i$. So, let $g(x) = \max[g\colon gAx \leqslant Bx]$. Now $g(\lambda x) = g(x)\ \forall\ \lambda > 0$ so that we can restrict our attention to the closed set $S = [x\colon x \geqslant 0, \Sigma_i x_i = 1]$. For a given $i$, $(gAx)_i$ is a continuous function of $x \in S$ and so $g(x)$ is continuous in $S$. Hence (see Burkill (1962), theorem 3.72, for example) $g(x)$ reaches a maximum $g'$ at some $x \in S$. Then $\forall\ g > g'$, the only feasible $x$ and $h$ in Q2 are $x = 0$ and $h = 0$, so that $h^o(g) = 0$ for $g > g'$. A1 and A2 imply that $h^o(g) > 0$ for some $g > 0$, and since the golden rule curve is not upward sloping, and is continuous (since the solution to Q2 is continuous in $g$) $g^+ \leqslant g'$ exists. Q.E.D.

It should be noted that, if A3 does not hold, $h^o(g)$ could be positive $\forall g > 0$ since there then exists $x \geqslant 0$ *s.t.* $Ax = 0$ and $Bx > 0$. So, $\forall\ g > 0$ $[B - (1 + g)A]x > 0$. Choosing $z$ so that $z_i > 0$ only for those $i$ for which $(Bx)_i > 0$ gives $[B - (1 + g)A]x \geqslant hz$ for some $h > 0$ and $\forall\ g > 0$. Thus A1 and A2 are not sufficient for a proof of the existence of $g^+$.

## III UNRESTRICTED AND RESTRICTED EFFICIENCY CURVES

In general, knowledge of the technique chosen by the golden rule programmes Q2 and P2 may not be useful in the determination of the technique to be chosen when $r$ and $g$ differ. For the price and quantity efficiency curves of a technique chosen in golden rule equilibrium may not exist at other growth or profit rates. In our numerical example in section I, the technique consisting of both activities with no overproduced goods is chosen in golden rule equilibrium with $r = g = 1$, but when $r = 1$ and $g = 0.55$ (between 1/2 and 5/9) this technique is not viable since the quantity efficiency curve does not exist at that value of $g$.

In some models, however, the choice of technique is independent of the growth rate: it depends only on the profit rate. These models are characterised by certain restrictions on the nature of the technology, and hence on the sizes of certain of the elements of $B$ and $A$. For example, in Hicks' neoAustrian model (1973) (which has been converted to activity analysis form by Burmeister (1974)), the technique is chosen according to the profit rate alone. So, if $r$ is fixed at $\bar{r}$, and we discover the golden rule technique for $\bar{r}$, the same technique will be chosen for any value of $g$ provided that $r$ remains equal to $\bar{r}$. The golden rule efficiency curve then tells us the relation between the real wage and the profit rate in any equilibrium, including those for which $g \neq r$. Because of this extension of the role of the golden rule curve beyond golden rule equilibria it is convenient to rename it the 'unrestricted efficiency curve' in line with Hicks' terminology.

Hicks then refers to the quantity efficiency curve for a particular technique as a 'restricted efficiency curve' since it describes the technical possibilities for the economy when it is restricted to choosing a particular technique. So, if $r$ and $g$ are specified, $w$ is given by the unrestricted curve at $r$, and $h$ is found from the restricted efficiency curve (for the technique chosen at profit rate $r$) at $g$.

The conclusion that the choice of technique depends only on the profit rate in certain models is a result of the dynamic non-substitution theorem (see Mirrlees (1969), Stiglitz (1970)). In terms of efficiency curves the non-substitution theorem implies that, if the quantity curve for a technique exists at a certain value of $g$ with $h > 0$, it will exist for any lower non-negative value of $g$ and for certain higher values up to some maximum growth rate for the technique. Such a theorem holds for a model in which all capital goods are circulating, and by extension in cases in which capital goods decay proportionately. Such models are well established in the literature: a model with general depreciation and non-shiftable capital is not so frequently used. Mirrlees (1969) has shown that the dynamic non-substitution theorem holds in such a model, which is also discussed by Bliss (1975). The simplest way of depicting such a model is to generalise the two sector model of Craven (1975), and define a *process j* to consist of streams of inputs $a_{ij}(u)$ of good $i$, outputs $b_{ij}(u)$ of good $i$ and inputs $c_j(u)$ of labour for each period $u = 1, \ldots, U_j$. We assume that there is no joint production of final goods so that $b_{ij}(u) > 0$ for only one $i$ for each $j$ (hence if $b_{ij}(u) > 0$, $b_{kj}(v) = 0 \ \forall \ k \neq i, \ \forall \ v$). Thus inputs of many kinds can flow into a process, but the only goods that can be transferred out are final goods. No used machinery or other equipment can be transferred from one process to another once it has been installed. This model can be transformed into activity analysis form by a generalisation of Burmeister's transformation of the neoAustrian model (1974), and such a transformation will result in $\Sigma_j U_j$ activities, one for each period of each process. The processes to be used, and their economic lives $T_j (\leqslant U_j)$ will be chosen by P2 for a given $r$.

We can now demonstrate that, if one process is chosen for the production of each good at profit rate $r$, the quantity efficiency curve, for the technique consisting of those chosen processes run for their chosen economic lives, exists for $g \in [0, r]$.

*Theorem 4* With non-shiftable capital, no joint production of final goods and process $j$ producing good $j$ with an economic life $T_j$ at profit rate $r$, A2 implies that Q1 has a solution $\forall \ g \in [0, r]$.

*Proof*: Define $\theta_j(t, g) = \Sigma_{u=t}^{T_j} \Sigma_i \ [p_i^o(b_{ij}(u) - (1 + g)a_{ij}(u))] (1 + g)^{t-u-1}$ where $p_i^o$ are the prices determined from P2. Then

(i) $(1 + g)\theta_j(t, g) - \theta_j(t + 1, g) \geqslant (1 + r)\theta_j(t, r) - \theta_j(t + 1, r)$ for $g \in [0, r]$.

(ii) $\theta_j(T_j, r) \geqslant 0$, else it is profitable to truncate process $j$ at least one period before $T_j$. See Hicks (1973) for a proof of this in the neo-Austrian case. This yields

(iii) $\theta_j(T_j, g) > \theta_j(T_j, r)$ for $g \in [0, r]$

(iv) $\theta_j(1, r) \geqslant 0$ since by the competitive equilibrium conditions in P2, $\theta_j(1, r) = \Sigma_{u=1}^{T_j} w^o c_j(u)(1 + r)^{-u} \geqslant 0$.

Using (iii) and (i) we have $\theta_j(T_j - 1, g) > \theta_j(T_j - 1, r)$, and repeated use of (i), together with (iv) implies $\theta_j(1, g) > 0$ for $g \in [0, r]$. Since this is true for each $j$, we have shown that

$$p^o[I - \bar{A}(g)] > 0$$

where

$$\bar{A}(g)_{ij} = \sum_{u=1}^{T_j} a_{ij}(u)(1+g)^{-u} / \sum_{u=1}^{T_j} b_{jj}(u)(1+g)^{-u}$$

The matrix $I - \bar{A}(g)$ therefore satisfies the Hawkins–Simon conditions (see Hawkins and Simon, 1949), and $\exists\ y \geqslant 0$ *s.t.* $[I - \bar{A}(g)]y = z$ and the theorem follows since A2 implies that $\Sigma_{u=1}^{T_j} \Sigma\, c_j(u)(1+g)^{-u} y_j > 0$. A suitable multiple of $y$ will use one labour unit and define the value of $h$.

This form of technology includes Hick's neoAustrian model, for which there is only one good and $a_{ii}(u) = 0$ for each $u$, and also the author's two sector model in Hicks (1975). The proof of theorem 4 therefore applies to these models also.

In *Capital and Time*, Hicks appeals (p. 67) to the social accounts to ensure that, in Fig. 3.1, the restricted curve for the technique chosen in golden rule equilibrium between B and C on the unrestricted curve does not enter the area *OABCD*. However, in theorem 1 we showed that it is not technically possible for this to happen, and so there is no need to draw upon the social accounts to prove that the curve remains above *AB* and to the east of *CD*. Indeed, we shall show in the next section that the social

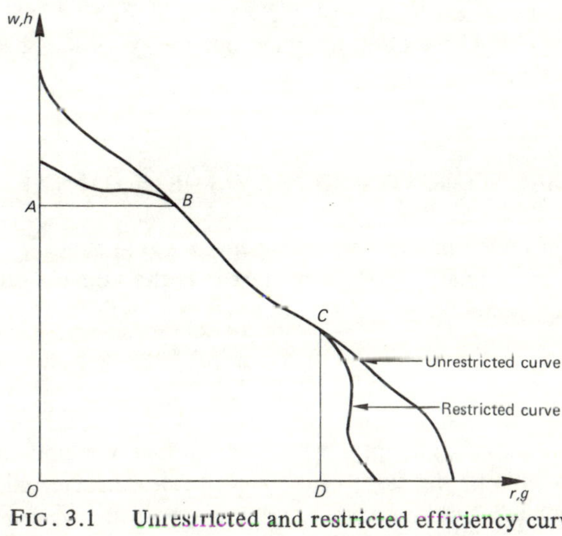


FIG. 3.1 Unrestricted and restricted efficiency curves

TABLE 3.1

| Period | 1 | 2 | 3 | 4 |
|---|---|---|---|---|
| Labour input | 1 | 1 | 8 | 2 |
| Corn output | 0 | 2 | 1 | 1 |

accounts are derivable from the technology using efficiency curves, so that these accounts cannot be used to limit the technical possibilities as Hicks would have us do.

In a model with circulating capital (or proportional decay of capital goods) it is possible to show via the Frobenius theorem (cf. Lancaster (1968) Review 7) that the restricted curves never slope upwards. However, this is not a general consequence of restricting the technology so that the non-substitution theorem holds.

For example, in the neoAustrian model with profiles shown in Table 3.1, the process will be extended to its full four periods when $r = 10$ and the real wage is 0.165. The restricted curve for this technique passes through the points

$$g = 0, h = 1/3;$$
$$g = 1, h = 11/30$$

with a maximum of $h$ at around $g = 1.14$. So, although we have shown that the restricted curve exists at least for $g < OD$ in Fig. 3.1, and that it cannot enter *OABCD*, we have not ruled out the particular shape illustrated in that figure.

## IV THE SOCIAL ACCOUNTS AND THE VALUE OF CAPITAL

We have already seen in theorem 1 that $h - w = (r - g)pAx$. $pAx$ is the value of the non-primary inputs – in short it is the value of capital per labour unit $k(r, g)$. So

$$k(r,g) = \frac{h - w}{r - g}$$

except in golden rule equilibrium where we can take the limit and show that $k(g, g)$ is (minus) the slope of the golden rule efficiency curve. The value of national income per labour unit $y(r, g)$ is then given by the

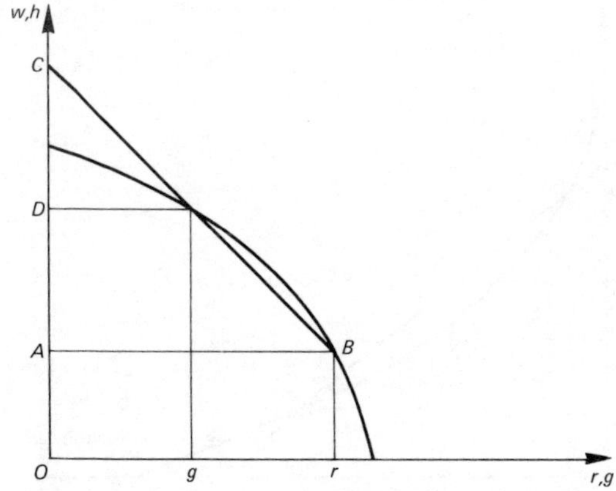


FIG. 3.2 The national accounts

formula

$$y(r, g) = rk + w = r\frac{h - w}{r - g} + w$$

which is equal to $gk + h$, the value of national output per labour unit. The national accounts can therefore be illustrated as in Fig. 3.2:

$$k = \tan ABC, y = OC + CA = OA = OD + DA.$$

The value of capital per labour unit clearly changes with $g$ and $r$ as long as efficiency curves are nonlinear. The latter effects, the Wicksell effects, are of two kinds: price effects occur when $r$ changes but the chosen technique does not, real effects occur when the technique changes. As shown in Craven (1977), each of these effects has its dual, and, as long as reswitching is possible, all four can have either sign. It is interesting to note that Harcourt's (1972) use of stationary states (he measures $y = OE$ and $k = \tan EBC$ in Figure 2) increases the possibility of capital reversal (that is, of $k$ increasing when we move to a technique chosen at higher values of $r$) as we see in Fig. 3.3 If $g = 0$, the real Wicksell effects as $r$ increases through $r_1$ and $r_2$ are of opposite sign:

$$k_I(r_1,0) = \tan FGD \quad k_{II}(r_1,0) = \tan EGD$$
$$k_I(r_2,0) = \tan FHC \quad k_{II}(r_2,0) = \tan EHC$$

So $k_{II}(r_1,0) - k_I(r_1,0) < 0$, while $k_I(r_2,0) - k_{II}(r_2,0) > 0$.
But when $g = \bar{g} \in (r_1,r_2)$ the real effects have the same sign:

$$k_{II}(r_1,g) - k_I(r_1,g) = \tan KBG - \tan JAG < 0$$
$$k_I(r_2,g) - k_{II}(r_2,g) = \tan CHA - \tan CHB < 0$$

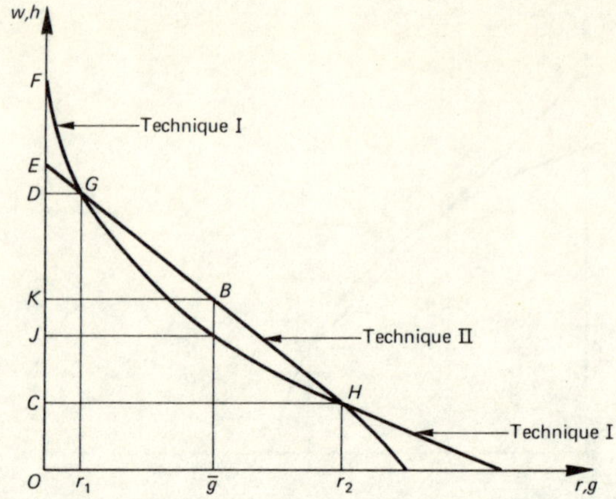


FIG. 3.3 Wicksell effects and reswitching

Multiple intersections of the efficiency curves for two techniques are then not sufficient for the real Wicksell effects to have opposite signs: the curves must intersect at two or more values between $r$ and $g$. In Craven (1977) the author has shown that Harcourt's restriction of $g$ to equal zero has serious implications for a critique of marginalist theories, and in the next section we shall see that, where a stationary equilibrium is possible, the distribution is exactly as measured in Marxian theory.

## V MARXIAN THEORIES

There has been a recent upsurge of interest in certain theoretical propositions implied by Marx in *Capital* (see, for example, Morishima (1973, 1975, 1976), Steedman (1975, 1976) and Wolfstetter (1973)). One of the points of interest has been the relation between the rate of exploitation and the profit rate. The former can be defined variously (see Morishima (1973), Ch. 5) as

$$E = \frac{\text{surplus labour}}{\text{necessary labour}} = \frac{\text{unpaid labour}}{\text{paid labour}} = \frac{\text{surplus value}}{\text{value of labour power}}$$

and is, in effect, a measure of the distribution of the product in terms of the labour time appropriated by capitalists divided by the labour time needed to produce the basket of consumption goods $w(r)z$ available to the labour force.

To produce $w(r)z$ with the chosen technique, and to replace the inputs used up requires cx units of labour where $(B - A)x \geqslant w(r)z$ and $x_i = 0\ \forall\ i \notin H$. The use of the chosen technique also requires that those goods in $J$ cannot be overproduced, so that $[(B - A)x]_i = w(r)z_i\ \forall\ i \in J$. Comparing these conditions with the constraints of Q1 indicates that the labour $cx$ required is equal to $w(r)/h(0)$, where $h(0)$ is the possible consumption output per labour unit when $g = 0$. So long as the quantity efficiency curve for the technique exists when $g = 0$ the necessary labour is given by $w(r)/h(0)$, and the surplus labour by $[h(0) - w(r)]/h(0)$. Hence the rate of exploitation is given by the formula

$$E = \frac{h(0) - w(r)}{w(r)}$$

and is illustrated as $BA/OA$ in Fig. 3.4 It is defined if and only if the quantity efficiency curve exists when $g = 0$.

An alternative way of measuring the rate of exploitation uses the price efficiency curve. For we may define a vector $v$ of *labour values* of the goods according to the formula $[v(B - A)]_i = c_i\ \forall\ i \in H$. $v$ then represents the amount of labour needed to produce each good and to replace the inputs used up in production using the chosen technique. If we also assume that the labour value of an overproduced good is zero,[6] we have $v_i = 0\ \forall\ i \notin J$ and the labour values $v$ are equal to $p(0)/w(0)$ derived from $P1$ when $r = 0$. Then the paid labour (the labour value of the goods received by the wage earners $w(r)vz$) is equal to $w(r)p(0)z/w(0) = w(r)/w(0)$ since $p(0)z = 1$. The rate of exploitation is then given by the alternative

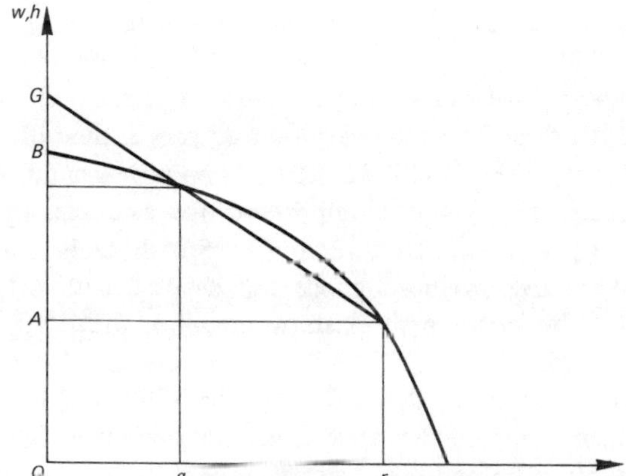


FIG. 3.4 Exploitation and distribution

formula

$$E = \frac{w(0) - w(r)}{w(r)}$$

whenever the price efficiency curve exists when $r = 0$. If the price efficiency curve does not exist, some of the labour values will be negative, a problem discussed by Steedman (1975). Where both the quantity and price curves exist at zero, the two measures of $E$ are the same since $w(0) = h(0)$.

In Fig. 3.4 we can compare the 'market price' measure of distribution $rk(r, g)/w(r) = GA/OA$ with the rate of exploitation $BA/OA$. It is clear that no general theorem can be established concerning which is the greater of the two, since that will depend upon the shape of the efficiency curve, and, in particular, on whether $G$ is to the north or south of $B$. The two measures of the distribution will be the same when the growth rate is zero.

The fundamental proposition that has been put forward by Morishima (1973) and others is that the rate of exploitation is positive if, and only if, the profit rate is positive. Thus it is the ability of capitalists to extract unpaid labour time from workers which enables them to earn profits. In this paper we are not concerned with these issues of political economy – whether the concept of exploitation is useful in explaining the origin of profits – but rather we shall investigate whether the fundamental proposition is true.

Provided that either the price efficiency curve exists when $r = 0$, or the quantity efficiency curve exists when $g = 0$, then with $0 < g < r$, $rk > 0$ implies $E > 0$. For $rk > 0$ and $g < r$ imply $h(g) > w(r)$[7]. If the price curve exists at zero, theorem 1 implies that $w(0) > h(g)$ and so $w(0) > w(r)$ so that $E > 0$. If the quantity curve exists at $g = 0$, theorem 1 ensures that $h(0) > w(r)$ so that $E > 0$. $E$ will be zero only if $h(0) = w(r)$: for example, if $B = \begin{pmatrix} 6 & 3 \\ 1 & 12 \end{pmatrix}$, $A = \begin{pmatrix} 5 & 0 \\ 0 & 10 \end{pmatrix}$ $c = (1\ 1)$ and $z = \begin{pmatrix} 1 \\ 1 \end{pmatrix}$ and if the technique chosen uses both activities and has no overproduced goods, then if $r = 1/10$ and $g = 1/20$, $w(r) = 1$, $h(g) = 15/14$ and $h(0) = 1$. *So* $rk > 0$ and $E = 0$.

The condition that $g \leqslant r$ is important: for example, if $B = \begin{pmatrix} 2 & 1 \\ 4 & 18 \end{pmatrix}$, $A = \begin{pmatrix} 1 & 0 \\ 0 & 6 \end{pmatrix}$, $c = (2\ 4)$, $z = \begin{pmatrix} 1 \\ 16 \end{pmatrix}$, $r = 1/2$ and $g = 5/6$, the technique using both activities and no overproduced goods can be used with $w(r) = 1/4$ and $h(g) = 17/140$. The price curve exists when $r = 0$, with $w(0) = 1/5$. $E$ is then equal to $-1/5$.

The reverse implication, that $E > 0$ implies $r > 0$ will hold when the quantity efficiency curve exists at zero, but not necessarily when the price curve does. For if $r < 0$, and the quantity curve exists at zero, $w(r)$ exceeds $h(0)$ and $E < 0$. But if the price curve exists the following example shows that $E > 0$ and $r < 0$ may coexist (in theory, although we could not expect to observe a capitalist economy in this situation, except perhaps temporarily). If $B = \begin{pmatrix} 6 & 1 \\ 3 & 12 \end{pmatrix}$, $A = \begin{pmatrix} 5 & 1 \\ 0 & 10 \end{pmatrix}$, $c = (4 \;\; 3)$, $z = \begin{pmatrix} 5 \\ 3 \end{pmatrix}$ then $r = -1/5$ yields $p = (7/41 \;\; 2/41)$ and $w(r) = 5/41$. When $r = 0$, $w(0) = 1/8$, and the labour values are $(1 \;\; 1)$. The rate of exploitation is $1/40$, and when $g = 1/5$, $h(g) = 1/19$, $x = \begin{pmatrix} 1/19 \\ 5/19 \end{pmatrix}$ and so $rk = -27/779$.

It is clear that, even when one or other of the curves exists at zero, the fundamental proposition may fail. Morishima achieves his original result with only circulating capital, in which case all the efficiency curves exist, and are downward sloping. In more complicated models, involving joint production and durable capital the proposition may be false either for the reasons illustrated in the above examples, or because neither of the quantity or price curves exists at zero, as in Steedman's (1975) example. In these cases, Morishima (1975) has suggested rescuing the fundamental proposition by defining the rate of exploitation and labour values in a different way.

Instead of seeking the labour necessary to produce $w(v)z$ with the chosen technique, he defines the necessary labour to be the minimum required by the economy to produce $w(r)z$. He solves the programme

$$\text{min. } cx \text{ s.t. } (B - A)x \geqslant w(r)z, \; x \geqslant 0.$$

If we compare this with Q2, we see that the minimum labour required to produce $w(r)z$ will be equal to $w(r)/h^o(0)$, where $h^o(0)$ is the solution of Q2 with $g = 0$. Surplus value is then $[h^o(0) - w(r)]/h^o(0)$ and the rate of exploitation (which we may usefully call the 'unrestricted' rate of exploitation since its definition is not restricted to the chosen technique) is

$$E' = \frac{h^o(0) - w(r)}{w(r)}.$$

If $r > g$ and $rk > 0$, $w(r) < h(g)$, which in turn must be less than or equal to $h^o(g)$ since the latter is the maximum that $h$ can be. Further, since the golden rule curve does not slope upwards $h^o(g) \leqslant h^o(0)$. Combining all of these inequalities ensures that $E' > 0$. Almost the same result can be reached when the non-substitution theorem holds even if $g$ exceeds $r$, for then $w(r) = w^o(r) = h^o(r) \leqslant h^o(0)$, and the only possibility that the theorem may fail is that $E'$ might equal zero if the golden rule efficiency curve is a constant function between zero and $r$. A negative unrestricted rate of exploitation can coexist with a positive rate only when $g > r$ and the non-substitution theorem does not hold. For example, when $B = \begin{pmatrix} 2 & 1 \\ 4 & 18 \end{pmatrix}$, $A = \begin{pmatrix} 0 & 0 \\ 0 & 6 \end{pmatrix}$, $c = (2 \;\; 4)$ and $z = \begin{pmatrix} 1 \\ 9 \end{pmatrix}$, $g = 3/4$ and $r = 1/6$ yield an equilibrium technique using the first activity and the first good not overproduced. The real wage is then 5/12, $h = 1/8$, the prices are (1 0) and $x = \binom{1/2}{0}$. For this economy, it can be shown that $h^o(0)$ is 4/13 so that $E' = -17/65$ while $rk = 1/12$. So there are circumstances in which the fundamental proposition can fail using the unrestricted definition of the rate of exploitation.

Other definitions of the rate of exploitation have been put forward, including one involving *synchronised labour costs* (see Samuelson and von Weisacker, and for a discussion in the context of circulating capital see Wolfstetter (1973). In this definition, the necessary labour includes the labour required not only to replace, but also to expand at rate $g$ the supply of inputs required to produce $w^o(r)z$ using the chosen technique. The necessary labour is therefore $cx$ where $[B - (1+g)A]x \geqslant w(r)z$, and if the synchronised labour cost of an overproduced good is zero, it can be shown that $cx = w(r)/h(g)$, and the corresponding rate of exploitation is $[h(g) - w(r)]/w(r)$ which is non-negative when $r$ exceeds $g$ and non-positive when $g$ exceeds $r$.

For completeness, we could define an unrestricted synchronised exploitation rate, in which the necessary labour is the minimum required by the economy to replace and expand the inputs at rate $g$, and the exploitation rate corresponding to this definition is $[h^o(g) - w(r)]/w(r)$. This exploitation rate reflects the inefficiency of capitalism noted by Nuti (1970), who demonstrated the actual consumption output $h(g)$ could be lower than the possible level $h^o(g)$ which would be obtained by planners seeking to maximise consumption output at a given growth rate.

We have no space to discuss the merits and demerits of the various measures of exploitation in Marxian theory (see the recent exchange between Steedman (1976) and Morishima (1976)). Our task has been merely to show that all of them can be illustrated by using efficiency curves and that $E$ (which takes historical precedence at least) will therefore be under- or over-estimated by the measured distribution at market prices ($rk/w$) according to the values of $g$ and $r$ and the shape of the efficiency curve. We have also shown that, in Harcourt's (1972) stationary equilibrium $rk/w = E$, and that his conclusions fail to have meaning in exactly the same circumstances as the first version of the fundamental proposition.

## VI SEVERAL PRIMARY FACTORS

In this section we make a few remarks on how the existence of more primary factors such as land and skilled labour affects the use of efficiency curves in capital theory. The notation is given in the first section, and we can change Q1 to read $\exists\ x \geqslant 0,\ h \geqslant 0$ such that $[B-(1+g)A]x \geqslant hz$, $Cx \leqslant b$, $[(B-(1+g)A)x]_i = hz_i\ \forall i \in J, x_j = 0\ \forall\ j \in H, (Cx)_k = b_k\ \forall\ k \in K$ where a technique is now defined by three sets, *H, J* and *K* where the last is the set of primary factors that must be fully employed. The quantity efficiency curve still relates *h* to *g*, and some such curve will exist with $h > 0$ for some $g > 0$ if A1 and a modified version of A2 hold. We can write A2 so that some primary factor is needed in production:

$$\text{A2}'\ \nexists\ x \geqslant 0\ s.t.\ (B-A)x \geqslant 0 \text{ and } Cx = 0.$$

This can be used to replace A2 wherever such an assumption is needed to prevent indefinitely large outputs.

The conditions for the existence of a price curve for the technique defined by *H, J* and *K* can be obtained as a modification of P1:

$$\exists p \geqslant 0, q \geqslant 0\ s.t.\ [p(B-(1+r)A)]_j = [qC]_j\ \forall j \in H, pz = 1,$$
$$p_i = 0\ \forall\ i \notin J, q_k = 0\ \forall\ k \notin K$$

so that any primary factor not fully employed must be free. The price curve is then defined to be the graph of the total payments to primary factors $qb$ against $r$. With these definitions of the quantity and price efficiency curves it can easily be shown that, when both of them exist for some $g = r$, $h(g) = q(r)b$. The golden rule efficiency curve still relates the maximum of *h* to *g* and the minimum value of payments to primary factors consistent with competitive equilibrium to *r*. Since the non-substitution theorem generally fails to hold (see Dorfman *et al.* (1958; p. 226)) when there is more than one primary factor, even if the technology is restricted to rule out joint production, it is unlikely that the simplifications of section III will be useful in this model.

The diagrammatic exposition of the national accounts discussed in section IV is still useful, but now gives only a partial view of the distribution of the product between the suppliers of the various factors. The national accounting equations give

$$y(r,g) = rk(r,g) + qb$$

$$y(r,g) = gk(r,g) + h$$

so that $k = (qb - h)/(g - r)$. We can therefore only discuss the distribution between capitalists and the owners of primary factors taken together, and not, for example, distinguish the wages of labour from the rents received by landlords. We need to know all of the components of *q* to separate these payments out.

Similarly we can develop a 'primary resource' theory of value and exploitation if either the price or quantity efficiency curve exists at zero. For then $[h(0) - q(r)b]/h(0)$ or $[q(0)b - q(r)b]/q(0)b$ tells us the proportion of the resources being appropriated by capitalists. The ratio between them can be considered only as a sort of rate of exploitation if the only primary factors receiving a positive income are various types of labour. Then $q(r)b/h(0)$ (or $q(r)b/q(0)b$) does measure the proportion of labour time which is used to produce the goods which workers can purchase. Even then the different types of labour will be exploited at different rates if $q_i(r) = q_j(r)$ for two types of labour $i$ and $j$. The ratio between the surplus labour and the necessary labour then gives an average of the individual rates of exploitation each weighted by its supply $b_i$. If land has a positive rent, this ratio does not include landlords' incomes in surplus value, so that the formula will underestimate the rate of exploitation of labour. Our efficiency curves then fail to illustrate the rate of exploitation just as they failed to detail the distribution of the product between various factor owners.

## VII CONCLUSION

In this paper we have seen how the efficiency curves of an economy can be used to illustrate the possibilities for steady state equilibria, to measure capital intensity and to show the distribution between capitalists and workers either in market prices or labour values. Apart from the pedogogic advantages of the two dimensional nature of the curves, they also enable us to answer certain major questions – on the value of capital and the distribution for example – without the ambiguities inherent in multi-dimensional analysis and without the pitfalls of aggregation. We have also seen that the affirmation (or otherwise) of the fundamental Marxian proposition is a corollary of the existence of the curves in certain ranges. The penultimate section showed that the valuation of capital can proceed despite the existence of several primary factors.

## NOTES

*I am grateful to participants in the Southampton Conference for helpful discussion.

1 Our vector inequality notation is such that $x \geqslant y$ allows $x = y$, $x > y$ implies $x \geqslant y$ but $x \neq y$.

2. *Nil posse creari de nilo* (Lucretius, *De Rerum Natura* i. 101) quoted by Marx, *Capital* vol. 1.

3. It is convenient to defer the question of the existence of price curves until the next section.
4. $^{o}$ denotes the optimal value of the variable.
5. Nuti (1970) allows 'bumps' in his frontier, because he includes certain government restrictions on the capitalists, such as the replacement of topsoil after open cast mining. Perfect competitors would not choose to be so concerned with the environment.
6. Some support may be obtained for this assumption from *Capital* vol. 1, p. 48 where Marx states: 'Lastly nothing can have a value without being an object of utility. If the thing is useless, so is the labour contained in it; the labour does not count as labour and therefore creates no value'.
7. A limiting argument establishes the result when $r = g$.

## REFERENCES

Bliss, C. J. (1975) *Capital Theory and the Distribution of Income* (Amsterdam: North-Holland).

Bruno, M. (1969), 'Fundamental Duality Relations in the Pure Theory of Capital and Growth', *Review of Economic Studies*, vol. 36.

Burkill, J. C. (1962), *A First Course in Mathematical Analysis* (Cambridge University Press).

Burmeister, E. (1974), 'Synthesising the NeoAustrian and Alternative Approaches to Capital Theory: A Survey', *Journal of Economic Literature*, vol. 12.

Burmeister, E., and Kuga, K. (1970), 'The Factor Price Frontier, Duality and Joint Production', *Review of Economic Studies*, vol. 37.

Craven, J. A. G. (1975), 'Capital Theory and the Process of Production', *Economica*, vol. 42.

Craven, J. A. G. (1977) 'On the Marginal Product of Capital', *Oxford Economic Papers*, vol. 29.

Dorfman, R., Samuelson, P. A., Solow, R. M. (1958), *Linear Programming and Economic Analysis* (New York: McGraw-Hill).

Gale, D. (1960), *The Theory of Linear Economic Models* (New York: McGraw-Hill).

Harcourt, G. C. (1972), *Some Cambridge Controversies in the Theory of Capital* (Cambridge University Press).

Hawkins, D. and Simon, H. A. (1949), 'Note: Some Conditions of Macroeconomic Stability', *Econometrica*, vol. 17.

Hicks, J. R. (1965), *Capital and Growth* (Oxford University Press).

Hicks, J. R. (1973), *Capital and Time* (Oxford University Press).

Lancaster, K. (1968), *Mathematical Economics* (London: Macmillan).

Marx, K., *Capital*, first published 1867.

Mirrles, J. A. (1969), 'The Dynamic Nonsubstitution Theorem', *Review of Economic Studies*, vol. 36.

Morishima, M. (1973), *Marx's Economics* (Cambridge University Press).

Morishima, M. (1975), 'Marx in the Light of Modern Economic Theory', *Econometrica*, vol. 42.

Morishima, M. (1976), 'Positive Profits with Negative Surplus Value: A Comment', *Economica Journal*, vol. 86.

Nuti, D. M. (1970), 'Capitalism, Socialism and Steady Growth', *Economic Journal,* vol. 80.

Samuelson, P. A. (1962), 'Parable and Realism in Capital Theory: the Surrogate Production Function', *Review of Economic Studies,* vol. 39.

Samuelson, P. A. and von Weisacker, C. C. (1971), 'A New Labor Theory of Value, for Rational Planning Through the Use of the Bourgeoise Profit Rate', *Proceedings of the National Academy of Science,* vol. 68.

Steedman, I. (1975), 'Positive Profits with Negative Surplus Value', *Economic Journal,* vol. 85.

Steedman, I. (1976), 'Positive Profits with Negative Surplus Value: A Reply', *Economic Journal*, vol. 86.

Stiglitz, J. E. (1970), 'Nonsubstitution Theorems with Durable Capital Goods', *Review of Economic Studies,* vol. 37.

Wolfstetter, E. (1973), 'Surplus Labour, Synchronised Labour Costs and Marx's Labour Theory of Value', *Economic Journal*, vol. 83.

# Part II

# Practice

# 4 The Stock of Fixed Assets in the United Kingdom: How to Make Best Use of the Statistics

TOM GRIFFIN

*Central Statistical Office*

## INTRODUCTION

There can be no doubting the importance of investment in fixed capital in an industrialised economy. The story of the industrial revolution could be written in terms of looms, steam-driven pumps and locomotives. Today, investment and the stock of fixed capital play a very important part in the consideration of the performance of all modern economies.

Fortunately the statistics of expenditure on fixed assets are fairly simply definable and fairly well understood, but the same degree of understanding cannot be claimed for statistics relating to the stock of fixed capital and the rate at which it is used up. These statistics add valuable further dimensions to the basic estimates of the flow of capital expenditure. But there are two distinct standard measures of the stock and two measures of the rate at which it is used up.

We have available to us in the United Kingdom a range of detailed estimates of the stock of fixed capital which are in some respects the most highly developed of their type in the world. Even in the USA, where a vast array of economic statistics are published, there are, for example, no estimates for industry groups within manufacturing. But it is clear from a number of published sources which quote and use capital stock estimates that they are often wrongly applied even by those who are relatively familiar with the subject. There are several reasons for the misunderstanding. Firstly there is the inescapable fact that capital stock is not a single concept capable of unique measurement. But further, the published series have not been as comprehensive as they might and are not accompanied by any explanatory notes, except those given in *Sources and Methods* (Maurice, 1968) which is the definitive account of how the UK National Accounts are compiled.

There is of course no uniquely correct worth or 'value' of fixed assets. The two types of estimate which are the main subject here, 'gross capital stock' and 'net capital stock', are each quite different in definition. Each has advantages over the other for specific purposes but neither can claim to be more intrinsically correct than the other. The estimates shown in the published accounts of business enterprises represent another value. Yet another, not discussed here at all, could be derived from the stock market evaluation of quoted companies.

The purpose of this article is simply to explain how to make best use of the National Accounts estimates of capital stock and derivatives such as capital consumption and, in doing so, to introduce some new series, of capital retirements, which have been published for the first time this year in the Blue Book (CSO, 1977). It is in the Blue Book that the most detailed tables of all these series are published. Very little is published elsewhere.

An article in *Economic Trends* (Griffin, 1975) described in detail, with examples, the methodological principles behind the estimates. The present article includes a description of the methodology in outline, sufficient only to enable anyone not familiar with the subject to follow the later arguments. The use of price deflators is discussed here a little more fully because they have such a crucial bearing on the definition of the series. Earlier comprehensive papers on the compilation of UK capital stock estimates were published in the *Journal of the Royal Statistical Society* (Redfern (1955) and Dean (1964)).

## GROSS CAPITAL STOCK AND RETIREMENTS ESTIMATES: HOW THEY ARE CALCULATED

The principles of the estimation of gross capital stock are simple. We begin with two kinds of data. First we know from the direct survey questionnaires on capital expenditure[1] how much each industry, let us say iron and steel for example, has spent each year on fixed assets. (The list of different industries and different types of asset for which we calculate gross capital stock are shown in copies of the Blue Book tables in Appendix IV.) Secondly we have estimates, less firmly based, of the life expectancy of plant and machinery and other assets in those industries. (Some of these are discussed in Appendix I.) To calculate gross capital stock we simply accumulated capital expenditures year by year and only deduct those capital expenditures from the past on assets which are assumed to have completed their expected lives. In order to calculate capital stock for 1947, the earliest year for which estimates are derived, it is necessary to establish very long historic series of capital expenditure estimates for prior years. This has been done on the basis of a range of data (see Redfern (1955)) which was generally less reliable and less detailed than the current capital expenditure estimates. Fortunately, the older the data the less impact it has on the resulting stock estimates.

A simplified example will illustrate the process best. Let us assume that an industry began in the year 1900 with an unknown stock of plant but we know that its plant had a service life of about three years. Let us also assume that from 1901 it spent £12 million each year on more assets with a life of about 3 years, and that prices did not change over the period. We now have enough information to calculate gross stock from 1904. At the end of 1901, the first year for which capital expenditure is known, the gross capital stock would have been at least £12 million (we must say 'at least' because the stock extant from before 1901 is unknown). In 1902 and 1903 another £12 million was spent and so at the end of the third year the gross capital stock will have amounted to £36 million. Since we know that the stock installed before 1901 lasted no more than three years we can now assume that it has been discarded. In the fourth year another £12 million was spent and so could be added to the £36 million already accumulated but, as the plant was expected to last only about three years, we can now assume that the plant bought in the first year will be retired in the fourth and so the gross capital stock at the end of 1904 was £36 million plus £12 million *minus* £12 million equals £36 million. Similarly in the fifth year £12 million would have been added to capital expenditure in that year and £12 million would have been deducted for retirements of plant now three years old and so gross capital stock will have remained at £36 million. This method of calculating gross capital stock is called the

TABLE 4.1 Example 1: The perpetual inventory method

*Assumed life three years*

| *in £m.* | *Gross capital formation* | *Retirements* | *Gross capital stock (end-year)* |
|---|---|---|---|
| 1901 | 12 | unknown | 12 minimum |
| 1902 | 12 | unknown | 24 minimum |
| 1903 | 12 | unknown | 36 |
| 1904 | 12 | 12 | 36 |
| 1905 | 12 | 12 | 36 |

perpetual inventory method and variants of it are used in most western industrialised countries.

The process applied in the CSO is in practice more complex than described here even for one kind of asset in one industry. The method was fairly complex from the beginning and is more sophisticated now especially in its treatment of asset lives and scrapping following the revisions to the model in 1975 (see Griffin, 1975). Allowance is made, for example, for war damage and for the fact that retirements are probably distributed over a number of years around the average: also, plant and machinery in a given industry is generally sub-divided into several classes each with their own life expectancies, and of course estimates for buildings and vehicles are each calculated separately. The distributions of retirements and the subdivisions of plant and machinery into several classes of life lengths are particularly important. The service lives for plant and machinery in manufacturing industries are given in Appendix I. In the chemical and allied industry group, for example, expenditure on plant is divided into five classes. For each of the five classes it is assumed that retirements are spread around the mean expected service life so that, taking the twenty-five year life class as an example, retirements are assumed to begin in the twenty-first year and end in the thirty-first.

Apart from the explanation below of how we arrive at constant price estimates, the outline descriptions above are sufficient for the present purpose. A more detailed description of the method is given (in Griffin (1975).

## NET CAPITAL STOCK AND CONSUMPTION ESTIMATES: HOW THEY ARE CALCULATED

The essential difference between gross capital stock described above and net capital stock is that, whereas for gross capital stock the whole of the original value of fixed assets is deemed to remain in stock until the year of retirement, for net capital stock the original value of assets is deemed to decline gradually over their service lives. If machinery is expected to last 20 years then it is assumed to be depreciated or consumed at the rate of one-twentieth per year. To illustrate the principle consider the same imaginary data used above for gross capital stock and retirements. So, an industry began in the year 1900 with an unknown stock of plant but it is known that its assets lasted about 3 years. It then spent £12 million each year up to 1905 on machines which were expected to last 3 years. Again, for the sake of simplicity, we will assume that prices did not change over the period. At the end of the first year, during which £12 million was

TABLE 4.2 Example 2: Relating the estimates

*Assumed life three years*

| *in £m.* | *Gross capital formation* | *Retire-ments* | *Gross capital stock (end-year)* | *Capital con-sumption* | *Net capital stock (end-year)* |
|---|---|---|---|---|---|
| 1901 | 12 | unknown | 12 min. | 4 min. | 8 min. |
| 1902 | 12 | unknown | 24 min. | 8 min. | 12 |
| 1903 | 12 | unknown | 36 | 12 | 12 |
| 1904 | 12 | 12 | 36 | 12 | 12 |
| 1905 | 12 | 12 | 36 | 12 | 12 |

spent, the net capital stock will have been at least £12 million *less* £4 million equals at least £8 million (*plus* the unknown stock remaining from before 1901). At the end of the second year, the first year's capital expenditure will be reduced again by £4 million so that the original £12 million will now have been reduced to £12 million – £4 million – £4 million equals £4 million. Meanwhile the second year's expenditure of a further £12 million will have been depreciated by £4 million leaving £12 million – £4 million equals £8 million. So the total net capital stock at the end of the second year is £4 million remaining from 1901 *plus* £8 million remaining from 1902 which equals £12 million in all. The pre-1901 stock will by now have retired. So, net capital stock at the end of each year is calculated by taking net stock at the end of the previous year, adding the year's gross capital expenditure and deducting the year's capital consumption.

The gross capital stock and retirements example can now be put together with the net capital stock and consumption example (See Table 4.2) to show how the four series relate.

Again it must be said that the process of calculating all these series is rather more complex than this simple illustration would suggest, for example, consumption is lagged by half a year, but the principles outlined are accurate enough for the present purpose.

To estimate an aggregate of capital stock it is necessary, especially over periods of high inflation, for the individual components of the stock to be valued consistently between years. To value each item of capital stock at the price at which it was originally bought (its historic cost) and to aggregate all such expenditure over a period of years, without revaluing them to the prices reigning in a single year, is like adding chalk and cheese. The stock of fixed assets in the published accounts of businesses, in particular their plaint and machinery is in most cases composed of just such a heterogeneous mixture of prices; although it should be noted that 'historic cost accounting', will probably give way in the next few years to an accounting system in which all assets are valued at current price levels (Sandilands, 1976). The accounts of individual enterprises are discussed further in the last section below.

Fixed capital stock in the National Accounts, on the other hand, from the introduction of the estimates in the 1950s, has as a matter of principle been valued as far as possible on a price basis which is consistent over time. For our estimates of capital stock in any year we either revalue to the prices current in the year or to prices of 1970 which happens to be the present reference year for most of our constant price series in national statistics. For capital stock at the end of 1975 at current prices, for example, we revalue all relevant past expenditures to end-1975 prices. The price indices used are discussed in some detail later.

It was for the purpose of estimating consumption to arrive at 'net national income' that the 'perpetual inventory' model was first used. (See Maurice, 1968.) By definition net national income is equal to gross national product *less* capital consumption.

## THE MEASUREMENT OF THE OUTPUT POTENTIAL OF FIXED CAPITAL

This is probably the commonest use to which estimates of capital stock are put, whether as explanatory variables in econometric models or as rule of thumb indicators of the relative capital intensity of an industry or of an economy. In practice both gross capital stock and net capital stock are often used for the purpose or more rarely, the two measures in combination but a closer look at the two different measures shows that, although neither is ideal, gross stock is superior to net stock in most respects as an indicator of potential rates of gross output.

The following arguments hold for the general case. It is not proposed to discuss here the complex and contentious issue of the precise role of aggregates of capital in production functions. As an illustration of the complexity of the relationship it may be noted that despite technical progress additions to the stock of fixed capital are commonly accompanied by less than proportionate extra output, although output per man may also be increased.

To put the comparison between the two measures of capital for this purpose in the simplest terms it may be said that to use net capital stock would mean assuming that productive potential declines in a straight line from the date of the capital expenditure so that for example a machine which is expected to last 20 years would be deemed to have become one-twentieth less productive after only one year of life, half as productive after 10 years, and nineteen-twentieths less productive after 19 years. The gross capital stock concept assumes on the other hand that productive potential is unaltered after one year, 10 years or 19 years[2]. The crucial question is which measure is most appropriate to the purpose at hand.

An analogy is often drawn between an asset familiar in our domestic lives, the motor-car, and manufacturers' plant: and it has been misleadingly concluded that both decline rapidly in their utility from the date of purchase. Analogies between domestic assets and industrial plant can of course be helpful but care has been taken to identify the relevant issues. In measuring capital for the purpose of estimating its productive potential in the short and medium-term it would be inappropriate to use for example market values, which are very much affected by the number of years of service left in an asset. It is also necessary to differentiate clearly between gross productive potential, and net productive potential, the latter taking account of higher running costs and any other expenditure which might be predicted to increase with the age of an asset. Usually one is considering potential production rates in gross quantity terms consistent with demand. Industrial plant and machinery, particularly the larger and more expensive production plant such as that used in the chemical, steel or paper industries, is generallyexpected to increase its production rate during the early years of its life. Later it may have to run a little more slowly or may be restricted to a narrower range of products while newer, faster or more versatile machinery is used for a wider range of products. But the likely effect of age on net, and more particularly gross, output potential should not be over-rated. Although it is difficult to generalise from any particular process, we can be sure that in its last few years of service most machinery will be capable of producing at much more than the small fraction of its original rate which would be implied by taking its written down value.

Indeed few enterprises can be expected to go on providing valuable factory space or to bear overhead and running costs for large quantities of plant with very low production potential. This general argument applies to plant that survives the whole or more, of its mean expected service life. It applies more strongly to plant which becomes obsolete before its expected life span is complete particularly when obsolescence is due to replacement of the product it manufactures.

Some of the arguments surrounding the measurement of capital stock confuse net with gross output potential. In particular it is sometimes suggested that older machinery should have reduced a weight in the aggregate because it may be more expensive in its use of labour and maintenance and repair bills. Certainly, higher running costs will reduce output per unit of total input but they do not affect gross output per unit of fixed capital employed. We are reminded that it is only in combination with other factors of production that fixed assets can produce anything and that a given level of capital stock can be combined with different levels of other inputs. In certain circumstances it will be preferable to consider a 'net' concept of output potential which would take into account demands on overheads and on other factors of production, but this is probably not the more common case.

Gross capital stock is therefore the better indicator of the current gross output potential of the current stock of fixed capital assets. Use of the estimates in studies of the medium term future, say the following five or so years, depends upon one's view of the balance of capital expenditures and retirements over that period. The perpetual inventory model can help by indicating the trend in retirements in the medium term future. (See table at Appendix II.)

It follows that the change in gross output potential is better indicated by the change in gross capital stock than by the change in net capital stock. Changes in gross capital stock, that is capital expenditures *less* retirements, are published for the first time in the 1977's Blue Book (CSO, 1977). The estimates are shown at current and 1970 prices and are analysed by industry group.

Net capital stock is however an indicator of the total future output potential of the present stock over the longer term because, as a measure of written down replacement cost, it is an estimate of the services remaining in the stock of fixed capital over the rest of its aggregate service life. The relationship over time of net stock to gross stock may therefore indicate the age trend of the stock and perhaps the increasing or impending need for replacement investment.

The general conclusion therefore is that for an indicator of the current gross output potential of fixed assets the more suitable series is gross capital stock in preference to net capital stock and therefore the growth in gross output potential is more suitably measured by capital expenditure *less* retirements rather than by capital expenditure *less* capital consumption. It is possible to modify the gross capital stock series and thereby perhaps to improve it, convert it to a 'vintage' series for example, as discussed briefly below, but one cannot be certain that the series is necessarily improved in that way. The modification of gross capital stock estimates for various purposes is still very much open to debate. (For example, see Denison (1972), Johansen and Sorsveen (1967), Jorgenson and Griliches (1969) and the OECD(1973).)

## CAPITAL CONSUMPTION AS A MEASURE OF OUTPUT POTENTIAL

Bearing in mind that in this context one is interested in the output potential from a flow of capital services there is another measure which could also be used; and that is capital consumption. A trivial example will illustrate the point. Let us assume that there are only two assets, each with a different function, installed in an industry. They cost £100 each but one is expected to last for ten years and the other for twenty. Both would contribute equally to our initial valuation of gross capital stock which would become £100 + £100 = £200. But their services are unlikely to be of equal value in any given year. The asset which is expected to last the longest will probably provide less service per year. If each were rented instead of being purchased then the respective rents would reflect the different durabilities. Capital consumption also reflects the different durabilities. In the first full year it would be (£100 *divided by* 10 years) *plus* (£100 *divided by* 20 years) = £15. Had both assets been expected to last only10 years then consumption would have been £20.

The practical difference between the two indicators, gross capital stock and consumption, in this context it is little more difficult to explain. Within a single industry, as far as we recognise it in our perpetual inventory model we assume that the mix of durabilities or expected asset lives remains the same over time. What evidence we have supports that general supposition (see Appendix I) and the result is that the growth rates of gross capital stock and capital consumption, within a single type of asset in a single industry, are the same. But insofar as the mix of investment between individual industries within manufacturing differs (say between textiles and food) then gross capital stock and consumption may not show quite the same rates of growth for the industries in aggregate so long as the mean lives in the two industries are different and so long as their individual growth rates are different. This is so because the ratio of consumption to gross stock will differ between the industries. It can be seen from the table in Appendix II that the difference between the growth rates of gross capital stock and consumption is not great for manufacturing as a whole.

It may be argued that any two industries are equally equipped with fixed assets if their gross capital stocks are equal but, since their levels of capital consumption may be different because their mean asset lives are different it may also be argued to the contrary that they are not equally served by fixed capital year by year. Two industries with dissimiliar proportions of buildings in their aggregates of gross capital stock may serve to illustrate the point. Buildings on the whole have longer service lives than do plant or vehicles. Therefore, an industry with a preponderance of buildings in its stock would be expected to have its stock last longer, but to get less service from it per year, than another industry with shorter-lived assets of similar value.

## PRICES AND TECHNICAL CHANGE

It is sometimes argued that net capital stock should be used as an indicator of the current output potential of fixed capital. It is claimed that by depreciating older plant in the estimation of net capital stock one is obliquely allowing for its relative lack of sophistication and its increasing inefficiency. The arguments for and against this contention can be complex but there are one or two points in relation to the application of price indices which, once established, can clarify the issues considerably.

Primarily, it is necessary to be clear about the principles, practices and problems underlying the price indices which are used to bring old and new capital expenditures to a common base[3]. It cannot be said too often that the compilation of price index series is inevitably complex, onerous and subjective. Further, there can be no unique series, for any collection of goods, which would suit all purposes.

To state the underlying principle most simply it may be said that price indices used here, which are mainly members of the family of wholesale price indices, are designed to measure changes in the average or total price of collections of goods of unchanged specification. The difficulty is of course that in practice assets are commonly discontinued or their specifications are changed and any effects of such changes on the prices of assets must be identified and removed when compiling each price index. In practice a variety of methods is used to deal with these changes. Most imply a competitive market in which additional utility will tend to be reflected in an equivalent addition to costs, which will in turn be reflected in an equivalent addition to price. Most of the methods depend too on discussions with the firms who supply the price quotations. In the case of plant and machinery, the firms who supply the data are generally the manufacturers.

Specification changes are of various kinds. For example, automatic control equipment may be included in new machines or they may be built on a bigger scale and higher prices may simply reflect these changes. Both types of change are very common and, in so far as they increase productive capacity in proportion to their additional cost then it can be said that, within the practical limits of price indexing, the effect on prices of such changes are removed in compiling the price indices, and consequently the changes appear as volume changes in the estimates of gross capital stock. The price indices do not, on the other hand, in practice generally take account of any 'costless' changes in machine specifications. That is to say if the quoted price of a machine is unchanged and it costs no more to produce but it is capable of higher production because of some costless design change then it may be argued that in a sense the price has fallen, but in practice the index will probably not fall on that account. (An example of a costless quality change may arise from the changeover to electronic components from mechanical ones.) Thus the price indices employed are adjusted so that they relate to constant specifications in the case of changes in fixed assets that involve extra costs to their manufacturers but generally not when the changes are costless.

Whether costless productivity changes ought to be allowed to influence price indices, in the context of capital stock, is a moot point for which there is not room for adequate discussion here. If the price effects of all changes and development in fixed assets were to be removed when compiling the price indices then the statistics could show no increase over time in the productivity of capital in the industry which uses it. It is arguable, depending on the intended use of the data, whether that is desirable. This is also discussed in Hibbert, Griffin and Walker (forthcoming). The weight of argument is probably in favour of the present practice in this general context. Denison (1972) and Jorgenson and Griliches (1969) have provided some of the fullest discussion on the subject of attributing productivity changes to capital.

In order to allow for unrecognised costless changes, and sometimes other technological improvements, and to allow for declining efficiency in ageing plant some researchers have constructed vintage models which are designed to give progressively less weight to older machinery. The main difficulty however has been in deciding the weights to be applied to different vintages and indeed there is conflicting evidence on the usefulness of introducing a vintage element (OECD, 1973). The following important consideration which has generally been overlooked in this context, will help to illustrate the possible pitfalls in having to assume that newer plant adds capital services to production at a higher rate than older plant.

## HEALTH, SAFETY AND MORE POLLUTION CONTROL

With increasing attention being given to health and safety at work and to reduction in environmental pollution more money is having to be spent by manufacturers on equipment designed to improve health, safety and the environment. Indeed one of the most common technical changes in machinery is the inclusion of safety equipment. In many cases legislation is forcing users of machinery both here and abroad see Segal and Rutledge, (1976) either to change their processes or to add special plant to their existing stock. Statistics on this subject are scarce but it has been claimed that as much as £100 million of the £800 million expected to be spent on fixed assets in the chemical industry in 1976 will be spent on equipment that does not contribute directly to production (Goldring, 1976). Expenditure on health, safety and pollution control is not new but the cost has certainly increased significantly in recent years to the extent that in some cases it is claimed that factories have had to close because it would have been uneconomic to have installed the necessary new plant. This is also discussed in Segal and Rutledge (1976).

In a sense such expenditures are productive insofar as the result may be to produce cleaner air or cleaner rivers but such production does not feature in conventional measures of output nor hence in the value added by the industry using the asset and so will also be missing from a typical production function.

## LEASING

It is not intended here to discuss every aspect of the strengths and weaknesses of capital stock measures but a word about leasing may be timely. It is widely recognised that the leasing of fixed assets has become more popular in recent years because of some tax and other advantages both to the users and to the lessors. The effect of increased leasing on the capital stock estimates, which are allocated to industry groups on the basis of ownership rather than use, is to put more under the heading of financial companies and less elsewhere. Some of these effects are quantified for the first time in the notes to the Blue Book published in September 1976[4].

Of the £500 million expenditure on fixed assets bought for leasing in 1975, at least £100 million was on assets leased to manufacturing industries. Investment equations for both users and lessors would be enhanced by allowing for this.

## THE MEASUREMENT OF REPLACEMENT INVESTMENT

As a rule of thumb in some economic models replacement investment in a given year is taken to be equal to a constant proportion of the gross capital stock at the end of the previous year. But it is very easy to show that such a measure is unlikely to be right (see Feldstein and Rothschild, 1974), and further, that there is a much better alternative readily available. 'Replacement investment' here is taken to mean the expenditure on new assets necessary to maintain gross output capacity.

Perhaps the easiest way to demonstrate the fallacy of the 'fixed proportion of gross capital stock' approach is to consider the following actual case. In the period from 1960 to 1970 the estimated gross capital stock of plant and machinery at 1970 prices of all manufacturing industries taken together went up by half (see Appendix II). Now, if replacement really were a fixed proportion of gross capital stock then that too would have increased by 50 per cent between the two dates. But, apart from a very small quantity of special equipment even the lightest plant and machinery last much longer than 10 years and, on average, they are expected to last more than 30 years (see Appendix I). The necessity to replace plant and machinery, therefore, in 1970 or 1971 is not much affected by the change in gross capital stock over the previous 10 years. Replacement investment could be a constant proportion of gross capital stock only if productive capacity deteriorated at a steady exponential rate but, as suggested above in the discussion of output potential, that condition does not hold. In essence for such a large group of industries as those that make up the whole of the manufacturing sector, replacement is a function of the capital expenditure of much earlier periods on equipment which is now becoming worn out or obsolete. That function is a complex one for which one needs to take into account how much was spent year by year over a period in excess of forty years previous to the year for which replacement investment is being calculated, together with the life expectancies of the assets purchased over those years and the expected spread of scrapping around each of the mean expected lives. Unfortunately that function cannot be surrogated by a simple equation employing a small number of variables: but, fortunately, it is just such a series of calculations which the CSO perpetual inventory model undertakes. Indeed, it is necessary to calculate retirements, which represent a more appropriate measure of replacement, in order to maintain the gross capital stock estimates.

For a number of reasons notional retirements as estimated in the perpetual inventory model are not the ideal measure of actual replacement investment. It is likely that retirements in practice are accelerated or held over particularly in the short run depending on the current circumstances of the industry. The considerations which bear on a decision to replace equipment are many and probably not entirely measurable. In particular, for a given industry, some major process may be undergoing rapid change so that an unusually large proportion of available investment funds is taken up with replacement and little is left over for the additions to the stock of fixed assets. Nevertheless, there is no better readily available measure of replacement investment than retirements, particularly as an indicator of the underlying trend.

It is sometimes argued that retirements are possibly poor estimators of replacement investment because they depend heavily on the assumptions one has to make about expected life lengths of fixed assets (see Appendix I). Certainly retirements do depend on those life assumptions, but then so do our estimate of gross capital stock, and therefore to take a fixed proportion of that is only compounding the problem. By definition, as long as gross captial stock is growing, retirements must be replacement investment. If gross capital stock is declining then it follows that retirements are not being fully replaced.

Some of the private fixed investment equations in the Treasury's macro-economic model of the United Kingdom now use retirements as a measure of the underlying trend in replacement. For their purpose however it was necessary for them to interpolate quarterly series from the annual series provided by the CSO perpetual inventory model.

Because the only significant volume of retirements in any year is likely to be fixed assets acquired several years previously it is possible, on the basis of what is known about past capital expenditures, to extend the estimated retirements series forward beyond the current year. In manufacturing industry in general, assets with the shortest service lives are expected to begin to be retired after three years (see Appendix I) and so it is possible to extend the retirements series three years further than the latest year for which capital expenditures are known (see Appendix II).

Estimates of retirements, analysed by industry group at current and at 1970 prices, were published for the first time in the Blue Book in September 1976. They have previously been available only on request to the Central Statistical Office.

## THE MEASUREMENT OF FIXED ASSETS IN BALANCE SHEETS AND AS WEALTH

The stock of fixed assets in the published balance sheets of business enterprises is generally shown as the aggregate of capital expenditures at their historic costs, that is an aggregate of the actual money costs at the time of each expenditure, *less* depreciation. It is common now for land and buildings to be revalued every few years but it is as yet uncommon for other fixed assets, plant and machinery and vehicles, ever to be revalued. The most usual method of depreciation used is the straight line method, that is to say the same money quantum of depreciation is deducted each year. The average period over which the depreciation is deducted is generally only about a half to one third of our estimate of average service lives (see Appendix I). It is common for fixed assets still to be in daily use and to have very many years of service left but to be completely written out of the balance sheet. In current practice the period over which an asset is to be depreciated is usually fixed at the beginning of its life and is not usually adjusted later even if it becomes clear, as it usually does, that the asset is going to last much longer.

The depreciation rate allowable for tax purposes is not relevant because it is varied in order to encourage fixed investment in plant and machinery, and indeed it is now usual to allow very rapid depreciation unrelated to the expected service life of the assets. The changes in accounting practice which are now just emerging and their possible effect on the official estimates of capital stock are discussed below in the section on the future measurement of capital stock.

The effect of these methods of depreciation and evaluation of fixed assets in the published accounts of businesses has been in general to understate very considerably the value (however the word is interpreted) of the stock of fixed assets. One result of this has been to allow businesses to be bought cheaply and their assets to be sold at a substantial profit.

These accounting methods are in principle intended to provide a conservative measure of the value of the stock of fixed assets to the owners of the business but because of the very short asset lives assumed, and because of infrequent revaluation, the balance sheet figures in aggregate would obviously be inappropriate for the purposes of macro-economic analysis. In our valuation of fixed assets in the CSO perpetual inventory model therefore we have from the outset tried to use realistic average, rather than minimum asset life assumptions and to revalue capital expenditure so that our 'net capital stock' estimates, that is accumulated capital expenditure *less* capital consumption or depreciation, represent useful measures of the value in terms of written down replacement cost of the stock of fixed assets in a given industry or in an institutional sector. We have not been constrained by considerations of prudence essential in the accounts of a single enterprise. Our estimates of net capital stock represent what might be called the 'unconsumed remainder' of the services provided by the stock of fixed assets so that if the method were to be applied in an 'average' enterprise and the enterprise were to be sold as a going concern one would reasonably expect the net capital stock estimate to equal approximately the value placed on the fixed assets. For example if the plant and machinery had completed one-third of its expected life then it would be valued at two-thirds of its purchase priced updated to present-day values. The net capital stock estimates are therefore useful in calculations of the rate of return on capital and profitability (discussed further below). They are also the most suitable for use in national and sector balance sheets which are now of national and international interest. (See UN Economic and Social Council, 1964.) Estimates of the value of fixed assets, in the National Accounts as in company accounts, are of course only very loosely related to the value put on a quoted company by the stock market.

## THE TREATMENT OF LAND AND OF SECOND-HAND ASSETS

The main drawback of the use of net capital stock estimates in this way is the treatment of land. As explained in the first section of this paper the perpetual inventory model functions broadly by accumulating annual estimates of fixed capital formation by industry. But the purchase of land does not enter into the calculation of capital stock which consists only of reproducible physical assets. This is associated with a further but less serious problem when land and buildings are transferred between different industries. Because in such transactions the land and buildings are rarely valued separately, it is not possible in practice to transfer the buildings from industry to industry within the capital stock in the National Accounts.

Sales of other second-hand assets between industries are not separately identified but simply deducted from the annual capital expenditure of the seller and added to that of the purchaser.

## THE MEASUREMENT OF RATES OF RETURN ON NET CAPITAL EMPLOYED

There are a number of ways of calculating rates of return on capital (see Walker, 1974), but in most cases a measure of the value of fixed assets will be required. Of the two estimates of capital stock which are derived from the perpetual inventory model, net capital stock is the more appropriate. The distinction between net and gross capital stock has been explained in the first part of this paper. Net capital stock, with the reservations already mentioned in relation to land, is a measure of the written down replacement cost of fixed assets. That value may be said to represent the wealth that remains tied up in fixed capital after deducting depreciation and therefore the capital (perhaps together with stocks of work in progress and other assets) upon which one may wish to calculate a rate of return. In the estimation of gross capital stock, on the other hand, an asset is deemed to contribute equally the total whether it is new or whether its service life is almost exhausted and its valuation is therefore inconsistent with that of work in progress and other assets.

## PROFITS NET OF THE DEPRECIATION OF FIXED CAPITAL

Capital consumption as derived from the perpetual inventory model is, in principle at least, the same as depreciation shown in the accounts of enterprises and indeed in the national accounts tables the term depreciation is used interchangeably with consumption (see CSO, 1977). The main differences between 'consumption' as derived from the CSO perpetual inventory model and 'depreciation' as derived from business accounts are in the periods over which they are calculated and the frequency of revaluation of the original capital expenditures. For the reasons already given above in the previous section capital consumption is the superior measure for most macro-economic purposes.

## THE FUTURE OF THE MEASUREMENT OF FIXED CAPITAL STOCK

Although it would not have been predictable, say five years ago, it now seems that the development of our estimates of capital stock is likely to emerge through revolutionary changes in the methods used in drawing up business accounts.

We of course go on polishing our perpetual inventory model and the data that goes into it but it should be admitted that significant improvements are rare now after about twenty years of development. Some landmarks have included the disaggregation of the manufacturing industries (Dean, 1964), computerisation and the developments of a year ago (Griffin, 1975), but it has been concluded that some apparently fertile areas are in practice not amenable to great improvement. For example it would be attractive to review comprehensively and systematically all the life length assumptions for every industry (Appendix I discusses some recent findings) but even if we were able to devote large resources to the job we would still be severely hampered by lack of detailed information at industry level. Fortunately, however, help appears to be imminent from the registered accounts of business. Extraordinarily rapid inflation in recent years has speeded the change from accounting at 'historic cost' to accounting in terms of current costs (see Sandilands, 1976). This inevitably implies that fixed assets must be regularly revalued and that depreciation must be based on more realistic estimates of assets' lives.

Many large enterprises are already embarked on the change and accountants and auditors throughout the profession are becoming increasingly convinced, with the majority of academic accountants (Perrin, 1976), that current cost accounting is both inevitable and desirable.

It is very unfortunate that the profession does not seem to be yet ready to receive the recommendations of the relevant accounting committees. The recommendations of both the Sandilands Committee, and the first report of Mr Douglas Morpeth's Steering Group which was established by the accounting profession to draw up an accounting standard based on the recommendations of the Sandilands Committee, have been ill-received by a narrow majority of the UK accounting profession. It is therefore not yet possible to predict precisely how the new style accounts, the methodology for which is still to be finalised, will be used to improve our estimates of capital stock. It may ultimately be possible for example to undertake occasional benchmark enquires seeking direct information on the stocks of fixed assets in business accounts and to link these benchmarks in intermediate years by means of the perpetual inventory model. It is too early to be more precise but there can be no doubt that better data will eventually emerge, although we shall be left with a host of conceptual problems[5].

It is also intended that the treatment of cars in the perpetual inventory model be changed to reflect the practice, common in business, of selling cars after only two or three years of their useful lives.

## NOTES

The author wishes to acknowledge the helpful comments of colleagues in the CSO and elsewhere and in particular those of Alan Armstrong at the University of Bristol and Ian Elliot at the NEDO. This paper is covered by Crown copyright and is reproduced with the permission of the Controller of MMSO and of the CSO; it was originally published in

*Economic Trends*, no. 276 (HMSO, October 1976). It is also republished in Central Statistical Office, *New Developments in Statistics*. Appendices II – IV have been updated for this volume.

1 The term capital expenditure is used here to refer to gross domestic capital formation as defined in Maurice (1968).

2 More precisely, since the model was revised as explained in Griffin (1975), expenditures with an attributed life of twenty years are deemed to retire not in their twenty-first year but over the period from the seventeenth to the twenty-fifth year.

3 Most of the indices used for plant and machinery in the capital stock estimates are compiled by the Department of Industry.

4 Further details are given in the Department of Trade and Industry (1976, p. 801).

5 Since this article was written, in October 1976, the Morpeth Group have completed their report. However, as the report has not received the acceptance that is due to it, the controversy over 'inflation accounting' has still not been resolved and it is not clear what form the new style company accounts will take. It is to be hoped that it is only a matter of time before current cost accounting becomes standard and that the delay will not be too long.

## APPENDIX I THE SERVICE LIVES OF FIXED ASSETS

Assessing the service lives of fixed assets is complex for a number of reasons. The component parts of process plant are replaced and modified at different times and even the definition of 'service life' is not entirely unambiguous. It has also been, on the whole, very difficult up to now to find good sources of data. The financial accounts of enterprises show depreciation and a value for fixed assets but estimates of asset lives based on these imply lives very far short of what we know to be reasonable on the basis of the data available to us. Engineers usually keep registers of machinery but they are seldom kept in such a way that information on service lives can readily be gleaned from them.

The length of life assumptions used in the original UK estimates of capital stock in the early 1950s (Redfern, 1955) were based on lengths of life used for accounting purposes in some parts of the public sector, on lengths of life underlying Inland Revenue depreciation allowances (Board of Inland Revenue, 1963), and on other miscellaneous data. The Inland Revenue data are of particular interest because they were adopted for some of the more important industries, including manufacturing. It has not been possible to get similar data from Inland Revenue more recently because it has been the policy of governments since the war to encourage fixed investment by allowing assets to be depreciated very quickly for tax purposes so that their owners could claim early tax relief on their expenditure. The same is true for example of the Internal Revenue Service data in the USA where, in their perpetual inventory model, they use a constant fraction of Bulletin F, 1942 lives: that is to say the lives agreed for depreciation purposes by the US Internal Revenue Service in 1942.

In the United Kingdom we have occasionally in the past cursorilly reviewed the Inland Revenue life lengths and those used on the advice of engineers and accountants in the utilities and other industries but little has been altered over the years (see, Dean, 1964), and it has not been practical to undertake a thorough comprehensive inquiry across all industries and all assets. We have therefore been particularly fortunate to have got together a wide range of representative data over the last year or so based, in some important cases, on large surveys conducted by the trade associations of the relevant industries.

The initial reaction of most who see for the first time the life assumptions that are used is to feel that they are probably far too long now even if they were correct at some earlier date. It has therefore been surprising to find from the large range of data collected in the last year that the existing life assumptions are remarkably accurate and that fixed assets appear to last as long now as they did thirty years ago despite the increasing pace of technical progress. Of course technical progress, particularly in metallurgy and plastics, has itself contributed to physical durability and the United Kingdom has a reputation for making its machinery last.

The life lengths used for all industries are very numerous but the assumptions used in manufacturing are given in Table 4.A1.

The industries within the maufacturing sector for which it has been possible to obtain substantial data over the last year or so include chemical and allied, iron and steel, engineering, vehicles, textiles, rubber and paper. In every case the data have been representative of a very large proportion of the industry. Some of the data were supplied confidentially and some are piecemeal and therefore difficult to summarise but those set out in the following paragraphs are representative of the full range.

The primary conclusion drawn from all the data brought together from a wide range of industries and assets is that plant and machinery is extremely durable such that there is some in excess of 70 years old and very little is retired in under 15 years. One large unexceptional manufacturer of very modern products has plant which was secondhand when it was installed 50 years ago. Obviously plant of that age will have been extensively overhauled and modified to some degree so that its age is in reality a composite of different ages, but substantial plant nevertheless survives such periods. Within the limitations imposed by physical dura-

TABLE 4.A1 Length of life assumptions for estimates of fixed capital stock in manufacturing industry

| *Percentages of investment in plant and machinery assumed to fall in each category*[1] | *Assumed average life lengths (years)*[2] | | | | | | |
|---|---|---|---|---|---|---|---|
| | *5* | *16* | *19* | *25* | *34* | *50* | *All* |
| Food, drink and tobacco | – | 2.0 | – | 22.0 | 68.0 | 8.0 | 100 |
| Coal and petroleum products | – | 3.4 | 2.7 | 6.8 | 56.9 | 30.2 | 100 |
| Chemicals and allied industries | – | 3.4 | 2.7 | 6.8 | 56.9 | 30.2 | 100 |
| Iron and steel | – | – | 13.8 | 3.7 | 77.9 | 4.6 | 100 |
| Other metals; Engineering; Metal goods (not elsewhere specified) | – | 1.4 | 10.0 | 20.0 | 56.5 | 12.1 | 100 |
| Aerospace | – | 3.0 | – | 13.0 | 69.0 | 15.0 | 100 |
| Motor vehicles[3] | 45.0 | 1.7 | – | 7.2 | 38.0 | 8.1 | 100 |
| Textiles | – | – | – | 2.6 | 89.7 | 7.7 | 100 |
| Bricks, pottery, glass, etc. | – | 5.0 | 24.0 | 19.0 | 14.0 | 38.0 | 100 |
| Rubber, leather, clothing, footwear | – | – | – | 73.0 | 4.0 | 23.0 | 100 |
| Paper, printing, publishing | – | – | – | 4.5 | 54.5 | 41.0 | 100 |
| Other manufacturing | – | – | – | 73.0 | 4.0 | 23.0 | 100 |
| Timber, furniture, etc. | – | – | – | 76.0 | 5.0 | 19.0 | 100 |

[1] For all manufacturing industries the assumed life length for buildings is 80 years and for road vehicles 10 years.

[2] The assumed lives are all averages so that some machines in each group are assumed to last longer, and some less, than the number of years given.

[3] In the motor vehicle industry certain tools, varying from year to year, are assumed to have a life of only five years.

bility the next limiting factor is the age of the process. New processes and new products generally require some new machinery which, once installed, will survive until it becomes too expensive to maintain or until the process it serves is superseded, whichever is the sooner. Basic preparation plant generally survives longer than other equipment and may survive a number of new products or new processes.

One interesting case is that of a major firm in a major industry which experienced more than one technical change in one of its main process during the 1960s causing unusually rapid obsolescence. The crucial conclusion for the perpetual inventory model is that the life assumptions for that industry were correct in the 1950s and are correct again now for recent expenditure. And, further, despite such a traumatic experience in an important process which brought some plant lives down to very low levels, the average for the industry over that period fell from around 35 years to a trough of no lower than about 25 years before returning again to 35 years.

Had the perpetual inventory model taken account of these rather violently changing life patterns then the gross capital stock of plant and machinery in that particular group would have been about 1½ per cent less than the figure calculated for 1974. The effect would of course be much less for all assets in aggregate for that industry and less still for all manufacturing industries taken together. Similar experiences could be occurring in other industries within manufacturing at any time and so, for those industries, the statistics are biased at those times; but for manufacturing as a whole the particular experience of one industry has much less impact.

For an individual manufacturer another important factor determining the age of his plant is the age of the company. For example a typical factory which is twenty five years old has never scrapped any machines although it has added to its stock of fixed assets and so the age of its plant ranges up to a maximum of twenty five years. In its accounts it uses only two periods over which it depreciates its plant; they are five years and ten years.

A piece of very important evidence in which the industries can be quoted by name is provided by the NEDO monograph *The Age of US and UK Machinery*. The study covered only machine tools, which represent about one eighth of plant and machinery used in manufacturing, but the conclusions are of considerable interest. To quote 'the very surprising result emerges that the life of plant has been very similar in the United States and the United Kingdom over the past 10 years, and this result holds for most types of machine tools over almost the entire range of user industries'. As (Table 4.A2) shows, the average service life was found to be

TABLE 4.A2 Machine tools – service lives and average ages in years by industry of use in the UK (1971) and in the USA (1968)

| | *Service life* | | *Average age* | |
|---|---|---|---|---|
| *Industry* | *UK* | *USA* | *UK* | *USA* |
| All industry | 25.0 | 23.5 | 12.00 | 12.75 |
| Farm machinery | 23.5 | 27.0 | 10.00 | 15.00 |
| Metal work | 22.5 | 24.0 | 11.00 | 12.50 |
| Construction | 24.5 | 24.5 | 12.50 | 13.00 |
| Engines | 23.0 | 25.0 | 11.75 | 13.25 |
| Precision | 25.0 | 22.0 | 11.75 | 11.75 |
| Electrical | 25.5 | 22.0 | 11.50 | 11.25 |
| Shipbuilding | 31.5 | 20.5 | 16.00 | 12.75 |
| Motor vehicles | 32.0 | 28.0 | 12.75 | 13.50 |
| Aerospace | 22.5 | 21.5 | 12.75 | 12.75 |
| Other metal | 23.5 | 22.5 | 11.75 | 12.50 |

*Source* NEDO Monograph 3 *The Age of US and UK Machinery* p. 50 (HMSO 1974).

about 25 years which matches the assumptions made in the perpetual inventory model.

The average age of machine tools in the United Kingdom is a little less than half the estimated service life because investment in them has been higher in recent years. Such machinery is of course comparatively light and could be renewed more readily than the major process plant used in for example the steel, paper or chemical industries.

Another quotable study is that undertaken on behalf of the British Paper and Board Industry Federation in 1975. In an analysis of the 384 paper and board making machines in the United Kingdom the start-up years were found to be as in Table 4.A3.

In the 15 years previous to the date of the survey 104, or 27 per cent, had been rebuilt and so it is not possible to make precise inferences from the start-up dates given in the table but clearly the implied ages (and therefore service lives) of these machines are very long indeed. They are

TABLE 4.A3 Paper and board making machines

| *Start-up dates* | % |
|---|---|
| 75 or more years ago | 5 |
| 50 to 74 years ago | 37 |
| 25 to 49 years ago | 26 |
| 24 or less years ago | 32 |

TABLE 4.A4 Metal founding industries age of plant and equipment in years

| *Industry* | *Iron* | *Steel* | *Bronze and brass* | *Aluminium* | *Zinc alloy* |
|---|---|---|---|---|---|
| Building average | 41 | 40 | 22 | 25 | 25 |
| *range* | – | – | *5–70* | *6–40* | *10–50* |
| Melting plant average | 19 | 21 | 17 | 12 | 13 |
| *range* | – | – | *5–30* | *2–20* | *5–25* |
| Sand plant average | 12 | 15 | 25 | 10 | – |
| *range* | – | – | *5–30* | *6–25* | – |
| Dressing average | 12 | 13 | 15 | 12 | – |
| *range* | – | – | *5–20* | *6–25* | – |
| Diecasting and trimming average | – | – | – | – | 10 |
| *range* | – | – | – | – | *7–15* |
| Ancillary equip. average | – | – | – | – | 11 |
| *range* | – | – | – | – | *8–20* |

certainly too long to suggest that any reduction is required in the lives assumed within the model for that industry group.

A further important series of recent studies in which the industries can be named are those which were undertaken in 1974 and 1975 on behalf of the National Economic Development Office (NEDO) by the relevant trade associations in the metal founding industries. Iron castings represent about two-thirds of the total output of these industries taken together.

In this table only ages and age ranges are given but approximate service lives may be inferred. The lower ages of plant in the aluminium and zinc industries is due, in part at least, to the relative newness of those industries.

Plant has been discussed here more than other types of asset because it receives most attention in the context of capital stock. Less information has been collected on buildings but what there is, for example the data above on metal founders, have again tended to confirm the existing life assumptions. For road vehicles however a change seems to be required. The average expected service life of road vehicles may still be ten years but, for cars in particular, it is rare for a company to keep a vehicle for more than about three years. It is therefore intended that the perpetual inventory model be adjusted to reflect the process of buying and selling business cars.

The general conclusion on asset lives is therefore that although it has not been possible to review all the assumptions as comprehensively as one would have liked there is nevertheless sufficient evidence to indicate that they are substantially right and that, surprising though it is, service lives have not changed appreciably in recent years. Only in very rare cases has evidence come to light which would suggest reductions in any of the life lengths used in the perpetual inventory model.

*Appendix II* TABLE 4.A5 Perpetual inventory of fixed assets in manufacturing industries

| | *At current prices* | | | | | |
|---|---|---|---|---|---|---|
| *All assets (manufacturing in £m.* | *Gross capital formation* | *Retirements* | *Gross stock (end-year prices)* | *Capital consumption* | *Net capital formation* | *Net stock (end-year prices)* |
| 1947 | – | – | 8325.5 | – | – | 4515.0 |
| 1948 | 320.2 | 124.1 | 9003.5 | 188.0 | 132.2 | 4926.4 |
| 1949 | 372.7 | 123.9 | 9459.4 | 200.0 | 172.8 | 5242.6 |
| 1950 | 442.9 | 123.9 | 10399.3 | 215.4 | 227.6 | 5848.6 |
| 1951 | 515.4 | 129.9 | 11953.7 | 249.7 | 265.7 | 6753.3 |
| 1952 | 553.2 | 137.9 | 13024.7 | 291.7 | 261.5 | 7377.2 |
| 1953 | 551.7 | 152.0 | 13523.0 | 309.9 | 241.9 | 7671.7 |
| 1954 | 589.9 | 164.9 | 14350.3 | 324.1 | 265.8 | 8181.0 |
| 1955 | 685.9 | 184.9 | 15667.8 | 354.4 | 331.6 | 8997.9 |
| 1956 | 837.9 | 208.3 | 16904.0 | 393.5 | 444.4 | 9910.1 |
| 1957 | 927.7 | 228.5 | 17985.4 | 429.3 | 498.5 | 10753.0 |
| 1958 | 908.6 | 240.2 | 18614.4 | 460.4 | 445.6 | 11293.4 |
| 1959 | 865.8 | 242.8 | 19046.9 | 477.5 | 388.3 | 11697.2 |
| 1960 | 1021.4 | 251.4 | 20228.0 | 503.2 | 518.2 | 12490.8 |
| 1961 | 1248.4 | 273.2 | 21663.3 | 550.1 | 698.3 | 13565.8 |
| 1962 | 1181.7 | 287.9 | 23006.8 | 590.9 | 590.8 | 14548.7 |
| 1963 | 1068.3 | 305.7 | 24370.2 | 630.9 | 437.4 | 15367.7 |
| 1964 | 1232.1 | 324.5 | 26040.7 | 669.0 | 563.1 | 16407.8 |
| 1965 | 1422.8 | 353.0 | 28178.6 | 730.7 | 692.1 | 17773.0 |
| 1966 | 1516.8 | 380.8 | 29881.2 | 791.3 | 725.5 | 18860.2 |
| 1967 | 1485.0 | 421.3 | 31583.9 | 826.3 | 658.7 | 19923.2 |
| 1968 | 1640.7 | 473.2 | 34055.8 | 892.4 | 748.3 | 21495.7 |
| 1969 | 1819.4 | 523.7 | 37517.1 | 965.7 | 853.7 | 23720.1 |
| 1970 | 2129.2 | 584.1 | 42403.8 | 1089.7 | 1039.5 | 26871.8 |
| 1971 | 2186.7 | 646.8 | 47501.4 | 1242.8 | 943.9 | 30067.2 |
| 1972 | 2044.4 | 697.5 | 53756.2 | 1372.5 | 671.9 | 33877.8 |
| 1973 | 2306.3 | 774.2 | 64442.9 | 1556.9 | 749.4 | 40450.8 |
| 1974 | 3153.7 | 944.7 | 82165.0 | 1906.3 | 1247.4 | 51421.2 |
| 1975 | 3428.9 | 1277.2 | 104172.3 | 2501.9 | 927.0 | 64704.5 |
| 1976 | 3954.2 | 1614.5 | 125365.8 | 3101.7 | 852.5 | 77211.1 |
| 1977 | – | – | – | – | – | – |
| 1978 | – | – | – | – | – | – |
| 1979 | – | – | – | – | – | – |
| *Increasing life assumptions by 20 per cent would produce the following results* | | | | | | |
| 1976 | 3954.2 | 1415.0 | 135438.4 | 2827.2 | 1127.0 | 86229.7 |
| *Reducing all life assumptions by 20 per cent would produce the following results* | | | | | | |
| 1976 | 3954.2 | 1936.1 | 112605.2 | 3431.2 | 523.0 | 66543.5 |

[1] Retirements can be calculated beyond the current year because they are based on expenditures of three or more years previously.
[2] The estimates do not purport to be accurate to the final digit shown.

| | | | | | |
|---|---|---|---|---|---|
| | | *At 1970 average prices* | | | |
| *Gross capital forma-tion* | *Retire-ments* | *Gross stock* | *Capital consump-tion* | *Net capital formation* | *Net stock* |
| – | – | 19322.6 | – | – | 10438.3 |
| 723.4 | 273.3 | 19736.4 | 423.4 | 300.0 | 10738.2 |
| 821.1 | 268.8 | 20227.5 | 439.0 | 382.1 | 11120.3 |
| 945.0 | 263.7 | 20845.0 | 458.5 | 486.5 | 11606.8 |
| 1010.7 | 255.1 | 21692.2 | 481.6 | 529.1 | 12135.9 |
| 972.2 | 248.9 | 22386.5 | 505.6 | 466.6 | 12602.5 |
| 950.6 | 264.9 | 23048.5 | 527.7 | 422.9 | 13025.4 |
| 1009.6 | 282.8 | 23733.5 | 549.0 | 460.6 | 13486.0 |
| 1109.1 | 299.5 | 24493.1 | 571.4 | 537.7 | 14023.6 |
| 1276.4 | 314.5 | 25133.5 | 595.7 | 680.7 | 14704.3 |
| 1358.2 | 327.7 | 25849.6 | 622.0 | 736.2 | 15440.5 |
| 1289.2 | 334.2 | 26502.1 | 648.8 | 640.4 | 16080.8 |
| 1233.1 | 340.0 | 27082.5 | 676.3 | 556.7 | 16637.6 |
| 1439.9 | 350.8 | 28135.8 | 708.0 | 731.9 | 17369.5 |
| 1702.9 | 368.3 | 29265.2 | 746.5 | 956.4 | 18325.8 |
| 1576.2 | 380.7 | 30215.8 | 785.6 | 790.6 | 19116.5 |
| 1386.9 | 395.7 | 31206.9 | 819.1 | 567.7 | 19684.2 |
| 1570.3 | 412.4 | 32364.9 | 852.7 | 717.7 | 20401.8 |
| 1737.9 | 429.0 | 33673.8 | 890.5 | 847.4 | 21249.3 |
| 1785.5 | 447.2 | 35012.1 | 930.0 | 855.5 | 22104.8 |
| 1743.7 | 493.0 | 36262.7 | 968.9 | 774.8 | 22879.5 |
| 1854.3 | 533.1 | 37583.8 | 1007.1 | 847.1 | 23726.7 |
| 1974.7 | 566.3 | 38992.2 | 1046.7 | 928.0 | 24654.7 |
| 2129.2 | 584.1 | 40537.3 | 1089.7 | 1039.5 | 25694.1 |
| 1994.1 | 589.1 | 41942.3 | 1132.4 | 861.7 | 26555.8 |
| 1740.1 | 593.7 | 43088.8 | 1168.0 | 572.1 | 27127.9 |
| 1769.5 | 600.7 | 44257.5 | 1200.4 | 569.0 | 27696.9 |
| 2033.4 | 621.3 | 45669.6 | 1237.5 | 795.8 | 28492.8 |
| 1727.3 | 653.8 | 46743.1 | 1270.2 | 457.1 | 28949.9 |
| 1642.7 | 680.7 | 47705.0 | 1294.6 | 348.1 | 29297.9 |
| – | 710.2 | – | – | – | – |
| – | 738.1 | – | – | – | – |
| – | 762.6 | – | – | – | – |
| 1642.7 | 597.9 | 51582.2 | 1181.1 | 461.6 | 32748.7 |
| 1642.7 | 811.4 | 42797.3 | 1430.5 | 212.2 | 25223.8 |

[3] The gross stock estimates up to 1961 are slightly inconsistent with the other series because the gross stock of the textile industry has been overwritten for that period.

*Appendix III: Net additions to fixed capital stock*

TABLE 4.A6 Gross domestic fixed capital formation less capital consumption (net domestic fixed capital formation) at 1970 prices by industry group[1]

| *in £m.* | *1966* | *1967* | *1968* | *1969* | *1970* | *1971* | *1972* | *1973* | *1974* | *1975* | *1976* |
|---|---|---|---|---|---|---|---|---|---|---|---|
| Agriculture, forestry and fishing | 45 | 55 | 82 | 63 | 62 | 77 | 107 | 131 | 127 | 78 | 54 |
| Mining and quarrying | 33 | 47 | 23 | 5 | 4 | 23 | 40 | 67 | 263 | 589 | 617 |
| Manufacturing | 844 | 770 | 793 | 982 | 1040 | 859 | 570 | 552 | 791 | 474 | 365 |
| Construction | 78 | 92 | 94 | 73 | 61 | 33 | 41 | 95 | 93 | 77 | 56 |
| Gas, electricity and water | 715 | 757 | 496 | 310 | 203 | 123 | 8 | –36 | –43 | –34 | –81 |
| Transport and communication | 189 | 310 | 471 | 413 | 438 | 439 | 479 | 559 | 370 | 301 | 101 |
| Distributive trades and other service industries | 631 | 675 | 768 | 860 | 944 | 1085 | 1166 | 1389 | 1333 | 950 | 869 |
| Dwellings | 1156 | 1320 | 1387 | 1286 | 1128 | 1222 | 1303 | 1182 | 1117 | 1214 | 1183 |
| Social and other public services | 765 | 927 | 1047 | 1032 | 1136 | 1193 | 1241 | 1302 | 1079 | 997 | 938 |
| Total | 4456 | 4953 | 5161 | 5024 | 5016 | 5054 | 4955 | 5241 | 5130 | 4646 | 4102 |

[1] That is, the change in net capital stock.

Source *National Income and Expenditure*, HMSO 1966–76.

TABLE 4.A7 Gross domestic fixed capital formation less retirements at 1970 prices by industry group[2]

| *in £m.* | *1966* | *1967* | *1968* | *1969* | *1970* | *1971* | *1972* | *1973* | *1974* | *1975* | *1976* |
|---|---|---|---|---|---|---|---|---|---|---|---|
| Agriculture, forestry and fishing | 95 | 104 | 131 | 111 | 110 | 124 | 154 | 184 | 187 | 141 | 120 |
| Mining and quarrying | 41 | 59 | 40 | 26 | 24 | 40 | 58 | 83 | 302 | 678 | 792 |
| Manufacturing | 1327 | 1246 | 1267 | 1463 | 1546 | 1402 | 1144 | 1152 | 1407 | 1090 | 979 |
| Construction | 128 | 145 | 150 | 129 | 119 | 90 | 94 | 149 | 149 | 134 | 113 |
| Gas, electricity and water | 957 | 1038 | 806 | 636 | 536 | 455 | 338 | 284 | 260 | 249 | 185 |
| Transport and communication[3] | 336 | 354 | 509 | 571 | 740 | 611 | 737 | 789 | 604 | 428 | 52 |
| Distributive trades and other service industries | 830 | 887 | 995 | 1108 | 1218 | 1383 | 1489 | 1748 | 1732 | 1377 | 1323 |
| Dwellings | 1469 | 1654 | 1736 | 1651 | 1506 | 1615 | 1714 | 1611 | 1562 | 1675 | 1657 |
| Social and other public services | 855 | 1026 | 1157 | 1155 | 1271 | 1341 | 1406 | 1484 | 1278 | 1216 | 1180 |
| Total | 6038 | 6513 | 6791 | 6850 | 7070 | 7061 | 7134 | 7484 | 7481 | 6988 | 6401 |

[2] That is, the change in gross capital stock

[3] The recent increase in retirements in the transport and communications industry is mainly caused by the retirement of ships.

Source *National Income and Expenditure*, HMSO 1966–76.

TABLE 4.A8 Gross capital stock at 1970 replacement cost by industry[1]

| *in £m.* | *1966* | *1967* | *1968* | *1969* | *1970* | *1971* | *1972* | *1973* | *1974* | *1975* | *1976* |
|---|---|---|---|---|---|---|---|---|---|---|---|
| Agriculture | 2.8 | 2.9 | 3.0 | 3.2 | 3.3 | 3.4 | 3.5 | 3.7 | 3.9 | 4.0 | 4.1 |
| Forestry and fishing | 0.3 | 0.3 | 0.3 | 0.3 | 0.3 | 0.3 | 0.3 | 0.3 | 0.3 | 0.3 | 0.4 |
| Mining and quarrying | 2.2 | 2.2 | 2.3 | 2.3 | 2.3 | 2.4 | 2.4 | 2.5 | 2.8 | 3.5 | 4.3 |
| Manufacturing | | | | | | | | | | | |
| Food, drink and tobacco | 3.8 | 4.0 | 4.2 | 4.3 | 4.5 | 4.7 | 4.9 | 5.2 | 5.4 | 5.5 | 5.7 |
| Coal, petroleum products, chemicals and allied industries | 5.9 | 6.2 | 6.6 | 6.9 | 7.3 | 7.7 | 8.0 | 8.1 | 8.3 | 8.6 | 8.8 |
| Iron and steel | 3.8 | 3.9 | 3.9 | 4.0 | 4.1 | 4.3 | 4.4 | 4.6 | 4.7 | 4.9 | 5.0 |
| Other metals, engineering and allied industries | 12.6 | 13.0 | 13.3 | 13.7 | 14.2 | 14.5 | 14.7 | 15.0 | 15.5 | 15.6 | 15.9 |
| Bricks, pottery, glass, cement, etc. | 1.4 | 1.4 | 1.5 | 1.6 | 1.7 | 1.7 | 1.8 | 1.9 | 1.9 | 2.0 | 2.0 |
| Timber, furniture, etc. | 0.5 | 0.5 | 0.6 | 0.6 | 0.6 | 0.6 | 0.7 | 0.7 | 0.7 | 0.8 | 0.8 |
| Paper, printing and publishing | 2.3 | 2.4 | 2.5 | 2.6 | 2.7 | 2.8 | 2.9 | 2.9 | 3.1 | 3.1 | 3.2 |
| Textiles, leather, clothing and other manufacturing | 4.7 | 4.9 | 5.0 | 5.3 | 5.4 | 5.6 | 5.7 | 5.9 | 6.1 | 6.2 | 6.3 |
| **Total** | 35.0 | 36.3 | 37.6 | 39.0 | 40.5 | 41.9 | 43.1 | 44.3 | 45.7 | 46.7 | 47.7 |

| | | | | | | | | | | | |
|---|---|---|---|---|---|---|---|---|---|---|---|
| Construction | 1.7 | 1.9 | 2.0 | 2.1 | 2.3 | 2.4 | 2.5 | 2.6 | 2.7 | 2.9 | 3.0 |
| Gas | 1.9 | 2.2 | 2.4 | 2.6 | 2.7 | 2.9 | 2.9 | 2.9 | 3.0 | 3.0 | 3.1 |
| Electricity | 9.8 | 10.5 | 11.0 | 11.4 | 11.8 | 12.0 | 12.3 | 12.5 | 12.7 | 12.8 | 12.9 |
| Water | 3.0 | 3.0 | 3.0 | 3.1 | 3.2 | 3.2 | 3.3 | 3.3 | 3.4 | 3.4 | 3.4 |
| Railways | 8.0 | 8.0 | 7.9 | 7.8 | 7.8 | 7.7 | 7.7 | 7.6 | 7.5 | 7.5 | 7.4 |
| Road passenger transport | 0.6 | 0.7 | 0.7 | 0.7 | 0.7 | 0.7 | 0.8 | 0.8 | 0.8 | 0.8 | 0.9 |
| Road haulage and storage | 0.9 | 1.0 | 1.1 | 1.2 | 1.2 | 1.3 | 1.4 | 1.4 | 1.5 | 1.5 | 1.5 |
| Shipping | 3.1 | 3.1 | 3.1 | 3.3 | 3.5 | 3.6 | 3.9 | 4.2 | 4.4 | 4.5 | 4.3 |
| Harbours, docks and canals | 1.5 | 1.5 | 1.6 | 1.6 | 1.6 | 1.6 | 1.6 | 1.6 | 1.6 | 1.6 | 1.6 |
| Air transport | 0.8 | 0.8 | 0.9 | 0.9 | 1.0 | 1.1 | 1.1 | 1.2 | 1.2 | 1.2 | 1.2 |
| Postal, telephone and radio communications | 3.8 | 4.1 | 4.4 | 4.7 | 5.1 | 5.5 | 5.8 | 6.3 | 6.7 | 7.1 | 7.3 |
| Distributive trades and other service industries | 14.7 | 15.5 | 16.5 | 17.7 | 18.9 | 20.3 | 21.8 | 23.5 | 25.2 | 26.5 | 27.8 |
| Private dwellings | 29.3 | 30.0 | 30.9 | 31.6 | 32.3 | 33.2 | 34.2 | 35.1 | 35.8 | 36.6 | 37.3 |
| Public dwellings | 15.1 | 15.0 | 16.9 | 17.8 | 18.6 | 19.4 | 20.0 | 20.8 | 21.6 | 22.5 | 23.4 |
| Roads[2] | 3.6 | 3.9 | 4.2 | 4.6 | 5.0 | 5.4 | 5.8 | 6.2 | 6.5 | 6.8 | 7.1 |
| Other public services | 13.9 | 14.6 | 15.6 | 16.3 | 17.2 | 18.1 | 19.2 | 20.3 | 21.3 | 22.3 | 23.2 |
| **Total gross capital stock** | 152.0 | 158.5 | 165.4 | 172.2 | 179.3 | 186.4 | 193.6 | 201.1 | 208.6 | 215.6 | 221.9 |

[1] For an account of the principles of valuation, see *National Accounts Statistics: Sources and Methods*, p. 383–7 and *Economic Trends*, October 1975. Figures relate to end of year.

[2] Excluding the non-renewable element more than 75 years old.

Source *National Income and Expenditure*, HMSO 1966–76.

TABLE 4.A9 Gross capital stock at 1970 replacement cost by type of asset[1]

| *in £m.* | *1966* | *1967* | *1968* | *1969* | *1970* | *1971* | *1972* | *1973* | *1974* | *1975* | *1976* |
|---|---|---|---|---|---|---|---|---|---|---|---|
| Road vehicles | 4.0 | 4.2 | 4.5 | 4.7 | 4.9 | 5.1 | 5.3 | 5.6 | 5.9 | 6.0 | 6.2 |
| Railway rolling stock, ships and aircraft | 6.2 | 6.1 | 6.1 | 6.2 | 6.5 | 6.6 | 6.8 | 7.1 | 7.3 | 7.3 | 7.1 |
| Plant and machinery | 44.5 | 47.1 | 49.6 | 52.1 | 54.8 | 57.4 | 59.8 | 62.5 | 65.3 | 67.8 | 70.4 |
| Dwellings | 44.4 | 46.0 | 47.8 | 49.4 | 50.7 | 52.5 | 54.3 | 55.9 | 57.4 | 59.1 | 60.6 |
| Other buildings and works | 52.9 | 55.1 | 57.4 | 59.8 | 62.2 | 64.8 | 67.4 | 70.0 | 72.7 | 75.4 | 77.6 |
| Total gross capital stock | 152.0 | 158.5 | 165.4 | 172.2 | 179.3 | 186.4 | 193.6 | 201.1 | 208.6 | 215.6 | 221.9 |

[1] For an account of the principles of valuation, see *National Accounts Statistics: Sources and Methods*, p. 383–7 and *Economic Trends*, October 1975. Figures relate to end of year.

Source *National Income and Expenditure*, HMSO 1966–76.

## REFERENCES


Board of Inland Revenue (1963), *Income Tax Wear and Tear Allowance for Machinery and Plant* (London: HMSO).

Central Statistical Office (1976), *National Income and Expenditure, 1965–75* (London: HMSO).

Central Statistical Office (1976), *Price Index Numbers for Current Cost Accounting*, no. 2, (London: HMSO).

Central Statistical Office (1977), *New Developments in Statistics* (London: HMSO).

Dean, G. A. (1964), 'The Stock of Fixed Capital in the United Kingdom', *Journal of the Royal Statistical Society*, series A, vol. 127, part 3.

Denison, E. F. (1972), 'Classification of Sources of Growth', *Review of Income and Wealth*, March.

Department of Trade and Industry (1976), *Trade and Industry*, (London: HMSO).

Feldstein, M. S. and Rothschild, M. (1974), 'Towards an Economic Theory of Replacement Investment', *Econometrica*, May.

Goldring, Mary (1976), 'The Cost of Staying Green and Pleasant', *Investors' Chronicle*, vol. 28, May.

Griffin, T. J. (1976), 'Revised Estimates of the Consumption and Stock of Fixed Capital', *Economic Trends*, no. 264, October (London: HMSO).

Hibbert, J., Griffin, T. J. and Walker, R. L. (1977), 'Development of Estimates of the Stock of Fixed Assets in the United Kingdom', *Review of Income and Wealth.*

Johansen, L. and Sorsveen, A. (1967), 'Notes on the Measurement of Real Capital in Relation to Economic Planning Models', *Review of Income and Wealth*, June.

Jorgenson, D. W. and Griliches, Z. (1969), 'The Explanation of Productivity Change', *Survey of Current Business*, May.

Maurice, Rita (ed.) (1968). *National Accounts Statistics: Sources and Methods* (London: HMSO).

National Economic Development Office (1974), *The Age of U.S. and U.K. Machinery*, Monograph 3 (London: HMSO).

Organisation for Economic Co-operation and Development (1973), *The Measurement of Domestic Cyclical Fluctuations* Outlook, Occasional Studies, July (Paris: OECD).

Perrin, J. R. (1976), 'Inflation Accounting : Survey of Academic Opinion', *Journal of Business Finance and Accounting*, vol. 3, no. 1.

Redfern, P. (1955), 'Net Investment in Fixed Assets in the United Kingdom, 1938–53', *Journal of the Royal Statistical Society*, series A, vol. 118, part 2.

Sandilands, F. C. P. (Chairman) (1976), *The Report of the Inflation Accounting Committee*, Cmnd. 6225 (London: HMSO).

Segal, F. W. and Rutledge, G. L. (1976), 'Capital Expenditures by Business for Air, Water and Solid Waste Pollution Abatement', *Survey of Current Business*, July.

United Nations Economic and Social Council (1964), *Draft International*

*Guidelines on the National and Sector Balance-Sheet and Reconciliation Accounts of SNA*, Paper E/CN.3/460, 24 July.

Walker, J. L. (1974), 'Estimating Companies' Rate of Return on Capital Employed, *Economic Trends*, November (London: HMSO).

# 5 Capital Stock in UK Manufacturing Industry: Disaggregated Estimates 1947–76

A. G. ARMSTRONG

*University of Bristol*

## 1 INTRODUCTION

There has been considerable discussion particularly in the theoretical literature concerning the concept of the stock of capital, and, in particular, doubts have been expressed about the validity of attempts to measure capital. Nevertheless, much use is made in empirical work in various areas of estimates of capital stock in industry. The aim of the present paper is not to enter into the controversy but to present estimates of the stock of capital in UK manufacturing industries in more detail than has been available previously.

The many uses to which capital stock data is put are outlined in an OECD monograph (Ward (1976)). Of these one may note particularly in a UK context the use of estimates of total capital stock to derive measures of capacity utilisation; the exact form of the capital series which is relevant is discussed in a paper by Griffin (1976). Capital stock data provide a vital ingredient to empirical work on production functions and on factor productivity and technical progress.

In this paper the existing available data on capital stock in UK manufacturing is outlined and in section 3 the method used to disaggregate the official series for buildings and for plant and machinery is described together with a new and different method for estimating the stock of vehicles. In section 4, the accuracy of the estimates is discussed.

## 2 EXISTING ESTIMATES OF CAPITAL STOCK

The official estimates by the CSO of the capital stock which are described by Hibbert, Griffin, and Walker (1977) give data for 23 production sectors of the economy of which 8 are in manufacturing industry. In a recent National Income Blue Book, (Table 11.14) (CSO (1977)) estimates are published, by type of asset, for these eight sectors of manufacturing industry. The published estimates are given to the nearest £10 million, but unpublished data is available for 11 sectors in manfacturing to the nearest £0.1 million and it is this which formed the basis of my estimates.

The important caveat should be made at this stage that neither I nor the CSO would claim that the estimates are accurate to the nearest £0.1 million, or even £1 million; it is, however, useful to use such detail in the working papers.

A few years ago I published estimates of the capital stock for 20 industries in manufacturing for the period 1947–68 (Armstrong (1974)). Since then those estimates have been out-dated not only by revisions to the basic data on capital formation but also by three changes in the official statistics: (i) the change from the 1958 to the 1968 SIC; (ii) the use of the establishment rather than the business unit as the basis for classifying capital formation by industry and (iii) the change in the assumption regarding the length of life of assets which is referred to below and is fully discussed by Griffin (1975). In addition, a further disaggregation of the engineering sector into three separate industries, which was not possible previously, has been made. The present estimates thus cover 23 industries within the manufacturing sector for the period 1947–76. Details of these industries and those in the official estimates are given in Table 5.A1 of the Appendix.

## 3 THE DISAGGREGATED ESTIMATES – METHODOLOGY

### 3.1 THE OFFICIAL ESTIMATES – METHODOLOGY

The CSO estimates of capital stock are based on the perpetual inventory method and are fully outlined in National Accounts Sources and Methods (CSO (1968) and by Griffin (1975, 1976)). For a full discussion of the perpetual inventory method, including its merits and demerits, the reader is referred to the monograph by Ward (1976) which also discusses other methods and the practice in other OECD countries.

The perpetual inventory method is fairly well known so that a brief description will suffice here. The value of gross capital stock at the end of the year $t$, $K_t$ is defined as:

$$K_t = K_{t-1} + V_t - S_t$$

where $V_t$ is gross fixed capital formation and $S_t$ is the gross value of assets scrapped during year $t$. All three series are valued at constant 1970 prices.

The method thus requires: (i) an initial estimate of the stock in some base year; (ii) a time series of capital formation and (iii) estimates of annual scrapping. In most simple models the assumption is made that $S_t = V_{t-L}$ where $L$ is the life of the asset. However, as noted by Griffin (1975) the CSO now use a more sophisticated and more realistic approach with the assumption that the scrapping of an asset is distributed over a range of $L^{\pm}3$ years after the date of acquisition.

## 3.2 THE OFFICIAL ESTIMATES – AVAILABLE DATA

As noted above official estimates of $K$ are available annually from 1947 for 11 sectors in manufacturing and also, of course, estimates of $V$ and $S$. Full estimates of $V$ are available from 1948 onwards for all the 23 industries distinguished here. Data on $V$ is actually available for 26 industries but in the present estimates some industries are combined: drink with tobacco; leather with clothing with footwear; paper and board with paper products, printing and publishing. The industrial order bricks, pottery and glass has been disaggregated with reference to Census of Production data. However, since official estimates of $V$ before 1948 are not available for the detail of the 23 industries official estimates of $S$ exist for no more than the 11 sectors.

It is useful at this stage to make the distinction between assets laid down before 1948 to which we can give a subscript 1 and those laid down in 1948 or later, subscript 2. For the 11 sectors there are estimates for all years of $S_1$ and $K_1$, the latter declining over the period as more of the pre-1948 stock is scrapped. For the full 23 industries (and by aggregation for the 11 sectors) there are estimates of $V_2$, $S_2$ and $K_2$. There is no scrapping of these assets until 1961 when some of the shortest-lived plant (with an assumed life of 16 ± 3 years) is scrapped, up to 1961 $K_2$ is simply the cumulative total of the annual $V_2$.

The official estimates of $K$ are obtained by adding $K_1$ to $K_2$ for the 11 sectors. More disaggregated estimates of $K$ thus require a disaggregation of $S_1$ and $K_1$ which then can be combined with the more detailed information available for $K_2$.

## 3.3 DISAGGREGATION FOR BUILDINGS AND PLANT

The method described here relates to only two assets, buildings and plant and machinery, where the procedure was to disaggregate the official estimates. In the case of road vehicles I did not use the official estimates and the method is described in section 3.5.

The estimates made here cover the industries distinguished by the Cambridge Growth Project in their input-output model although it was necessary to combine some pairs of industries as adequate data on investment was not fully available. The numbering and titling of the industries follow the current practice of the Cambridge group and the correspondence of these industries with SIC and with the sectors distinguished in the official estimates is shown in Table 5.A1 of the Appendix. It will be noted there that five of the Cambridge industries correspond with those in the official statistics and thus no disaggregation was necessary for chemicals; iron and steel; textiles; timber, furniture, etc.; paper, printing and publishing. It was thus necessary to disaggregate the official estimates for the other six sectors into 18 industries.

As was noted in the previous section the main requirement is to disaggregate the official estimates of $K_1$ and $S_1$. This was done by disaggregating the estimates of $K_1$ (i.e. pre-1948 assets) at end-1947 and by disaggregating the time series of $S_1$, the scrapping of those assets. By combining the two the (declining) time series of $K_1$ was obtained; since there is no investment $K_t = K_{t-1} - S_t$.

The original Cambridge estimates which formed the basis of this disaggregation were described by Pyatt (1974) and it probably is useful to quote directly from his description:–

> Our main supplementary source of information (*i.e. in addition to the work of Redfern (1955) which was Pyatt's basic source for the whole of manufacturing*) was Barna's work (1957) on the gross stocks of buildings and plant and machinery owned by various manufacturing industries in mid-1955. Barna's estimates cover roughly the same range of activities as our industries 5 to 28, which constitute our manufacturing group: in estimating the capital series for these industries we could thus use him as a guide. First, three series for gross investment at constant prices by the manufacturing group as a whole, each series going back $S$ years from 1948, were constructed on the basis of Redfern, one for industrial buildings one for commercial buildings and one for plant and machinery: for plant and machinery, which are allotted life-spans of up to 45 years, $S \leqslant 45$ and so the series was

constructed back to 1903; for industrial buildings $S = 50$ and for commercial buildings $S = 75$, and the respective series were constructed accordingly. Second, the total gross stock of each of these three types of asset held by the manufacturing group in the first stage, and then allocated among the twenty-one industries according to the proportions implied by Barna's estimates. Third, each industry's investment in each of the three assets during the period 1948 to mid-1955 was subtracted from the corresponding stock held by that industry in mid-1955 to yield that part of the stock which was attributable to investments made before 1948. Finally, for each industry this last magnitude was expressed as a proportion of the total stock of that asset held by the manufacturing group as a whole; these proportions were then applied to the series of total gross investments in that asset constructed in the S years before 1948.

These estimates by Pyatt were made independently of any official work although they were published at about the same time. It would have been possible to use the earlier Pyatt methods simply to extend his disaggregated series but it seems much more desirable to combine his estimates with the more accurate official estimates.

The first stage was to adjust the original series to allow for two classification changes: (i) the change from the business unit to the establishment basis and (ii) the change from the 1958 to the 1968 SIC. This was done by comparing the official estimates of capital formation both before and after each change took place. Since this comparison was used to adjust $K_1$ and $S_1$ in 1947 there is an implicit assumption that changes in the classification would have the same effect on the estimates of capital formation for the many years before 1948 as in the years after 1948. There is obviously scope for error here; however, in only 3 cases was the adjustment more than 5 per cent so that any errors in the adjustment factors would not be significant when related to the total for the industry in question.

These adjusted Cambridge estimates were not used directly but were used in order to allocate the official estimates of $K_1$ and $S_1$ for each sector into the 2, 3 and 4 component industries in the more detailed classification. The estimates of $K_1$ for 1947 and the time series of $S_1$ were combined to provide a time series of $K_1$.

Full data on $V_2$, $S_2$ and $K_2$ for all the industries was provided by the CSO. The estimates of $K$ were obtained by adding $K_1$ to $K_2$ and are shown in Tables 5.A2 and 5.A3 of the Appendix.

## 3.4 DISAGGREGATION OF THE ENGINEERING INDUSTRY

In the original Cambridge work and in my earlier estimates engineering and electrical goods constituted a single industry. With the introduction of the 1968 SIC this industrial order was divided into three: – mechanical, instrument and electrical (Orders VII, VIII, and IX). In view of the size of these sectors in the economy and the interest expressed in them by NEDO it seemed desirable to attempt a further disaggregation.

Full data on capital formation since 1948 and scrapping of these post-1947 assets were available in the official estimates for each of three industries so that estimates of $K_2$ were readily available. However, neither in the official estimates nor in the earlier Cambridge work was there any disaggregated data on $S_1$ and $K_1$.

The starting-point was to divide the estimate of $K_1$ in 1947 for the engineering sector across the three industries. The capital-output ratio (ACOR) was known for engineering and output data was available for each of the three industries; thus, an appropriate assumption about the capital-output ratio in each of the three industries would enable estimation of the stock in each. The simplest possible assumption that the capital-output ratios were the same did not seem acceptable. The method used was to calculate incremental capital-output ratios (ICOR) in each industry over the period 1948–58. The 'relative capital-intensity' of each industry was then obtained by dividing the individual ICOR's by that of engineering; the values of this ratio for mechanical, instrument and electrical engineering were respectively 1.10, 0.90 and 1.05 for plant and 1.12, 1.12 and 0.88 for buildings. It was assumed that this estimate of relative capital intensity derived from ICOR's could be applied to the ACOR for engineering in 1948 in order to obtain estimates of the ACOR in the three industries; these were then combined with output figures to yield estimates of these capital stock. Some further details are given in Appendix A.

The justification should be considered for using values of ICOR's from the period 1948–58 to estimate ACOR's in 1948, which relates to investment accumulated before that date. This method does not imply that the capital intensity of each industry was the same in 1948–58 as it was before 1948. The key assumption is that in respect of capital-intensity the relative position of three industries within engineering was the same before and after 1948; in other words, it makes the reasonable assumption that the three sectors were similarly affected by technical progress.

Scrapping of pre-1948 assets, $S_1$, was allocated to the three sub-industries in proportion to their estimated stock of assets in 1948 and in this way the time-series of the declining $K_1$ was built up. This series was combined with the official estimates of $K_2$ to obtain the required series.

## 3.5 ROAD VEHICLES

The official estimates of the stock of road vehicles use the perpetual inventory method and assume a life of 10 years (with an even distribution of 3 years on either side). I would suggest that the life of 10 years assumed in the official estimates is too long for the majority of commercial vehicles. Nor is the assumption of a constant life easily justified in view of the fact that the timing of the scrapping and replacement of road vehicles is to a certain extent dependent on underlying economic conditions. In the present estimates, therefore, use has been made of the data given in the *Annual Abstract of Statistics* on the number of commercial vehicles currently licensed and the number of new registrations. By subtracting the change in the number of current licences from the number of new registrations an estimate can be obtained of the total number of vehicles scrapped in all industries in each year.

A figure for the average value per vehicle (at 1970 prices) was obtained by dividing the value of gross investment by the number of new registrations. This figure varies as the product-mix of annual capital formation changes. After falling in the first post-war decade the value rises by some 50 per cent by 1970, reflecting an increase in the average size of vehicle. The value of scrapping (at 1970 prices) was obtained by multiplying the number of vehicles scrapped in year $t$ by the value per vehicle in capital formation in year $t$-7. This total value of scrapping was allocated across industries in direct proportion to their investment seven years earlier.

The life of seven years was chosen after discussion with people in the industry who suggested that this was a reasonably typical life span for a commercial vehicle. The actual 'life' assumed here is not so important as in the official methods because its use is to determine which year's investment should be used to allocate a previously estimated total scrapping figure across industries and the pattern of investment between industries does not change much over a few years.

This method for allocating scrapping across industries could not be used for 1954 and earlier years since detailed capital formation data is not available before 1948. The procedure which was used to allocate the small amounts of scrapping (no more than 7 per cent of capital stock) in the years 1948–54 is described in Appendix B.

Estimates of the capital stock in 1947, were obtained, as in the case of plant and buildings, by allocating the CSO estimates across industries in proportion to the earlier Cambridge estimates by Pyatt (1964). These starting-point estimates were combined with the official data on capital formation and my estimates of scrapping to build up the time series of capital stock. It can be noted here than any inaccuracies made in the initial allocation of the official estimates of stock across industries cease to be relevant after 1954; the assumption of a seven year life means that after 1954 all the necessary data is available from official sources.

The main difference between the present estimates and the official series lies in the series for scrapping. In the present estimates the annual value of scrapping is higher and fluctuates more than the official estimates where the value of scrapping increases steadily in every year. The result is that from the same starting point of £0.21 thousand million in 1947 the official estimates for the whole of manufacturing reach £0.72 thousand million in 1965 and £1.17 thousand million in 1976 (CSO (1977) Table 11.14); my estimates are £0.54 thousand million in 1965 and £0.82 thousand million in 1976. The CSO estimate is some 40 per cent higher than mine but since vehicles are a small part of the total stock this difference amounts to no more than 0.8 per cent of total stock.

## 4 ACCURACY OF THE ESTIMATES

### 4.1 STOCK OF PRE-1948 ASSETS

The reliability of any capital stock estimates using the perpetual inventory method depends on the accuracy of capital formation data and the use of the correct assumption regarding scrapping of assets. The description above has shown that official estimates of capital formation are available for all the industries in the post-war period. This, however, is not the case with earlier data and it was necessary to treat pre-1947 assets separately. The official estimates of the stock in 1947 are based on the less reliable pre-1948 and pre-war capital formation data for broad industry groups. The estimates presented here make use of the earlier Cambridge disaggregated estimates. In both cases the estimates of the stock in 1947 depend solely on the early capital formation data. However, as time passes more post-1947 stock is accumulated for which reliable data is available and more of the pre-1948 stock is scrapped.

It is useful, therefore, to enquire as to what proportion of the total stock is made up of pre-1948 assets. The data and the method used here make this information readily available. From 100 per cent in 1947 this declined in the case of buildings to 74 per cent in 1957 and 36 per cent in 1976, and in the case of plant and machinery to 47 per cent in 1957 and 7 per cent in 1976. For buildings and plant combined the figures are 57 per cent and 16 per cent. The proportion varies across industries and is highest in the slower growing industries where there has been less investment – coal and oil products, shipbuilding, other vehicles, and leather, clothing, footwear.

It can thus be seen that any inaccuracies arising from inadequacies of the earlier capital formation data now affect no more than one sixth of the total stock and only 8 per cent of the stock of plant and machinery. Any inaccuracies due to errors in the post-1947 capital formation data or due to incorrect assumptions about scrapping obviously remain.

## 4.2 ASSUMED LIFE OF ASSETS

Since there is virtually no data measuring actual scrapping some assumptions about lives are vital. If the perpetual inventory method uses an assumed life of assets which is too long any initial estimate or indeed the estimate of stock in any single year will be too high since this will assume more stock still in existence than the actual. Similarly, with a rising trend in capital formation, an overlong life assumption will underestimate scrapping and thus will overestimate the annual change in stock.

Correct assumptions about the life of assets are obviously important since errors may affect comparisions of capital-intensity and rate of growth of capital stock between industries within the UK or between the UK and other countries. Further, although annual scrapping is little over 1 per cent of total stock in manufacturing it amounts to about 30 per cent of annual capital formation (with a larger proportion for plant and machinery and with, in all assets, cyclical variations). Thus, any errors in the estimates of the annual increase in stock will have implications for the use of capital stock data in studies of capacity utilisation.

The change in practice introduced by the CSO in 1975 was important in producing a smoother and improved scrapping series. As described by Griffin (1975) the assumption now used is that the scrapping of an asset (with a life of $L$ years) purchased in year $t$ is distributed over the years $t + L - 3$ to $t + L + 3$ rather than being concentrated in year $t + L$. The effect of this change on the estimates of the stock in any year or on the long-run growth was insignificant but it is a valuable change in order to avoid echo-effects on scrapping of previous bunching of investment.

Some recent research in which I have been involved in the European Economic Commission revealed marked differences in the capital-output ratios between British, French and German manufacturing industries which could not be explained by differences in the structure of industry or in post-war investment performance. The low capital-output ratios for France would appear to be due to the assumption of shorter lives of assets which as Ward (1976) notes: 'In the case of construction capital goods the average and extreme service lives are respectively 35, and 10 to 80 years; whereas in the case of machinery it is 16, and 4 to 10 years.' Similarly in Germany one may expect smaller estimates of stock than in UK (other things being equal) since 'only a very small proportion of fixed assets in the present German capital stock is officially regarded as being older than 25 years'. (Ward (1976) p. 109).

Since the assumed life of assets is much higher in the UK – 80 years for buildings and around 30 years for plant (with a range from 16 to 50) – the evidence supplied by Griffin (1976) on actual lives of assets in parts of UK manufacturing industry is particularly interesting and important and we may conclude this section by quoting Griffin:

> The general conclusion on assests lives is therefore that although it has not been possible to review all the assumptions as comprehensively as one would have liked there is nevertheless sufficient evidence to indicate that they are substantially right and that, surprising though it is, service lives have not changed appreciably in recent years. Only in very rare cases has evidence come to light which would suggest reductions in any of the life lengths used in the perpetual inventory model.

## 5 THE FINAL ESTIMATES

The detailed estimates are presented in Tables 5.A2–5.A5 at the end of this paper. These show gross capital stock at 1970 replacement cost for 23 industries from 1947 to 1976 separately for plant and machinery, buildings and road vehicles and also for all assets. As can be seen from Table 5.A1 the estimates given here for 5 industries are the official estimates (except for vehicles) and it would not be amiss to repeat the word of caution given in section 2 on the accuracy of these figures. It should be noted that although the estimates are given here correct to the nearest £1 million the CSO feels able to publish the statistics correct to only £10 million.

It is hoped that these tables will form a useful addition to the industrial data available in the UK and I shall be pleased to hear from any users of the data any comments on the methods used here or any apparent inconsistencies in the figures.

NOTES

I am indebted to Mr Tom Griffin of the Central Statistical Office for making available the full information on their estimates of capital formation, scrapping and stock in much greater detail than published in the National Income Book. Without this information the preparation of these estimates would not have been possible although, of course the CSO accepts no responsibility for the data presented here.

Disaggregated estimates covering 1957–75 were originally prepared for the National Economic Development Office and have been used in the NEDO monographs on UK and West German industry (Panić (1976)) and on capacity utilisation in the UK (Panić (1978)).

Also I must thank David Mitchell for much useful computing assistance, often of a rather tedious nature, in the preparation of these estimates.

## APPENDIX A DISAGGREGATION OF ENGINEERING – DETAILS OF METHOD

The average capital-output ratio for 1948, $k$, is defined as the value of the gross capital stock at 1970 replacement cost at the end of 1947, $K$, divided by the value of net output at 1970 prices in 1948, $y$.

The incremental capital-output ratio, ICOR, was obtained by dividing the total capital formation at 1970 prices, $v$, over the years 1948–57 by the increase in the trend value in net output, $y^*$, at 1970 prices from 1948 to 1958.

The values of net output at 1970 prices in 1948–58 were obtained by combining the indices of production in *Economic Trends*, November 1973 with the value of net output by industry in 1970 given in the 1977 Blue Book Table 3.2.

The method can be summarised:

$$\text{ICOR} = \frac{\Sigma v_t}{y^*_{58} - y^*_{48}} \qquad t = 48 \ldots 57$$

$$\alpha_i = \frac{\text{ICOR}_i}{\text{ICOR}}$$

$$k_i = \alpha_i k$$

$$K_i = k_i y_i$$

where subscript refers to three industries within engineering which is denoted by absence of subscript.

## APPENDIX B SCRAPPING OF VEHICLES, 1948–54

As noted in section 3.5 the method used to allocate scrapping across industries in later years could not be used for 1948–54 due to the absence of capital formation data for years seven years earlier.

For the years 1948–51 the total was first allocated across the 11 CSO sectors in proportion to CSO estimates of scrapping for these groups for 1948 and 1949 (presumably equal to capital formation in 1938 and 1939). The estimates for the sectors were split across industries with reference to the earlier stock estimates for 1947.

For the years 1952–54 the total was first allocated across the 11 sectors in proportion to CSO estimates of scrapping in 1955–57 which are based on capital formation in 1945–47, these being the appropriate on my assumption of a seven year life. Again the sector figures were allocated across industries in proportion to 1947 stock.

APPENDIX C

Table 5.A1 Industry classification

| *Cambridge Industry* | *SIC (MLH)* | *23 Industries* | *11 Sectors* |
|---|---|---|---|
| 5/6 | 211–229 | Food processing | Food, drink, tobacco |
| 7/8 | 231–240 | Drink and tobacco | |
| 9 | 261 | Coal and other petroleum products | Coal and all petroleum products |
| 10 | 262–263 | Mineral oil refining | |
| 11 | Order V | Chemicals | Chemicals |
| 12 | 311–313 | Iron and steel | Iron and steel |
| 13 | 321–323 | Non-ferrous metals | Other metals and engineering |
| 14 | Order VII | Mechanical engineering | |
| 15 | Order VIII | Instrument engineering | |
| 16 | Order IX | Electrical engineering | |
| 17 | Order X | Shipbuilding | |
| 21 | Order XI | Metal goods n.e.s. | |
| 18 | 381 | Motor vehicles | Vehicles |
| 19 | 383 | Aerospace equipment | |
| 20 | 380, 382, 384–5 | Other vehicles | |
| 22/23 | Order XIII | Textiles | Textiles |
| 24 | Orders XIV, XV | Leather, clothing, footwear | Leather, clothing, and other manufacturing |
| 29 | 491 | Rubber | |
| 30 | 492–496 | Manufacturing n.e.s. | |
| 25(a) | 461, 464, 469 | Building materials | Bricks, pottery, glass |
| 25(b) | 462, 463 | Pottery and glass | |
| 26 | Order XVII | Timber | Timber |
| 27/28 | Order XVIII | Paper, printing, etc. | Paper, printing, etc. |

TABLE 5.A2 Gross capital stock at 1970 replacement cost: Buildings
(*£m at year-end*)

| *S.A.M.* | *Industry* | *1947* | *1948* | *1949* | *1950* | *1951* | *1952* | *1953* | *1954* | *1955* | *1956* |
|---|---|---|---|---|---|---|---|---|---|---|---|
| 5/6 | Food processing | 527 | 536 | 548 | 560 | 570 | 585 | 598 | 614 | 637 | 668 |
| 7/8 | Drink and tobacco | 403 | 404 | 405 | 409 | 414 | 416 | 418 | 423 | 429 | 435 |
| 9 | Coal, other petroleum products | 180 | 176 | 173 | 170 | 169 | 167 | 167 | 171 | 175 | 179 |
| 10 | Mineral oil refining | 0 | 3 | 11 | 42 | 50 | 62 | 75 | 79 | 82 | 89 |
| 11 | Chemicals | 508 | 519 | 533 | 555 | 583 | 614 | 649 | 678 | 710 | 754 |
| 12 | Iron and steel | 693 | 705 | 723 | 740 | 757 | 773 | 783 | 793 | 805 | 823 |
| 13 | Non-ferrous metals | 154 | 157 | 163 | 168 | 172 | 173 | 176 | 180 | 186 | 195 |
| 14 | Mechanical engineering | 639 | 649 | 659 | 666 | 679 | 689 | 700 | 716 | 734 | 769 |
| 15 | Instrument engineering | 51 | 52 | 54 | 55 | 57 | 58 | 59 | 59 | 61 | 64 |
| 16 | Electrical engineering | 204 | 210 | 218 | 225 | 232 | 242 | 256 | 269 | 286 | 309 |
| 17 | Shipbuilding | 123 | 125 | 127 | 130 | 134 | 136 | 140 | 146 | 151 | 157 |
| 18 | Motor vehicles | 171 | 175 | 179 | 186 | 192 | 201 | 209 | 217 | 237 | 260 |
| 19 | Aerospace | 110 | 113 | 117 | 121 | 125 | 135 | 148 | 157 | 165 | 176 |
| 20 | Other vehicles | 170 | 170 | 167 | 167 | 167 | 166 | 166 | 165 | 164 | 162 |
| 21 | Metal goods n.e.s | 387 | 390 | 394 | 402 | 403 | 408 | 413 | 421 | 433 | 445 |
| 22/23 | Textiles | 798 | 802 | 814 | 827 | 834 | 837 | 839 | 847 | 859 | 867 |
| 24 | Leather, clothing, footwear | 411 | 415 | 418 | 418 | 421 | 421 | 422 | 424 | 426 | 430 |
| 25(A) | Building materials | 154 | 159 | 162 | 167 | 172 | 175 | 178 | 184 | 191 | 198 |
| 25(B) | Pottery and glass | 60 | 63 | 67 | 71 | 73 | 77 | 79 | 81 | 84 | 87 |
| 26 | Timber | 163 | 165 | 167 | 171 | 174 | 176 | 177 | 182 | 187 | 192 |
| 27/28 | Paper, printing, etc. | 466 | 472 | 475 | 478 | 483 | 489 | 496 | 507 | 522 | 547 |
| 29 | Rubber | 98 | 99 | 101 | 103 | 103 | 103 | 104 | 105 | 109 | 112 |
| 30 | Manufacturing n.e.s. | 84 | 86 | 89 | 92 | 94 | 95 | 95 | 97 | 99 | 100 |
| *Total* | | 6554 | 6645 | 6764 | 6923 | 7058 | 7198 | 7347 | 7515 | 7732 | 8018 |

| | | *1957* | *1958* | *1959* | *1960* | *1961* | *1962* | *1963* | *1964* | *1965* | *1966* |
|---|---|---|---|---|---|---|---|---|---|---|---|
| 5/6 | Food processing | 700 | 725 | 749 | 775 | 802 | 831 | 858 | 897 | 930 | 954 |
| 7/8 | Drink and tobacco | 444 | 454 | 465 | 484 | 506 | 527 | 550 | 572 | 599 | 626 |
| 9 | Coal, other petroleum products | 182 | 181 | 181 | 180 | 181 | 181 | 182 | 183 | 184 | 185 |
| 10 | Mineral oil refining | 99 | 107 | 112 | 115 | 119 | 122 | 125 | 128 | 132 | 139 |
| 11 | Chemicals | 799 | 846 | 882 | 916 | 955 | 994 | 1019 | 1046 | 1079 | 1108 |
| 12 | Iron and steel | 842 | 860 | 876 | 913 | 971 | 1029 | 1050 | 1065 | 1079 | 1092 |
| 13 | Non-ferrous metals | 203 | 206 | 211 | 215 | 220 | 229 | 234 | 239 | 245 | 252 |
| 14 | Mechanical engineering | 806 | 827 | 847 | 868 | 900 | 927 | 944 | 972 | 1004 | 1035 |
| 15 | Instrument engineering | 66 | 69 | 72 | 75 | 80 | 85 | 89 | 94 | 97 | 104 |
| 16 | Electrical engineering | 329 | 347 | 365 | 383 | 405 | 419 | 436 | 456 | 477 | 496 |
| 17 | Shipbuilding | 166 | 178 | 189 | 197 | 204 | 209 | 213 | 221 | 224 | 227 |
| 18 | Motor vehicles | 281 | 300 | 310 | 334 | 369 | 401 | 433 | 456 | 483 | 513 |
| 19 | Aerospace | 188 | 199 | 216 | 223 | 227 | 235 | 240 | 246 | 250 | 254 |
| 20 | Other vehicles | 164 | 166 | 166 | 168 | 169 | 169 | 168 | 167 | 165 | 167 |
| 21 | Metal goods n.e.s. | 457 | 468 | 480 | 491 | 511 | 522 | 536 | 548 | 567 | 584 |
| 22/23 | Textiles | 874 | 877 | 882 | 888 | 899 | 905 | 906 | 916 | 932 | 943 |
| 24 | Leather, clothing, footwear | 432 | 434 | 435 | 439 | 444 | 448 | 450 | 456 | 461 | 465 |
| 25(A) | Building materials | 207 | 215 | 221 | 232 | 248 | 263 | 271 | 286 | 309 | 331 |
| 25(B) | Pottery and glass | 89 | 91 | 94 | 97 | 100 | 104 | 107 | 110 | 115 | 121 |
| 26 | Timber | 196 | 200 | 204 | 212 | 218 | 224 | 231 | 241 | 249 | 256 |
| 27/28 | Paper, printing, etc. | 572 | 591 | 608 | 627 | 648 | 671 | 690 | 710 | 736 | 753 |
| 29 | Rubber | 115 | 118 | 121 | 124 | 126 | 127 | 129 | 133 | 137 | 143 |
| 30 | Manufacturing n.e.s. | 102 | 104 | 106 | 110 | 115 | 119 | 124 | 128 | 135 | 144 |
| *Total* | | 8313 | 8563 | 8792 | 9066 | 9417 | 9741 | 9985 | 10270 | 10589 | 10892 |

Table 5A.2 continued.

| *S.A.M.* | *Industry* | *1967* | *1968* | *1969* | *1970* | *1971* | *1972* | *1973* | *1974* | *1975* | *1976* |
|---|---|---|---|---|---|---|---|---|---|---|---|
| 5/6 | Food processing | 983 | 1015 | 1048 | 1071 | 1090 | 1112 | 1131 | 1156 | 1174 | 1187 |
| 7/8 | Drink and Tobacco | 654 | 682 | 703 | 727 | 758 | 804 | 838 | 874 | 897 | 911 |
| 9 | Coal, other petroleum products | 185 | 184 | 184 | 184 | 185 | 186 | 185 | 184 | 184 | 184 |
| 10 | Mineral oil refining | 146 | 156 | 159 | 162 | 174 | 181 | 185 | 197 | 210 | 214 |
| 11 | Chemicals | 1136 | 1162 | 1196 | 1243 | 1279 | 1306 | 1330 | 1361 | 1397 | 1422 |
| 12 | Iron and steel | 1098 | 1105 | 1115 | 1141 | 1180 | 1209 | 1224 | 1243 | 1276 | 1304 |
| 13 | Non-ferrous metals | 256 | 263 | 277 | 289 | 296 | 300 | 303 | 306 | 310 | 311 |
| 14 | Mechanical engineering | 1064 | 1094 | 1122 | 1154 | 1178 | 1194 | 1215 | 1239 | (1262) | (1280) |
| 15 | Instrument engineering | 110 | 117 | 121 | 125 | 128 | 129 | 131 | 134 | (136) | (138) |
| 16 | Electrical engineering | 515 | 538 | 561 | 589 | 609 | 622 | 637 | 659 | (676) | (691) |
| 17 | Shipbuilding | 228 | 234 | 242 | 248 | 254 | 259 | 269 | 280 | (290) | (298) |
| 18 | Motor vehicles | 531 | 546 | 576 | 603 | 621 | 634 | 650 | 665 | (678) | (690) |
| 19 | Aerospace | 259 | 266 | 275 | 281 | 285 | 287 | 290 | 293 | (295) | (298) |
| 20 | Other vehicles | 167 | 166 | 164 | 162 | 160 | 158 | 156 | 154 | (152) | (149) |
| 21 | Metal goods n.e.s. | 598 | 615 | 630 | 645 | 659 | 671 | 682 | 697 | 709 | 715 |
| 2/23 | Textiles | 951 | 963 | 979 | 989 | 995 | 993 | 999 | 1011 | (1015) | (1012) |
| 24 | Leather, clothing, footwear | 467 | 469 | 473 | 475 | 477 | 479 | 482 | 488 | (491) | (491) |
| 25(A) | Building materials | 345 | 359 | 375 | 383 | 391 | 399 | 408 | 417 | (423) | (429) |
| 25(B) | Pottery and glass | 124 | 129 | 138 | 146 | 150 | 154 | 161 | 170 | (175) | (178) |
| 26 | Timber | 262 | 270 | 281 | 289 | 298 | 309 | 321 | 335 | (340) | (344) |
| 27/28 | Paper, printing, etc. | 768 | 783 | 806 | 833 | 850 | 864 | 877 | 896 | 909 | 914 |
| 29 | Rubber | 148 | 153 | 164 | 169 | 180 | 186 | 190 | 192 | 193 | (191) |
| 30 | Manufacturing n.e.s. | 150 | 158 | 172 | 179 | 186 | 193 | 200 | 209 | (217) | (226) |
| *Total* | | 11145 | 11427 | 11761 | 12087 | 12383 | 12629 | 12864 | 13160 | 13409 | 13577 |

*Note:* The figures in brackets include my estimates of the allocation of capital formation in groups of industries in Blue Book Table 10.8 across individual industries.

TABLE 5.A3 Gross capital stock at 1970 replacement cost: Plant
(£m. at year-end)

| *S.A.M.* | *Industry* | *1947* | *1948* | *1949* | *1950* | *1951* | *1952* | *1953* | *1954* | *1955* | *1956* |
|---|---|---|---|---|---|---|---|---|---|---|---|
| 5/6 | Food processing | 508 | 540 | 573 | 617 | 654 | 694 | 729 | 770 | 813 | 860 |
| 7/8 | Drink and tobacco | 201 | 213 | 227 | 240 | 257 | 269 | 280 | 288 | 298 | 308 |
| 9 | Coal, other petroleum products | 286 | 287 | 289 | 296 | 307 | 318 | 332 | 349 | 369 | 387 |
| 10 | Mineral oil refining | 0 | 12 | 46 | 83 | 148 | 211 | 258 | 282 | 301 | 329 |
| 11 | Chemicals | 984 | 1025 | 1077 | 1147 | 1234 | 1312 | 1398 | 1492 | 1581 | 1711 |
| 12 | Iron and steel | 1041 | 1071 | 1112 | 1166 | 1125 | 1274 | 1320 | 1394 | 1459 | 1536 |
| 13 | Non-ferrous metals | 129 | 143 | 161 | 172 | 187 | 196 | 210 | 220 | 234 | 253 |
| 14 | Mechanical engineering | 985 | 1008 | 1031 | 1063 | 1108 | 1159 | 1204 | 1250 | 1299 | 1346 |
| 15 | Instrument engineering | 77 | 80 | 84 | 89 | 93 | 97 | 99 | 102 | 106 | 109 |
| 16 | Electrical engineering | 329 | 351 | 373 | 395 | 422 | 455 | 486 | 521 | 565 | 610 |
| 17 | Shipbuilding | 336 | 337 | 342 | 342 | 347 | 350 | 352 | 357 | 358 | 361 |
| 18 | Motor vehicles | 387 | 418 | 445 | 484 | 529 | 571 | 604 | 638 | 689 | 751 |
| 19 | Aerospace | 266 | 265 | 269 | 283 | 326 | 379 | 429 | 453 | 470 | 492 |
| 20 | Other vehicles | 134 | 140 | 147 | 151 | 154 | 162 | 167 | 171 | 175 | 180 |
| 21 | Metal goods n.e.s. | 604 | 623 | 641 | 664 | 683 | 701 | 717 | 737 | 761 | 793 |
| 22/23 | Textiles | 1276 | 1308 | 1357 | 1408 | 1458 | 1483 | 1505 | 1539 | 1577 | 1605 |
| 24 | Leather, clothing, footwear | 241 | 254 | 266 | 271 | 273 | 272 | 274 | 273 | 274 | 274 |
| 25(A) | Building materials | 170 | 186 | 202 | 205 | 217 | 227 | 242 | 257 | 273 | 293 |
| 25(B) | Pottery and glass | 84 | 91 | 100 | 111 | 118 | 125 | 131 | 139 | 144 | 151 |
| 26 | Timber | 60 | 71 | 82 | 92 | 102 | 108 | 113 | 121 | 128 | 133 |
| 27/28 | Paper, printing, etc. | 861 | 878 | 895 | 916 | 939 | 953 | 963 | 983 | 1008 | 1047 |
| 29 | Rubber | 163 | 170 | 175 | 178 | 184 | 190 | 189 | 195 | 204 | 216 |
| 30 | Manufacturing n.e.s. | 106 | 112 | 111 | 117 | 120 | 121 | 124 | 128 | 133 | 136 |
| *Total* | | 9228 | 9583 | 10005 | 10490 | 10985 | 11627 | 12126 | 12659 | 13219 | 13881 |

TABLE 5.A3 continued.

| *S.A.M.* | *Industry* | *1957* | *1958* | *1959* | *1960* | *1961* | *1962* | *1963* | *1964* | *1965* | *1966* |
|---|---|---|---|---|---|---|---|---|---|---|---|
| 5/6 | Food processing | 909 | 958 | 1005 | 1056 | 1111 | 1169 | 1227 | 1293 | 1352 | 1412 |
| 7/8 | Drink and tobacco | 322 | 337 | 355 | 381 | 409 | 436 | 466 | 497 | 539 | 572 |
| 9 | Coal, other petroleum products | 402 | 431 | 440 | 440 | 443 | 444 | 444 | 450 | 457 | 459 |
| 10 | Mineral oil refining | 383 | 418 | 431 | 482 | 509 | 529 | 558 | 587 | 614 | 670 |
| 11 | Chemicals | 1858 | 2016 | 2150 | 2267 | 2418 | 2567 | 2682 | 2835 | 3039 | 3276 |
| 12 | Iron and steel | 1642 | 1764 | 1869 | 2035 | 2269 | 2450 | 2546 | 2614 | 2666 | 2705 |
| 13 | Non-ferrous metals | 274 | 284 | 299 | 314 | 334 | 355 | 367 | 381 | 402 | 433 |
| 14 | Mechanical engineering | 1397 | 1446 | 1483 | 1537 | 1592 | 1640 | 1687 | 1756 | 1820 | 1890 |
| 15 | Instrument engineering | 112 | 114 | 117 | 122 | 128 | 133 | 139 | 148 | 156 | 167 |
| 16 | Electrical engineering | 652 | 694 | 735 | 784 | 829 | 871 | 922 | 985 | 1053 | 1120 |
| 17 | Shipbuilding | 364 | 371 | 379 | 384 | 385 | 383 | 384 | 382 | 381 | 378 |
| 18 | Motor vehicles | 815 | 860 | 922 | 992 | 1099 | 1195 | 1283 | 1364 | 1448 | 1535 |
| 19 | Aerospace | 511 | 524 | 534 | 549 | 564 | 576 | 583 | 592 | 598 | 612 |
| 20 | Other vehicles | 186 | 191 | 196 | 201 | 207 | 212 | 213 | 214 | 217 | 220 |
| 21 | Metal goods n.e.s. | 819 | 839 | 869 | 905 | 947 | 981 | 1007 | 1036 | 1077 | 1119 |
| 22/23 | Textiles | 1634 | 1647 | 1660 | 1689 | 1736 | 1770 | 1800 | 1852 | 1920 | 1985 |
| 24 | Leather, clothing, footwear | 273 | 271 | 273 | 278 | 283 | 287 | 294 | 303 | 314 | 324 |
| 25(A) | Building materials | 312 | 332 | 351 | 377 | 407 | 440 | 467 | 495 | 535 | 579 |
| 25(B) | Pottery and glass | 157 | 164 | 168 | 176 | 188 | 201 | 213 | 224 | 239 | 255 |
| 26 | Timber | 138 | 143 | 152 | 159 | 165 | 170 | 178 | 187 | 196 | 202 |
| 27/28 | Paper, printing, etc. | 1093 | 1130 | 1164 | 1203 | 1252 | 1297 | 1347 | 1409 | 1477 | 1536 |
| 29 | Rubber | 226 | 233 | 239 | 247 | 254 | 268 | 278 | 302 | 324 | 348 |
| 30 | Manufacturing n.e.s. | 141 | 146 | 155 | 167 | 183 | 198 | 213 | 232 | 259 | 289 |
| *Total* | | 14620 | 15316 | 15967 | 16745 | 17712 | 18572 | 19298 | 20138 | 21083 | 22086 |

| S.A.M. | Industry | 1967 | 1968 | 1969 | 1970 | 1971 | 1972 | 1973 | 1974 | 1975 | 1976 |
|---|---|---|---|---|---|---|---|---|---|---|---|
| 5/6 | Food processing | 1488 | 1573 | 1654 | 1738 | 1814 | 1892 | 1973 | 2068 | 2114 | 2183 |
| 7/8 | Drink and tobacco | 614 | 657 | 698 | 755 | 820 | 875 | 946 | 1025 | 1082 | 1132 |
| 9 | Coal, other petroleum products | 460 | 456 | 453 | 451 | 459 | 456 | 450 | 443 | 440 | 443 |
| 10 | Mineral oil refining | 774 | 882 | 970 | 1036 | 1118 | 1200 | 1226 | 1249 | 1277 | 1304 |
| 11 | Chemicals | 3461 | 3642 | 3851 | 4133 | 4378 | 4539 | 4645 | 4780 | 4956 | 5134 |
| 12 | Iron and steel | 2763 | 2811 | 2859 | 2931 | 3067 | 3196 | 3304 | 3438 | 3591 | 3758 |
| 13 | Non-ferrous metals | 457 | 478 | 507 | 585 | 634 | 660 | 678 | 703 | 725 | 734 |
| 14 | Mechanical engineering | 1954 | 2017 | 2071 | 2144 | 2197 | 2244 | 2303 | 2376 | (2426) | (2465) |
| 15 | Instrument engineering | 178 | 190 | 202 | 216 | 229 | 243 | 260 | 280 | (297) | (312) |
| 16 | Electrical engineering | 1185 | 1257 | 1331 | 1399 | 1464 | 1531 | 1610 | 1712 | (1791) | (1862) |
| 17 | Shipbuilding | 370 | 362 | 352 | 345 | 337 | 331 | 330 | 334 | (333) | (330) |
| 18 | Motor vehicles | 1623 | 1685 | 1760 | 1864 | 1910 | 1910 | 1953 | 1999 | (2022) | (2054) |
| 19 | Aerospace | 630 | 648 | 667 | 680 | 679 | 679 | 678 | 686 | (689) | (691) |
| 20 | Other vehicles | 219 | 217 | 214 | 211 | 207 | 202 | 198 | 194 | (189) | (185) |
| 21 | Metal goods n e.s. | 1157 | 1201 | 1240 | 1280 | 1316 | 1347 | 1384 | 1436 | 1462 | 1474 |
| 22/23 | Textiles | 2030 | 2113 | 2205 | 2289 | 2356 | 2404 | 2491 | 2585 | (2637) | (2666) |
| 24 | Leather, clothing, footwear | 330 | 337 | 345 | 353 | 360 | 367 | 376 | 385 | (387) | (385) |
| 25(A) | Building materials | 613 | 652 | 693 | 724 | 755 | 788 | 823 | 859 | (887) | (912) |
| 25(B) | Pottery and glass | 267 | 284 | 305 | 323 | 341 | 359 | 376 | 403 | (419) | (434) |
| 26 | Timber | 210 | 225 | 234 | 245 | 258 | 275 | 300 | 326 | (335) | (344) |
| 27/28 | Paper, printing, etc. | 1597 | 1658 | 1720 | 1793 | 1852 | 1907 | 1972 | 2048 | 2107 | 2153 |
| 29 | Rubber | 374 | 404 | 446 | 471 | 498 | 519 | 540 | 552 | 558 | (564) |
| 30 | Manufacturing n.e.s. | 310 | 342 | 380 | 410 | 442 | 472 | 513 | 553 | (577) | (602) |
| *Total* | | 23064 | 24091 | 25157 | 26376 | 27491 | 28396 | 29329 | 30434 | 31301 | 32121 |

*Note:* The figures in brackets include my estimates of the allocation of capital formation in groups of industries in Blue Book Table 10.3 across individual industries.

TABLE 5.A4 Gross capital stock at 1970 replacement cost: Vehicles
*(£m. at year end)*

| *S.A.M.* | *Industry* | *1947* | *1948* | *1949* | *1950* | *1951* | *1952* | *1953* | *1954* | *1955* | *1956* |
|---|---|---|---|---|---|---|---|---|---|---|---|
| 5/6 | Food processing | 47 | 56 | 61 | 66 | 69 | 71 | 74 | 77 | 79 | 81 |
| 7/8 | Drink and tobacco | 21 | 24 | 26 | 27 | 27 | 28 | 28 | 28 | 29 | 30 |
| 9 | Coal, other petroleum products | 3 | 3 | 4 | 4 | 4 | 4 | 4 | 4 | 4 | 4 |
| 10 | Mineral oil refining | 0 | 0 | 0 | 0 | 0 | 0 | 1 | 1 | 1 | 1 |
| 11 | Chemicals | 14 | 17 | 21 | 23 | 25 | 27 | 28 | 30 | 32 | 33 |
| 12 | Iron and steel | 9 | 9 | 10 | 11 | 12 | 12 | 13 | 14 | 15 | 16 |
| 13 | Non-ferrous metals | 3 | 5 | 5 | 5 | 5 | 6 | 7 | 7 | 7 | 7 |
| 14 | Mechanical engineering | 22 | 25 | 28 | 31 | 33 | 36 | 38 | 40 | 42 | 44 |
| 15 | Instrument engineering | 2 | 2 | 2 | 3 | 3 | 3 | 4 | 4 | 4 | 5 |
| 16 | Electrical engineering | 6 | 8 | 9 | 10 | 11 | 13 | 14 | 16 | 17 | 18 |
| 17 | Shipbuilding | 2 | 2 | 2 | 4 | 4 | 4 | 3 | 4 | 4 | 4 |
| 18 | Motor vehicles | 4 | 4 | 4 | 6 | 7 | 8 | 8 | 9 | 10 | 11 |
| 19 | Aerospace | 4 | 4 | 4 | 5 | 6 | 6 | 6 | 7 | 8 | 9 |
| 20 | Other vehicles | 1 | 1 | 2 | 3 | 3 | 4 | 5 | 5 | 5 | 5 |
| 21 | Metal goods n.e.s. | 6 | 8 | 10 | 12 | 14 | 17 | 19 | 21 | 22 | 24 |
| 22/23 | Textiles | 18 | 21 | 23 | 25 | 27 | 29 | 29 | 29 | 31 | 31 |
| 24 | Leather, clothing, footwear | 5 | 7 | 10 | 12 | 14 | 15 | 17 | 19 | 20 | 20 |
| 25(A) | Building materials | 7 | 8 | 10 | 12 | 14 | 16 | 17 | 19 | 20 | 21 |
| 25(B) | Pottery and glass | 2 | 2 | 4 | 5 | 5 | 6 | 6 | 5 | 6 | 6 |
| 26 | Timber | 19 | 22 | 25 | 28 | 30 | 31 | 31 | 32 | 32 | 32 |
| 27/28 | Paper, printing, etc. | 9 | 10 | 12 | 14 | 15 | 17 | 18 | 21 | 23 | 24 |
| 29 | Rubber | 3 | 3 | 4 | 4 | 4 | 4 | 4 | 4 | 5 | 5 |
| 30 | Manufacturing n.e.s. | 1 | 1 | 1 | 2 | 2 | 3 | 3 | 4 | 4 | 5 |
| *Total* | | 208 | 242 | 277 | 312 | 334 | 360 | 377 | 400 | 420 | 436 |

| S.A.M. | Industry | 1957 | 1958 | 1959 | 1960 | 1961 | 1962 | 1963 | 1964 | 1965 | 1966 |
|---|---|---|---|---|---|---|---|---|---|---|---|
| 5/6 | Food processing | 80 | 84 | 87 | 92 | 95 | 99 | 105 | 112 | 112 | 114 |
| 7/8 | Drink and tobacco | 30 | 30 | 30 | 31 | 34 | 35 | 37 | 38 | 40 | 41 |
| 9 | Coal, other pertroleum products | 5 | 5 | 5 | 5 | 5 | 5 | 5 | 5 | 5 | 5 |
| 10 | Mineral oil refining | 1 | 2 | 2 | 2 | 2 | 2 | 1 | 1 | 1 | 1 |
| 11 | Chemicals | 33 | 34 | 34 | 36 | 38 | 38 | 41 | 44 | 47 | 50 |
| 12 | Iron and steel | 16 | 15 | 15 | 15 | 15 | 15 | 15 | 16 | 16 | 17 |
| 13 | Non-ferrous metals | 8 | 8 | 7 | 6 | 7 | 7 | 7 | 8 | 8 | 9 |
| 14 | Mechanical engineering | 44 | 44 | 42 | 42 | 42 | 42 | 43 | 45 | 48 | 51 |
| 15 | Instrument engineering | 5 | 5 | 4 | 4 | 4 | 4 | 4 | 4 | 4 | 5 |
| 16 | Electrical engineering | 18 | 18 | 18 | 18 | 18 | 17 | 19 | 23 | 25 | 26 |
| 17 | Shipbuilding | 3 | 3 | 3 | 3 | 3 | 3 | 3 | 3 | 3 | 4 |
| 18 | Motor vehicles | 10 | 9 | 9 | 12 | 12 | 12 | 13 | 14 | 15 | 15 |
| 19 | Aerospace | 8 | 6 | 7 | 7 | 6 | 5 | 5 | 5 | 5 | 6 |
| 20 | Other vehicles | 5 | 5 | 5 | 3 | 3 | 3 | 2 | 2 | 2 | 1 |
| 21 | Metal goods n.e.s. | 24 | 24 | 24 | 25 | 26 | 26 | 28 | 30 | 31 | 31 |
| 22/23 | Textiles | 30 | 28 | 26 | 26 | 25 | 25 | 26 | 27 | 27 | 28 |
| 24 | Leather, clothing, footwear | 18 | 17 | 18 | 18 | 17 | 17 | 17 | 18 | 18 | 18 |
| 25(A) | Building materials | 20 | 19 | 19 | 20 | 21 | 23 | 28 | 33 | 36 | 38 |
| 25(B) | Pottery and glass | 6 | 7 | 6 | 8 | 9 | 8 | 9 | 9 | 10 | 10 |
| 26 | Timber | 30 | 28 | 29 | 31 | 30 | 29 | 32 | 36 | 40 | 38 |
| 27/28 | Paper, printing, etc. | 24 | 24 | 24 | 25 | 26 | 27 | 30 | 33 | 35 | 37 |
| 29 | Rubber | 5 | 5 | 5 | 6 | 5 | 5 | 6 | 6 | 6 | 6 |
| 30 | Manufacturing n.e.s. | 5 | 5 | 5 | 6 | 6 | 6 | 7 | 8 | 9 | 11 |
| *Total* | | 428 | 425 | 424 | 441 | 449 | 453 | 483 | 520 | 543 | 562 |

TABLE 5.A4 continued

| S.A.M. | Industry | 1967 | 1968 | 1969 | 1970 | 1971 | 1972 | 1973 | 1974 | 1975 | 1976 |
|---|---|---|---|---|---|---|---|---|---|---|---|
| 5/6 | Food processing | 121 | 122 | 124 | 128 | 129 | 130 | 128 | 126 | 120 | 117 |
| 7/8 | Drink and tobacco | 44 | 44 | 45 | 47 | 49 | 49 | 50 | 50 | 53 | 54 |
| 9 | Coal, other petroleum products | 6 | 6 | 6 | 5 | 5 | 5 | 4 | 4 | 3 | 3 |
| 10 | Mineral oil refining | 1 | 1 | 1 | 1 | 1 | 2 | 1 | 2 | 2 | 2 |
| 11 | Chemicals | 53 | 55 | 57 | 61 | 62 | 62 | 61 | 64 | 65 | 66 |
| 12 | Iron and steel | 18 | 17 | 18 | 21 | 22 | 23 | 23 | 25 | 25 | 24 |
| 13 | Non-ferrous metals | 9 | 9 | 10 | 11 | 11 | 11 | 11 | 12 | 13 | 13 |
| 14 | Mechanical engineering | 56 | 59 | 67 | 76 | 81 | 84 | 88 | 94 | (94) | (95) |
| 15 | Instrument engineering | 6 | 7 | 9 | 10 | 11 | 12 | 12 | 13 | (15) | (16) |
| 16 | Electrical engineering | 27 | 28 | 31 | 34 | 35 | 35 | 37 | 41 | (42) | (41) |
| 17 | Shipbuilding | 4 | 3 | 4 | 5 | 5 | 5 | 5 | 6 | (6) | (6) |
| 18 | Motor vehicles | 15 | 15 | 16 | 18 | 19 | 20 | 21 | 23 | (23) | (22) |
| 19 | Aerospace | 6 | 7 | 7 | 7 | 7 | 7 | 7 | 8 | (7) | (6) |
| 20 | Other vehicles | 1 | 0 | 0 | 1 | 1 | 0 | 0 | 1 | (1) | (1) |
| 21 | Metal goods n.e.s. | 34 | 34 | 36 | 40 | 43 | 46 | 49 | 55 | 58 | 59 |
| 22/23 | Textiles | 29 | 30 | 33 | 35 | 36 | 36 | 37 | 41 | (41) | (42) |
| 24 | Leather, clothing, footwear | 18 | 18 | 19 | 20 | 21 | 22 | 24 | 27 | (27) | (28) |
| 25(A) | Building materials | 39 | 40 | 42 | 40 | 40 | 41 | 44 | 49 | (49) | (50) |
| 25(B) | Pottery and glass | 10 | 10 | 10 | 11 | 10 | 10 | 9 | 10 | (10) | (10) |
| 26 | Timber | 40 | 43 | 44 | 46 | 47 | 50 | 58 | 62 | (64) | (68) |
| 27/28 | Paper, printing, etc | 39 | 41 | 43 | 46 | 48 | 51 | 54 | 61 | 61 | 63 |
| 29 | Rubber | 6 | 7 | 7 | 8 | 9 | 9 | 10 | 10 | 10 | (10) |
| 30 | Manufacturing n.e.s. | 12 | 14 | 16 | 18 | 19 | 20 | 22 | 23 | (23) | (24) |
| *Total* | | 594 | 610 | 645 | 689 | 711 | 730 | 755 | 809 | 812 | 820 |

*Note*: The figures in brackets include my estimates of the allocation of capital formation in groups of industries in Blue Book Table 10.8 across individual industries.

TABLE 5.A5 Gross capital stock at 1970 replacement cost: Total assets
(*£m. at year end*)

| *S.A.M.* | *Industry* | *1947* | *1948* | *1949* | *1950* | *1951* | *1952* | *1953* | *1954* | *1955* | *1956* |
|---|---|---|---|---|---|---|---|---|---|---|---|
| 5/6 | Food processing | 1082 | 1132 | 1182 | 1243 | 1293 | 1350 | 1401 | 1461 | 1529 | 1609 |
| 7/8 | Drink and tobacco | 625 | 641 | 658 | 676 | 698 | 713 | 726 | 739 | 756 | 773 |
| 9 | Coal, other petroleum products | 469 | 466 | 466 | 470 | 480 | 489 | 503 | 524 | 548 | 570 |
| 10 | Mineral oil refining | 0 | 15 | 57 | 125 | 198 | 273 | 334 | 362 | 384 | 419 |
| 11 | Chemicals | 1506 | 1561 | 1631 | 1725 | 1842 | 1953 | 2075 | 2200 | 2323 | 2498 |
| 12 | Iron and steel | 1743 | 1785 | 1845 | 1917 | 1894 | 2059 | 2116 | 2201 | 2279 | 2375 |
| 13 | Non-ferrous metals | 286 | 305 | 329 | 345 | 364 | 375 | 393 | 407 | 427 | 455 |
| 14 | Mechanical engineering | 1646 | 1682 | 1718 | 1760 | 1820 | 1884 | 1942 | 2006 | 2075 | 2159 |
| 15 | Instrument engineering | 130 | 134 | 140 | 147 | 153 | 158 | 162 | 165 | 171 | 178 |
| 16 | Electrical engineering | 539 | 569 | 600 | 630 | 665 | 710 | 756 | 806 | 868 | 937 |
| 17 | Shipbuilding | 461 | 464 | 471 | 476 | 485 | 490 | 495 | 507 | 513 | 522 |
| 18 | Motor vehicles | 562 | 597 | 628 | 676 | 728 | 780 | 821 | 864 | 936 | 1022 |
| 19 | Aerospace | 380 | 382 | 390 | 409 | 457 | 520 | 583 | 617 | 643 | 677 |
| 20 | Other vehicles | 305 | 311 | 316 | 321 | 324 | 332 | 338 | 341 | 344 | 347 |
| 21 | Metal goods n.e.s. | 997 | 1021 | 1045 | 1078 | 1100 | 1126 | 1149 | 1179 | 1216 | 1262 |
| 22/23 | Textiles | 2092 | 2131 | 2194 | 2260 | 2319 | 2349 | 2373 | 2415 | 2467 | 2503 |
| 24 | Leather, clothing, footwear | 657 | 657 | 694 | 701 | 708 | 708 | 713 | 716 | 720 | 724 |
| 25(A) | Building materials | 331 | 353 | 374 | 384 | 403 | 418 | 437 | 460 | 484 | 512 |
| 25(B) | Pottery and glass | 146 | 156 | 171 | 187 | 196 | 208 | 216 | 225 | 234 | 244 |
| 26 | Timber | 242 | 258 | 274 | 291 | 306 | 315 | 321 | 335 | 347 | 357 |
| 27/28 | Paper, printing, etc. | 1336 | 1360 | 1382 | 1408 | 1437 | 1459 | 1477 | 1511 | 1553 | 1618 |
| 29 | Rubber | 264 | 272 | 280 | 285 | 291 | 297 | 297 | 304 | 318 | 333 |
| 30 | Manufacturing n.e.s. | 191 | 199 | 201 | 211 | 216 | 219 | 222 | 229 | 236 | 241 |
| *Total* | | 15990 | 16470 | 17046 | 17725 | 18377 | 19185 | 19850 | 20574 | 21371 | 22335 |

TABLE 5.A5 continued

| *S.A.M.* | *Industry* | *1957* | *1958* | *1959* | *1960* | *1961* | *1962* | *1963* | *1964* | *1965* | *1966* |
|---|---|---|---|---|---|---|---|---|---|---|---|
| 5/6 | Food processing | 1689 | 1767 | 1841 | 1923 | 2008 | 2099 | 2190 | 2302 | 2394 | 2480 |
| 7/8 | Drink and tobacco | 796 | 821 | 850 | 896 | 949 | 998 | 1053 | 1107 | 1178 | 1239 |
| 9 | Coal, other petroleum products | 589 | 604 | 617 | 625 | 629 | 630 | 631 | 638 | 646 | 649 |
| 10 | Mineral oil refining | 483 | 543 | 575 | 599 | 630 | 653 | 684 | 716 | 747 | 810 |
| 11 | Chemicals | 2690 | 2896 | 3066 | 3219 | 3411 | 3599 | 3742 | 3925 | 4165 | 4434 |
| 12 | Iron and steel | 2500 | 2639 | 2760 | 2963 | 3255 | 3494 | 3611 | 3695 | 3761 | 3814 |
| 13 | Non-ferrous metals | 485 | 498 | 517 | 535 | 561 | 591 | 608 | 628 | 655 | 694 |
| 14 | Mechanical engineering | 2247 | 2317 | 2372 | 2447 | 2534 | 2609 | 2674 | 2773 | 2872 | 2976 |
| 15 | Instrument engineering | 183 | 188 | 193 | 201 | 212 | 222 | 232 | 246 | 257 | 276 |
| 16 | Electrical engineering | 999 | 1059 | 1118 | 1185 | 1252 | 1307 | 1377 | 1464 | 1555 | 1642 |
| 17 | Shipbuilding | 533 | 552 | 571 | 584 | 592 | 595 | 600 | 606 | 608 | 609 |
| 18 | Motor vehicles | 1106 | 1169 | 1241 | 1338 | 1480 | 1608 | 1729 | 1834 | 1946 | 2063 |
| 19 | Aerospace | 707 | 729 | 757 | 779 | 797 | 816 | 828 | 843 | 853 | 872 |
| 20 | Other vehicles | 355 | 362 | 367 | 372 | 379 | 384 | 383 | 383 | 384 | 388 |
| 21 | Metal goods n.e.s. | 1300 | 1331 | 1373 | 1421 | 1484 | 1529 | 1571 | 1614 | 1675 | 1734 |
| 22/23 | Textiles | 2538 | 2552 | 2568 | 2603 | 2660 | 2700 | 2732 | 2795 | 2879 | 2956 |
| 24 | Leather, clothing, footwear | 723 | 722 | 726 | 735 | 744 | 752 | 761 | 777 | 793 | 807 |
| 25(A) | Building materials | 539 | 566 | 591 | 629 | 676 | 726 | 766 | 814 | 880 | 948 |
| 25(B) | Pottery and glass | 252 | 262 | 268 | 281 | 297 | 313 | 329 | 343 | 364 | 386 |
| 26 | Timber | 364 | 371 | 385 | 402 | 413 | 423 | 441 | 464 | 485 | 496 |
| 27/28 | Paper, printing, etc. | 1689 | 1745 | 1796 | 1855 | 1926 | 1995 | 2067 | 2152 | 2248 | 2326 |
| 29 | Rubber | 346 | 356 | 365 | 377 | 385 | 400 | 413 | 441 | 467 | 497 |
| 30 | Manufacturing n.e.s. | 248 | 255 | 266 | 283 | 304 | 323 | 344 | 368 | 403 | 444 |
| *Total* | | 23361 | 24304 | 25183 | 26252 | 27578 | 28766 | 29766 | 30928 | 32215 | 33540 |

| S.A.M. | Industry | 1967 | 1968 | 1969 | 1970 | 1971 | 1972 | 1973 | 1974 | 1975 | 1976 |
|---|---|---|---|---|---|---|---|---|---|---|---|
| 5/6 | Food processing | 2592 | 2710 | 2826 | 2937 | 3033 | 3134 | 3232 | 3350 | 3408 | 3487 |
| 7/8 | Drink and tobacco | 1312 | 1383 | 1446 | 1529 | 1627 | 1728 | 1834 | 1951 | 2032 | 2097 |
| 9 | Coal, other petroleum products | 651 | 646 | 643 | 640 | 649 | 647 | 639 | 631 | 627 | 630 |
| 10 | Mineral oil refining | 921 | 1039 | 1130 | 1199 | 1293 | 1383 | 1412 | 1448 | 1489 | 1520 |
| 11 | Chemicals | 4650 | 4859 | 5104 | 5437 | 5719 | 5907 | 6036 | 6205 | 6418 | 6622 |
| 12 | Iron and steel | 3879 | 3933 | 3992 | 4093 | 4269 | 4428 | 4551 | 4706 | 4892 | 5086 |
| 13 | Non-ferrous metals | 722 | 750 | 794 | 885 | 941 | 971 | 992 | 1021 | 1048 | 1058 |
| 14 | Mechanical engineering | 3074 | 3170 | 3260 | 3374 | 3456 | 3522 | 3606 | 3709 | (3782) | (3840) |
| 15 | Instrument engineering | 294 | 314 | 332 | 351 | 368 | 384 | 403 | 427 | (448) | (466) |
| 16 | Electrical engineering | 1727 | 1823 | 1923 | 2022 | 2108 | 2188 | 2284 | 2412 | (2509) | (2594) |
| 17 | Shipbuilding | 602 | 599 | 598 | 598 | 596 | 595 | 604 | 620 | (629) | (634) |
| 18 | Motor vehicles | 2169 | 2246 | 2352 | 2485 | 2550 | 2564 | 2624 | 2687 | (2723) | (2766) |
| 19 | Aerospace | 895 | 921 | 949 | 968 | 971 | 973 | 975 | 987 | (991) | (995) |
| 20 | Other vehicles | 387 | 383 | 378 | 374 | 368 | 360 | 354 | 349 | (342) | (335) |
| 21 | Metal goods n.e.s. | 1789 | 1850 | 1906 | 1965 | 2018 | 2064 | 2115 | 2188 | 2229 | 2248 |
| 22/23 | Textiles | 3010 | 3106 | 3217 | 3313 | 3387 | 3433 | 3527 | 3637 | (3693) | (3720) |
| 24 | Leather, clothing, footwear | 815 | 824 | 837 | 848 | 858 | 868 | 882 | 900 | (905) | (904) |
| 25(A) | Building materials | 997 | 1051 | 1110 | 1147 | 1186 | 1228 | 1275 | 1325 | (1359) | (1391) |
| 25(B) | Pottery and glass | 401 | 423 | 453 | 480 | 501 | 523 | 546 | 583 | (604) | (622) |
| 26 | Timber | 512 | 538 | 559 | 580 | 603 | 634 | 679 | 723 | (739) | (756) |
| 27/28 | Paper, printing, etc. | 2404 | 2482 | 2569 | 2672 | 2750 | 2822 | 2903 | 3005 | 3077 | 3130 |
| 29 | Rubber | 528 | 564 | 617 | 648 | 687 | 714 | 740 | 754 | 761 | (765) |
| 30 | Manufacturing n.e.s. | 472 | 514 | 568 | 607 | 647 | 685 | 735 | 785 | (817) | (852) |
| *Total* | | 34803 | 36128 | 37563 | 39152 | 40585 | 41755 | 42948 | 44403 | 45522 | 46518 |

*Note*: The figures in brackets include my estimates of the allocation of capital formation in groups of industries in Blue Book Table 10.8 across individual industries.

## REFERENCES

Armstrong, A. G., (1974), Structural Change in the British Economy, 1948–1968, vol. 12 of Stone, R. (ed.), *A Programme for Growth*, (London: Chapman and Hall).

Barna, T. (1957), 'The Replacement Cost of Fixed Assets in British Manufacturing Industry in 1955', *Journal of the Royal Statistical Society*, series A, vol. 120, part 1.

Central Statistical Office, (1977), *National Income and Expenditure 1966–76* (London: HMSO).

Griffin, T. (1975), 'Revised Estimates of the Consumption and Stock of Fixed Capital', *Economic Trends*, no. 264, October (London: HMSO).

Griffin, T. (1976), 'The Stock of Fixed assets in the U.K.: How to Make Best Use of the Statistics', *Economic Trends*, no. 276, October (London: HMSO).

Hibbert, J., Griffin, T. and Walker, J. L. (1977), 'The Development of Estimates of the Stock of Fixed Assets in the U.K. *Review of Income and Wealth*, pp. 117–35.

Maurice, Rita (ed.) (1968), *National Accounts Statistics: Sources and Methods* (London: HMSO).

P̄anić, M. (1976), *The U.K. and West German Manufacturing Industry, 1954–72*, Monograph 5 (London: HMSO).

P̄anić, M. (1978), *Capacity Utilisation in Manufacturing Industry*, Monograph 6 (London: HMSO).

Pyatt, G. (1964), *Capital, Output and Employment*, 1948–1960, vol. 4 of *A Programme for Growth* (London: Chapman and Hall).

Redfern, P. (1955) 'Net Investment in Fixed Assets in the UK, 1938–1958', *Journal of the Royal Statistical Society*, series A, vol. 118, part 2.

Ward, M. P. (1976), *The Measurement of Capital: the methodology of Capital Stock Estimates in OECD Countries (Paris: OECD).*

# 6 Estimates of the Capital Stock of Welsh Manufacturing, 1949–70

D. E. L. THOMAS

*University College of Swansea*

## INTRODUCTION

The analysis of the economic development of the regions of the United Kingdom has always been handicapped by the almost complete unavailability of statistics of regional capital stock. Although the theoretical validity of the empirical measures that are available, chiefly at the national level, may be severely criticised, the estimates continue to be extensively employed for purposes such as economic forecasting, examining differences and trends in productivity and technical progress and evaluating the extent of economies of scale. In the absence of stock figures, an evaluation of the performance of regional economies has to rely almost exclusively on a single input, labour and, as a result, many existing as well as potentially new theories of regional development cannot be adequately tested. Moreover, without estimates of the stock of capital it is impossible to assess fully the contribution which is made by the government through its policy of subsidising investment, to the build-up of the capital stock of manufacturing industry and the efficiency with which this stock is employed. Any light that might be shed on this and other issues would obviously be beneficial in appraising the effectiveness or otherwise of current regional policy and hence would have direct relevance for the formulation of future government action.

## METHODS OF ESTIMATING CAPITAL STOCK

There are three chief methods of obtaining estimates of capital stock:

(i) perpetual inventory;

(ii) conducting a capital census; and
(iii) employing a surrogate, of which the most popular is probably statistics of electricity consumption.

In the present paper, a variation of the perpetual inventory technique only is employed for deriving estimates of the stock of buildings and plant and machinery (including vehicles) by industry group in Welsh manufacturing for the period 1949–70. The conceptual and statistical difficulties involved in compiling estimates of capital stock by this (and the other two) method(s) have been discussed at length elsewhere and are not considered here. Nor is an attempt made to justify the theoretical appropriateness or otherwise of the estimates, especially in the face of criticisms by Joan Robinson and others concerning the ambiguity of the unit in which capital is measured in the aggregate production function. It should be appreciated at the outset, of course, that the immense difficulties inherent in the concept of a stock of capital mean that any estimates that may be derived are arbitrary and cannot be expected to provide more than general orders of magnitude.

## PERPETUAL INVENTORY

The perpetual inventory method of estimating capital stock involves cumulating annual totals of investment at constant prices over assumed lengths of lives of the assets. Either a gross or a net measure of capital stock may be adopted; the latter allowing for capital consumption (or depreciation).

Let $K_t$ = gross stock of capital at end of year $t$;
$\bar{K}_t$ = net stock of capital at end of year $t$;
$I_j$ ($j = t \ldots t - m + 1$) = annual value of gross investment at constant prices, where $m$ denotes the number of years for which data on gross investment are available;
$C_j$ ($j = t \ldots t - m + 1$) = capital consumption during the year; $\ell$ = average length of life of assets.

Applying the perpetual inventory method yields

$$K_t = \sum_{j=t}^{t-l+1} I_j \tag{1}$$

and

$$\bar{K}_t = \sum_{j=t}^{l} [I_j - C_j] \tag{2}$$

It is well known that there is a number of theoretical and empirical difficulties associated with measuring gross investment at constant prices, establishing the average length of life of assets and deciding what depreciation procedure to adopt. Probably the most serious practical problem, however, in applying the perpetual inventory method for deriving regional estimates of capital stock is the difficulty of obtaining adequate and reliable data on annual gross investment ($I_j$) for different classes of assets for a sufficiently long period of time. Frequently, the number of years ($m$) for which figures of gross investment are available from official statistics is less than the average length of life of assets ($\ell$). One approach when $m < \ell$ is to fill in the missing figures of gross fixed capital formation for the $\ell - m$ years on the basis of fragmentary evidence or proxies of various kinds. But in the case of Wales (as well as the other regions of the United Kingdom) such 'indicators' are just not available and hence $K_t$ and $\bar{K}_t$ cannot be estimated by equations (1) and (2).

$K_t$, however, may be expressed as

$$K_t = f_g K_{t-m} + K_s \tag{3}$$

where $K_{t-m}$ is the gross stock of capital in existence at the end of $t - m$ and $K_s$ is the gross stock acquired since the beginning of $t - m + 1$, which exists at the end of year $t$. $f_g$ is the fraction of $K_{t-m}$ that remains at the end of the year $t$.

Similarly,

$$\bar{K}_t = f_n \bar{K}^*_{t-m+1} + \bar{K}_s \tag{4}$$

where $\bar{K}^*_{t-m+1}$ is the amount of the net stock of capital in existence at end of $t - m$ ($\bar{K}_{t-m}$) which exists at the end of $t - m + 1$ and $f_n$ is the fraction of $\bar{K}^*_{t-m+1}$ that remains in year $t$. $\bar{K}_s$ equals the net stock of capital acquired since the beginning of $t - m + 1$, which exists at the end of year $t$.

Now

$$K_s = \overset{t-m+1}{\underset{j=t}{I'_j}} \tag{5}$$

and

$$\bar{K}_s = \sum_{j=t}^{t-m+1} I'_t \tag{6}$$

where $I'_j$ and $\bar{I}'_j$ represent the gross and net investment respectively acquired since the beginning of $t - m + 1$.

If data can be obtained on gross investment for $m$ years, $K_s$ and $\bar{K}_s$ (provided, of course, a particular depreciation procedure is adopted) can be computed. However, $f_g$, $K_{t-m}$, $f_n$ and $\bar{K}^*_{t-m+1}$ are not known and have to be estimated.

In the next section, estimates are derived of gross fixed capital formation in buildings (*B*) and plant and machinery (*PM*) by industry group in Welsh manufacturing for the period 1949–70 (that is, $m$ equals 22 years). Section III illustrates how the gross and net stock of capital acquired since the beginning of 1949 (that is, the equivalent of $K_s$ and $\bar{K}_s$ in equations (3) and (4) respectively) are calculated and outlines the problems of estimating, and derives figures for the net stock of capital in existence at the end of 1948 which remains at the end of 1949 ($\bar{K}^*_{49}$). This section also includes estimates of the fraction ($f_n$) of $\bar{K}^*_{49}$ which exists each year between 1950 and 1970 and concludes by considering an alternative method of estimating the gross stock of capital which exists prior to the time when data on gross fixed capital formation become available (that is, $K_{t-m}$). The final section compares the different estimates of $K_t$ and $\bar{K}_t$ ($t$ = 1949, . . . , 1970), tests them for variations in some of the assumptions that are employed in their derivation and uses them to provide tentative estimates of capital intensity.

## II GROSS INVESTMENT BY INDUSTRY, 1949–70: CENSUSES OF PRODUCTION AND CHANGES IN THE SIC

One source of information on gross fixed capital formation in Welsh manufacturing is the various censuses of production that have been taken for Great Britain under the Statistics of Trade Act 1949. Since 1947 full (or detailed) censuses have been conducted for six years: 1948, 1951, 1954, 1958, 1963 and 1968. In some of the intervening years up until 1970, when the first of a new annual series of censuses of production was introduced, simpler censuses were taken providing a much more limited amount of data. Owing to changes in coverage, definition and scope, the information contained even in the detailed censuses has not remained strictly comparable from one report to another and additional difficulties arise from the non-disclosure of information relating to individual enterprises and the revisions made in 1958 and 1968 to the Standard Industrial Classification (SIC), first introduced in 1948.

The first requirement for obtaining a measure of consistency and comparability in the estimates for different sectors within manufacturing through time is to adjust for revisions to the SIC. The major changes that have occurred are summarised in Table 6.1 where the 1948 and 1968 SICs are reclassified according to the 1958 framework. In so far as the 1948 and 1958 editions are concerned Table 6.1, however, does not capture all the

TABLE 6.1 Classification of manufacturing industry 1948–68

| | *Standard Industrial Classification* | | |
|---|---|---|---|
| *Industry group* | (1) *1958* | (2) *1948* | (3) *1968* |
| Food, drink and tobacco | III | XIII | III excl. MLH 221 |
| Chemicals and allied | IV | IV | IV, V and III (MLH 221) |
| Metal manufacture | V | V | VI |
| Engineering and electrical | VI | VI and IX (MHLs 100 and 101) | VII, VIII, IX, XII (MLH 390) |
| Shipbuilding and marine engineering | VII | | X |
| Vehicles | VIII | VII | XI |
| Other metals | IX | VIII & IX (MLH 102) | XII excl. MLH 390 |
| Textiles | X | X | XIII |
| Leather, leather goods and fur | XI | XI | XIV |
| Clothing and footwear | XII | XII | XV |
| Bricks, pottery, glass, cement, etc. | XIII | III | XVI |
| Timber, furniture, etc. | XIV | XIV | XVII |
| Paper, printing and publishing | XV | XV | XVIII |
| Other manufacturing | XVI | XVI and IX (MLH 103) | XIX |

*Note*: In the 1948 SIC, motor vehicle repairs, garages and filling stations and boot and shoe repairs were included under manufacturing in orders VII and XII respectively. In the 1958 (and 1968) editions these activities were transferred to miscellaneous services. Similarly, the repairing and cleaning of watches and clocks, which in 1948 had been included with watch and clock manufacture in order IX, was classified separately in 1958 and 1968 under then distributive trades. Repair activities, which are applicable to Welsh manufacturing have been excluded, where possible, from the estimates given below.

modifications in coverage and scope that were introduced in the 1958 SIC and the information that may be compiled on the basis of this table therefore, even for the detailed censuses, is still not strictly comparable. Fortunately, some allowance can be made for these additional discrepancies, since the data for 1954, which are based on the 1948 SIC in the 1954 census are reproduced in the 1958 census according to the 1958 classification. As a result bridges may be constructed for those orders for which data are disclosed for converting the 1954 census figures from the 1948 SIC to the 1958 SIC, which were also employed for recalculating the data for 1949 and 1951 on the 1958 basis.

Information on capital expenditure in the Census of Production relates to new building work (*B*), plant and machinery (*PM*) and vehicles (*V*). Expenditure on *B* covers the cost incurred during the year in which the census is taken of new buildings, extension or reconstruction of old buildings and newly-constructed buildings purchased. The expenditure figures for *PM* and *V* represent the cost, including transport and installation of both new and second-hand assets, less the amount received for disposals.

Figures of capital expenditure by Welsh manufacturing industry were recorded for the first time in the 1949 census. This census provided data, classified according to the 1948 SIC, on expenditure by larger establishments on each of the three categories of assets (*B*, *PM* and *V*), but since it was not a full census the number of industries for which information was not disclosed was much greater than in the subsequent detailed ones. Statistics of the value of gross investment of larger establishments in 1951 and 1954 and of all firms in 1954 are available in the Summary Tables of the 1954 census but, in contrast to the census of 1949, that of 1954 did not provide a breakdown of the total value between *B*, *PM* and *V*. Figures for total fixed investment by all establishments for 1954 and for *B*, *PM* and *V* for all establishments in 1958 and 1963 compiled according to the 1958 SIC, are recorded in the Summary Tables of the 1958 and 1963 censuses. The 1968 census provided separate figures on *B*, *PM* and *V* for all establishments classified according to the 1968 SIC for both 1963 and 1968 and data for total investment by all firms in 1970 are contained in the census for that year.

## ESTIMATES FOR ALL FIRMS, 1949 AND 1951

The procedure for estimating values of fixed investment by all firms in 1949 and 1951 was, firstly, to amend the census figures in accordance with column (2) of Table 6.1 and then scale up the data for larger establishments by the ratio of employment in all firms to employment in larger establishments. These values were supplemented by estimates for the undisclosed trades,which were derived by multiplying the value of fixed investment (less disposals) per person in these trades in the United Kingdom by the number employed in these trades in Wales. The resulting totals were then converted to a 1958 basis using the ratio of the capital expenditure figures for 1954 from the 1958 census to the 1954 figures from the 1954 census.

In 1949 information was disclosed for all trades in only two orders (VII and XII) and the proportion of fixed investment accounted for by the undisclosed trades was particularly high in orders IV, X, XIII and XVI. By contrast, details were disclosed in 1951 for all trades in 9 of the 14 orders and, in two others (VII and XI) with only a single undisclosed trade in each, the estimated value of fixed investment was negligible (less than £.01m). However, orders X and XII and, to a lesser extent order XVI, contained a high proportion of undisclosed trades in 1951. It follows that there may be a considerable margin of error attached to the estimates for orders IV and XVI (1949) and X and XIII (1949 and 1951)[1]. This is especially true of order X (textiles), where the proportion of investment attributable to undisclosed trades is about 90 per cent.

## THE YEARS 1954, 1958, 1963, 1968 AND 1970

Figures of capital expenditure for all firms in 1954 and 1958, compiled according to the 1958 SIC, are available for 12 of the 14 orders in the Summary Tables of the 1958 census. Subtracting the sum of gross fixed investment for the twelve orders that are included from the total for manufacturing as a whole, yields a residual for shipbuilding and marine engineering (order VII) and vehicles (order VIII) of £1.1 million in 1954 and £1.6 million in 1958. Since the definition of the trades included in the vehicles group is similar in both the 1948 and 1958 SICs (with the exception of the exclusion of repair activity from the 1958 SIC), the figure for vehicles in 1954 (1958 SIC) was assumed to equal that recorded in the 1958 census (less the value of repairs). This came to £0.5 million, leaving a residual of £0.6 million for shipbuilding and marine engineering.

During 1958 the total area of industrial building completed in engineering and electrical goods, shipbuilding and marine engineering and other metals was 393 thousand square feet or 39.2 per cent of the total for the four orders combined. The total value of gross investment by these four orders equalled £0.4 million and if the proportion accounted for by vehicles is assumed to be the same as its proportion of the square footage of buildings completed, its share works out at £1.57 million, leaving a residual of £0.03 million for shipbuilding and marine engineering. Given the relatively high figure for the total area of building completed in the vehicles industry and that the census reveals that £2.4 million out of the total capital expenditure of £4.0 million was accounted for by engineering and electrical goods and other metals, the negligible value for shipbuilding and marine engineering does not seem unreasonable. Consequently, the entire value of the residual in 1958 (£1.6 million) was allocated to vehicles.

The values for 1963 are taken from the 1968 census (after reclassifying the information in accordance with column (3) of Table 6.1). Only the total value of investment is given for shipbuilding and marine engineering (order VII) and other metals (order IX) in 1968. It is assumed that the total for order VII (£0.1m) is attributed to *PM*, which enables the distribution among *B* and *PM* for order IX to be derived as a residual. Capital expenditure figures by manufacturing orders in 1970 are published in the report on the census of production for that year for all orders except chemicals and allied industries, mechanical and instrument engineering, shipbuilding and marine engineering, vehicles, textiles and bricks, pottery, glass and cement. However, details are disclosed for a number of individual trades within these orders and, when this information is combined with the data in *Welsh Economic Trends* (Welsh Office, 1974), on the total for all engineering and allied industries and the category 'other manufacturing industries', it is again possible to derive a number of other values as residuals.

## METAL MANUFACTURE, 1949–1970

Except for 1949, 1951, 1954, 1958, 1963 and 1970 the only other years for which there is census information on capital expenditure in Welsh manufacturing are 1952, 1953, 1955, 1956 and 1957, when sample censuses were conducted. The data on manufacturing in the sample censuses are confined to fourteen selected trades (out of a total of about 130) and the total for all establishments (1955, 1956 and 1957 only). The only order for which there are reasonably complete statistics is metal manufacture, where the proportion of the total value of gross investment accounted for by the disclosed trades is 90 per cent or more (except in 1953, when it is about 85 per cent). In 1952 and 1953 the figures for metal manufacture are published for larger establishments only and allocated between *B, PM* and *V*, whereas in 1955, 1956 and 1957 they cover all establishments, but relate only to total investment: Since the ratio of employment in all firms to that in larger establishments in metal manufacture was unity in both 1951 and 1954 the figures for all establishments in the disclosed trades in 1952 and 1953 were assumed to the same as the published values for larger establishments. Estimates for the two undisclosed trades in this order (blast furnaces and wrought iron and steel tubes) were derived by the same procedure as that adopted for undisclosed trades in other years.

The value of total investment in metal manufacture for 1950 may be obtained from Nevin's (1957) *Social Accounts of the Welsh Economy* and for B and PM in 1966, 1967 and 1969 from Tomkins' (1971) *Income and Expenditure Accounts for Wales 1965–1968* and the procedure outlined on pp. 168–9 respectively. For the remaining six years between 1949 and 1970 (1959–1962 and 1964 and 1965) the annual reports of the Iron and Steel Board (British Steel Corporation since 1967) provide the value of capital expenditure on development schemes costing over £100,000 in the iron and steel industry. Separate figures are published for South Wales, but those for North Wales are included with the values for Lancashire (other than the North West) and Cheshire and were obtained separately from the British Steel Corporation and Brymbo Steel Works Ltd. Order *V* also covers privately owned steelworks and the enterprises engaged in the manufacture of other metals including aluminium, copper, lead and zinc. There is no information on the amount of capital expenditure undertaken by these activities, but an arbitary allowance for investment in metal manufacture other than by the nationalised iron and steel industry was made by multiplying public investment in iron and steel by the average ratio, derived from the censuses of production, of total expenditure in metal manufacture to expenditure in the category 'iron and steel (general)' in 1963 and 1968 (1.15).

## TOTAL FOR ALL MANUFACTURING, 1949–70

The total value of gross fixed investment in all manufacturing establishments for 1955, 1956 and 1957 are included in the census reports for these years. The reports exclude certain trades that were covered in the censuses taken for the years 1948 to 1953 but of these, only one: bread and flour confectionery, seems to be among the trades incorporated in the present study. In 1954 and 1958 investment in this activity was about one per cent of the total for all manufacturing industries and, in order to allow for the exclusion of bread and flour confectionery, the figures for 1955, 1956 and 1957 have all been increased by one per cent. The resultant figures were then converted to a 1958 basis by multiplying them by the ratio of gross investment in all manufacturing in 1954, classified according to the 1958 SIC, to that in 1954 classified according to the 1948 SIC.

The value of total gross fixed investment in manufacturing as a whole for 1950, 1952 and 1953 were taken from Nevin's (1957) *Social Accounts* and also converted to a 1958 basis. For 1959 to 1969, with the exception of 1963 and 1968, the value of total investment – distributed among *B* and *PM* (including *V*) was obtained from *Welsh Economic Trends*, (Welsh Office, 1974).

## INVESTMENT IN PM, 1966, 1967 AND 1969

Under the 1966 Industrial Development Act, grants were provided to manufacturing firms in respect of approved capital expenditure incurred on new plant and machinery. In addition to encouraging investment generally a major purpose of the grants was to provide a special inducement for firms to invest in the Development Areas. Accordingly, there was a standard rate of grant which was fixed at a rate of 20 per cent of approved expenditure during the Act's first year of operation (1966), but raised to 25 per cent in December 1966 and a Development Area rate, initially fixed at 40 per cent, but increased to 45 per cent in December 1966. *The Digest of Welsh Statistics*, (Welsh Office, 1974), publishes details of the amount of investment grants paid at both rates to each industry group classified according to the 1968 SIC for the four year period 1966 to 1969.

The data on investment grants were employed for estimating investment in plant and machinery annually between 1966 and 1969 by manufacturing industry group. Estimates for each group were obtained by grossing up the figures of the amount of grant paid according to the relevant rate of grant. For all manufacturing industries the totals in 1966 and 1967 are close to the figures published in *Welsh Economic Trends* : £63m. and £80m. respectively, which relate to acquisitions less disposals of vehicles, plant, machinery and other capital equipment, but the amount for 1968 is about £20m. higher than the figure in *Welsh Economic Trends* and £24m. higher than the figure for expenditure on plant and machinery in the census. The estimate derived on the basis of investment grants for 1969 is over £11m. less than the figure in *Welsh Economic Trends*. The investment grants-based estimates for 1968 by industry group may be compared with the census values for that year. The latter are less than the former in every group with the exception of coal and petroleum products. The relative discrepancy in food, drink and tobacco, metal manufacture, mechanical and electrical engineering and vehicles is particularly marked. There is probably no evidence available on the relative degree of reliability of census and investment grants-based estimates, but part of the discrepancy may probably be explained by the fact that not all the grants paid in a particular year are spent in that year. The census figures are adopted for 1968 with investment grants providing the basis for the estimates for 1966, 1967 and 1969. The grossed-up figures for each order in 1966, 1967 and 1969 were adjusted by multiplying by a factor which ensured that the totals for all manufacturing equalled the total given in *Welsh Economic Trends* and then converted to the 1958 SIC in accordance with the schemation in column (3) of Table 6.1.

## INDUSTRIAL DISTRIBUTION

Statistics of gross investment in buildings are available for individual SIC orders only for the four census years: 1949, 1958, 1963 and 1968. For plant and machinery there is an industrial distribution for the same four years and also for 1966, 1967 and 1969, where estimates were derived as a by-product of the allocation of investment grants. The problem that remains is to allocate the value of total gross investment for manufacturing as a whole among individual orders for the other years in the period of study.

### *(i) Replacement expenditure*

In allocating total investment among industries a distinction needs to be made between the replacement of existing assets on the one hand and additions on the other. The ratio of the amount of investment required for replacing an asset to total gross investment in that asset in year $t$, $(R/{,}I)$, depends upon the length of life of the asset ($\ell$) and the rate of growth of investment in the asset ($r$) during the previous $\ell$ years. More specifically, E.

TABLE 6.2 Ratio of replacement investment and capital consumption to gross investment[2]

| $r.\ell$ | 0.1 | 0.3 | 0.5 | 1.0 | 1.5 | 2.0 | 2.5 | 3.0 | 3.5 |
|---|---|---|---|---|---|---|---|---|---|
| $R/I$ | 0.91 | 0.74 | 0.61 | 0.37 | 0.22 | 0.14 | 0.08 | 0.05 | 0.03 |
| $C/I$ | 0.95 | 0.86 | 0.79 | 0.63 | 0.52 | 0.43 | 0.37 | 0.32 | 0.28 |

Domar (1953) has indicated how $(R/I)$ varies inversely with the product $rl$, according to Table 6.2.

There is also, as a comparison of the first and third rows reveals, an inverse relationship between $r\ell$ and the ratio of capital consumption to gross investment $(C/I)$ and a knowledge of either ratio therefore – for a given value of $r\ell$ – enables the other to be determined. The ratio $C/I$ for certain manufacturing industries in the United Kingdom between 1949 and 1970 may be computed using G. Dean's (1964) figures of capital

TABLE 6.3 Ratio of capital consumption to gross investment in UK manufacturing, 1949–70

| | *Buildings* | | | *Plant and Machinery* | | |
|---|---|---|---|---|---|---|
| *Industry group* | *1949–59* | *1960–70* | *1949–70* | *1949–59* | *1960–70* | *1949–70* |
| Food, drink and tobacco | .43 | .30 | .36 | .44 | .49 | .47 |
| Chemicals and allied | .24 | .38 | .31 | .35 | .43 | .39 |
| Iron and steel | .51 | .56 | .53 | .46 | .78 | .62 |
| Metal-using industries and metal manufacture other than iron and steel | .41 | .38 | .39 | .74 | .66 | .70 |
| Bricks, pottery, glass, cement etc. | .35 | .28 | .31 | .44 | .40 | .42 |
| Timber, construction | .36 | .31 | .33 | .37 | .46 | .41 |
| Paper, printing and publishing | .53 | .39 | .46 | .55 | .48 | .51 |
| Leather, clothing and other manufacture | .75 | .43 | .59 | .62 | .45 | .54 |
| Manufacturing and construction, excluding textiles | .38 | .37 | .37 | .53 | .54 | .53 |

*Sources*:
(i) Gross domestic fixed capital formation: Blue Book (various issues)
(ii) Capital consumption: 1949–62:
Geoffrey Dean 'The Stock of Fixed Capital in the United Kingdom in 1961', *Journal of the Royal Statistical Society*, Series A (General), vol. 127 part 3 (1964), appendix to Section 11, Table IV, p. 350.
1963–70:
(a) Buildings: gross capital stock at 1963 replacement cost (Blue Book) ÷ 80,
(b) Plant and machinery: gross capital stock at 1963 replacement cost ÷ average length of lives assumed by Dean *op. cit.* (appendix to section 11, Tables 1, p. 346).

consumption, his assumptions about average asset lives and the Blue Book statistics of gross capital stock and capital formation (Table 6.3). For manufacturing as a whole (including construction) the ratio for buildings is 0.37 and for plant and machinery, 0.53. The ratio for both categories of assets differs by only one hundredth between the first and second 11 years of the 22-year period. There are a number of significant inter-industrial variations in the ratio, with iron and steel and the other metal industries yielding the highest figure and chemicals, bricks, pottery glass, cement, etc., and timber and construction, the lowest. In the case of a number of industries there is also a sizeable difference between the values of the ratio in the two sub-periods.

Given the values of $C/I$ for manufacturing as a whole (0.37 for *B* and 0.53 for *PM*). Table 6.2 suggests that $R/I$ is about 8 per cent for *B* and between 20 and 25 per cent for *PM*. In the light of these figures, and bearing in mind the large number of arbitrary assumptions and approximations that are involved in deriving estimates anyway, it was decided to regard all investment in *B* as additions to existing assets and assume that the proportion of total replacement expenditure to total gross investment in *PM* in Welsh manufacturing equalled that for the United Kingdom. The latter figure was taken as 20 per cent and expenditure on replacements by individual manufacturing industries in Wales was then obtained by distributing the total in proportion to the number of employees.

(ii) *Buildings*

One series of data that has a degree of relevance as a proxy for distribution of investment by industry in *B* is the statistics on the area of industrial building completed, which are available annually from the Department of Trade and Industry. In a study of regional development between 1945 and 1962 Maton (1968) concluded 'that the proportion of new building by manufacturing industry devoted to particular industries was very broadly similar for the period 1951 to 1962 whether measured by the area of buildings completed or by expenditure (at 1958 prices) on them, though there are some significant differences'. That these differences exist is not surprising of course, bearing in mind that new factories or extensions to existing ones vary in height and in the type and quality of the materials employed in their construction.

For manufacturing as a whole in Wales, the coefficient of correlation between expeniture on new building work (1958 prices) and the area of industrial building completed between 1961 and 1971 was 0.66. This was higher, however, than the coefficient of correlation between the proportion of total expenditure by SIC order (obtained from the census) and the proportion of total industrial building completed by each SIC order in both 1963 and 1968. In 1963 the coefficient of correlation for all industries equalled only 0.42, but if vehicles are excluded (the square footage of factory space completed in this industry in 1963 was well out of line with the figures recorded for the other years – 1.145 million square feet compared to an annual average between 1960 and 1962 and 1964 and 1968 of 0.104 and 0.090 million square feet respectively) its value is 0.91. In 1968 the value of the coefficient obtained by using all groups (except shipbuilding and marine engineering and other metals, for which data are not disclosed) classified according to the 1968 SIC is only 0.25.

C. R. Tomkins (1971) derived estimates of expenditure on *B* for Welsh manufacturing industries classified according to the 1958 SIC for the four-year period 1965 to 1968 by dividing the United Kingdom figure for each industry as shown in the Blue Book between Wales and the rest of the United Kingdom on the basis of industrial building completed each year. The figures are scaled up so that they equal in aggregate the total value of *B* in Welsh manufacturing as a whole. A comparison of Tomkins' estimates for 1968 with the census figures for the same year reveals that the coefficient of correlation between the two sets of figures is about 0.6. The estimates for each group with the exception of timber and furniture diverge by 30 per cent or more from the values given in the census.

Unfortunately, there is no entirely satisfactory procedure for estimating the distribution of expenditure on *B* among industries, and it may even be argued that since the values of the coefficient of correlation indicate that a substantial proportion of the variation in actual expenditure is unexplained by employing statistics of area of industrial building as a proxy, the method has little or nothing to commend it. However, in the absence of other sources of information it was decided to adopt the approach adopted by Tomkins, with a presumption that, while it probably yields annual estimates for each industry with relatively large errors, it provides some indication of the change from one year to another as well as the order of magnitude of the gross addition to the existing stock of *B* over a period of time.

The estimates of gross investment in buildings by industry groups that have been derived by the various methods outlined are included in Table 6.4.

### (iii) *Additions to plant and machinery*

The problem remains of distributing expenditure on additions to PM among the various industry groups excluding metal manufacture. In the absence of a suitable alternative, recourse was again made to the statistics

TABLE 6.4 Estimated gross investment in buildings, 1949–70
(*£m. at current prices*)

| *SIC Order* | | '49 | '50 | '51 | '52 | '53 | '54 | '55 | '56 | '57 | '58 | '59 | '60 | '61 | '62 | '63 | '64 | '65 | '66 | '67 | '68 | '69 | '70 |
|---|---|---|---|---|---|---|---|---|---|---|---|---|---|---|---|---|---|---|---|---|---|---|---|
| III | Food, drink and tobacco | 0.1 | 0.1 | 0.4 | 0.1 | 0.0 | 0.8 | 1.4 | 0.3 | 1.1 | 0.5 | 1.2 | 1.0 | 2.4 | 1.4 | 1.0 | 1.7 | 1.0 | 1.3 | 0.9 | 0.8 | 1.7 | 0.5 |
| IV | Chemicals and allied industries | 1.4 | 2.3 | [illegible] | 0.6 | 1.6 | 0.3 | 1.0 | 0.4 | 1.9 | 1.1 | 1.1 | 9.2 | 1.1 | 1.6 | 1.4 | 1.3 | 1.9 | 1.1 | 1.3 | 3.3 | 1.0 | 2.9 |
| V | Metal manufacture | 1.1 | 0.7 | 2.6 | 2.3 | 1.9 | 2.8 | 1.5 | 2.4 | 4.3 | 5.5 | 2.3 | 12.0 | 11.8 | 3.7 | 3.6 | 0.2 | 2.0 | 0.7 | 1.3 | 3.1 | 4.0 | 6.1 |
| VI | Engineering and electrical goods | 0.1 | 0.4 | 0.2 | 0.3 | 0.1 | 1.3 | 1.0 | 1.0 | 0.8 | 0.3 | 2.1 | 0.9 | 4.4 | 1.4 | 1.3 | 1.1 | 1.7 | 2.2 | 3.9 | 1.0 | 2.6 | 8.7 |
| VII | Shipbuilding and marine engineering | 0.0 | 0.1 | 0.0 | 0.0 | 0.0 | 0.2 | 0.1 | 0.1 | 0.1 | 0.0 | 0.5 | 0.0 | 0.0 | 0.0 | 0.0 | 0.2 | 0.0 | 0.0 | 0.0 | 0.0 | 0.2 | 0.3 |
| VIII | Vehicles | 0.0 | 0.1 | 0.1 | 0.2 | 0.2 | 0.5 | 0.8 | 0.4 | 0.5 | 0.6 | 1.2 | 0.2 | 0.7 | 0.9 | 0.9 | 1.9 | 0.0 | 0.7 | 0.3 | 0.8 | 1.2 | 2.9 |
| IX | Other metals | 0.2 | 0.3 | 0.1 | 0.1 | 0.0 | 0.4 | 0.4 | 0.3 | 0.2 | 0.2 | 0.7 | 0.4 | 1.1 | 1.4 | 0.5 | 1.0 | 0.8 | 0.7 | 1.4 | 1.6 | 0.8 | 1.0 |
| X | Textiles | 0.8 | 1.2 | 0.1 | 0.1 | 0.5 | 0.8 | 1.5 | 1.7 | 0.1 | 0.9 | 0.4 | 0.4 | 0.1 | 4.7 | 0.3 | 0.3 | 0.3 | 0.6 | 0.6 | 0.3 | 0.4 | 0.8 |
| XI | Leather, leather goods and fur | 0.0 | 0.0 | 0.0 | 0.0 | 0.0 | 0.0 | 0.0 | 0.1 | 0.0 | 0.1 | 0.0 | 0.0 | 0.0 | 0.0 | 0.0 | 0.0 | 0.0 | 0.1 | 0.1 | 0.0 | 0.2 | 0.2 |
| XII | Clothing and footwear | 0.0 | 0.1 | 0.1 | 0.0 | 0.0 | 0.0 | 0.1 | 0.1 | 0.2 | 0.0 | 0.2 | 0.1 | 0.1 | 0.4 | 0.2 | 0.3 | 0.4 | 0.3 | 0.5 | 0.2 | 0.3 | 0.0 |
| XIII | Bricks, pottery, glass, cement, etc. | 0.3 | 0.2 | 0.1 | 0.0 | 0.1 | 0.3 | 0.2 | 0.3 | 0.3 | 0.3 | 0.2 | 0.4 | 0.5 | 0.1 | 0.5 | 0.5 | 0.7 | 1.0 | 1.0 | 0.5 | 1.2 | 0.3 |
| XIV | Timber, furniture, etc. | 0.0 | 0.1 | 0.0 | 0.0 | 0.0 | 0.0 | 0.0 | 0.1 | 0.1 | 0.1 | 0.2 | 0.1 | 0.1 | 0.1 | 0.1 | 0.0 | 0.5 | 0.1 | 0.3 | 0.2 | 0.3 | 0.1 |
| XV | Paper, printing and publishing | 0.1 | 0.3 | 0.1 | 0.1 | 0.0 | 0.5 | 0.2 | 0.5 | 0.7 | 0.4 | 0.0 | 0.9 | 0.4 | 2.1 | 0.5 | 0.4 | 0.2 | 0.2 | 1.5 | 0.7 | 0.9 | 2.4 |
| XVI | Other manufacturing | 0.1 | 0.1 | 0.3 | 0.0 | 0.2 | 0.2 | 0.0 | 0.2 | 0.1 | 0.2 | 0.0 | 0.2 | 0.1 | 0.1 | 0.2 | 0.1 | 0.5 | 1.0 | 0.9 | 2.4 | 1.4 | 0.7 |
| *All manufacturing* | | 4.2 | 6.0 | 4.2 | 3.9 | 4.7 | 8.1 | 8.3 | 7.7 | 10.7 | 10.2 | 10.0 | 26.0 | 23.0 | 18.0 | 10.5 | 9.0 | 10.0 | 10.0 | 14.0 | 14.9 | 16.0 | 27.0 |

of the area of building completed under industrial development certificates. For each United Kingdom order, estimates were derived of the value of additions to *PM* by subtracting, from the total value of gross fixed capital formation, estimates of the replacement component derived by applying the *R*/*I* ratios listed in Table 6.3.

The resulting United Kingdom figures were then distributed among Welsh industries according to the ratios:

$$\frac{\text{area of industrial building completed in order } i \text{ in Wales}}{\text{area of industrial building completed in order i in the United Kingdom.}}$$

and the figures for each industry adjusted so that the aggregate equalled the estimated total additions for all industries, excluding metal manufacture in Wales.

This method of distributing investment on additions to *PM* is, conceptually and empirically, probably the weakest of all the estimating procedures invoked in generating the present estimates. The expectation is, of course, that the square footage of industrial building completed provides a less satisfactory indication of investment in *PM* than in *B*. It was not possible, however, to find a more suitable proxy and it is noteworthy that V. H. Woodward (1970) was also forced to rely upon statistics of the area of building completed for distributing expenditure on additions to *PM* by manufacturing industries among regions in 1961. The estimates of total gross investment (replacement plus additions) that were derived by the methods outlined are given in Table 6.5.

## III ESTIMATES OF GROSS AND NET CAPITAL STOCK

### (i) GROSS STOCK ACQUIRED SINCE 1949 ($K_s$)

The annual series of gross investment in *B* and *PM* in current prices for each industry between 1949 and 1970 were deflated by the aggregate UK price indices for *B* and *PM* (1958 = 100). For 1949–65 the index numbers were taken from C. H. Feinstein (1965) and for 1966–70 from the Blue Book. The values of $K_s$ (gross stock of capital acquired since the beginning of 1949) for each industry were then obtained by cumulating the annual figures of deflated real expenditure (Appendix, Table 6.A1).

### (ii) NET STOCK ACQUIRED SINCE 1949 ($\bar{K}_s$)

In order to estimate the net stock of capital it was necessary to derive values of capital consumption, which in turn required figures for the

TABLE 6.5 Estimated gross investment in plant and machinery, 1949–70 (£m. at current prices)

| SIC Order | | '49 | '50 | '51 | '52 | '53 | '54 | '55 | '56 | '57 | '58 | '59 | '60 | '61 | '62 | '63 | '64 | '65 | '66 | '67 | '68 | '69 | '70 |
|---|---|---|---|---|---|---|---|---|---|---|---|---|---|---|---|---|---|---|---|---|---|---|---|
| III | Food, drink and tobacco | 0.8 | 0.5 | 0.6 | 0.9 | 0.6 | 0.8 | 3.0 | 1.1 | 2.6 | 1.0 | 3.1 | 1.9 | 0.6 | 1.5 | 2.6 | 5.2 | 3.4 | 1.0 | 3.1 | 2.8 | 2.5 | 4.9 |
| IV | Chemicals and allied industries | 4.9 | 2.4 | 7.7 | 4.5 | 7.7 | 8.5 | 3.6 | 2.1 | 9.0 | 10.8 | 6.0 | 12.7 | 0.7 | 2.2 | 13.1 | 10.4 | 16.2 | 16.3 | 26.9 | 22.7 | 17.5 | 59.4 |
| V | Metal manufacture | 4.5 | 23.3 | 3.6 | 6.8 | 8.5 | 26.9 | 25.8 | 21.8 | 31.8 | 32.2 | 31.5 | 57.7 | 94.9 | 61.2 | 15.4 | 12.1 | 11.8 | 21.8 | 27.9 | 30.4 | 34.5 | 69.0 |
| VI | Engineering and electrical goods | 0.5 | 0.8 | 1.0 | 1.3 | 0.8 | 0.3 | 2.3 | 2.3 | 2.4 | 0.7 | 4.3 | 3.2 | 1.4 | 3.1 | 2.8 | 5.4 | 7.2 | 4.4 | 5.6 | 5.1 | 11.8 | 4.5 |
| VII | Shipbuilding and marine engineering | 0.1 | 0.3 | 0.4 | 0.3 | 0.2 | 0.4 | 0.3 | 0.3 | 0.5 | 0.0 | 0.9 | 0.3 | 0.2 | 0.3 | 0.1 | 0.4 | 0.2 | 0.1 | 0.0 | 0.1 | 0.0 | 0.0 |
| VIII | Vehicles | 0.2 | 0.6 | 0.3 | 1.5 | 0.9 | 0.0 | 1.4 | 1.2 | 1.7 | 1.0 | 2.1 | 1.2 | 0.5 | 1.1 | 3.1 | 5.6 | 0.7 | 3.8 | 3.5 | 2.0 | 5.0 | 10.6 |
| IX | Other metals | 0.6 | 0.6 | 0.9 | 0.7 | 0.5 | 0.6 | 1.1 | 0.9 | 1.1 | 1.2 | 1.7 | 1.5 | 0.6 | 1.6 | 1.6 | 4.6 | 3.3 | 2.1 | 2.6 | 4.1 | 5.0 | 6.1 |
| X | Textiles | 2.9 | 1.2 | 3.6 | 1.0 | 2.9 | 3.7 | 3.6 | 5.8 | 1.0 | 2.2 | 1.4 | 1.6 | 0.5 | 4.2 | 2.7 | 2.7 | 2.4 | 7.0 | 3.0 | 4.6 | 5.1 | 5.9 |
| XI | Leather, leather goods and fur | 0.0 | 0.0 | 0.1 | 0.2 | 0.1 | 0.1 | 0.1 | 0.2 | 0.1 | 0.0 | 0.1 | 0.1 | 0.0 | 0.1 | 0.1 | 0.1 | 0.1 | 0.1 | 0.1 | 0.1 | 0.2 | 0.8 |
| XII | Clothing and footwear | 0.1 | 0.4 | 0.1 | 0.4 | 0.3 | 0.1 | 0.7 | 0.6 | 1.0 | 0.1 | 0.8 | 0.9 | 0.4 | 0.8 | 0.1 | 1.4 | 2.0 | 0.3 | 0.3 | 0.5 | 0.4 | 1.0 |
| XIII | Bricks, pottery, glass, cement, etc. | 0.7 | 0.4 | 0.9 | 0.3 | 0.7 | 0.3 | 0.8 | 1.1 | 1.1 | 1.1 | 0.8 | 1.1 | 0.3 | 0.6 | 2.0 | 2.7 | 2.9 | 2.4 | 1.7 | 1.8 | 1.7 | 4.4 |
| XIV | Timber, furniture, etc. | 0.2 | 0.3 | 0.2 | 0.5 | 0.1 | 0.2 | 0.3 | 0.4 | 0.6 | 0.4 | 0.6 | 0.5 | 0.2 | 0.3 | 0.2 | 0.8 | 1.2 | 0.2 | 0.3 | 0.6 | 0.5 | 0.8 |
| XV | Paper, printing and publishing | 0.6 | 0.6 | 1.1 | 1.1 | 0.1 | 0.1 | 0.6 | 1.3 | 2.0 | 0.7 | 0.3 | 1.3 | 0.3 | 1.4 | 1.8 | 2.1 | 1.4 | 0.8 | 1.8 | 3.9 | 3.4 | 5.8 |
| XVI | Other manufacturing | 0.1 | 0.2 | 0.3 | 0.1 | 1.2 | 0.3 | 0.3 | 1.3 | 0.7 | 0.5 | 0.4 | 0.9 | 0.3 | 0.7 | 1.6 | 3.3 | 4.2 | 2.8 | 3.4 | 4.2 | 3.2 | 4.0 |
| *All manufacturing* | | 16.2 | 31.4 | 20.8 | 20.3 | 24.6 | 42.3 | 43.8 | 40.3 | 55.9 | 51.9 | 54.0 | 85.0 | 101.0 | 79.0 | 47.2 | 57.0 | 57.0 | 63.0 | 80.0 | 82.9 | 91.0 | 177.0 |

average length of life of *B* and *PM*. The life span of an asset depends upon numerous factors including the quality of the materials and components employed in its manufacture, intensity of its use, degree of obsolescence, possibility of destruction by fire and storms and the scrapping policy of individual firms. It follows that actual lengths of life, even of identical assets, are likely to vary at a moment in time as well as over a period of years. In empirical work, assets employed in manufacturing are usually divided into a small number of heterogeneous categories, such as buildings, plant and machinery and vehicles. 'Buildings' sometimes includes land and other fixed assets, including furniture, office machinery and containers of the cask and crate type, all of which are subject to widely different lengths of life. Similarly, the category termed plant and machinery, if it also includes vehicles, embraces cars, lorries, dumpers, excavators as well as plant and machinery generally, each of which might reasonably be expected to have an unequal life-span.

Unfortunately there is little direct information in the United Kingdom on the true lengths of life both of those assets that have been used in the past and of those that are currently extant. Following P. Redfern (1955), most of the work on the estimation of capital stock has relied heavily on the life-spans that are implicit in the treatment of depreciation for taxation purposes, in which the length of life of particular categories of assets is assumed to be unique and constant overtime. In the case of manufacturing, Redfern adopted lives of 50, 75 and 10 years for industrial buildings, commercial buildings and road vehicles respectively and classified plant and machinery into five categories with lives of 45, 30, 22, 17 and 14 years, corresponding to basic rates of depreciation on the reducing balance principle of 5, 7½, 10, 12½ and 15 per cent respectively. Opinion, as well as some empirical work since, seem to suggest that these figures underestimate the true lives. T. Barna (1957) without citing direct evidence though 'that a large amount of assets must be in existence' which have lasted longer than the time assumed by Redfern, 1955. C. H. Feinstein (1972) observed that 'it seems likely that the accounting assumptions frequently employed in estimating depreciation tend on the whole to be conservative, so that the phenomenon of fully depreciated assets still in use, particularly as reserve capacity, may be quite usual'. A similar conclusion was supported by E. T. Nevin (1963), who estimated average lives of assets in manufacturing in Ireland, Norway and the United Kingdom from figures of annual investment and a direct estimate of the stock of assets in existence at a particular moment in time. For buildings an average life of 93 years in Ireland compared with either 66 or 133 years for the United Kingdom (depending upon whether the capital stock figure employed was gross or net). The corresponding figures for plant and machinery were 37 years and 36 (or 72) years respectively.

In empirical studies, mainly because of the absence of direct information on the actual life of assets, the values of $l$ that are adopted do not diverge substantially from the values employed by accountants – in spite of the dissatisfaction concerning their reliability. The estimates of average lives which are employed in the official estimates of capital consumption and of the gross and net capital stock of the United Kingdom are those computed by G. Dean. The figures for buildings and vehicles are 80 years and 10 years respectively and for five groups of plant and machinery the estimated lives are 16, 19, 25, 34 and 50 years. Dean provides data on the distribution among industries of plant and machinery according to these five classes of asset life and the mean length of life for each industry varies between 31 and 40 years, except for timber and construction which has an average life of 26 years. C. H. Feinstein adopts a life of 60 years for $B$ and notes that the typical figure implied by accounting practices in the period 1920–38 for $PM$ in manufacturing is about 30 years. E. W. Henry (1971–72) agrees that 'for plant and machinery one might expect that 30 years or less is fairly typical, with technological change giving improved performance of new machines, and thus encouraging scrapping of machines which are operable, but increasingly obsolescent'. Finally, C. W. Jefferson (1968), 'in the absence of a detailed knowledge of composition of assets', assumed a value of 80 for $l$ in buildings and 30 in plant and machinery in Northern Ireland manufacturing.

There is also no information on the length of life of assets in Welsh manufacturing. For each industry a figure of 80 years was arbitrarily adopted for $B$ and one of 30 years for $PM$. Bearing in mind that $PM$ in the present study includes vehicles, a value of 30 years would be close to the average life of $PM$ and $V$ combined that would be obtained for most industries from using Dean's assumptions.

Estimates for the net stock of capital acquired since the end of 1948 (at 1958 prices) in Welsh manufacturing are given in Table 6.A2.

## GROSS AND NET STOCK AT A POINT IN TIME

When the number of years for which figures of real gross investment are available is less than the length of life of the assets (that is, $m < l$), the following considerations are involved in estimating the stock existence at a given point in time[3].

First, the gross stock in existence at the end of $t - m$ ($K_{t-m}$) decreases annually between $t - m + 1$ and $t$ by the amount of assets scrapped during each year.

Secondly, the net stock in existence at end of $t - m$ ($\bar{K}_{t-m}$) reduces as time passes until at $t$ it equals $f_n \bar{K}^*_{t-m+1}$, where $\bar{K}^*_{t-m+1}$ is the amount of $\bar{K}_{t-m}$ which exists at the end of $t - m + 1$ and $f_n$ represents the fraction of $\bar{K}^*_{t-m+1}$ remaining in year $t$.

In follows that

$$\bar{K}_t = f_n \bar{K}^*_{t-m+1} + \bar{K}_s \tag{7}$$

where $\bar{K}_s$ is the net stock of capital acquired since the beginning of $t - m + 1$, which exists at the end of year $t$. As was demonstrated in the previous section, $\bar{K}_s$ in equation (7) can be computed, but estimates must somehow be obtained for $f_n$ and $\bar{K}^*_{t-m+1}$.

C. W. Jefferson estimated $\bar{K}^*_{t-m+1}$ for manufacturing industries in Northern Ireland by assuming that the changes in the capital output ratios between $t - m + 1$ and $t$ were the same as the changes in the capital-output ratios of the corresponding industries in the United Kingdom and employing a value for $f_n$ which can reasonably be assumed to lie within certain limits (see below). Another, and similar, approach would be to assume equal changes in the capital-labour ratios. In both cases, the degree of validity of the assumption that capital-labour and/or capital-output ratios of industry groups in a region change to the same extent as those in the corresponding UK industries depends upon a number of considerations.

To begin with, the ratios may differ from one area to another and from the overall national figure because of varying rates of technological progress, different composition of trades within each manufacturing sector, variations in the degree of utilisation of the existing stock and unequal rates of expansion of capacity reflecting perhaps differences in the ratio of the price of labour to the price of capital. In particular, government policy in the development regions by providing grants to encourage investment reduces in effect the cost of capital relative to that of labour and these regions might be expected to become more capital-intensive relative to the nation. Furthermore, it is possible, because of the time lags involved in the adjustment of investment, labour and output to one another, that for some industries in certain regions the ratio of capital stock to labour or output (or both) either at the beginning or at the end of the period of study may diverge from the desired (or optimal) figure. The likelihood is, of course, that the extent of the discrepancy is not the same for the economy as a whole as it is for a particular regional economy. However, since individual SIC orders contain a broad spectrum of trades each of which in the majority of regions contains a number of separate firms the capital labour/output ratios of firms and trades might well change in opposite directions. The net result therefore, might be that the change in the ratio for each order in the various regions may not in fact differ much.

The last observation is obviously speculative, but in order to generate estimates of capital stock for Welsh manufacturing the assumption was nevertheless made that changes in the capital-labour and capital-output ratios in the various industries in Wales between the end of 1948 and the end of 1970 were equal to those for the corresponding industries in the United Kingdom during the same period. By adopting both capital-labour and capital-output ratios two series of gross and net capital stock were derived for each industry. The general method of approach was as follows.

Let $C$ = ratio of the capital-labour/output ratio in $t$ to $t - m + 1$ calculated for the United Kingdom (with year $t - m + 1$ taken as unity). Then

$$C = \frac{\overline{K}_t}{H_t} \bigg| \frac{\overline{K}_{t-m+1}}{H_{t-m+1}}$$

$$= \frac{f_n \overline{K}^*_{t-m+1} + \overline{K}_s}{H_t} \Bigg| \frac{\overline{K}^*_{t-m+1} + \overline{I}'_{t-m+1}}{H_{t-m+1}} \qquad (8)$$

where $\overline{I}'_{t-m+1}$ equals the net investment undertaken in $t - m + 1$ and H equals labour (or net output).

In this equation, $C, \overline{K}_s, \overline{I}'_{t-m+1}, H_{t-m+1}$ and $H_t$ are known. There are two unknowns: $f_n$ and $\overline{K}^*_{t-m+1}$.

## JEFFERSON'S METHOD OF ESTIMATING $f_n$

In order to calculate $f_n$, C. W. Jefferson derives a relationship between gross and net capital stock which is based on the mechanics of the perpetual inventory method. Given an asset with a life of $l$ years, the value of $\overline{K}_t$ depends upon the distribution of $I_j$ over the previous $l$ years. $\overline{K}_t$ is relatively high when the greater proportion of the total gross investment over the $l$ year period occurs in the latter years and relatively low when it occurs in the earlier years. Jefferson experimented with various series of $I_j$ assuming $l$ values of 80 and 30 and the linear method of depreciation. His results indicate for instance that when the proportion of the total gross investment undertaken over an 80-year period is the same in the first half as it is in the second half, the ratio $\bar{K}_t/\bar{K}_t$ equals 0.49, but when the proportion in the latter period is ten times that in the earlier one this ratio rises to 0.70. Similar limits in the $\bar{K}_t/K_t$ ratio were also obtained for assets with lives of 30 years.

Although the distribution of $I_j$ in *B* over an 80-year period varies from industry to industry it does not appear, on the basis of the evidence available (chiefly based on censuses of production stretching back to 1907), that the proportion in the 40-year period immediately prior to 1949 to that in the 40 years before 1909 was outside the limits 1:1 and 10:1 for any industry. This implies that the limits for $\bar{K}_t/K_t$ are roughly between 0.5 and 0.7. For his calculations, Jefferson adopted a ratio of 0.6, but in the majority of cases the choice of any ratio between 0.5 and 0.7 does not greatly affect the results.

The gross stock of capital in existence at the end of $t-m$, $(K_{t-m})$, reduces in amount between $t-m+1$ and $t$ because of the discarding of assets acquired $l$ years previously. Since $K_{t-m}$ is not known there is, of course, no information on the magnitude of the annual reduction. However, if $l$ is long and the value of $I_j$ had been growing more or less annually the ratio of $I_j$, undertaken $l$ years previously, to current $I_j$, will be small. The proportionate reduction in $K_{t-m}$ between $t-m+1$ and $t$ will, therefore, also be small. Given that all the broad industry groups covered by the 1958 SIC (with the exception of shipbuilding and marine engineering) have been expanding in Wales since long before the beginning of the present century, the type of situation that has been outlined is probably not untypical of buildings in general. By contrast, it is unlikely to be sufficiently representative of investment in *PM* where, because $l$ is much less, the proportionate reduction in $K_{t-m}$ between $t-m+1$ and $t$ is expected to be relatively greater.

It follows that it might not be too unreasonable to assume that the annual depreciation between $t-m+1$ and $t$ on the stock of buildings, which was in existence at the end of $t-m$ $(K_{t-m})$ is constant and equal to that in $t-m+1$, in which case

$$f_n = \left\{1 - \frac{10}{6\ell}\right\} \tag{9}$$

in $t-m+2$ and

$$f_n = \left\{1 - \frac{[t-(t-m+1)]\,10}{6\ell}\right\} \tag{10}$$

in period $t$.

However, a similar assumption for $f_n$ in the case of PM would probably over estimate the annual rate of depreciation, in which case it would be desirable to consider some alternative possibilities for allowing for depreciation. One approach, for example, would be to assume that $K_{t-m}$ decreases annually in the form of a geometric progression (that is, by a reducing balance system), another would be to assume that depreciation equals $(10/6\ell)\bar{K}^*_{t-m+1}$ for a certain number of years, but is then halved (that is, falls to $(10/12\ell)\bar{K}^*_{t-m+1}$, say for the remainder of the period. It is the latter assumption that is adopted in the present study.

## ESTIMATES OF THE AMOUNT REMAINING BETWEEN 1949 AND 1970 OF THE GROSS AND NET CAPITAL STOCK IN EXISTENCE IN WELSH MANUFACTURING AT THE END OF 1948

The net stock of capital existing at the end of 1948 ($\bar{K}_{t-m}$ – $\bar{K}_{1970-22} = \bar{K}_{1948}$) which was in existence at the end of 1949 ($\bar{K}^*_{t-m+1} = \bar{K}^*_{1949}$) was computed using equation (8). However, before this equation could be adopted, it was necessary to compute net capital-labour and net capital-output ratios for the various United Kingdom manufacturing groups. It was possible to obtain figures for the net capital stock of both *B* and *PM* for eight United Kingdom industry groups by subtracting estimates of the accrued capital consumption of each category of asset from the gross stock figures provided by Dean (1949–62) and in the Blue Book (1963–70). The accrued values of capital consumption were computed by the extrapolating backwards over the assumed average length of life of assets the annual figures of capital consumption published by Dean and those derived from the figures of gross stock. The 'labour' component of the United Kingdom capital-labour ratio relates to the number of insured employees and the 'output' component of the capital-output ratio, to the index of industrial production. The estimates of the capital-labour and capital-output ratios that were derived from these sources are listed in Table 6.A3.

Equation (8) also requires data on the labour input and output of Welsh manufacturing. The data adopted for labour relate to the number of insured employees and the figures for output were derived from a variety of sources including Nevin's *Social Accounts*, the Welsh index of industrial production (available from 1963 onwards) and a number of miscellaneous indicators.

The two sets of estimates of $\bar{K}^*_{1949}$ for the various Welsh manufacturing industry groups that are generated by letting *C* in equation (8) equal the change, firstly, in the UK capital-labour ratio (denoted by I) and, secondly, in the UK capital-net output ratio (denoted by II) appear in Table 6.A4 (in the columns under 1949). In each case, in order to reduce some of the bias inherent in the relationship between two individual years, that is, 1949 and 1970, *C* relates to the averages of the two four-year periods 1949–52 and 1967–70.

## ASSUMED VALUES OF $f_n$

In order to estimate the values between 1949 and 1970 of the net stock of *B* and *PM* that were in existence at the end of 1948, it was necessary to assume certain values for $f_n$. In the case of *B* it was assumed that the annual capital consumption on the 'end of 1948' stock of capital remaining between 1949 and 1970 was constant and equal to the depreciation in 1949, that is, equal to $(1/80)\,K^*_{49}$ or $(10/(6 \times 80))\,\bar{K}^*_{49}$ assuming a ratio of net to gross stock of 0.6. It follows that $f_n$ in 1950 equals (47/48) (that is, $1 - (10/(6 \times 80))$ and decreases each year by (1/48) to give a figure of 27/48 for 1970. For *PM* it was assumed that depreciation is at the rate of $(10/(6 \times 30))\,\bar{K}^*_{49}$ for the first 11 years and at the rate of $(10/(12 \times 30))\,\bar{K}^*_{49}$ for the remaining 11 years. This implies that the value of $f_n$ decreases from 17/18 in 1950, by equal annual decrements of 1/18 to 8/18 in 1959 and from 15/36 in 1960 to 5/36 in 1970. The estimates for a selected number of years between 1949 and 1970, for the various manufacturing industries in Wales, of the values at 1958 prices of the net stock of B and PM that were in existence at the end of 1948 that are derived on the basis of these assumed values of $f_n$ are provided in Table 6.A4.

## CAPITALISED VALUE OF NET OUTPUT LESS WAGES AND SALARIES

Another method of obtaining a measure of capital stock at a given point in time is to capitalise the income that the stock is receiving at this date. Given the statistics available, the income of capital for the purpose of the present study may be defined as the value of net output less wages and salaries and therefore includes, in addition to profits, rent, rates and taxes, advertising and other selling expenses as well as depreciation. The capitalisation factor for each industry group is the United Kingdom ratio of net output less wages and salaries to capital stock. Capital income, which is derived from the censuses of production, represents the average figures for

1948, 1951 and 1954, revalued at 1958 prices and the capital stock data are the mean values for 1949, 1951 and 1954 of G. Dean's perpetual inventory estimates at 1958 replacement cost. It is assumed that the average values of both income and stock relate to the position at the end of 1951 and the measure of stock is a proxy for gross capital stock ($K_{51}$)[4]. The distribution of the total stock for each industry group in Wales in 1951 between *B* and *PM* was assumed to be in the same proportion as that for the corresponding industry group in the United Kingdom (Table 6.A5).

The limitations of the capitalised value of net output less wages and salaries as a measure of capital stock are apparent. The concept is obviously not the same as the physical measure that is implied in the notion of the production function and the capitalisation factor is identical with marginal physical product of capital only under equilibrium conditions in a perfectly competitive world. The value of the stock for a particular industry at a given time depends upon the level of gross profits, which in turn depends upon the efficiency of the industry as well as the overall state of the economy. Applying the United Kingdom capitalisation factor to Welsh manufacturing is valid only to the extent that the ratio of income to the stock of capital in Wales is the same as that throughout the country. Whether this in fact is the case, however, is not known and indeed, one of the reasons for requiring estimates of regional capital stock is to throw light on this very question.

Bearing in mind these limitations, the figures of gross stock in the post-1951 period ($t = 1952, \ldots, 1970$) may be computed from the equation:

$$K_t = f_g K_{51} + K_s' \tag{11}$$

where $K_s'$ = gross capital stock acquired since the end of 1951. Since there is no information on the amount of assets scrapped in the years following 1951, $f_g$ is unknown. In the case of *B*, with an assumed length of life of 80 years, it was postulated that the gross stock at the end of the 1951 ($K_{51}$) remains intact until 1970, in which case $f_g$ equals 1.0 in every year between 1952 and 1970. This implies that the estimated values of *B* are inflated somewhat – especially towards the end of the period of study. For *PM* it was arbitrarily assumed that $K_{51}$ remains constant until the end of 1960, but is then halved and remains at this lower level until the end of 1970. The effect of this assumption is to provide estimates of *PM* that are too high in the years immediately prior to 1960 and ones that are too low in the immediate post 1960 years.

Estimates of the net stock of capital may be generated by assuming a particular ratio of net to gross stock at the end of 1951. The ratio that was adopted was again 0.6, which makes $f_n$ for $B$ equal to 47/48 in 1952 and 29/48 in 1970. In the case of *PM*, $f_n$ decreases from 17/18 in 1952 by equal annual increments of 1/18 to 9/18 in 1960 and from 17/36 in 1961, by annual increments of 1/36 to 8/36 in 1970.

## IV RESULTS

The estimates of gross and net capital stock by industry groups for each year between 1949 and 1970 are obtained by adding the gross and net stock acquired since 1949 to the amount in existence at the end of 1948 which still remains between 1949 and 1970[5]. The estimates for 1951, 1956, 1964 and 1970 appear in Tables 6.6 and 6.7, where columns I and II refer to the figures obtained by employing the United Kingdom capital-labour and capital-output ratios respectively and column III to those derived from employing the capitalised value of net output less wages and salaries as a proxy for the gross stock in existence in 1951.

A comparison of the results for methods I and II shows that the figures generated by the former are higher than those yielded by the latter for every industry with the exception of other metals, for which they more or less coincide. The discrepancies are particularly marked in the early years, but converge with the passage of time and by 1970 the ratio: I/II equals 1.1 for the majority of industries. The reason for the wide gap in the figures for 1949 is that the value of $\bar{K}^*_{49}$ (the value at the end of 1949 of net stock in existence at the end of 1948) for each industry in estimating equation (8) differs markedly according to whether it is estimated by method I or method II. In the years following 1949 the gap diminishes since, for both sets of estimates, the value of the net stock in existence at the end of 1948 falls with each succeeding year and the proportion of capital acquired since 1949 increases. The estimates of $\bar{K}^*_{49}$ in turn are closely associated with the differences in the values of the capital-labour and capital-output ratios that are employed in their calculation. As Table 6.A3 reveals, the change in the net capital-labour ratio between 1949–52 and 1967–70 for each of the eight industry groups was greater than the corresponding change in the net capital-net output ratio. The ratio of the net stock of $B$ to labour increased during the period in each industry but, by contrast, the ratio of the net stock of $B$ to net output fell in all industry groups with the exception of food, drink and tobacco and bricks, pottery, glass and cement. In the case of *PM* the change in the ratio of

TABLE 6.6 Estimates of the gross stock of capital in Welsh manufacturing (£m. at 1958 prices)[1]

| Industry | 1951 | | | 1956 | | | 1964 | | | 1970 | | |
|---|---|---|---|---|---|---|---|---|---|---|---|---|
| | *I*[2] | *II* | *III* | *I* | *II* | *III* | *I* | *II* | *III* | *I* | *II* | *III* |
| Food, drink and tobacco | 52.3 | 37.0 | 19.7 | 62.7 | 47.4 | 30.1 | 77.2 | 65.7 | 53.3 | 96.1 | 84.6 | 72.2 |
| Chemicals and allied | 145.9 | 86.3 | 33.1 | 181.4 | 121.8 | 68.6 | 217.3 | 179.7 | 139.0 | 348.9 | 311.3 | 270.6 |
| Metal manufacture | 617.8 | 398.8 | 217.1 | 732.9 | 513.9 | 332.2 | 885.6 | 745.9 | 635.4 | 1048.8 | 909.1 | 798.6 |
| Engineering and electrical goods | 57.9 | 46.4 | 66.0 | 70.9 | 69.4 | 79.0 | 86.4 | 78.9 | 92.0 | 132.7 | 125.2 | 138.3 |
| Shipbuilding and marine engineering | – | – | 10.7 | – | – | 12.8 | – | – | 12.8 | – | – | 13.6 |
| Vehicles | 96.1 | 70.2 | 16.7 | 104.2 | 78.3 | 24.8 | 92.1 | 75.0 | 41.5 | 116.1 | 99.0 | 65.5 |
| Other metals | 67.3 | 57.6 | 38.7 | 73.1 | 73.4 | 44.5 | 68.2 | 68.5 | 50.4 | 91.2 | 91.5 | 73.4 |
| Textiles | 97.6 | 45.5 | – | 122.1 | 70.0 | – | 115.7 | 81.2 | – | 140.1 | 105.6 | – |
| Leather, leather goods and fur | 6.1 | 2.6 | 0.6 | 7.0 | 3.5 | 1.4 | 5.8 | 3.3 | 2.1 | 7.5 | 5.0 | 3.8 |
| Clothing and footwear | 26.4 | 18.6 | 3.8 | 29.0 | 21.2 | 6.4 | 28.5 | 23.2 | 13.4 | 33.7 | 28.4 | 18.6 |
| Bricks, pottery, glass, cement, etc. | 26.9 | 16.7 | 9.6 | 31.6 | 21.4 | 14.3 | 36.7 | 29.4 | 23.8 | 52.2 | 44.9 | 39.3 |
| Timber, furniture, etc. | 7.1 | 3.7 | 0.9 | 8.8 | 5.4 | 2.6 | 11.9 | 9.3 | 6.7 | 16.2 | 13.6 | 11.0 |
| Paper, printing and publishing | 35.3 | 15.9 | 8.5 | 40.3 | 20.9 | 13.5 | 44.6 | 31.7 | 25.7 | 62.4 | 49.5 | 43.5 |
| Other manufacturing | 25.7 | 13.6 | 3.8 | 30.0 | 17.9 | 8.1 | 29.5 | 22.0 | 16.3 | 52.2 | 44.7 | 39.0 |

[1] Buildings plus plant and machinery.
[2] Numbers I, II and III refer to different methods of estimation.

TABLE 6.7 Estimates of the net stock of capital in Welsh manufacturing (*£m. at 1958 prices*)

| | *1951* | | | *1956* | | | *1964* | | | *1970* | | |
|---|---|---|---|---|---|---|---|---|---|---|---|---|
| *Industry* | *I* | *II* | *III* | *I* | *II* | *III* | *I* | *II* | *III* | *I* | *II* | *III* |
| Food, drink and tobacco | 30.2 | 21.8 | 11.9 | 33.8 | 27.0 | 19.0 | 48.4 | 43.8 | 37.8 | 54.7 | 51.5 | 46.7 |
| Chemicals and allied | 89.9 | 57.5 | 19.9 | 100.9 | 76.8 | 43.5 | 137.1 | 122.5 | 93.6 | 219.9 | 210.9 | 184.5 |
| Metal manufacture | 355.6 | 236.3 | 130.2 | 373.1 | 284.0 | 200.9 | 554.3 | 500.4 | 440.1 | 550.4 | 516.8 | 469.9 |
| Engineering and electrical goods | 33.4 | 27.1 | 39.6 | 37.6 | 32.9 | 42.6 | 55.9 | 53.0 | 58.4 | 84.8 | 83.1 | 86.3 |
| Shipbuilding and marine engineering | – | – | 6.4 | – | – | 6.6 | – | – | 7.0 | – | – | 5.6 |
| Vehicles | 53.1 | 38.9 | 10.0 | 47.2 | 36.5 | 14.9 | 49.5 | 42.9 | 29.7 | 57.8 | 53.5 | 45.1 |
| Other metals | 38.2 | 38.4 | 23.2 | 34.1 | 34.3 | 23.0 | 38.2 | 38.3 | 30.9 | 48.6 | 48.6 | 43.7 |
| Textiles | 58.9 | 30.4 | – | 68.3 | 46.8 | – | 66.4 | 52.9 | – | 70.1 | 61.5 | – |
| Leather, leather goods and fur | 3.3 | 1.5 | 0.4 | 3.5 | 2.0 | 1.2 | 3.1 | 2.1 | 1.6 | 3.7 | 3.1 | 2.7 |
| Clothing and footwear | 15.0 | 10.7 | 2.3 | 13.8 | 10.5 | 4.0 | 15.7 | 13.7 | 9.3 | 16.3 | 14.9 | 11.8 |
| Bricks, pottery, glass, cement, etc. | 16.3 | 10.7 | 5.8 | 17.2 | 12.9 | 8.5 | 22.5 | 19.6 | 15.7 | 30.8 | 28.8 | 25.3 |
| Timber, furniture, etc. | 4.4 | 2.6 | 0.5 | 5.1 | 3.5 | 1.6 | 7.2 | 6.3 | 4.5 | 9.4 | 8.7 | 7.1 |
| Paper, printing and publishing | 20.8 | 10.3 | 5.1 | 20.7 | 12.7 | 8.0 | 27.0 | 22.0 | 17.8 | 36.7 | 33.5 | 29.6 |
| Other manufacturing | 14.6 | 8.0 | 2.3 | 14.9 | 10.1 | 5.7 | 17.9 | 15.1 | 12.1 | 33.3 | 31.6 | 29.5 |

capital to labour and capital to net output was positive in five and four of the industries respectively. The absolute value of the discrepancy between the two ratios in *B* ranged from 0.34 for iron and steel to 0.95 for chemicals and allied industries. For *PM* the difference ranged from 0.27 for metal using and other metal manufacture to 1.11 for chemicals and allied industries.

The greater the magnitude of $\bar{K}^*_{49}$, given the assumed values for $f_n$ in equation (8), the larger is the annual reduction in the post 1948 years in the value of the net stock existing at the end of 1948. In the case of *PM*, in particular, this reduction in the years following 1948 is greater for some industries than the addition to the stock since the beginning of 1949. As a result, the figures for the total net stock diminish or remain more or less constant for a number of years from 1949 onwards. This phenomenon is more characteristic of method I with its higher estimates of $\bar{K}^*_{49}$ and all industries, with the exception of chemicals and allied trades and timber and furniture, are subject to it. With method II, the non-rising trend in the estimates, where it occurs, disappears from about 1954–55 onwards for all industries except vehicles and other metals, where it continues until about 1960.

During most of the 1950s and, for some industries throughout the entire period, the estimates that employ the capitalised value of net output less wages and salaries as a proxy for the gross stock in 1951 (method III) are below those generated by methods I and II for all industries with the exception of engineering and electrical goods. From about 1955 onwards, both the absolute values and the trends in the figures of net stock derived from methods II and III are close together for nine of the thirteen industries. The exceptions are engineering and electrical goods, vehicles, other metals and clothing and footwear, all of which exhibit large absolute differences, particularly in the earlier years and two of which – vehicles and other metals – reveal different trends up to about 1960.

Given the assumption that the *PM* in existence in 1949 (or 1951 in the case of method III) remains fully intact during the first half of the 1949–70 (1951–70) period, but is then halved for the remainder of the time, the estimates of the total gross stock are too high towards the end of the first half and too low at the beginning of the second half. As a result, each of the three methods of estimation yields a time series for every industry with a trough in the middle, which is not likely to be there in practice – judging at least from the gross capital stock series which are published for the corresponding United Kingdom manufacturing groups, all of which exhibit a continually rising trend. In applied work involving the use of the estimates of gross stock some allowance may be made for this limitation by interpolating across the middle years of the period.

Each series of estimates derived from methods I and II is subject to at least three other limitations. First, since figures of capital stock are published for only eight United Kingdom manufacturing groups the capital-labour (output) ratios employed in deriving estimates for individual Welsh industries do not in all cases relate specifically to those industries. Thus the estimates for engineering and electrical goods, vehicles and other metals are all based on the United Kingdom capital-labour (output) ratio for the composite category: metal-using industries and metal manufacture other than iron and steel, which contains shipbuilding and marine engineering and metal manufacture (other than iron and steel) in addition to engineering and electrical goods, vehicles and other metals. Similarly, the change in the United Kingdom ratio for leather, clothing and other manufacturing combined was employed in obtaining separate estimates for the four Welsh industries: textiles, leather, leather goods and fur, clothing and footwear and other manufacturing and the change in the ratio for iron and steel was used to yield estimates of the capital stock of metal manufacture in Wales. Unfortunately, there is no way of discovering to what extent the changes in the capital-labour (output) ratios for individual industries in the United Kingdom are different from those of the composite group of which they are members. However, a glance at the ratios for the eight manufacturing groups listed in Table 6.A3 reveals that there is a considerable range in their values and it follows therefore that a significant amount of variation in the ratios for individual industries within broad groups also cannot be ruled out.

Secondly, the assumption that the changes in the Welsh capital-labour (output) ratios over the period 1949–70 are identical with those in the corresponding United Kingdom industries may be invalid. Again, it was not possible to ascertain quantitatively the extent of any differences that might have existed. An examination of employment figures, however, did not suggest that significant errors had resulted from variations in the rate of capital utilisation between Welsh and United Kingdom industries. In particular, there were no industries in Wales in which the trend in employment between 1967 and 1970 compared to that in the preceding years was markedly out of line with the trend in the corresponding industries in the United Kingdom.

Some indication of the effect on the estimates of errors in the assumed values of the capital-labour (output) ratios may be gleaned from comparing the results of method I with those of method II.

As has already been noted the effect of different values in the ratios is greatest during the early years of the period of study and even the largest discrepancies that occur do not cause the capital stock figures to diverge by more than about 10 per cent around 1970. It is hardly necessary to add that if the two possible sources of error in the assumed changes in the capital-labour (output) ratios for individual industries were numerically small the estimates, even in the early years, would not be affected unduly.

Thirdly, the estimates that are derived from all three methods incorporate the assumption that the ratio of the net stock of capital to gross stock in 1949 ($\bar{K}^*_{49}/K_{49}$) or 1951 for method III equals 0.6. In order to obtain some indication of how critical this assumption is for the magnitude of the results the figures for method II were re-calculated with ($\bar{K}_{49}/K_{49}$) equal to first, 0.5 and secondly to 0.7 (Table 6.A6). This range, according to C. W. Jefferson, represents more or less the extreme limits for the ratio in the United Kingdom.

In general, the effect of a change of one tenth in either direction in ($\bar{K}_{49}/K_{49}$) has a greater impact on the estimates for *PM* than on those for *B*. The reason for this may be attributed chiefly to the different length of life of the two categories of asset: owing to its shorter life-span, the proportion of the amount of *PM* in existence at the end of 1948 which still remains in 1970 is much less than the corresponding proportion for *B*. This in turn implies that a given change in the ($\bar{K}_{49}/K_{49}$) ratio effects the value of $f_n$ for *PM* much more than it does for *B* and hence causes greater variations in the estimates of *PM*. When the ratio is assumed to equal 0.5 the figures for total net stock are affected to a greater extent in 1955 than in 1970 (except for leather, leather goods and fur), although it is only in three industries in 1955: vehicles, other metals and clothing and footwear and two in 1970: vehicles and other metals, that the estimates fall below 90 per cent of those that are derived on the basis of value of 0.6 for ($\bar{K}_{49}/K_{49}$). When the ratio equals 0.7 the estimates for both 1955 and 1970 are between 101 and 108 per cent of those when it is 0.6, except for vehicles, other metals and clothing and footwear, where the range is between 110 and 115 per cent.

## CAPITAL INTENSITY

Given the overwhelming importance of the estimates of $\bar{K}^*_{49}$ in the value of the stock figures in 1949 and in the years immediately following and given that they are sensitive to the value of the capital – labour or capital – output ratios employed in their computation, little faith may be placed in the estimates from methods I and II for the early years of the period of study. Consequently, in order to obtain an indication of the magnitude of the capital intensity – defined as gross capital stock per

TABLE 6.8 Gross capital stock per employee at 1958 prices

| | Wales | | | | | |
|---|---|---|---|---|---|---|
| | | | | | *% increase* | |
| | *1964* | | *1970* | | *1964–70* | |
| *Industry (in £000s)* | *II* | *III* | *II* | *III* | *II* | *III* |
| Food, drink and tobacco | 3.0 | 2.4 | 3.9 | 3.4 | 30 | 42 |
| Chemicals and allied | 7.6 | 5.9 | 11.5 | 10.0 | 51 | 69 |
| Metal manufacture | 7.8 | 6.6 | 9.9 | 8.7 | 27 | 32 |
| Engineering and electrical goods | 1.5 | 1.7 | 1.8 | 2.0 | 20 | 18 |
| Shipbuilding and marine engineering | – | 2.9 | – | 5.0 | – | 72 |
| Vehicles | 4.1 | 2.2 | 4.3 | 2.8 | 5 | 27 |
| Other metals | 3.1 | 2.3 | 3.6 | 2.9 | 16 | 26 |
| Textiles | 4.5 | – | 5.4 | – | 20 | – |
| Leather, leather goods and fur | 1.7 | 1.1 | 3.3 | 2.5 | 94 | 127 |
| Clothing and footwear | 1.5 | 0.9 | 1.7 | 1.1 | 13 | 22 |
| Bricks, pottery, glass, cement, etc. | 2.8 | 2.2 | 4.1 | 3.6 | 46 | 64 |
| Timber, furniture, etc. | 1.5 | 1.1 | 1.4 | 1.2 | –7 | 9 |
| Paper, printing and publishing | 2.6 | 2.1 | 3.4 | 3.0 | 31 | 43 |
| Other manufacturing | 1.5 | 1.1 | 2.2 | 1.9 | 47 | 73 |

| | United Kingdom | | |
|---|---|---|---|
| *Industry* | *1964* | *1970* | *% increase 1964–70* |
| Food, drink and tobacco | 2.8 | 3.7 | 32 |
| Chemicals and allied | 6.8 | 8.9 | 31 |
| Iron and steel | 5.3 | 6.2 | 17 |
| Metal using industries | 2.1 | 2.5 | 19 |
| Leather, clothing and other manufacturing | 1.1 | 2.3[1] | |
| Bricks, pottery, glass, cement | 2.1 | 3.1 | 48 |
| Timber, furniture, etc. | 1.0 | 1.2 | 20 |
| Paper, printing and publishing | 2.4 | 2.9 | 21 |

[1] Including textiles.

employee – of Welsh manufacturing industries, the figures were computed for only two years (1964 and 1970) in the second half of the period (Table 6.8). The overall picture that emerges, using the estimates from methods II and III[6] is that the most capital-intensive sectors of Welsh industry are chemicals, metal manufacture and textiles and that, where direct comparisons are possible, Welsh industries with the exception of food, drink and tobacco, were more capital-intensive in 1970 than their counterparts in the United Kingdom as a whole. The figures also suggest that the rate of increase in capital intensity between 1964 and 1970 was higher in Wales in all industries with the exception of timber and furniture and perhaps also food, drink and tobacco.

## NOTES

1 Estimates of gross investment for all orders for each year between 1949 and 1970 are recorded in Tables 6.4 and 6.5 in the text.

2 Replacement investment constitutes expenditure on replacing assets of a particular vintage that have reached the end of their working lives. Capital consumption is the amount of assets consumed during the process of production.

3 See also pp. 161–2. Equation (7) on this page is identical with equation (4) on p. 161.

4 Since Dean's estimates of capital stock are published for only eight United Kingdom industry groups, the capitalisation factor for each of the four Welsh SIC groups: engineering and electrical goods, shipbuilding and marine engineering, vehicles and other metal goods was assumed to be the same as that derived for Dean's composite category: metal-using industries and metal manufacture other than iron and steel. Similarly, the capitalisation factor for leather, clothing and other manufacturing combined was adopted for the three separate industries: leather, leather goods and fur, clothing and footwear and other manufacturing. The capitalisation factor for iron and steel was employed to capitalise the value of net output less wages and salaries for metal manufacture.

5 The gross stock of 'pre-1949' buildings which exists at the end of 1949 equals $\overline{K}^*_{49} \cdot (10/6)$. It is assumed that the stock at the end of 1949 remains intact until 1970. For plant and machinery the 'pre-1949' stock in 1949 is assumed to remain intact until the end of 1959, when it is reduced by one-half.

6 The figures of capital intensity using the results of method I would be higher than those of methods II and III for all industries with the exception of engineering and electrical goods and other metals. On the other hand, the rates of increase in capital intensity implied by estimates I would in general be lower than those resulting from the other two methods.

TABLE 6.A1 Gross stock of capital acquired since end of 1948 (*£m. at 1958 prices*)

| *Industry* / *End of year* | *1949* | | | *1959* | | | *1964* | | | *1970* | | |
|---|---|---|---|---|---|---|---|---|---|---|---|---|
| | *B* | *PM* | *T* | *B* | *PM* | *T* | *B* | *PM* | *T* | *B* | *PM* | *T* |
| Food, drink and tobacco | 0.1 | 1.2 | 1.3 | 6.6 | 16.9 | 23.5 | 13.7 | 27.9 | 41.6 | 18.7 | 41.8 | 60.5 |
| Chemicals and allied | 2.0 | 7.4 | 9.4 | 14.1 | 78.4 | 92.5 | 28.5 | 115.1 | 143.6 | 37.7 | 237.5 | 275.2 |
| Metal manufacture | 1.6 | 6.8 | 8.4 | 29.8 | 244.6 | 274.4 | 60.7 | 474.6 | 535.3 | 74.2 | 624.3 | 698.5 |
| Engineering and electrical goods | 0.1 | 0.8 | 0.9 | 8.5 | 19.6 | 28.1 | 17.3 | 34.5 | 51.8 | 33.0 | 65.1 | 98.1 |
| Shipbuilding and marine engineering | 0.0 | 0.2 | 0.2 | 1.1 | 4.3 | 5.4 | 1.3 | 5.6 | 6.9 | 1.7 | 6.0 | 7.7 |
| Vehicles | 0.0 | 0.3 | 0.3 | 4.8 | 12.3 | 17.1 | 9.1 | 22.9 | 32.0 | 13.6 | 42.4 | 56.0 |
| Other metals | 0.3 | 0.9 | 1.2 | 3.3 | 11.4 | 14.7 | 7.5 | 20.6 | 28.1 | 12.6 | 38.5 | 51.1 |
| Textiles | 1.1 | 4.4 | 5.5 | 9.5 | 35.0 | 44.5 | 15.1 | 45.9 | 61.0 | 17.5 | 67.9 | 85.4 |
| Leather, leather goods and fur | 0.0 | 0.0 | 0.0 | 0.2 | 1.1 | 1.3 | 0.2 | 1.5 | 1.7 | 0.7 | 2.7 | 3.4 |
| Clothing and footwear | 0.0 | 0.2 | 0.2 | 0.8 | 6.1 | 6.9 | 1.9 | 9.6 | 11.5 | 3.4 | 13.3 | 16.7 |
| Bricks, pottery, glass, cement, etc. | 0.4 | 1.1 | 1.5 | 2.6 | 9.6 | 12.2 | 4.6 | 15.9 | 20.5 | 8.4 | 27.6 | 36.0 |
| Timber, furniture, etc. | 0.0 | 0.3 | 0.3 | 0.6 | 4.2 | 4.8 | 1.0 | 6.1 | 7.1 | 2.3 | 9.1 | 11.4 |
| Paper, printing and publishing | 0.1 | 0.9 | 1.0 | 3.1 | 10.0 | 13.1 | 7.3 | 16.5 | 23.8 | 11.9 | 29.7 | 41.6 |
| Other manufacturing | 0.1 | 0.2 | 0.3 | 1.6 | 6.1 | 7.7 | 2.3 | 12.5 | 14.8 | 7.8 | 29.7 | 37.5 |
| *All manufacturing* | 5.8 | 24.7 | 30.5 | 86.6 | 459.6 | 546.2 | 170.5 | 809.2 | 979.7 | 243.5 | 1235.6 | 1479.1 |

TABLE 6.A2 Net stock of capital acquired since end of 1948
(*£m. at 1958 prices*)

| *Industry* / *End of year* | *1949* | | | *1959* | | | *1964* | | | *1970* | | |
|---|---|---|---|---|---|---|---|---|---|---|---|---|
| | *B* | *PM* | *T* | *B* | *PM* | *T* | *B* | *PM* | *T* | *B* | *PM* | *T* |
| Food, drink and tobacco | 0.1 | 1.2 | 1.3 | 6.4 | 14.1 | 20.5 | 12.9 | 21.4 | 34.3 | 16.7 | 28.2 | 44.9 |
| Chemicals and allied | 2.0 | 7.1 | 9.1 | 12.9 | 62.8 | 75.7 | 25.7 | 83.0 | 108.7 | 32.4 | 170.3 | 202.7 |
| Metal manufacture | 1.6 | 6.6 | 8.2 | 27.9 | 204.0 | 231.9 | 55.3 | 364.5 | 419.8 | 63.8 | 405.4 | 469.2 |
| Engineering and electrical goods | 0.1 | 0.8 | 0.9 | 8.0 | 16.4 | 24.4 | 15.9 | 26.6 | 42.5 | 29.8 | 46.6 | 76.4 |
| Shipbuilding and marine engineering | 0.0 | 0.2 | 0.2 | 1.1 | 3.5 | 4.6 | 1.3 | 3.8 | 5.1 | 1.7 | 3.0 | 4.7 |
| Vehicles | 0.0 | 0.3 | 0.3 | 4.6 | 10.2 | 14.8 | 8.4 | 17.9 | 26.3 | 12.2 | 31.1 | 43.3 |
| Other metals | 0.3 | 0.9 | 1.2 | 3.3 | 9.2 | 12.5 | 7.0 | 15.7 | 22.7 | 11.3 | 27.7 | 39.0 |
| Textiles | 1.1 | 4.2 | 5.3 | 8.8 | 27.4 | 36.2 | 13.6 | 31.5 | 45.1 | 14.8 | 41.8 | 56.6 |
| Leather, leather goods and fur | 0.0 | 0.0 | 0.0 | 0.2 | 1.1 | 1.3 | 0.2 | 1.3 | 1.5 | 0.7 | 2.0 | 2.7 |
| Clothing and footwear | 0.0 | 0.2 | 0.2 | 0.8 | 5.1 | 5.9 | 1.9 | 7.2 | 9.1 | 3.4 | 8.5 | 11.9 |
| Bricks, pottery, glass, cement, etc. | 0.4 | 1.1 | 1.5 | 2.6 | 7.7 | 10.3 | 4.3 | 11.8 | 16.1 | 7.5 | 19.0 | 26.5 |
| Timber, furniture, etc. | 0.0 | 0.3 | 0.3 | 0.6 | 3.4 | 4.0 | 1.0 | 4.3 | 5.3 | 2.3 | 5.7 | 8.0 |
| Paper, printing and publishing | 0.1 | 0.9 | 1.0 | 3.1 | 7.9 | 11.0 | 6.8 | 12.1 | 18.9 | 10.8 | 20.7 | 31.5 |
| Other manufacturing | 0.1 | 0.2 | 0.3 | 1.6 | 5.0 | 6.6 | 2.3 | 10.0 | 12.3 | 7.3 | 22.7 | 30.0 |
| *All manufacturing* | 5.8 | 24.0 | 29.8 | 81.9 | 377.8 | 459.7 | 156.6 | 611.1 | 767.7 | 214.7 | 832.7 | 1047.4 |

TABLE 6.A3 Capital-labour and capital-output ratios by industry group in the UK: average 1967–70*

| *Industry group* | *Type of asset* | *Capital-labour ratio* | *Capital-output ratio* |
|---|---|---|---|
| Food, drink and tobacco | *B* | 1.46 | 1.06 |
| | *PM* | 1.44 | 1.03 |
| Chemicals and allied | *B* | 1.58 | 0.63 |
| | *PM* | 1.86 | 0.75 |
| Iron and steel | *B* | 1.21 | 0.87 |
| | *PM* | 1.44 | 1.04 |
| Metal using and other metal manufacture | *B* | 1.26 | 0.84 |
| | *PM* | 0.82 | 0.55 |
| Leather, clothing and other manufacturing | *B* | 1.08 | 0.65 |
| | *PM* | 0.91 | 0.58 |
| Bricks, pottery, glass, etc. | *B* | 1.75 | 1.00 |
| | *PM* | 1.93 | 1.10 |
| Timber, furniture and construction | *B* | 1.32 | 0.93 |
| | *PM* | 2.24 | 1.56 |
| Paper, printing and publishing | *B* | 1.15 | 0.73 |
| | *PM* | 0.78 | 0.48 |

*Source*: see text, p. 181.
*average 1949–52 = 1.00

TABLE 6.A4 appears on facing page.

TABLE 6.A5 Capitalised values of net output less wages and salaries end of 1951

(*£m. at 1958 prices*)

| *Industry group* | *B* | *PM* | *Total* |
|---|---|---|---|
| Food, drink and tobacco | 10.6 | 9.1 | 19.7 |
| Chemicals and allied trades | 11.3 | 21.8 | 33.1 |
| Metal manufacture | 84.7 | 132.4 | 217.1 |
| Engineering and electrical goods | 23.1 | 42.9 | 66.0 |
| Shipbuilding and marine engineering | 3.7 | 7.0 | 10.7 |
| Vehicles | 5.8 | 10.9 | 16.7 |
| Other metals | 13.5 | 25.2 | 38.7 |
| Leather, leather goods and fur | 0.3 | 0.3 | 0.6 |
| Clothing and footwear | 2.1 | 1.7 | 3.8 |
| Bricks, pottery, glass, cement, etc. | 4.3 | 5.3 | 9.6 |
| Timber, furniture, etc. | 0.5 | 0.4 | 0.9 |
| Paper, printing and publishing | 3.0 | 5.5 | 8.5 |
| Other manufacturing | 2.1 | 1.7 | 3.8 |
| *All manufacturing* | 165.0 | 264.2 | 429.2 |

*Source*: see text, p. 182.

TABLE 6.A4 Values between 1949 and 1970 of the net stock of buildings and plant and machinery in existence at end of 1948

(*£m. at 1958 prices*)

| | *1949* | | | | *1959* | | | | *1964* | | | | *1970* | | | |
|---|---|---|---|---|---|---|---|---|---|---|---|---|---|---|---|---|
| | *B* | | *PM* | | *B* | | *PM* | | *B* | | *PM* | | *B* | | *PM* | |
| *Industry* | *I* | *II* | *I* | *II* | *I* | *II* | *I* | *II* | *I* | *II* | *I* | *II* | *I* | *II* | *I* | *II* |
| Food, drink and tobacco | 13.5 | 8.9 | 15.8 | 11.2 | 10.7 | 7.0 | 7.0 | 5.0 | 9.3 | 6.1 | 4.8 | 3.4 | 7.6 | 5.0 | 2.2 | 1.6 |
| Chemicals and allied | 17.0 | 7.6 | 54.5 | 28.1 | 13.5 | 6.0 | 24.2 | 12.5 | 11.7 | 5.2 | 16.7 | 8.6 | 9.6 | 4.3 | 7.6 | 3.9 |
| Metal manufacture | 80.2 | 43.9 | 260.0 | 164.9 | 63.5 | 34.8 | 115.6 | 73.3 | 55.1 | 30.2 | 79.4 | 50.4 | 45.1 | 24.7 | 36.1 | 22.9 |
| Engineering and electrical goods | 9.5 | 7.4 | 22.5 | 17.8 | 7.5 | 5.9 | 10.0 | 7.9 | 6.5 | 5.1 | 6.9 | 5.4 | 5.3 | 4.2 | 3.1 | 2.5 |
| Vehicles | 15.6 | 10.6 | 41.0 | 30.4 | 12.4 | 8.4 | 18.2 | 13.5 | 10.7 | 7.3 | 12.5 | 9.3 | 8.8 | 6.0 | 5.7 | 4.2 |
| Other metals | 10.1 | 10.2 | 28.0 | 28.1 | 8.0 | 8.1 | 12.4 | 12.5 | 6.9 | 7.0 | 8.6 | 8.6 | 5.7 | 5.7 | 3.9 | 3.9 |
| Textiles | 15.5 | 5.4 | 34.7 | 13.5 | 12.3 | 4.3 | 15.4 | 6.0 | 10.7 | 3.7 | 10.6 | 4.1 | 8.7 | 3.0 | 4.8 | 1.9 |
| Leather, leather goods and fur | 1.3 | 0.5 | 2.3 | 1.0 | 1.0 | 0.4 | 1.0 | 0.4 | 0.9 | 0.3 | 0.7 | 0.3 | 0.7 | 0.3 | 0.3 | 0.1 |
| Clothing and footwear | 5.3 | 3.6 | 9.9 | 6.9 | 4.2 | 2.9 | 4.4 | 3.1 | 3.6 | 2.5 | 3.0 | 2.1 | 3.0 | 2.1 | 1.4 | 1.0 |
| Bricks, pottery, glass, cement, etc. | 5.5 | 2.9 | 8.4 | 4.9 | 4.4 | 2.3 | 3.7 | 2.1 | 3.8 | 2.0 | 2.6 | 1.5 | 3.1 | 1.6 | 1.2 | 0.7 |
| Timber, furniture, etc | 2.2 | 1.1 | 1.4 | 0.5 | 1.7 | 0.9 | 0.6 | 0.2 | 1.5 | 0.8 | 0.4 | 0.2 | 1.2 | 0.6 | 0.2 | 0.1 |
| Paper, printing and publishing | 6.1 | 2.3 | 12.7 | 4.9 | 4.8 | 1.8 | 5.6 | 2.2 | 4.2 | 1.6 | 3.9 | 1.5 | 3.4 | 1.3 | 1.8 | 0.7 |
| Other manufacturing | 3.1 | 1.4 | 11.4 | 5.9 | 2.5 | 1.1 | 5.1 | 2.6 | 2.1 | 1.0 | 3.5 | 1.8 | 1.7 | 0.8 | 1.6 | 0.8 |
| *All manufacturing (excluding shipbuilding and marine engineering)* | 184.9 | 105.8 | 502.7 | 318.1 | 146.5 | 83.9 | 223.2 | 141.3 | 127.0 | 72.8 | 153.6 | 97.2 | 103.9 | 59.5 | 69.9 | 44.3 |

TABLE 6.A6 Effect on estimates of net capital stock of varying ratio of net to gross stock in 1949[1]

| Industry | $\bar{K}_{49}/K_{49} = 0.5$ | | | | | | $\bar{K}_{49}/K_{49} = 0.7$ | | | | | |
|---|---|---|---|---|---|---|---|---|---|---|---|---|
| | *1955* | | | *1970* | | | *1955* | | | *1970* | | |
| | *B* | *PM* | *T* | *B* | *PM* | *T* | *B* | *BM* | *T* | *B* | *PM* | *T* |
| Food, drink and tobacco | 94.7 | 92.2 | 93.2 | 95.3 | 94.8 | 95.1 | 102.7 | 105.9 | 104.5 | 103.2 | 105.1 | 104.3 |
| Chemicals and allied | 98.1 | 96.4 | 96.7 | 97.8 | 97.6 | 97.6 | 102.6 | 102.9 | 102.9 | 101.6 | 102.2 | 102.1 |
| Metal manufacture | 94.1 | 92.3 | 92.6 | 94.3 | 94.6 | 94.6 | 104.7 | 106.3 | 106.0 | 104.4 | 105.2 | 105.1 |
| Engineering and electrical goods | 97.2 | 90.8 | 92.9 | 97.9 | 95.8 | 96.5 | 102.8 | 107.8 | 106.2 | 101.5 | 104.0 | 103.2 |
| Vehicles | 91.2 | 80.9 | 84.1 | 92.9 | 88.3 | 89.8 | 106.1 | 119.1 | 115.1 | 105.5 | 114.2 | 111.3 |
| Other metals | 92.6 | 81.4 | 84.9 | 92.9 | 87.5 | 89.4 | 106.5 | 118.6 | 114.9 | 105.9 | 114.7 | 111.6 |
| Textiles | 97.2 | 95.0 | 95.6 | 97.2 | 95.7 | 96.1 | 102.8 | 103.7 | 103.4 | 102.8 | 104.1 | 103.7 |
| Leather, leather goods and fur | 100.0 | 92.3 | 94.1 | 90.0 | 93.3 | 92.0 | 100.0 | 107.7 | 105.9 | 100.0 | 113.3 | 108.0 |
| Clothing and footwear | 88.6 | 87.1 | 87.6 | 92.6 | 90.3 | 91.1 | 105.7 | 112.9 | 110.5 | 107.4 | 110.7 | 109.5 |
| Bricks, pottery, glass, cement, etc. | 97.5 | 94.8 | 95.7 | 96.7 | 96.1 | 96.3 | 105.0 | 105.2 | 105.1 | 103.3 | 103.3 | 103.3 |
| Timber, furniture, etc. | 90.0 | 100.0 | 96.9 | 96.5 | 98.3 | 97.7 | 100.0 | 104.8 | 103.1 | 103.4 | 100.0 | 101.1 |
| Paper, printing and publishing | 100.0 | 92.5 | 94.8 | 98.3 | 97.0 | 97.5 | 102.9 | 105.0 | 104.3 | 100.8 | 102.9 | 102.2 |
| Other manufacturing | 100.0 | 94.0 | 95.5 | 98.8 | 96.7 | 97.2 | 104.5 | 107.5 | 106.7 | 101.2 | 103.3 | 102.8 |

[1] The figures in this table are percentages of the values of capital stock that are derived from method II (see text) with $\bar{K}_{49}/K_{49}$ equal to 0.6.

REFERENCES

Barna, T. (1957), 'The Replacement Cost of Fixed Assets in British Manufacturing Industry in 1955', *Journal of the Royal Statistical Society*, Series A (General), vol. 120.

Dean, G. A. (1964), 'The Stock of Fixed Assets in the United Kingdom in 1961', *Journal of the Royal Statistical Society*, Series A (General), vol. 127.

Domar, E. D. (1953), 'Depreciation, Replacement and Growth', *Economic Journal*, vol. LXIII, Table 1, p. 8.

Feinstein, C. H. (1965), *Domestic Capital Formation in the United Kingdom, 1920–1938*, Studies in the National Income and Expenditure of the United Kingdom, No. 4 (Cambridge University Press).

Feinstein, C. H. (1972), *National Income, Expenditure and Output of the United Kingdom 1855–1965* Cambridge University Press) Table 63.

Henry, E. W. (1971–72), 'Estimation of Capital Stock in Irish Industry 1953 to 1968', *Journal of the Statistical and Social Inquiry Society of Ireland*, vol. XXIII, part IV, p. 6.

Jefferson, C. W. (1968), *A Method of Estimating the Stock of Capital in Northern Ireland Manufacturing Industry; Limitations and Applications* (Dublin: The Economic and Social Research Institute).

Maton, J. M. (1966), Manufacturing Output, Employment and New Building. Regional Analysis: 1948–1958, *Board of Trade Journal*, 28 January, p. vi.

Nevin, E. T. (ed.) (1957), *The Social Accounts of the Welsh Economy, 1948–56*, Welsh Economic Studies No. 2 (University of Wales Press), Table XIV, p. 12.

Nevin, E. T. (1963), 'The Life of Capital Assets: An Empirical Approach', *Oxford Economic Papers*, vol. 15.

Redfern, P. (1955), 'Net Investment in Fixed Assets in the United Kingdom 1938–1953', *Journal of the Royal Statistical Society*, Series A (General), vol. 118.

Tomkins, C. R. (1971), *Income and Expenditure Accounts for Wales 1965–1968* (Welsh Council), Table 35, p. 109.

Welsh Office (1974), *Welsh Economic Trends*, No. 1 (London: HMSO).

Welsh Office (1972–73), *Digest of Welsh Statistics*, No. 19 (London: HMSO), Table 185, p. 140.

Woodward, V. H. (1970), *Regional Social Accounts for the United Kingdom*, NIESR, Regional Papers (Cambridge University Press).

# 7 The Stock of Human Capital in the UK 1975: A Preliminary Estimate

E. R. CHANG, K. HILTON and H. A. YASEEN

*Universities of Southampton and Zagazig*

From the broadest and most general point of view 'a nation's wealth consists of all its sources that contribute to output' (NBER, 1964). As such, both human and non-human resources are included in the concept of national wealth. Human beings provide varying contributions to output depending upon their precise characteristics, or skills, many of which may be induced by 'investment' expenditure.

However, some writers (see NBER (1964), Abraham (1969) and Revell (1967)) suggest that measures of wealth should be limited to non-human forms. Revell (1967) for example, defines national wealth as 'the value of physical assets situated within national boundaries plus the net foreign balance'. This definition clearly ignores human capital. Among the reasons which are offered to justify the confinement of national wealth to non-human forms are the following.

(i) In a society without slaves, human resources cannot be purchased or owned, and therefore could not be recognised as assets. As Lev and Schwartz (1971) pointed out, this is obviously true with respect to individual employees who can resign at will, but in practice this is not so obvious with respect to the firm's labour force as a whole.

In this context they asserted that:

> As long as employees can be replaced it does not matter for our purpose whether the labour force always contains the same person or is a rapidly changing group. The labour force as a whole is constantly associated with the firm, and it can be constructively regarded as 'owned' by it. In modern economies where firms are usually purchased

as going concerns, payment is often made for intangible assets such as a stable and high quality labour force.

This argument is even stronger from a macro-economic point of view. At the macro level, one can argue that, apart from migration, the labour force as a whole is one of the country's resources and could be regarded as belonging to it. It is true that a human being is not purchased but he is 'reared'. Rearing expenditures on education, training, and health are likely to increase the future productivity of human beings. These expenditures may thus be regarded as sources of future income, and as such they represent investment expenditures. On the other hand, the value of a human in terms of the net present value of the flow of future services derived from skills already embodied in that individual decreases with advancement in age. This means that human capital is subject to deterioration or depreciation which has many of the characteristics of the depreciation of physical assets.

(ii) It is morally repugnant to treat human beings as 'capital'. Schultz, for example, attributed the absence of the notion of human capital from the mainstream of economic thought to moral reasons. In this context he asserted:

> The mere thought of investment in human beings is offensive to some among us... Hence, to treat human beings as wealth that can be augmented by investment runs counter to deeply held values. It seems to reduce man once again to a mere material component, to something akin to property. And for man to look upon himself as a capital good, even if it did not impair his freedom, may seem to debase him. No less a person than J. S. Mill at one time insisted that the people of the country should not be looked upon as wealth because wealth existed only for the sake of people. But surely Mill was wrong; there is nothing in the concept of human wealth contrary to his idea that it exists only for the advantage of people. By investing in themselves, people can enlarge the range of choice available to them. It is one way free men can enhance their welfare.

Indeed, the freedom and dignity of man may be successfully preserved even if his productive potential is analysed like that of capital goods. The recognition of the notion of human capital helps since expenditures which increase labour productivity are now analysed within a formal framework. This treatment makes man more valuable than at least some physical assets even from an economic point of view. As H. von Thünen argued in 1875, the failure to apply the concept of human capital was especially immoral in wars: 'for here . . . one will sacrifice in a battle a hundred human beings in the prime of their lives without a thought in order to save one gun . . . the purchase of a cannon causes an outlay on public funds, whereas human beings are to be had for nothing by means of a mere conscription decree'.

(iii) The third and most common reason which has induced many writers to disregard the value of human assets is that the difficulties of measurement are too great. Abraham (1969) suggested that measures of wealth have to be limited to the non-human forms because 'the stock of wealth can only be added together in value terms and human capital is so difficult to value'. However, these difficulties are not peculiar to human capital alone; most, if not all of the alleged difficulties of measurement of human capital have their counterpart in the difficulties arising in the measurement of non-human capital.

We argue that human capital is an integral part of the national wealth. It is a form of capital because it can be viewed as a source of either future earnings or of future satisfaction, or both. The recognition of human resources as an integral part of capital is certainly consistent with Fisher's (1927) definition of capital. He asserted that wealth in its broadest sense includes not only slaves who are owned by other human beings, but also freemen who are their own masters. Indeed, Kendrick (1971) states 'if the concept of "wealth" is broadened to include not only tangible non-human assets, but also human capital including the real investments designed to enhance the quality or efficiency of factors, then economic growth can be largely explained by the trends in total capital'. Moreover, the measurement of both direct and indirect rearing expenses could help in correcting the measurement of the gross national product and its allocation between consumption and capital formation. The current practice governing the preparation of national income accounts treats direct costs of education as consumption expenditures and ignores the foregone income of students and trainees, which could be regarded as indirect investment. The recognition of the notion 'human capital' could help in correcting both our measures of GNP, to include indirect investment, and our allocation of GNP between consumption and capital formation. Furthermore, the recognition of this notion would also permit the correction of our measures of national income to make allowance for the deterioration of human capital.

It follows from the above discussion that the recognition of the notion 'human capital' is significant for measures of the national wealth, and the national income (and its allocation between consumption and capital formation). We do not deny that it may be helpful to distinguish between different types of capital, either for pedogogical or utilitarian reasons. We see essential differences between human and non-human capital lying simply in the place of embodiment of the capital. We may, following Johnson (1968) make the distinction between consumption capital and production capital, but this distinction exists in relation to capital embodied in physical as well as in a human form. We feel it is more appropriate a procedure to analyse human capital in terms of the nature and impact of the form of embodiment rather than on other features of human beings. All the 'unique' features of human capital do have analogues in at least some kinds of physical capital.

Having argued that sensible estimates of human capital *can* be made, one may still question *why* they should be made. The simplest way of answering this question is to argue that estimates of human capital are required for broadly the same reasons as those for physical capital. Examples of such reasons are: in the estimation of (aggregate) production functions; in making international or intertemporal comparisons of wealth; in a whole range of economic analysis where stocks of wealth are required. The neglect of human capital may indeed yield misleading results. For example, it is pointed out by Kenan (1970) that there is a common explanation for the apparent paradox of the trade of a capital-rich country such as the US being labour-using and capital-conserving: the US has a high level of human (as well as physical) capital, which is not reflected in the conventional measures of the labour stock. Many examples of this kind can be found in the literature.

The interest of economists in measuring the money value of a human being can be traced back to the second half of the seventeenth century when Sir William Petty estimated the value of the stock of 'human capital' in England at the end of the seventeenth century. He estimated this value by capitalising the total contribution of labour to the national income at an interest rate. In the absence of actual statistical data representing the total contribution of labour to the national income, he proceeded indirectly. He estimated this contribution by deducting both the rent of land and the yearly profit on other sources of income from the total national expenditure. The following quotation summarises both the procedure he performed and the purposes of his estimation.

> Suppose the people of England to be 6 millions in number, that their expense at £7 per head be £42 millions: suppose also that the rent of lands be £8 millions, and the yearly profit of all the personal estate be £8 millions more; it must needs follow, that the labour of the people

must have supplied the remaining £26 millions, the which multiplied by 20 (the mass of mankind being worth 20 years purchase as well as land) makes £520 millions, as the value of the whole people: which number divided by 6 millions, makes above £80 to be the value of each head of man, woman and child; and of adult persons twice as much; from whence we may learn to compute the loss we have sustained by the plague, by the slaughter of men in war, and by sending them abroad into the service of foreign princes.

Petty's work on the concept and measurement of human capital was followed and criticised by Adam Smith in the eighteenth century, and by Marshall, and many others in the nineteenth century. These works have been quoted, summarised and appraised by many writers of the present century, such as Irving Fisher (1927), L. Dublin and A. Lotka (1946). Hundreds of professional papers and monographs have also appeared during the 1960s and the 1970s and an extended bibliography of this work is given in Schultz (1972). It is generally accepted in the recent literature that current market prices provide the most useful and understandable basis for valuing and combining components of the capital stock. However, current market prices cannot be readily determined for human resources in a non-slave society, but neither can they be determined for the majority of non-human tangible assets. In such a situation, present-day values are necessarily approximated. Two main approaches have been suggested for estimating the monetary value of human capital at any given point in time:

(i) Estimating the costs (inputs) going into the formation of the current stock of human capital and accumulating these costs to arrive at the value of gross investment currently embodied in human beings. As with physical capital, an allowance needs to be made for the deterioration of human capital in order to arrive at the sum of the net investment currently embodied in the stock of human capital.

(ii) capitalising the net earnings power of human resources.

Each of the above two approaches has its advantages and its shortcomings. The superiority of one approach over the other depends upon the purpose for which the estimate is made. The capitalised value approach *could* be considered appropriate if we are interested in an assessment of the value of the working population (i.e., the utilised part of human capital).

Yet, if we wish to use the value of the capital stock as an argument in the estimation of economic relationships, there is a danger that the flow of benefits (reflected in the capitalised value of the stream of future earnings) will be used to explain the same flow of benefits i.e. the analysis becomes circular. Furthermore, apart from the special problems of the appropriate discount rate for human capital flows, there is the problem, most acute in the case of human capital, that the capitalised value is conditional upon the utilisation of the capital stock. To make *ex ante* estimates requires us to make difficult judgements about the probability distributions of the utilisation rate of the capital stock over the whole life of the human resources involved.

The use of the costs going into the formation of human capital may be considered as the relevant approach if we are interested in correcting some of our measures of GNP (to include the indirect costs of education and training), and correcting the classification of GNP between consumption and capital formation accounts. Furthermore, this approach could help in specifying the main components of human capital and determining how much of society's resources have gone into the formation of the different components of human capital.

In this paper, we are mainly concerned with the cost approach for:

(i) it is considered (as argued above) that it is the appropriate approach for purposes of national income accounts.

(ii) The estimation of the value of human capital in cost terms is consistent with the current practices (of national accounting) used in measuring the value of non-human tangible assets; and we can make reasonable comparisons of the relative value of human compared with non-human capital if we use the same principles of valuation.

(iii) aggregation in cost units has a certain practical appeal in that it involves the use of costs that have in fact been incurred.

In this context, it should be noted that we do not treat all expenditures on human beings as investment expenditures, i.e. we do not follow Engels as reported in Kiker (1966) and Dublin and Lotka (1946) in their treatment of all expenditures on human beings as investment. Neither do we follow the current practice of most existing systems of national accounting which treat all expenditures on human beings as consumption expenditures. We treat only expenditures that are expected to enhance future productivity (the equivalent of productive assets) or yield a stream of future enjoyments (the equivalent of consumer durables) as investment expenditures. It follows that we do not treat expenditures on food, clothing, and shelter as investment expenditures because they are not devoted to the maintenance and improvement of the *skills* of human beings; they rather represent consumption expenditures because they are devoted to maintaining the *stock* of human beings.

It is generally agreed that expenditures on education constitute both investment and consumption. Unfortunately the distinction between the consumption and the investment aspects of education is by no means clear cut, and it seems impossible to quantify these components on conceptual grounds. As Mark Blaug rightly states: 'there can be no magic formula, the discovery of which will suddenly permit us to quantify the consumption components of education' (Blaug, 1970). However, most writers and empirical investigators on this topic suggest that expenditure relating to the consumption benefits from the educational process is very small relative to the investment aspect of education. Even when all costs of schooling are counted, rates of return from schooling have been estimated to be of the same order of magnitude as those from investment in physical assets. As these returns disregard the immediate consumption benefits, it could be argued that given decision takers optimise, the immediate consumption elements are small.

The total cost of education can be measured as the sum of direct and indirect costs. Since – in principle – students could contribute to GNP if they were participating in the labour force, the income foregone is an indirect measure of the cost of schooling. However, it may be convenient to distinguish between foregone earnings (i.e., private sacrifice involved in schooling) and foregone output or income (public sacrifice). From the point of view of an individual, the amount of his private sacrifice (foregone earnings) involved in his schooling depends among other things on the minimum legal age of joining the labour force (which differs from one country to another). But from the point of view of the society the education of individuals of over 6 years old involves a real cost in terms of alternative output foregone. In principle, one has to take into consideration the state of employment in the society. It is clearly sensible to speak about income foregone in a country where people are fully employed and there is excess demand for labour. On the other hand, it could be argued that if there is unemployment in a country, the opportunity cost is zero. Yet, in practice, although there may be unemployment in a country, positive wages are paid. Hence, if we are to treat education costs on the same basis as employment costs only in the most extraordinary circumstances will the relevant cost of labour be zero.

Even if we ignore indirect costs, education and training costs represent only part of the total costs incurred in embodying human capital in individuals. For practical reasons, the possible contributions of health for example, to the *skills* embodied in human capital cannot be readily included in measures of such capital. This implies that such measures would represent only a partial measurement of the value of human capital; namely, the value of investment in education and training. The purpose of adding up educational or training expenditures is to be able to obtain a lower bound for the total cost of producing human capital relative to the costs of physical capital. This is not to say that an annual comparison of the amount spent in physical capital with the amount spent on education (or on training) is sufficient, because the distribution of the lengths of working lives of educated persons is different from the distribution of the lengths of lives of physical equipment, as Vaizey (1962) notes; hence the depreciation rates will be different.

In this paper we consider only the measurement of investment in general education (i.e. primary and secondary education) which is currently embodied in the stock of human resources in England and Wales. In this context, it should be noted that the value of human capital embodied in an individual does not last beyond his death. It is also assumed that the economic value of an individual approaches zero at the age of retirement. This is based on the assumption that the value of the stock of services embodied in an individual after his retirement is negligible compared with the value of services existing during his productive work before retirement although certainly 'consumer durable' type elements will last normally till death. It is also assumed that the value of part-time services rendered by an individual while in school is relatively small compared with the value of his services after leaving school. On the other hand, we assume that an individual is capable of rendering services as soon as he finishes his schooling. Hence, it is assumed that the productive life of an individual (who has finished his schooling) starts when he is 17 years of age (i.e. the assumed age of finishing schooling), and lasts until he is 65 years old (i.e. the assumed retirement age). The series of expenditures on investment in general education embodied in an individual thus covers 12 years; its first element was made when he was 5–6 years old, and its last element was made when he was 16–17 years old. This means that educating an individual of age 65 has started when he was five years old (i.e. 60 years previously at $t = 0$). He finished his schooling when he was 17 (i.e. at $t = 11$). If all expenditure on investment in general education is allocated to a human capital account and if depreciation is deducted from this account, the balance of this account would give the sum of net investment currently embodied in the stock of human resources. This implies that if we are interested in estimating the value of investment in general education currently embodied in human resources, an aggregation should be made over a period of 60 years from $t = 0$ up to $t = 59$ (the period preceding the period of estimation). The current practice of national accounting is such that normally in respect of physical capital only actual *not* opportunity costs are used. Furthermore, indirect costs of education are not included in estimates of expenditure on education (which are allocated to consumption accounts under existing practice); hence here we exclude indirect cost of education in GNP.

We can make estimates of the cost of education at the then current prices, and as with physical capital make adjustments to provide estimates of the capital stock embodied in human beings. The kind of adjustments that may be involved are listed below.

(i) *Relating to length of education process* The treatment in the national accounts of physical assets that require some years for their construction varies from asset to asset and from country to country. For example, expenditure on some assets, such as that on ships, is treated in the UK as representing an addition to the fixed capital stock during a particular year even though the ship may not be completed by the end of that year. In the case of many other assets, such expenditure is treated as work-in-progress, and so provides addition to working capital rather than fixed capital. Hence, it is not clear how education expenditures should be treated for them to be consistent with the treatment of expenditure on physical assets; we treat it here in the way that ships are treated in the national income accounts.

There is a further difficulty relating to interest costs. National income accountants normally treat interest as a transfer payment and so interest costs are not included directly in the cost of the assets contributing to the physical capital stock. Yet, as the cost of assets reflects prices paid for those assets, and as the costs of assets in part at least reflects a rate of time preference, it is clear that implicitly the interest rate does have some impact on the valuation of the capital stock. This can be easily recognised if one considers a project with alternative methods of production, one of which involves an expenditure of $100 in each of two years, and the other involves nil expenditure in the first year and $201 in the second year. The choice between the two methods will depend on the rate of interest and so the value of the assets will depend on the rate of interest, yet the rate of interest does not enter into the national accounts. In the case of physical capital, the problem may not be important for there are relatively few assets that have a very long construction period. In the case of human capital there is a long gestation period: should an interest charge be added to the payments before the age when the individual becomes an addition to the actual capital stock? According to the UN standard for physical assets (see United Nations (1968)) the answers would be clearly negative on the grounds that interest in excluded wherever it can be identified. Yet, it could be argued that human assets have such different characteristics as to warrant a special treatment. Hence, below we include estimates for which an interest addition has been made to costs incurred in the earlier years, to indicate the size of the difference that would be involved, with this alternative treatment.

(ii) *In relation to the depreciation of human capital* For physical capital, the value of an asset at a point of time is normally assumed to be a decreasing function of time. Sometimes the value of an asset completed in a particular year is not regarded as an addition to the physical capital stock even at the end of the year (i.e. the total cost is written off during the year of construction) but this may be regarded as a special case of a decreasing function. The approach used by (national income) accountants is not intended to provide precise estimates of the rate of consumption of fixed capital; the general rule, is described by the United Nations (1968) in the following terms: '. . It seems reasonable . . . to value consumption of fixed capital on a straight line basis with reference to the expected economic lifetime of the individual asset . . .'.

For human capital, various arguments can be put forward to treat the consumption of human capital in a different way. It could, for example, be argued that there is some appreciation of the stock of human capital at least in the earlier years that arises from its use, but in the later years the rate of depreciation accelerates. One could find many alternative plausible depreciation profiles. As a first approximation we have assumed below that the depreciation of a straight line varies from age 17 to 65; in practice because the 1975 stock is dominated by the expenditures in recent years, alternative depreciation assumptions (e.g. reducing balance basis) have little effect on the estimates.

(iii) *In relation to changing price levels* Alternative candidates for use as deflators are available, but they are sufficiently highly correlated for it to make little difference whichever one is used. We have used the deflator for the gross domestic product.

For a particular point in time, say at the end of year, $t$, estimates may be constructed of the cost of general education 'embodied' in the working population thus:

(a) Given information about the total expenditure on general education and the number of pupils, we can construct estimates of the average historical cost per pupil being taught in each of the years, $(t - x), x < 60$; this historical cost may be adjusted for price level changes by the use of a price index.

(b) He may assume that the average cost per pupil in each year is the same for all pupils of all ages (the effect of this approximation can be shown to be small).

(c) He can estimate the cost of general education embodied in a person born in a particular year, $q$, $(16 < (t-q) < 66)$ by summing the average cost of general education in each of the years $(q + v)$, $v = 56 \ldots 15, 16$. i.e. by summing the average cost when the person born in year $q$ was being educated.

(d) If we wish to allow for an interest charge during the period of education, we need to discount each of the yearly costs by $(1 + r)^{(16 - v)}$ where $r$ is the rate of interest and $v$ is the age when the education cost was incurred for the cohort born in $q$. Hence for an individual born in $q$ the discounted sum of costs is:

$$\sum_{v=5}^{16} \frac{C_{(q+v)}}{(1 + r)^{(16-v)}} \tag{i}$$

(e) In time period, $t$ these costs can then be depreciated by means of a scaling factor $[(65 - (t - q))]/[(65 - 16)]$ given we use a straight line depreciation approach.

(f) The cost for the $i$ individuals of the cohort born in $q$ may then be summed to provide the total depreciated cost in time period $t$ of educating that cohort.

(g) The depreciated costs for all the relevant cohorts alive at time period $t$ may then be summed to provide the total value of education embodied in the population.

The data available is crude and for some periods of time, in particular 1914–19 and 1939–45 estimates based on interpolative methods have been used. The basic source of data is the UK. Government publication *Statistics of Education*: this source together with the interpolative approximations yielded historical costs per pupil of £6.84 in 1916 and £225.20 in 1975. Table 7.1 shows the estimates of the general educational content of human capital.

The table shows that the value of net investment in general education embodied in the current stock of human capital in England and Wales is estimated to be in the range of £36–60 thousand millions at 1975 prices. This suggests that the value of the general educational content of human capital depends on the views taken of the various conceptual issues, in particular on *deterioration* and on the *time preference* procedures. The results are not in practice very sensitive to the depreciation assumption for most of the expenditure is of recent origin. Nearly 60 per cent of the gross historical expenditure on general education is embodied in people aged (at the time of our analysis) between 17 and 26. If we adjust our figures for price level changes we find that 50 per cent of the gross investment in general education is embodied in this group, (i.e. people aged 17–26), and 27 per cent of the gross investment in general education is embodied in people aged 27–36. Only 23 per cent of the gross investment in general

TABLE 7.1 The educational content of human capital

| *in £000 m.* | *0% interest rate* | *4% interest rate* | *8% interest rate* |
|---|---|---|---|
| Net investment at current prices | 13 | 17 | 22 |
| Net investment at constant (1975) prices | 36 | 46 | 60 |

education is embodied in people between 37 and 65 years old. On the other hand, the results are fairly sensitive to adjustments to allow for the long 'production' period. With no discounting and straight-line depreciation, the general education content of human capital in England and Wales is estimated at £36 thousand million. A discount rate of 4 per cent has increased this value by 29 per cent to be £46 thousand million. If the discount rate is 8 per cent the value of net investment in general education increases by 68 per cent to be £60 thousand million.

Estimates of the general educational content of human capital, based on the above, are subject to a wide margin of error. More than this – they depend on the views taken of the various conceptual issues, and not just on 'depreciation', and on the time preference procedure.

Yet this represents only the general education expenditures content of human capital. We could engage in a similar but more difficult procedure for other educational expenditure. An alternative means of estimating the aggregate value of human capital is to make use of the US studies in this area. We could assume that the ratio of total educational capital to general educational capital is the same in each country and then our estimate for the total educational capital would be in the range £175–380 thousand million.

This may be compared with the £210 thousand million value placed on the non-human capital. *In other words these estimates suggest that the value of human capital is of the same order of magnitude as non-human capital.* More sophisticated analyses for the US suggest similar results for that country; Kendrick's (1971) results imply the ratio of total human to non-human capital in the US is 1.15.

Many alternative approaches to this measurement process are possible. The above is merely illustrative. To perform a satisfactory analysis would take many man years, and access to much unpublished data. All that has been attempted here is to show the possibility and the relative importance of the various parameters.

Nevertheless, it is important to note that the methods proposed for evaluating the value of human capital have a direct counterpart in the methods currently used to measure the physical capital stock. It could be that – if one believes in a market mechanism operating in respect of capital goods – the costs of capital assets may more closely reflect their value. Yet, the approaches to physical capital measurement are used in non market orientated societies. Certainly, in cases such as these the human capital approach here described is as readily justified as the physical capital approach. The scheme is not perfect; but neither are the current arrangements. The recognition and inclusion of human capital is surely an improvement on its complete exclusion.

## REFERENCES

Abraham, W. (1969), *National Income and Economic Accounting* (Prentice-Hall).

Blaug, M. (1970), *An Introduction to the Economics of Education* (Allen Lane, The Penguin Press).

Dublin, L. I. and A. J. Lotka (1946), *The Money Value of a Man*, revised edition (New York: Ronald Press).

Fisher, Irving (1927), *The Nature of Capital and Income* (London: Macmillan).

Johnson, H. G. (1968), 'Towards a Generalised Capital Accumulation Approach to Economic Development', in M. Blaug (ed.) *Economics of Education* 1 – Selected Readings, (Penguin).

Kendrick, J. W. (1971), 'The Accounting Treatment of Human Investment and Capital', *Review of Income and Wealth*, vol. 17.

Kenen, P. B. (1970), 'Skills, Human Capital and Comparative Advantage', in W. Lee Hanson (ed.), *Education Income of Human Capital*, Studies in Income and Wealth vol. 35 (Columbia University Press).

Kiker, B. F. (1966), 'The Historical Roots of the Concept of Human Capital', *Journal of Political Economy*, vol. 74.

Lev, B. and Schwartz, A. (1971), 'On the Use of Economic Concept of Human Capital in Financial Statements', *Accounting Review*, vol. 46 (January).

National Bureau of Economic Research (1964), 'Measuring the Nation's Wealth', *Studies in Income and Wealth*, vol. 29.

Petty, Sir William (1699), *Political Arithmetic, or a Discourse Concerning the Extent and Value of Lands, People, Buildings, etc.* (London: Robert Clavel).

Revell, J. (1967), *The Wealth of the Nation – The National Balance Sheet of the U.K., 1957–1961* (Cambridge University Press).

Schultz, T. W. (1960), 'Capital Formation by Education', *Journal of Political Economy*, vol. 68.

Schultz, T. W. (1961), 'Investment in Human Capital', *American Economic Review*, vol. LI, March.

Schultz, T. W. (1972) 'Human Capital: Policy Issues and Research Opportunities', in *Human Resources*, (National Bureau of Economic Research), pp. 73–84.

Solomon, L. C. (1971) 'Capital Formation by Expenditures on Education in 1960, *Journal of Political Economy*, vol. 79.

United Nations (1968), *A System of National Accounts*, Studies in Method F2(R3).

von Thünen, H. (1875), *Der Isolierte Staat*, 3rd ed. vol. 2, part 2, trans. B. F. Hoselitz, reproduced by the Comparative Education Centre, University of Chicago.

Vaizey, J. (1962), *The Economics of Education* (London: Faber and Faber.)

# 8 Total Factor Productivity in the UK: A Disaggregated Analysis

WILLIAM PETERSON

*Cambridge University*

## INTRODUCTION

This paper presents a set of estimates of the growth of total factor productivity for the United Kingdom during the period 1954–68. The growth of total factor productivity is defined as the difference between the growth rate of final output and that of a suitably weighted combination of productive inputs, both evaluated at constant prices: this difference, or 'residual' (Denison, 1967), can thus be thought of as showing the contribution of unidentified variables, such as economies of scale and advances in technical knowledge, to the process of economic growth. The estimates to be presented in this paper are for 35 distinct industries, covering the whole of the productive sector of the UK economy: government and non-profit making bodies such as charities have been excluded. The aim is to evaluate the contribution which each of these industries has made to the overall growth of productivity, using the information provided by a series of input-output tables to ensure that indirect effects of technical advance, through the provision of cheaper inputs to other industries, are taken into account. Thus the paper can be regarded as complementary to the large body of work, surveyed by Nadiri (1970, 1972), which has attempted to evaluate the aggregate contribution of factors such as the improved design of plant or the spread of higher education. A second aim is to assess the contribution of capital accumulation to technical advance. The conventional treatment of capital in estimating total factor productivity growth is to regard the services of capital as a primary input, on an equal footing with labour: in this approach changes in the efficiency with which capital goods are themselves produced can be taken into account only through corrections for quality change. The deficiencies of such a methodology have been convincingly propounded by Rymes (1971), building on the extensive recent criticism of neo-classical capital theory (Harcourt, 1972). The approach adopted in this paper leads naturally to the alternative treatment suggested by Rymes, in which capital goods are regarded as a form of intermediate product and labour is the sole primary input. The resulting indices of total factor productivity also have the advantage that they provide a more appropriate measure of each industry's contribution to the rate of technical advance for the economy as a whole.

I

Following Jorgenson and Griliches (1967) we make use of the accounting identity for total output and total input to define an index of total factor productivity for the economy as a whole. For $m$ inputs and $n$ outputs this identity can be expressed as

$$p'c = w'v \tag{1}$$

where $p_i$ is the price of the $i$th final output
$c_i$ is the quantity of the $i$th final output
$w_j$ is the price of the $j$th primary input
$v_j$ is the quantity of the $j$th primary input.

Total factor productivity can now be defined by totally differentiating equation (1). Using the identity

$$dx = \hat{x} d \log x \tag{2}$$

(where $\hat{x}$ is a matrix with the elements of $x$ on the diagonal and zeros elsewhere), and dividing through by $p'c$ or $w'v$ we derive

$$(p'c)^{-1} p'\hat{c}(d \log c + d \log p) = (w'v)^{-1} w'\hat{v}(d \log v + d \log w) \tag{3}$$

Define the vectors

$$\begin{aligned} a' &= (p'c)^{-1} p'\hat{c} \\ b' &= (w'v)^{-1} w'\hat{v} \end{aligned} \tag{4}$$

where $a_i$ is the value share of the $i^{\text{th}}$ output in total output and $b_j$ the value share of the $j^{\text{th}}$ input in total input. Then the rate of growth of total factor productivity for the economy as a whole is defined as

$$d \log T = a'd \log c - b'd \log v = -(a'd \log p - b'd \log w) \tag{5}$$

and in index of total factor productivity can be derived from (5) by suitable choice of a base year. It is clear that (5) is equivalent to Jorgenson and Griliches's definition of total factor productivity as the ratio of Divisia indices of final outputs and primary inputs.

Consider now the application of this definition to an economy where technology at any moment of time can be represented by the following input-output relationships and associated dual price equations

$$
\begin{aligned}
c &= (I - A)q \\
v &= Bq \\
p' &= p'A + w'B
\end{aligned}
\tag{6}
$$

where $q$ is the vector of gross outputs, $A$ and $B$ matrices of unit input requirements for intermediate goods and primary inputs respectively. We now totally differentiate the first two equations of (6) and substitute the results into (5) to obtain

$$
\begin{aligned}
d \log T = (p'c)^{-1} p'(I - A)dq - (w'v)^{-1} w'Bdq - (p'c)^{-1} p'dAq \\
- (w'v)^{-1} w'dBq.
\end{aligned}
\tag{7}
$$

From (1) $p'c = w'v$, and from (6) $p'(I - A) - w'B = 0'$, so that

$$d \log T = -(p'c)^{-1} (p'dA + w'dB)q. \tag{8}$$

Thus it is clear that a change in one or other of the input-output coefficient matrices is necessary (but not sufficient) for there to be a change in total factor productivity.

It is clearly desirable, in a multi-sectoral analysis, to derive an index of total factor productivity for an individual industry with the property that the index for the economy as a whole is a suitably weighted sum of the indices for individual industries. To do this, we start from the identity between total output and total input for a particular industry

$$p_k q_k = \sum_i p_i q_{ik} + \sum_j w_j v_{jk} \tag{9}$$

where $q_{ik}$ is the input of the $i^{th}$ commodity into the $k^{th}$ industry, and $v_{jk}$ the input of the $j^{th}$ primary input. Taking logarithms and totally differentiating

$$
\begin{aligned}
d \log p_k + d \log q_k = (p_k q_k)^{-1} \Big[\sum_i p_i q_{ik}(d \log q_{ik} + d \log p_i) \\
+ \sum_j w_j v_{jk}(d \log v_{jk} + d \log w_j)\Big].
\end{aligned}
\tag{10}
$$

Rearranging (10) and separating price and quantity changes as before,

$$d \log t_k = d \log q_k - (p_k q_k)^{-1} \sum_i p_i q_{ik} \, d \log q_{ik}$$
$$- (p_k q_k)^{-1} \sum_j w_j v_{jk} \, d \log v_{jk}. \qquad (11)$$

But by our assumption that the underlying technology is given by the input-output relations (6)

$$\begin{aligned} d \log q_{ik} &= d \log a_{ik} + d \log q_k \\ d \log v_{jk} &= d \log b_{jk} + d \log q_k. \end{aligned} \qquad (12)$$

Substituting from (12) into (11) and simplifying

$$d \log t_k = -p_k^{-1} \sum_i p_i a_{ik} \, d \log a_{ik} - p_k^{-1} \sum w_j b_{jk} \, d \log b_{jk} \qquad (13)$$

$$p_k \, d \log t_k = -(\sum_i p_i da_{ik} + \sum_j w_j db_{jk}). \qquad (14)$$

It has been shown by Domar (1961) that equation (14) is a continuous analogue of the 'measure of structural change' put forward by Leontief (1953) and used by him to analyse changes over time in input-output coefficients. However because the definition of total factor productivity for an industry implied by (14) does not distinguish between intermediate and primary inputs a weighted average of the indices for individual industries will tend to underestimate the overall growth rate of productivity. This can be shown by considering the index $d\log T'$ formed by combining the Leontief indices using final demand weights: from equation (14)

$$\begin{aligned} d \log T' &= -(p'c)^{-1} \sum_k p_k c_k \, d \log t_k \\ &= -(p'c)^{-1} (p'dA + w'dB)c \\ &< -(p'c)^{-1} (p'dA + w'dB)q = d \log T \end{aligned} \qquad (15)$$

since the vector $q$ of gross outputs is uniformly greater than the vector $c$ of final demands, and the assumption of technical advance implies that $p'dA + w'dB \leqslant 0$.

However this problem of aggregation can easily be overcome. Consider the modified index for industry $k$, $d\log \tilde{t}_k$, defined by

$$d \log \tilde{t}_k = c_k^{-1} q_k \, d \log t_k \qquad (16)$$

Then we see that

$$-(p'c)^{-1}\sum_k p_k c_k \, d\log \tilde{t}_k = -(p'c)^{-1}(p'dA + w'dB)q$$
$$= d\log T. \tag{17}$$

Thus for each industry the Leontief index of structural change must be multiplied by the ratio of gross output to final demand: the growth of total factor productivity for the economy as a whole is the mean of the adjusted indices, each weighted by the industry's share in total final output. It is intuitively clear why this adjustment to the original indices is necessary: if the original indices were combined using final demand weights the contribution to growth of industries predominantly producing intermediate goods will be underestimated, because their indirect effect on industries 'downstream' will be ignored. The limiting case would be when an industry did not sell to final demand at all, since such an industry would apparently make no contribution to productivity growth however rapidly its techniques of production were changing.

An alternative approach to the problem raised by the existence of intermediate goods is to redefine the underlying technology in terms of vertically integrated sectors. In this system each sector produces one type of final output, making use only of primary inputs to do so. The disadvantage of using this approach to construct indices of total factor productivity is that the indices relate to the unobservable vertically integrated sectors rather than to the industries originally defined by the statisticians. Thus rapid technical progress in the integrated 'engineering' sector does not necessarily imply that the establishments classified to engineering are experiencing exceptional success in research or innovation, since they may merely be benefiting from such success in their supplying industries. Nevertheless it is true that indices of productivity change for the vertically integrated sectors do reflect the extent to which technical progress is leading to the increased availability and lower cost of individual final products.

The system of vertically integrated sectors corresponding to the input-output technology described in equation (6) can be set out as

$$v = B(I-A)^{-1}c$$
$$p' = w'B(I-A)^{-1}. \tag{18}$$

The first equation of (17) can be totally differentiated by making use of the fact that for any non-singular matrix $G$,

$$dG^{-1} = -G^{-1}dG\,G^{-1}. \tag{19}$$

The resulting expression can be simplified using the price dual to give an expression for the growth of total factor productivity

$$d \log T^* = -(p'c)^{-1} (w'dB(I-A)^{-1}c + p'dA(I-A)^{-1}c) \qquad (20)$$

Since

$$(I-A)^{-1}c = q,$$

it is clear that this is identical to the expression given in (3).

Equation (20) can be regarded as a final demand weighted average of productivity growth rates for the individual vertically integrated sectors. To show this we define the $m \times n$ matrix $M$, such that,

$$M = B(I-A)^{-1} \qquad (21)$$

and $M_{jk}$ gives the total direct and indirect requirements of primary input $j$ per unit of final good $k$. Then

$$d \log T^* = -(w'Mc)^{-1} w'dMc. \qquad (22)$$

For each vertically integrated sector the equality of total input and total output can be written as

$$p_k c_k = \sum_j w_j m_{jk} c_k \qquad (23)$$

and the growth of total factor productivity can be defined as

$$d \log t_k^* = d \log c_k - (\sum_j w_j m_{jk} c_k)^{-1} \sum_j w_j m_{jk} c_k (d \log m_{jk} + d \log c_k) \qquad (24)$$

$$= -(\sum_j w_j m_{jk} c_k)^{-1} \sum_j w_j dm_{jk} c_k.$$

Thus the growth of total factor productivity for the economy is

$$d \log T^* = a'd \log t^* \qquad (25)$$

and the growth rates for the vertically integrated sectors are related to the Leontief indices for the individual industries by

$$d \log t^* = (I - A')^{-1} d \log t. \qquad (26)$$

Although equations (17) and (25) both express aggregate productivity growth as final demand weighted means of growth rates for individual industries, the two decompositions are not the same. This is because, as can be seen from (17), $d \log \bar{t}$ itself depends on the structure of final demand whereas $d \log t^*$ depends solely on changes in technology. For this reason the equality of the aggregate measures does not imply that the two indices should be the same for any individual industry. It is possible, as the empirical analysis of this paper will show, for an industry to be making a substantial contribution to economic growth, by producing an important intermediate good more efficiently, while at the same time the corresponding vertically integrated sector is becoming less productive.

The analytical framework set out above to assess the effects of interdependence between industries can also be applied to the problem of measuring the contribution of capital goods to economic growth. To see this it is only necessary to reinterpret the input-output technology as a simple circulating capital model without joint production. Then conventional neoclassical measures of total factor productivity, based on an approach which treats labour and capital symmetrically as primary factors of production, will tend to under-estimate the rate of technical progress because, as has been pointed out by Rymes (1971), capital goods are themselves produced by processes which become more efficient through time as the result of technical change. It is for this reason that, as Rymes shows, capital input should be measured as 'real capital' rather than commodity capital: where 'real capital' is the sum of dated labour, cumulated using the current rate of profit, that would be required to reproduce the existing stock of plant using currently available technology.

It is easy to see how these 'Harrodian' measures of technical change can be computed using the information available in a set of input-output tables. Suppose we define, in addition to the conventional $n$ final outputs, a vector of $k$ investment goods $(y_1 \,.\,.\, y_k)$ and an $n \times k$ matrix $G$ giving the unit input requirements of intermediate goods per unit of investment good output (we assume that the fictitious processes used to produce investment goods do not require primary input). Then the system of production equations becomes

$$\begin{aligned} \tilde{c} &= (I - A)q - Gy \\ 0 &= -B_1 q + y \\ \tilde{v} &= B_2 q \end{aligned} \tag{27}$$

where we have partitioned the $B$ matrix to distinguish the submatrices for capital goods $B_1$ and other primary inputs $B_2$: the vector $\tilde{c}$ is a vector of final demands *excluding* investment and $\tilde{v}$ is the $(m - k)$ vector of non-produced primary inputs. Then the first two equations can be written as

$$\begin{bmatrix} \tilde{c} \\ 0 \end{bmatrix} = (I - A^*)\begin{bmatrix} q \\ y \end{bmatrix}. \tag{28}$$

where $A^*$ is the augmented matrix

$$\begin{bmatrix} A & G \\ B_1 & 0 \end{bmatrix}$$

and the analysis of total factor productivity presented in this paper is equally applicable to the transformed system.

II

As part of the work of constructing a multi-sectoral model of the UK economy, the Cambridge Growth Project has constructed disaggregated national accounts for the period 1954–68. These accounts give detailed information about production and demand for 45 different commodities and 35 industries: a full account of their construction is given in Barker (1972). In addition the project has compiled time series data on primary inputs in both volume and value terms, and this information has been published by Armstrong (1974). These sources were used to construct matrices of intermediate input requirements and primary input requirements for each year, assuming that the underlying technology exhibited constant returns to scale.

The accounting system used to construct these matrices distinguishes four primary inputs: labour, capital services, direct imports and net indirect taxes. A row for net indirect taxes is necessary because the commodity flows in the system are valued at producers' prices rather than market prices. However the most important indirect taxes in the UK economy (purchase tax (later replaced by VAT) and duties on drink, tobacco and petrol) are treated as though they were paid directly by consumers. Thus indirect taxes on industry (mainly rates, some motor and petrol taxes, and agricultural subsidies) are comparatively small. In order to avoid attributing the effects of changes in indirect tax rates to technical progress the 1963 rates were assumed to be in force throughout the period: thus the only effect of indirect taxes on the results comes through their influence on the weights used to aggregate the indices for individual industries to give a measure of technical progress for the economy as a whole.

Direct industry imports (principally charter payments for shipping) have been treated explicitly as a primary input. However the only industry for which they are a significant proportion of total input is transport, and here there was little change in the unit input requirement over the period. Thus the effect of their inclusion on the overall result is likely to be small. Other imports are treated as negative final demand for the commodity in question. While this is consistent with our accounting framework, it has the disadvantage that, for some industries, the ratio of gross output to final demand (domestic output plus net exports) changes sign during the period, and domestic output becomes less than intermediate demand. In cases where this happens it is inappropriate to use formula (17) to measure the industry's contribution to the overall growth of total factor productivity. To cope with this difficulty, the treatment of imports was modified by assuming that the import share was the same for domestic final demand and for intermediate demand, so that all industries produce some output for final consumption as well as intermediate products. It would perhaps be more satisfactory to treat foreign trade as a fictitious industry, as was originally done by Leontief (1941), since this would enable us to analyse the effects of changes in the terms of trade on total factor productivity.

Although the measure of labour input used incorporates the effects of changes in hours worked (except for the service industries where the appropriate data is not available), no attempt has been made to allow for improvements in the quality of the labour force. There is no official data on his subject: and in any case the main aim of this paper is to study the importance of industrial interdependence rather than the contributions of individual primary inputs. However it is worth pointing out that the two are not mutally exclusive, since the methods adopted here do not preclude a detailed analysis of changes in the composition and quality of primary inputs provided the necessary information is available.

The capital stock series used in the calculations is a slight disaggregation of that published by Armstrong (1974), making use of unpublished data to extend the coverage to 35 industries. In accordance with the distinction made earlier in this paper between neoclassical and Harrodian concepts of capital accumulation and technical change, two alternative treatments of capital stock were adopted. The neo-classical approach considers capital services (assumed proportionate for each industry to the capital stock) as a non-reproducible primary input. The alternative treatment assumes that, in each year, the gross investment undertaken by each industry represents the flow of capital goods required to maintain the industry on its current growth path. Since the commodity flows required to produce investment goods are also known, the input-output matrix is augmented by additional rows and columns, using the framework set out in (28), and the appropriate indices of total factor productivity are constructed for the augmented system.

Table 8.1 sets out the average annual growth rates of productivity for 35 industries and for the productive sector of the British economy. These growth rates, which are discrete approximations to the formulae given above, have been evaluated adopting the neoclassical convention that

TABLE 8.1 Total factor productivity growth, 1954–68: Neoclassical

| *Industry* | *Intermediate inputs* $-p'\delta A$ | *Primary inputs* $-w'\delta B$ | $d \log \tilde{t}$ | $d \log t^*$ |
|---|---|---|---|---|
| 1 Agriculture, etc | 1.52 | 1.22 | 2.11 | 3.96 |
| 2 Coal mining | –0.03 | 1.53 | 5.69 | 2.01 |
| 3 Mining n.e.s. | –1.36 | 1.54 | 0.06 | 1.00 |
| 4 Cereal processing | 0.13 | 0.15 | 0.51 | 2.20 |
| 5 Food processing n.e.s. | 0.75 | 0.21 | 0.78 | 3.15 |
| 6 Drink | –0.68 | 0.90 | 0.26 | 1.02 |
| 7 Tobacco manufacture | –0.57 | –0.87 | –1.45 | 0.35 |
| 8 Coke ovens | 0.45 | –0.31 | 0.37 | 1.77 |
| 9 Mineral oil refining | 0.85 | 0.41 | 2.04 | 2.38 |
| 10 Chemicals, etc. | 1.27 | 0.90 | 4.34 | 3.79 |
| 11 Iron and steel | 1.08 | 0.17 | 7.55 | 2.63 |
| 12 Non-ferrous metals | 0.19 | 0.06 | 0.63 | 0.38 |
| 13 Engineering | –0.21 | 0.89 | 1.02 | 1.49 |
| 14 Shipbuilding, etc. | 1.14 | 0.87 | 2.86 | 3.28 |
| 15 Motor vehicles, etc. | 0.83 | 1.10 | 2.75 | 3.47 |
| 16 Aerospace equipment | 0.08 | 0.57 | 0.92 | 1.41 |
| 17 Vehicles n.e.s. | 1.18 | 0.41 | 2.56 | 2.91 |
| 18 Metal goods | –0.27 | 0.05 | –0.75 | 0.71 |
| 19 Textile fibres | 2.17 | 5.08 | 5.89 | 8.99 |
| 20 Textiles n.e.s. | –0.52 | 0.24 | –0.55 | 2.37 |
| 21 Leather, clothing, etc. | 1.57 | 0.97 | 2.77 | 4.27 |
| 22 Bricks, etc. | 0.29 | 1.19 | 10.85 | 2.52 |
| 23 Pottery and glass | 1.17 | 1.73 | 7.12 | 3.78 |
| 24 Timber and furniture | –0.73 | 0.54 | –0.34 | 0.40 |
| 25 Paper and board | 1.29 | 0.56 | 2.65 | 3.58 |
| 26 Printing and publishing | –0.77 | 0.96 | 0.68 | 1.36 |
| 27 Rubber | 1.51 | 1.27 | 7.78 | 4.42 |
| 28 Manufactures n.e.s. | –1.12 | 0.70 | –0.85 | 0.76 |
| 29 Construction | –0.88 | 0.40 | –0.64 | 0.19 |
| 30 Gas | –0.28 | –0.41 | –1.38 | 0.33 |
| 31 Electricity | 1.36 | 1.62 | 6.84 | 3.92 |
| 32 Water | 0.44 | 0.45 | 1.68 | 1.29 |
| 33 Transport and comms. | –0.04 | 1.67 | 2.86 | 2.20 |
| 34 Distribution | 0.50 | 0.05 | 0.68 | 0.81 |
| 35 Services | –0.97 | –0.02 | –1.52 | –0.66 |
| *All industries* | 0.04 | 0.53 | 1.47 | 1.47 |

capital services are non-reproducible primary inputs. The first and second columns of the table are partial indicators of productivity growth and ignore the effects of industrial interdependence: they represent the contributions of the reduction in input requirements for intermediate goods and primary inputs respectively, and can thus be related to the decomposition of productivity change for an individual industry given in equation (14). The third column is the adjusted Leontief index of structural change $d\log\bar{t}_k$, defined in equation (16), and therefore shows the contribution of each industry to the overall rate of productivity growth, allowing for indirect contributions through the provision to the rest of the economy of cheaper intermediate goods. Finally the fourth column gives the rate of productivity growth for the vertically integrated sector producing each commodity: this growth rate, which is defined as $d\log t_k^*$ by equation (24), gives the total improvement in the efficiency with which primary inputs can be combined to produce each commodity without distinguishing the industry in which the improvement has occurred.

It is clear from Table 8.1 that, for the economy as a whole, changes in the matrix of intermediate input requirements have contributed relatively little to improvements in total factor productivity. This is because such changes have been small, and reflect not only technical change but also substitution between alternative raw materials and, unfortunately, changes in statistical coverage and methodology. However it is clear that certain industries have reduced their intermediate input requirements substantially over the period, and where such industries are themselves producers of intermediate goods such technical change may make a major contribution to the growth of the economy: this effect is particularly noticeable for chemicals, iron and steel and electricity.

In contrast, reductions in primary input requirements have contributed to productivity growth for all but four of the 35 industries. However it is clear that for the majority of industries the improvement has been relatively small, with only the comparatively unimportant textile fibre industry attaining a rapid rate of technical advance. Of the four industries with declining productivity, two (tobacco and coke) are small and suffered from a very slow growth rate of demand during the period: the same problem of stagnant demand also afflicted the gas industry before the switch to supplies of cheap natural gas at the end of the 1960s. The very small decline in productivity in series probably reflects the difficulty of measuring output correctly for this industry.

The general sluggishness of productivity growth indicated by the small reductions in intermediate input requirements for most industries is confirmed by the slow rate of technical change for the economy as a whole. Table 8.1 indicates that, for the non-government sector, total factor productivity grew at 1.47 per cent per year: this estimate is rather smaller than that of 1.98 per cent given by Christensen *et al.* (1975) for the period 1955–68. Their figure is based on aggregate data for gross private domestic product and factor outlay: thus the coverage excludes public corporations but includes the services of owner-occupied housing and consumer durables. It is possible that these differences are sufficient to account for the discrepancy.

It is clear from columns 3 and 4 of the table that productivity change in a particular industry need not imply that the industry's product has become cheaper to produce. Thus in several industries such as metal goods or textiles there was a decline in industry productivity, usually because an increase in intermediate input requirements, possibly resulting from a move towards buying raw materials in semi-finished form, was not matched by a corresponding decrease in primary input requirements. However in almost all cases technical progress in the supplying industries was such that the total primary input required to produce the industry's output fell. Thus industrial interdependence can be thought of as spreading the gains arising from technical progress in particular industries through the economy. The table also shows the importance in the dissemination of technical progress of basic industries such as coal, chemicals, steel, bricks and electricity: although the underlying rate of productivity growth for these industries may be small the high ratio of gross output to final demand magnifies its effect on the economy.

Table 8.2 presents alternative estimates of the growth in total factor productivity based on a treatment of capital goods as reproducible intermediate inputs. For the economy as a whole the rate of growth increases from 1.47 per cent to 1.53 per cent: this increase would be greater if it were not for the apparent decline in productivity in mining and gas, which merely reflects the fact that our period includes the first North Sea investment boom, but excludes the corresponding increase in output. Column 3 of the table shows that most of the basic industries retain their importance within this frame of analysis, although in some industries (notably mineral oil refining and electricity) the change in treatment of capital inputs reduces the apparent rate of technical progress: this is because our definition of capital requirements is now based on gross investment undertaken rather than an estimate of services provided by the capital stock and hence the capital input coefficients are less stable.

Although the method which has been used in this paper to generate estimates of total factor productivity requires very much more information than the aggregative approach adopted by Denison (1967), Jorgenson and

TABLE 8.2 Total factor productivity growth, 1954–68: Harrodian

| *Industry* | *Intermediate inputs* $-p'\delta A$ | *Primary inputs* $-w'\delta B$ | $d \log \tilde{t}$ | $d \log t^*$ |
|---|---|---|---|---|
| 1 Agriculture, etc. | 1.30 | 1.70 | 2.32 | 4.20 |
| 2 Coal mining | −0.18 | 1.91 | 6.52 | 2.17 |
| 3 Mining n.e.s. | −3.41 | 1.70 | −0.41 | −1.25 |
| 4 Cereal processing | 0.11 | 0.32 | 0.78 | 2.37 |
| 5 Food processing n.e.s. | 0.69 | 0.37 | 0.86 | 3.28 |
| 6 Drink | −0.95 | 0.77 | −0.20 | 0.52 |
| 7 Tobacco manufacture | −0.71 | 0.08 | −0.64 | 1.23 |
| 8 Coke ovens | 0.91 | −0.03 | 2.80 | 2.43 |
| 9 Mineral oil refining | 0.74 | 0.34 | 1.76 | 0.42 |
| 10 Chemicals, etc. | 1.32 | 0.90 | 4.45 | 3.68 |
| 11 Iron and steel | 1.32 | 0.42 | 10.98 | 2.95 |
| 12 Non-ferrous metals | 0.16 | 0.25 | 0.96 | 0.05 |
| 13 Engineering | −0.20 | 0.95 | 1.15 | 1.54 |
| 14 Shipbuilding, etc. | 1.22 | 1.03 | 3.16 | 3.54 |
| 15 Motor vehicles, etc. | 0.95 | 0.95 | 2.70 | 3.39 |
| 16 Aerospace equipment | 0.19 | 0.82 | 1.45 | 1.87 |
| 17 Vehicles n.e.s. | 1.03 | 0.50 | 2.49 | 2.76 |
| 18 Metal goods | −0.34 | 0.21 | −0.49 | 0.72 |
| 19 Textile fibres | 2.91 | 2.00 | 3.93 | 6.47 |
| 20 Textiles n.e.s. | −0.65 | 0.40 | −0.47 | 1.68 |
| 21 Leather, clothing, etc. | 1.55 | 0.93 | 2.70 | 3.91 |
| 22 Bricks, etc. | 0.11 | 1.22 | 10.17 | 1.94 |
| 23 Pottery and glass | 1.03 | 1.87 | 7.13 | 3.51 |
| 24 Timber and furniture | −0.79 | 0.62 | −0.31 | 0.28 |
| 25 Paper and board | 1.56 | 0.51 | 3.04 | 3.72 |
| 26 Printing and publishing | −0.79 | 0.92 | 0.50 | 1.28 |
| 27 Rubber | 1.38 | 1.18 | 7.18 | 4.04 |
| 28 Manufactures n.e.s. | −1.33 | 0.81 | −0.99 | 0.55 |
| 29 Construction | −1.04 | 0.71 | −0.46 | 0.22 |
| 30 Gas | −3.06 | 0.17 | −4.96 | −2.06 |
| 31 Electricity | −0.07 | 1.37 | 3.13 | 1.99 |
| 32 Water | −0.01 | 0.05 | 0.29 | 0.46 |
| 33 Transport and comms. | −0.44 | 1.44 | 1.74 | 1.44 |
| 34 Distribution | 0.16 | 0.60 | 0.93 | 0.94 |
| 35 Services | −1.44 | 0.53 | −1.45 | −0.66 |
| *All industries* | −0.07 | 0.76 | 1.53 | 1.53 |

Griliches (1967) and many others, it would not be impossible to carry out such calculations for other countries for which suitable input-output data is available. The advantages of doing this would be considerable, since the measures defined and constructed in this paper are capable of providing the information needed to identify those industries which are suffering from technical stagnation or where small improvements in productivity would lead to substantial gains for the economy. In addition they can provide useful detail on the extent to which technical progress has led to differential movements in primary input requirements for different commodities, and hence, if we are prepared to assume a stable pattern of wage differentials across industries, to changes in relative prices.

## REFERENCES


Armstrong, A. G. (1974), *Structural Change in the British Economy 1948–68*, vol. 12 of Stone, R. (ed), *A Programme for Growth* (London: Chapman and Hall).

Barker, T. S. (1972), *Updated Social Accounting Matrices: U.S. Commodity Accounts 1954–68*, Cambridge Growth Project Paper 363.

Christensen, L. R., Cummings, D. and Singleton, K. (1975), *Real Product, Real Factor Input and Productivity in the United Kingdom, 1955–73*, Social Systems Research Institute, Wisconsin, Workshop Paper 7530.

Denison, E. F. (1967), *Why Growth Rates Differ* (Washington: Brookings Institution).

Domar, E. D. (1961), 'On the Measurement of Technical Change', *Economic Journal*, December, pp. 709–29.

Harcourt, G. C. (1972), *Some Cambridge Controversies in the Theory of Capital* (Cambridge University Press).

Jorgenson, D. W. and Griliches, Z. (1967), 'The Explanation of Productivity Change', *Review of Economic Studies*, July, pp. 249–83.

Leontief, W. W. (1941), *The Structure of American Economy, 1919–29* (Harvard University Press).

Leontief, W. W. (1953), *Studies in the Structure of the American Economy* (Oxford University Press).

Nadiri, M. I. (1970), 'Some Approaches to the Theory and Measurement of Total Factor Productivity: A Survey', *Journal of Economic Literature*, December, pp. 1137–77.

Nadiri, M. I. (1972), 'International Studies of Factor Inputs and Total Factor Productivity: A Brief Survey', *Review of Income and Wealth*, June, pp. 129–54.

Rymes, T. K. (1971), *On Concepts of Capital and Technical Change* (Cambridge University Press).

# 9 Capital Utilisation and Input Substitution

DAVID HEATHFIELD

*University of Southampton*

It has long been recognised that production studies have lacked any satisfactory treatment of capital utilisation. Perhaps the paucity of data discouraged theoretical developments or perhaps little effort was expended on gathering data until some theoretical case was made for doing so.

The theoretical neglect has to some extent been rectified by Winston (see for example Winston and McCoy (1974)). Others, notably Marris (1964) and Aberg (1964) have worked in terms of labour shift working which has direct bearing on capital utilisation.

The empirical problems have been greatly eased by Foss (1963) upon whose method the estimates of capital utilisation used here are based. These estimates use electricity consumption data and purport to measure utilisation as a percentage of maximum. (See Heathfield (1972)).

Some attempt at explaining changes in capital utilisation over time is made by Heathfeld (1976). It is intended in this paper to investigate the relation between output, capital and labour when capital utilisation can be explicitly allowed for.

The obvious approach is to enter capital utilisation as a separate argument in an aggregate production function. Whatever the merits and demerits of such functions might be, they do seem adequately to describe data at many levels of aggregation.

Few would now want to argue that aggregate production functions do more than describe historical (or cross sectional) data – there is no presumption of putty-putty capital. Explanations of the empirical success of such functions have then to be couched in tems of a vintage model in which capital is either clay-clay or putty-clay.

It is possible in a clay world to have disembodied technical progress but for the moment we assume fixed coefficients. If fixed coefficients mean anything they must relate the flow of output, the flow of labour services and the flow of capital services of a machine. By 'machine' is meant the smallest physical piece of capital which can be used to produce output. To divide a machine further would deprive it of its power to produce at all. That is not to say that a machine is a unit of capital. Some machines may 'contain' many units of capital, others few. We do not here consider the problems of defining or measuring capital (nor labour nor output for that matter), we simply assume that we know what it is and that our data adequately represent it. Our reason for delineating a machine is simply that it is to a machine that fixed coefficients apply.

Substitution is possible, even for a given machine, if by that is meant the substitution of capital stock for labour services. If one machine working for three hours with one man produces the same output as three machines each working for one hour with one man each, then no unique capital stock can be deduced from knowledge of output or labour services: there is no fixed capital stock-coefficient.

Substitution between labour-services and capital-services will appear to be possible, for any given *set* of machines, if machines have different coefficients and utilisation rates are varied. The set of machines will have fixed coefficients only if utilisation rates are in fixed proportion. If the assumption of common utilisation rates is dropped then capital stock will behave, in aggregate, as if there were substitution between capital and labour – as indeed in this sense there is. Capital utilisation is of course limited to lie between zero and one hundred per cent and most of the work done in this area deals only with these extremes: machines are either fully used or they are idle[1]. Switching machines into and out of the operating capital stock gives rise to a number of aggregate relationships which have been fully investigated by Johansen (1972).

One model of particular interest is that of Houthakker (1955–56) who assumes that the coefficients are distributed as a Pareto distribution and shows that as the zero quasi rent plane is moved some machines are discarded and others activated, and the relationship between aggregate variables will be that of a Cobb-Douglas.

In all these models, and in particular the Houthakker model, it is difficult to see why there should be idle capital at both ends of the vintage structure. Obviously, as relative prices move, some existing processes will be rendered unprofitable and hence obsolete, but why there should be unused machines which have never been profitable and will continue to be unprofitable unless relative prices continue to move in their favour, is not clear.

Solow (1967) has a somewhat different model. He assumes two sectors, one producing capital with only labour and the other producing consumer goods with capital and labour. The supply function for new capital is such that the *ex-ante* production function (the range of machines from which an investing entrepreneur may choose) is Cobb-Douglas. In order for this to be reflected in his *ex-post* (clay) observations it is necessary to consider only long run equlibria in each of which all machines are identical. Thus unless the cost of capital function is as assumed and unless there is rapid adjustment to 'best practice' coefficients, this model is unlikely to be of any interest empirically.

A somewhat different derivation of the Cobb-Douglas function from a set of fixed coefficient machines would be as follows.

Let a machine (i) be denoted by a list of coefficients e.g. an output-capital ratio

$$\gamma i = \frac{Yi}{KuiKsi} \tag{1}$$

and a labour-capital ratio

$$\rho i = \frac{LuiLsi}{KuiKsi} \tag{2}$$

where $Kui$ is the utilisation of the $i$th machine

$Ksi$ is the amount of capital in the $i$th machine
$Yi$ is the output of the $i$th machine
$Lsi$ is the number of men operating the $i$th machine
$Lui$ is the average number of hours worked per man on the $i$th machine.

For a set of '$n$' such machines we have an aggregate output/capital ratio:

$$\gamma a = \frac{\sum^{n} Yi}{\sum^{n} KuiKsi} \tag{3}$$

Assuming that each machine has the same utilisation we have

$$\gamma a = \frac{Ya}{KuKsa} \tag{4}$$

and similarly for the aggregate labour-capital ratio:

$$\rho i = \frac{(LuLs)a}{KuKsa} \tag{5}$$

Thus, provided each machine has the same utilisation aggregate capital stock, aggregate output and aggregate man hours can be related by aggregate coefficients. Ignoring subscripts, (4) can be rewritten as:

$$Y = \gamma\, KuKs \tag{6}$$

or

$$Y = \gamma\, (KuKs)^{\alpha}\, (KuKs)^{1-\alpha} \tag{7}$$

substituting (5) into (7) we get

$$Y = \gamma\rho^{\alpha-1}\, (KuKs)^{\alpha}\, (LuLs)^{1-\alpha} \tag{8}$$

which is Cobb-Douglas with constant returns to scale.
The weakness of this derivation is that any value of $\alpha$ should satisfy (8) and yet empirically $\alpha$ always seems to approximate to 0.3 – capital's share in national output. One possible reason for this might be that if (9) is estimated as:

$$Y = A(KsKu)^{\alpha}\, (LsLu)^{1-\alpha} \tag{9}$$

then $\gamma\rho^{\alpha-1}$ is contrained to be a constant.

For any particular machine or, on our assumptions, any given group of machines, the coefficients are indeed fixed but over a cross section of machines or over time when new machines will be added and old ones abandoned there will be changes in $\rho$ and $\gamma$. Taking the simplest possible case where both coefficients follow an exponential growth path we have:

$$\rho = e^{nt} \tag{10}$$

$$\gamma = e^{mt} \tag{11}$$

Now in order for $\gamma\rho^{\alpha-1}$ to be constant $e^{(m-(1-\alpha)n)t}$ = constant

or

$$(1-\alpha)n = m \tag{12}$$

or

$$(1-\alpha) = \frac{m}{n}$$

That is to say $(1-\alpha)$ is determined by the proportionate rates of growth of output, labour and capital. This is similar to Mendeihausen's (1938) comment on the Cobb-Douglas function that linear time trends in variables gives rise to spurious results. However, detrended variables seem to work equally well. The CES function can be similarly derived.
From (5) we have

$$Y^{\theta} = \gamma^{\theta}\, (KsKu)^{\theta}$$

or

$$Y^{\theta} = \gamma^{\theta}\, \{\delta(KsKu)^{\theta} + (1-\delta)\,(KsKu)\}^{\theta} \tag{13}$$

and substituting (5) we have:

$$Y^{\theta} = \gamma^{\theta} \{\delta(KsKu)^{\theta} + (1-\delta)\rho^{-\theta}(LsLu)\} \tag{14}$$

which is CES with constant return to scale.

Given then that we live in a clay-clay or putty-clay world, the use of Cobb-Douglas or CES functions to summarise production data may be successful if the underlying distribution of coefficients is Pareto or if the proportionate rates of growth are constant. Should the success of such functions be due solely to the omission of capital utilisation figures we would expect their introduction radically to alter the estimates.

The paucity of our data constrained us to examine the simplest possible functions with the most tractable error structures. Thus we chose a Cobb-Douglas function with an exponential error term and with labour and capital exogenous.

$$Y = A(K)^{\alpha} (LuLs)^{\beta} e^{u} \tag{15}$$

or

$$Y = A(KsKu)^{\alpha} (LsLu)^{\beta} e^{u} \tag{16}$$

or

$$Y = AKs^{\alpha 1} Ku^{\alpha 2} Ls^{\beta 1} Lu^{\beta 2} e^{u} \tag{17}$$

or

$$Y = AKs^{\alpha 1} Ls^{\beta 1} Lu^{\beta 2} e^{u} \tag{18}$$

The first equation (15), from which capital utilisation is omitted, is the usually estimated form of the function. The second introduces capital utilisation but imposes perfect substitutability between capital stock and capital usage on the one hand and between labour stock and labour usage on the other. The third releases the function from these substitutability constraints and the fourth is an attempt to match the equation used by Feldstein (1967) when investigating the differences between men and hours in the production process. The same equations were estimated with a time trend to capture technical progress and we have then eight equations in all.

Our results together with an account of the data, are given in Table 9.1. They are very mixed; often none of the forms offered is satisfactory – yielding significant negative coefficients.

Paper and printing and iron and steel meet with some success for the standard forms (equations 15) and this success is not disrupted by the introduction of a capital utilisation variable. Equations of a more general form do not yield sensible results – coefficients are often negative and very sensitive to the introduction of a time trend. For chemicals the

TABLE 9.1 Regression results for different Cobb-Douglas production functions

(a) *Paper and printing*

| *Const.* | *Ku* | *Ks* | *Lu* | *Ls* | *t* | $R^2$ | *D.W.* | *Equation* |
|---|---|---|---|---|---|---|---|---|
| −12.44 | – | 0.83 | 2.49 | 1.21 | – | 0.9896 | 1.24 | |
| (4.3) | – | (10.0) | (4.9) | (5.45) | – | | | (18) |
| −11.06 | – | 0.15 | 2.47 | 0.94 | 0.03 | 0.9892 | 1.31 | |
| (3.3) | – | (0.2) | (4.8) | (2.3) | (0.81) | | | |
| −9.85 | 0.11 | 0.25 | 2.3 | 0.81 | 0.03 | 0.9880 | 1.21 | |
| (1.7) | (0.3) | (0.3) | (3.1) | (1.3) | (0.7) | | | (17) |
| −10.74 | 0.15 | 0.94 | 2.30 | 1.03 | – | 0.9886 | 1.10 | |
| (1.94) | (0.4) | (3.1) | (3.1) | (1.9) | – | | | |
| −8.89 | – | 1.25 | 1.47 | | −0.02 | 0.9827 | 1.28 | |
| (2.1) | – | (1.3) | (3.27) | | (0.6) | | | (15) |
| −7.0 | – | 0.71 | 1.27 | | – | | | |
| (2.8) | – | (8.1) | (4.6) | | – | | | |
| 8.53 | 1.82 | | −4.23 | | | 0.9615 | 1.37 | |
| (1.1) | (4.6) | | (0.5) | | – | | | (16) |
| −2.30 | 0.26 | | 0.75 | | 0.02 | 0.9801 | 1.27 | |
| (0.4) | (0.5) | | (1.1) | | (3.4) | | | |

(b) *Chemicals*

| *Const.* | *Ku* | *Ks* | *Lu* | *Ls* | *t* | $R^2$ | *D.W.* | *Equation* |
|---|---|---|---|---|---|---|---|---|
| 22.17 | – | 0.80 | −2.45 | −1.35 | – | 0.9847 | 2.03 | |
| (3.4) | – | (7.2) | (2.2) | (2.8) | – | | | (18) |
| 10.8 | – | 0.01 | −0.75 | −0.58 | 0.05 | 0.9856 | 1.67 | |
| (1.0) | – | (0.02) | (0.4) | (0.7) | (1.3) | | | |
| 13.3 | 0.63 | 0.62 | −1.1 | −0.76 | – | 0.9916 | 1.71 | |
| (2.4) | (3.0) | (6.2) | (1.2) | (1.9) | – | | | (17) |
| 11.4 | 0.60 | 0.47 | −0.84 | −0.63 | 0.01 | 0.9907 | 1.61 | |
| (1.3) | (2.4) | (0.9) | (0.6) | (1.0) | (0.3) | | | |
| 17.0 | – | 0.91 | −1.34 | | – | 0.9844 | 1.70 | |
| (3.8) | – | (17.6) | (2.7) | | – | | | (15) |
| 9.5 | – | −0.2 | −0.52 | | 0.06 | 0.9870 | 1.62 | |
| (1.6) | – | (0.05) | (0.8) | | (1.8) | | | |
| 11.4 | 0.65 | | −0.74 | | – | 0.993 | 1.57 | |
| (3.6) | (26.4) | | (2.1) | | – | | | (16) |
| 11.1 | 0.58 | | −0.71 | | 0.006 | 0.9924 | 1.60 | |
| (3.3) | (2.6) | | (1.9) | | (0.3) | | | |

TABLE 9.1 continued

(c) *Engineering*

| Const. | Ku | Ks | Lu | Ls | t | $R^2$ | D.W. | Equation |
|---|---|---|---|---|---|---|---|---|
| −3.1 | – | 0.72 | 0.11 | 0.56 | – | 0.9558 | 1.17 | |
| (0.6) | – | (3.6) | (0.11) | (1.3) | – | | | (18) |
| 14.8 | – | −3.00 | 2.74 | 0.47 | 0.17 | 0.9851 | 2.09 | |
| (3.9) | – | (3.6) | (3.4) | (1.8) | (4.5) | | | |
| 4.1 | 0.52 | 0.42 | −0.86 | −0.02 | – | 0.9544 | 1.10 | |
| (0.4) | (0.83) | (1.0) | (0.6) | (0.02) | – | | | (17) |
| −15.5 | −0.05 | −3.00 | 2.85 | 0.52 | 0.17 | 0.9832 | 2.16 | |
| (2.0) | (0.1) | (3.4) | (2.2) | (1.0) | (4.1) | | | |
| −4.4 | – | 0.8 | 0.48 | | – | 0.9591 | 1.03 | |
| (1.3) | – | (15.2) | (1.3) | | – | | | (15) |
| −6.6 | – | −1.71 | 0.72 | | 0.1 | 0.9763 | 1.53 | |
| (2.4) | – | (2.0) | (2.4) | | (3.0) | | | |
| 1.92 | 0.55 | | −0.20 | | – | 0.9601 | 0.83 | |
| (0.5) | (15.4) | | (0.5) | | – | | | (16) |
| −6.92 | −0.15 | | 0.75 | | 0.04 | 0.9669 | 1.30 | |
| (1.2) | (0.4) | | (1.2) | | (1.8) | | | |

(d) *Food, etc.*

| Const. | Ku | Ks | Lu | Ls | t | $R^2$ | D.W. | Equation |
|---|---|---|---|---|---|---|---|---|
| 7.03 | – | 0.47 | −0.52 | −0.002 | – | 0.9972 | 1.96 | |
| (3.1) | – | (13.5) | (1.2) | (0.02) | – | | | (18) |
| 7.23 | – | 0.21 | 0.52 | 0.05 | 0.1 | 0.9971 | 1.79 | |
| (3.2) | – | (0.7) | (1.2) | (0.4) | (0.9) | | | |
| 10.64 | 0.20 | 0.43 | −0.95 | −0.36 | – | 0.9980 | 1.44 | |
| (4.2) | (2.2) | (12.5) | (2.2) | (1.9) | – | | | (17) |
| 12.0 | 0.29 | 0.75 | −1.14 | −0.47 | −0.02 | 0.9979 | 1.53 | |
| (4.0) | (2.1) | (2.0) | (2.4) | (2.0) | (0.9) | | | |
| 4.5 | – | 0.52 | 0.01 | | – | 0.9970 | 1.72 | |
| (4.3) | – | (65.4) | (0.1) | | – | | | (15) |
| 5.0 | – | 0.20 | −0.04 | | 0.01 | 0.9970 | 1.61 | |
| (4.3) | – | (0.7) | (0.3) | | (1.0) | | | |
| 11.86 | 0.44 | | −0.79 | | – | 0.9962 | 1.22 | |
| (9.8) | (58.2) | | (6.0) | | – | | | (16) |
| 7.38 | 0.14 | | −0.30 | | 0.02 | 0.9972 | 1.29 | |
| (3.2) | (1.0) | | (1.2) | | (2.2) | | | |

TABLE 9.1 continued

(e) *Iron and steel*

| *Const.* | *Ku* | *Ks* | *Lu* | *Ls* | *t* | $R^2$ | *D.W.* | *Equation* |
|---|---|---|---|---|---|---|---|---|
| −9.30 | – | 0.41 | 2.56 | 0.45 | – | 0.7183 | 1.20 | (18) |
| (2.3) | – | (4.6) | (2.4) | (1.1) | – | | | |
| −11.50 | – | −0.34 | 2.65 | 0.85 | 0.04 | 0.9121 | 2.48 | |
| (5.0) | – | (2.1) | (4.5) | (3.4) | (4.8) | | | |
| −6.80 | 0.64 | 0.33 | 2.01 | 0.47 | – | 0.8834 | 2.68 | (17) |
| (2.5) | (3.9) | (5.4) | (2.9) | (1.7) | – | | | |
| −9.76 | 0.27 | −0.14 | 2.39 | 0.73 | 0.03 | 0.9169 | 2.75 | |
| (3.7) | (1.2) | (0.6) | (3.9) | (2.8) | (2.1) | | | |
| −4.32 | – | 0.3 | 0.97 (Lu+Ls) | | – | 0.6819 | 1.04 | (15) |
| (1.6) | – | (5.1) | (3.4) | | – | | | |
| −7.38 | – | −0.46 | 1.30 (Lu+Ls) | | 0.05 | 0.8718 | 1.89 | |
| (4.1) | – | (2.5) | (6.6) | | (4.2) | | | |
| −4.03 | 0.29 (Ku+Ks) | | 0.94 (Lu+Ls) | | – | 0.8078 | 1.37 | (16) |
| (2.0) | (7.1) | | (4.3) | | – | | | |
| −5.2 | 0.11 (Ku+Ks) | | 1.07 (Lu+Ls) | | 0.01 | 0.7954 | 1.30 | |
| (1.8) | (0.3) | | (3.4) | | (0.6) | | | |

coefficients on labour are always negative which reflects the labour saving nature of investment rather than the marginal productivity of labour.

There is little evidence of technical progress as proxied by a time trend and often the introduction of time is at the expense of some other variable – usually capital. Occasionally, for example in paper and printing equation (16), the introduction of time 'improved' the coefficients on labour and capital but there seems to be no reason for accepting the general proposition that technical progress explains some part of output.

There is evidence to suggest that capital stock is not a perfect substitute for capital utilisation. Similarly labour hours is not a perfect substitute for men; in every case the elasticity of output with respect to hours was greater than that with respect to men, which conforms with Feldstein's results even when capital utilisation is introduced. Insofar as any significance can be attached to these results, they therefore allay the suspicion that the different elasticities of Feldstein arose from the omitted capital utilisation effect.

## AN ALTERNATIVE APPROACH

Describing aggregate relationships between output, capital and labour by Cobb-Douglas functions may be defensible simply as a method of summarising data or, if one of the derivations given here were accepted, on the grounds that the estimated coefficients have some analytical force in that something can be inferred about the micro relations which underlie them. The danger of using such functions simply to summarise data is that the unwary are invited by the very form of the function partially to differentiate it with respect to either capital or labour and even to give some economic significance to the results of doing so. The fact that additional capital alone can add nothing to output is lost to view. A number of less obvious pitfalls are given by Samuelson (1976).

Furthermore as a method of gaining insight into the underlying structure of the economy it is unduly restrictive. If one is interested in how aggregate coefficients change over time it would seem sensible to deal with them directly. Input-output models provide a respectable precedent for describing production processes as a list of coefficients. The slight modification to the usual input-output approach suggested here is that the common denominator of input-output coefficients (output) is replaced by a common denominator of capital coefficients (capital services). Replacing output by capital services focuses attention on the set of machines being considered rather than on any particular product or industry.

If we adopt this direct, or 'listing' approach we can compute and analyse each coefficient separately. Using our data we can derive 14 annual observations of the output-capital and the labour-capital coefficients for each of our five industry groups. The labour-capital coefficients are shown in Figs. 9.1 to 9.5.

In every case the labour/capital coefficient ($\rho$) decreases secularly as might be expected. The output-capital coefficients are shown in Figs. 9.6 to 9.10 and these on the other hand decrease over time exept for that of paper and printing. The decreasing output-capital coefficients are some what difficult to accept since it is unlikely that new capital produces less per hour than does existing stock. A possible explanation would be if capital were taking over more and more jobs previously performed by labour and for which capital is progressively less well fitted . The fluctuations in the output-capital coefficients suggest that the vintage tail of capital stock is not as stabilising as originally assumed – capital characteristics might be responding quite quickly to relative price changes. Alternatively, the assumption of uniform utilisation has to be questioned. Fluctuations in the labour-capital coefficients may arise additionally from labour hoarding which is not allowed for in our measure of labour services.

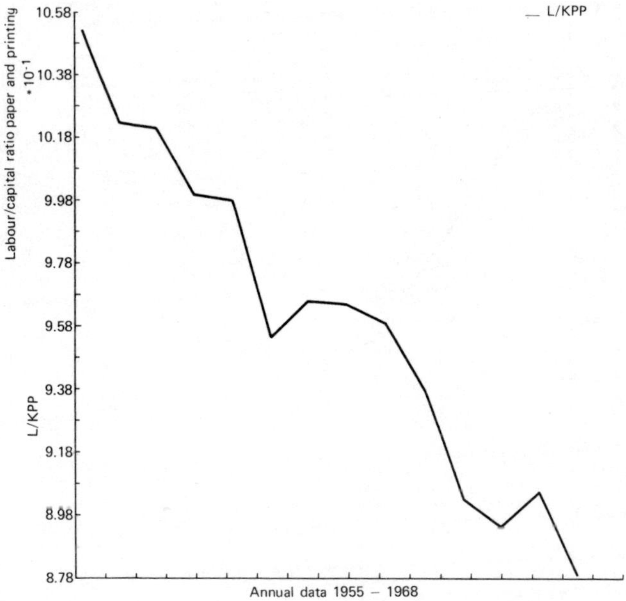


FIG. 9.1 Labour capital ratio: Paper and printing[3]

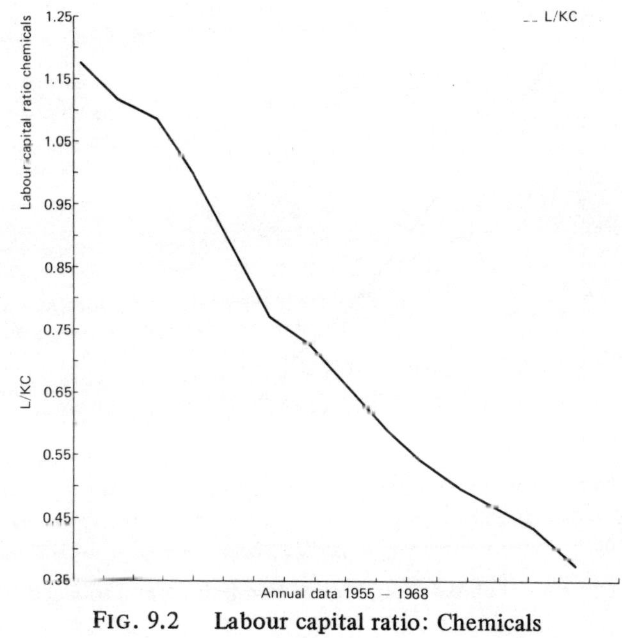


FIG. 9.2 Labour capital ratio: Chemicals

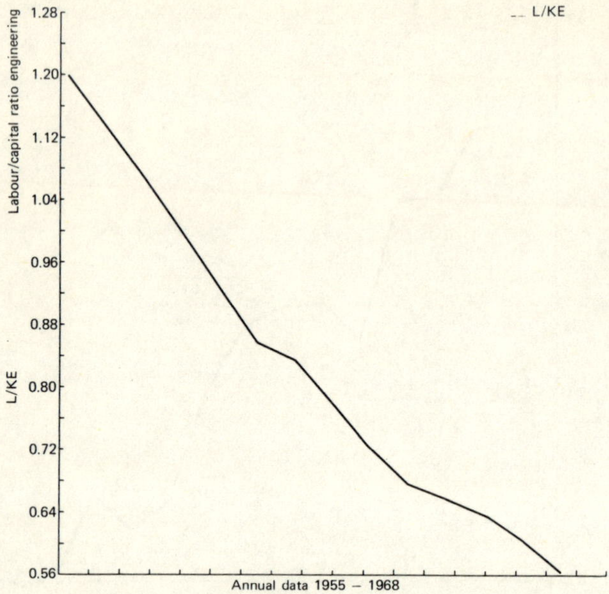


FIG. 9.3 Labour capital ratio: Engineering

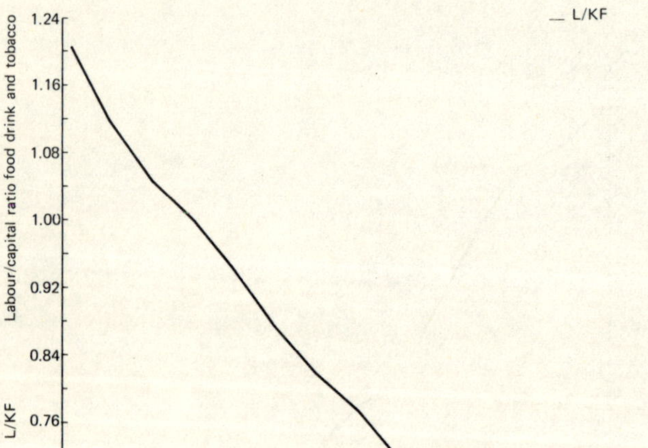


FIG. 9.4 Labour capital ratio: Food, drink and tobacco

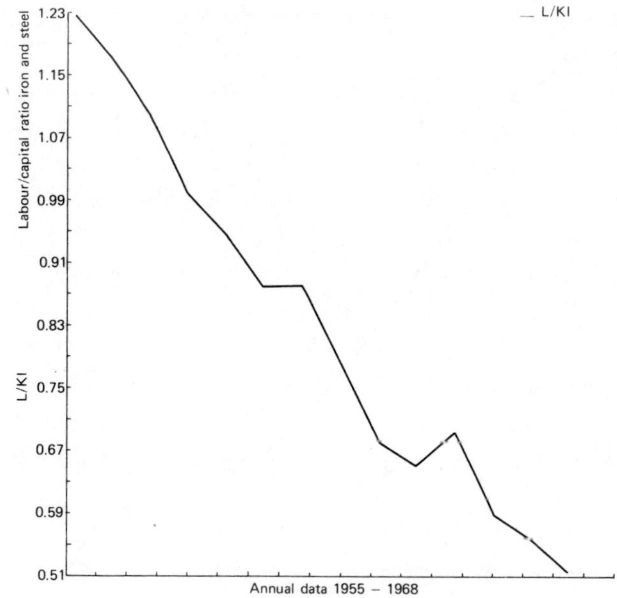


FIG. 9.5 Labour capital ratio: Iron and steel

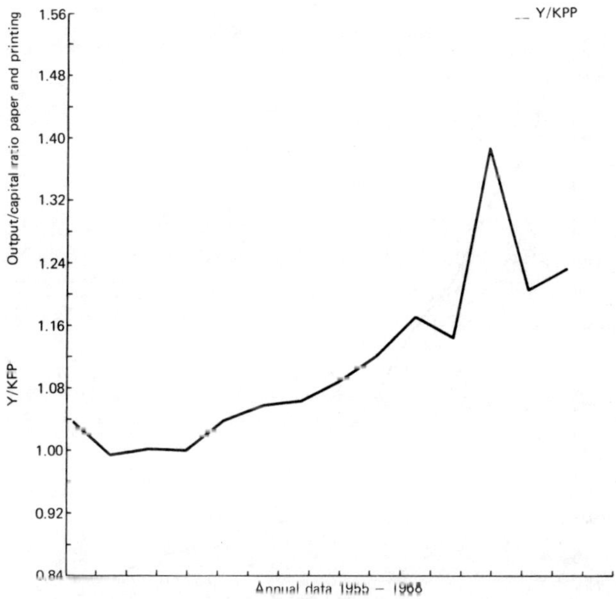


FIG. 9.6 Output capital ratio: Paper and printing

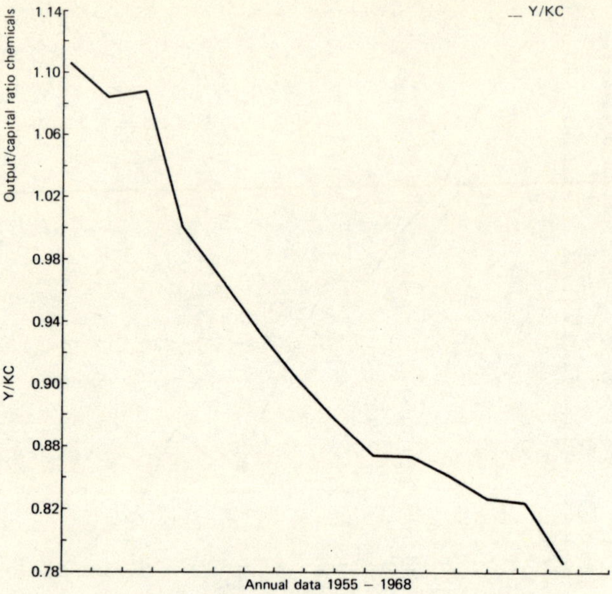


**FIG. 9.7 Output capital ratio: Chemicals**

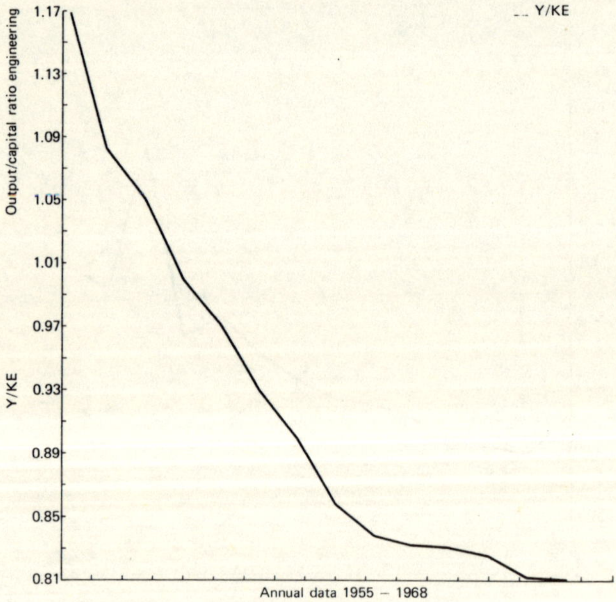


**FIG. 9.8 Output capital ratio: Engineering**

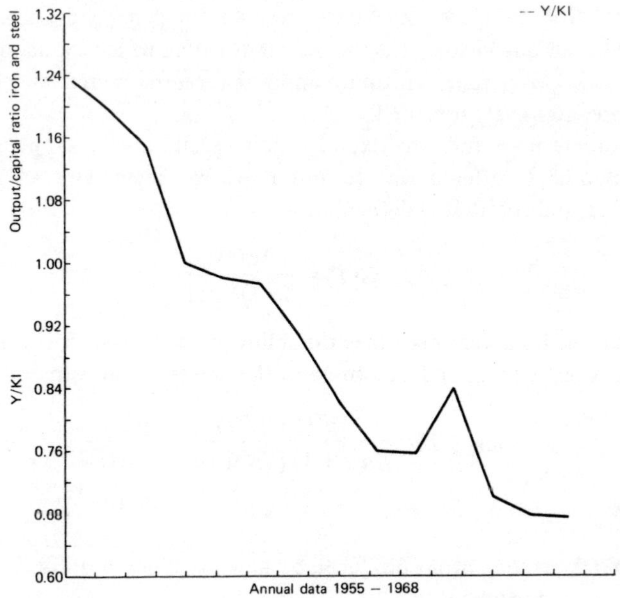


FIG. 9.9 Output capital ratio: Iron and steel

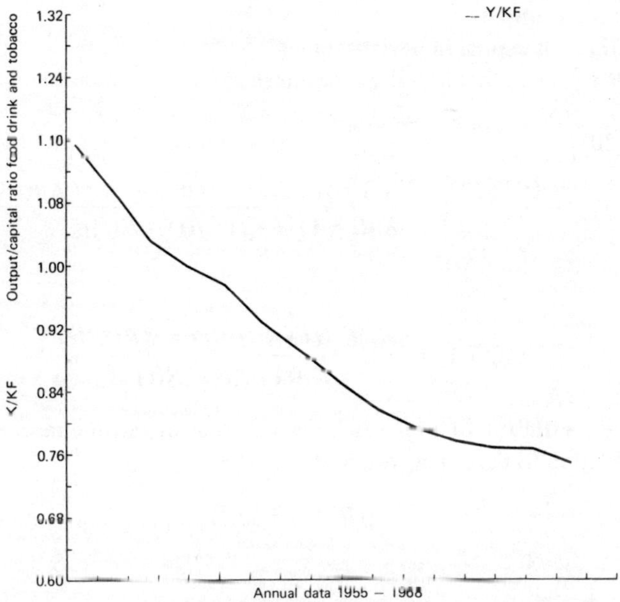


FIG. 9.10. Output capital ratio: Food, drink and tobacco

Apart from its increasing output-capital ratio, paper and printing is also the odd man out in that it is the only industry in which capital utilisation is decreasing over time. This may imply that capital is used less efficiently the more intensively it is used.

In order more fully to explore these results a very simple model is developed and 'offered up' to our data. We begin with an aggregate output-capital coefficient defined as:–

$$\gamma a(T) = \frac{Ya(t)}{Ku(t)Ks(t)} \tag{19}$$

With one-hoss-shay machines the following period will lose those machines of oldest vintage and gain those of the newest by investment.

$$\gamma a(t+1) = \frac{Ya(t) + YI(t) - YR(t)}{Ku(t+1)\{Ks(t) + I(t) - R(t)\}} \tag{20}$$

where

- $YI(t)$ is the output produced by new machines at utilisation $Ku(t+1)$
- $YR(t)$ is the output which the retired machines would have produced at utilisation $Ku(t+1)$ had they not been retired
- $I(t)$ is capital in new machines
- $R(t)$ is capital in retired machines

from (20)

$$\gamma a(t+1) = \frac{\gamma a(t)Ku(t+1)Ks(t) + \gamma(It)Ku(t+1)I(t) - \gamma(Rt)Ku(t+1)R(t)}{Ku(t+1)\{Ks(t) + I(t) - R(t)\}} \tag{21}$$

or

$$\gamma a(t+1) = \frac{\gamma a(t)Ks(t) + \gamma(It)I(t) - \gamma(Rt)R(t)}{Ks(t) + I(t) - R(t)} \tag{22}$$

Let the coefficient of new machines and that of retiring machines be in fixed relation to that of aggregate stock. Then:

$$\gamma(It) = \gamma + \gamma a(t)$$

and (23)

$$\gamma(Rt) = -\gamma + \gamma a(t)$$

Substituting (23) into (22) yields

$$\gamma a(t+1) = \frac{\gamma a(t)Ks(t) + \gamma a(t)I(t) - \gamma a(t)I(t) + \gamma(I(t) + R(t))}{Ks(t+1)} \tag{24}$$

$$\gamma a(t+1) = \gamma a(t) + \frac{\gamma I(t)}{K(t+1)} + \frac{\gamma R(t)}{K(t+1)} \tag{25}$$

If retirement can be regarded as a constant proportion of capital stock ($\delta$) we have:–

$$\gamma a(t+1) = \gamma a(t) + \gamma\delta + \frac{\gamma I(t)}{K(t+1)} \tag{26}$$

In general:

$$\gamma a(T) = \gamma ao + \gamma\delta + \gamma \sum_{o}^{T} \left\{ \frac{I(t)}{K(t+1)} \right\} \tag{27}$$

This fairly simple explanatory equation is based on some assumptions which may seem questionable[4]. In particular we assume that: (1) all machines have the same utilisation, although utilisation can be changed over time, (2) no disembodied technical progress, and (3) a fixed relation between the coefficients of old and new machines. The first two of these can be somewhat relaxed by *ad hoc* additions to equation (27). Disembodied technical change, which affects all existing machines equally, is proxied by a simple time trend. The possible variation in utilisation of different vintages is captured by including a capital utilisation term in (27). This, on the basis that, as utilisation falls, the other vintages would fall idle first and hence bias upward the aggregate coefficients. For estimation purposes this equation (27) becomes

$$\gamma a(t) = (\gamma o + \delta\gamma) + \gamma \sum_{o}^{T} \frac{I(t)}{Ks(t+1)} + \alpha_1 Ku(T) + \alpha_2 T \tag{28}$$

An exactly similar equation is used to explain the labour capital coefficient ($\rho$) which can be similarly derived. The results are shown in Table 9.2.

The most striking feature about these results is that all but one of the coefficients are negative. This implies that new machines produce less output per capital-hour and require fewer men per unit of capital than do older machines. It is difficult unambiguously to regard this as technical progress since similar results would be obtained by simply substituting labour for capital. In the language of neoclassical production functions, entrepreneurs, when choosing new machines from an *ex-ante* production

TABLE 9.2 Regression results for a simple model

| | *Const.* | $\Sigma I/\Sigma K$ | *t* | *Ku* | $R^2$ | *D.W.* |
|---|---|---|---|---|---|---|
| (a) *Paper* | | | | | | |
| $\gamma$ | 147 | −0.79 | −2.0 | −0.14 | 0.9293 | 1.95 |
| | (7.0) | (2.8) | (5.8) | (0.7) | | |
| $\rho$ | 1253 | −1.43 | −153 | −2371 | 0.9601 | 1.41 |
| | (11.6) | (0.1) | (8.6) | (2.3) | | |
| (b) *Chemicals* | | | | | | |
| $\gamma$ | 200 | −0.46 | −1.65 | −39.3 | 0.9422 | 0.97 |
| | (4.1) | (2.3) | (2.1) | (1.4) | | |
| $\rho$ | 25889 | −58.1 | −422 | −860 | 0.9800 | 0.61 |
| | (3.6) | (2.0) | (3.6) | (2.1) | | |
| (c) *Engineering* | | | | | | |
| $\gamma$ | 2.02 | −0.0019 | −0.0085 | −0.65 | 0.9086 | 1.25 |
| | (4.3) | (1.0) | (1.1) | (2.3) | | |
| $\rho$ | 21811 | −24.0 | −288 | −7240 | 0.9856 | 1.30 |
| | (6.6) | (1.8) | (5.3) | (3.5) | | |
| (d) *Food* | | | | | | |
| $\gamma$ | 239 | −1.20 | −2.00 | −73.6 | 0.9983 | 1.75 |
| | (27.0) | (6.1) | (29.0) | (12.5) | | |
| $\rho$ | 23084 | −107 | −386 | −7309 | 0.9978 | 1.45 |
| | (15.0) | (3.1) | (32.1) | (7.1) | | |
| (e) *Iron and steel* | | | | | | |
| $\gamma$ | 153 | −0.50 | −0.432 | −5.72 | 0.9538 | 2.05 |
| | (3.7) | (2.6) | (13.5) | (0.2) | | |
| $\rho$ | 17501 | −47.2 | −527 | −3210 | 0.9868 | 1.64 |
| | (6.4) | (3.8) | (25.3) | (1.7) | | |

function are substituting capital for labour. This represents movement along an isoquant rather than movement of an isoquant.

The time trend, which was introduced as a proxy for disembodied technical progress, again suggests that what changes there are in the coefficients of existing machines are not due to technical progress. The falling output-capital ratio may be due to wear and tear eroding the productive potential of capital and thus brings into question our one-hoss-shay assumption. The falling labour requirement of existing machines may suggest some organisational improvements or even the possibility of some *ex-post* flexibility in labour-capital ratios.

The existence or otherwise of technical progress is not clarified by the estimated Cobb-Douglas functions, none of which seems particularly to suggest that time is a sensible variable to include in these functions. It is often insignificant and usually enters at the expense of some other variable – typically capital.

It may well be that the widely held view that technical progress is both capital and labour saving may have arisen from output-capital stock data with no allowance being made for utilisation.

The capital utilisation term was included to capture the effects of changing the composition of active capital stock in the face of demand variations – older machines were expected to be laid off before new ones if demand fell. This would suggest that falling utilisation would have an effect similar to that of investment. In this case, falling utilisation would lower both the output-capital ratio and the labour-capital ratio. The negative coefficients found here suggest otherwise. The rising labour-capital ratio may be explained in terms of labour hoarding. There is plenty of evidence to suggest that labour is not dismissed when demand is felt to be temporarily low. If this is so then the case for laying off older machines before new ones is also weakened. The labour has to be paid and hence there is no saving by shutting down relatively labour using machines. Assuming uniform capital utilisation may be quite reasonable. It may further follow that as the amount of hoarded labour increases, those machines which are operated can be operated more efficiently – either by using more labour per machine hour or by having the slack to choose the most appropriate machines for the task.

In general, the explanatory power of these equations is high, although Durbin-Watson statistics suggest some misspecification. With rather more data, it may be possible to test a less naïve model. Perhaps this is enough to suggest that dealing directly with output-capital, labour-capital ratios is a profitable method of approaching production problems.

## CONCLUSIONS

We have attempted in this paper to make use of capital utilisation data to throw some light on the relation between aggregate output and aggregate inputs into five UK industries. Though now largely discredited as anything more than a data describing device having little analytical value, the Cobb-Douglas function, if fitted to aggregate data, can imply something about the underlying micro relations. Apart from the dangers of interpreting a distribution as a functional relationship, this device is unduly restrictive and can be made to conform to at least three different micro worlds. A more natural and less restrictive approach would seem to be to deal directly with the input/output/capital coefficients and seek to explain how those of aggregate processes change over time. The case for moving directly to these coefficients is reinforced in this paper by the failure of the Cobb-Douglas to explain the aggregate data used. Explanations of changes in aggregate coefficients were more successful (though not without puzzles). We ought to add that not too much can be made of the empirical evidence submitted since there are so few data upon which to base any rigorous tests or alternative model specifications. The evidence is offered in the spirit of suggesting what might profitably be done now that the aggregate production function is becoming less acceptable.

## NOTES

This is a revised version of a paper presented to the Southampton Conference on the Measurement of Capital, 14–16 July 1976.

1. I have been unable to discover if Solow (1967) fulfilled his expressed intention of introducing capital utilisation into his models.
2. The capital stock figures were supplied by Alan Armstrong, University of Bristol. Labour and output figures were supplied by the Southampton Econometric Model Building Unit. The equations were estimated using an OLS program developed as part of HASH – a general program due to Tim Harrison.
3. These graphs plotted using a program SLIDE developed by S. P. Chakravarty, University of Southampton.
4. They are not, however, as strong as those necessary to deal with aggregate production functions in a putty-putty world. See Fisher (1969).

## REFERENCES

Aberg, Y. (1964), *The Effects of Reductions in Hours of Work*, SOU. As reviewed in Osterberg (1964).

Brown, M., Sato, K. and Zarembka, P. (eds.), (1976), *Essays in Modern Capital Theory* (Amsterdam: North Holland).

Feldstein, M. S., (1967), 'Specification of the Labour Input in the Aggregate Production Function', *Review of Economic Studies*, vol. 34.

Fisher, F. M. (1969), 'The Existence of Aggregate Production Functions', *Econometrica*, vol. 37.

Foss, M. (1963), 'The Utilisation of Capital Equipment', *Survey of Current Business*, vol. 43.

Heathfield, D. F. (1972), 'The Measurement of Capital Usage Using Electricity Consumption Data for the U.K.', *Journal of the Royal Statistical Society*, vol. 135.

Heathfield, D. F. (1976), 'Capital Utilisation', Paper presented at the *Colloque International, Le Capital dans le Fonction de Production*, Paris, November.

Houthakker, J. (1955–56), 'The Pareto Distribution and the Cobb-Douglas Production Function in Activity Analysis', *Review of Economic Studies*, vol. 23.

Johansen, L. (1972), *Production Functions* (Amsterdam: North Holland).

Marris, R. (1964), *The Economics of Capacity Utilisation*, (Cambridge University Press).

Menderhausen, J. (1938), 'On the Significance of Professor Douglas' Production Function', *Econometrica*, vol. 6.

Osterberg, G. (1964), 'The Effects of Reductions in the Hours of Work – A Review Article', *Economisk Tidskrift*, vol. 66.

Samuelson, P. A. (1976), 'Interest Rate Determinations and Oversimplifying Parables : A Summing Up' in Brown, Sato and Zarembka (eds.) (see above).

Solow, R. M. (1967), 'Heterogeneous Capital and Smooth Production Functions: An Experimental Study', *Econometrica*.

Winston, G. C. and McCoy, T. O. (1974), 'Investment and the Optimal Idleness of Capital', *Review of Economic Studies*, vol. 41.

# 10 Capital Stock, Capital Services and the Use of Fuel Consumption Proxies: An Appraisal

DEREK L. BOSWORTH
*Loughborough University of Technology*

## 1 INTRODUCTION

It has become fashionable in the recent economic literature to use electricity data as proxy for the consumption of capital services. Taylor (1967), for example, reported a high correlation across regions of the UK between electricity consumption and the stock of active capital. Heathfield (1972) has compared the consumption of electricity with the stock of capital in an attempt to derive measures of capital usage. Heathfield adopted the book value of the capital stock as a measure of the potential supply of capital services. More recently still, Moody (1974) and Bosworth (1974, 1976) have estimated neoclassical production functions using fuel proxies for the capital input. After comparing the results of using a traditional measure of the capital input with those of a proxy variable, Moody was able to conclude that electricity consumption was a better measure of the capital input than the book value of the capital stock.

Given the current popularity of the fuel proxies, it seems an opportune time to consider a number of very important problems associated with such measures. The next section considers whether, because fuel can be measured in its own technical units (i.e., therms) which are independent of prices, the 'measurement of capital problem' is avoided? The third section of this paper attempts to emphasise that the underlying technology of production (about which we have scant knowledge at the present time) is central to our understanding and interpretation of any empirical results.

The fourth section reviews a number of problems of measurement and misspecification that have arisen in the literature and which form potential problems to the general approach. The problems discussed in this paper are associated both with the use of fuel proxies for the input of capital services into the production process and with the measurement of capital usage. A general conclusion is that, while fuel consumption proxies have certain attributes which favour their usage, they are associated with new problems that in turn require solutions.

The final section of this paper reports some early results arising from an empirical investigation of the relationship between fuel consumption and the capital input. They are preliminary in several senses. First, new measures of fuel consumption by type of fuel and by industry are currently being produced and are nearing completion. The new data will be for manufacturing industries at the level of aggregation used in the Cambridge Growth Model. Second, not all of the links between fuel and capital suggested in the earlier theoretical sections have been investigated and it seems sensible at this stage to await the completion of the new data. Finally, a more rigorous investigation of the usefulness of matching certain types of fuel with certain types of capital requires further econometric sophistication that has not been attempted to date (e.g. in particular more rigorous comparisons entail nesting the alternative specifications).

## 2. THE MEASUREMENT OF CAPITAL PROBLEM

In principle, the measurement of the input of capital services presents no problem: we require a measure, $K$, in physical units of the amount of capital 'used up' in the production of output over some stated period. This is inserted into a production relationship,

$$Y = f(K, L)$$

in order to determine the marginal physical products of capital and labour and thereby the distributive shares of capital and labour. Where such a measure exists, if we believe in the neoclassical postulate, then we have a concise and elegant theory of production and distribution.

The problem has been that capital is measured in value terms in empirical studies. Value in this instance is calculated as the price that must be paid to purchase a machine (or, more accurately, the lifetime of services that it promises to yield) multiplied by the number of machines bought. Joan Robinson (1970) has called the use of this measure of capital 'the strangest part of the whole affair'. While the value of capital may be a useful measure of the store of wealth, it is unlikely to play a meaningful role in the empirical analysis of production or distribution. To the neoclassicist, the value of capital is the value of the marginal physical product of capital multiplied by the physical quantity of capital. Under competitive conditions, the value of the marginal physical product of capital is the marginal physical product multiplied by the going price of final output. The marginal physical product, however, is obtained by estimating the production relationship and is not available for use in estimating the production function. Without a physical measure of the capital input, the neoclassicist cannot estimate a production relationship and, in turn, cannot calculate the value of capital. The traditionally accepted route around these problems – in this case to assume that capital is paid the value of its marginal product – is still open. The price to which we refer in this instance, however, is not the purchase price associated with securing the machine's lifetime services, but the rental that the producer would have to pay under competitive conditions to secure the machine's services during a single production period.

Fuel consumption appears to offer a way out of this dilemma: it can be measured in its own technical units and we might expect there to be a relationship between the physical stock of capital in active use and the amount of fuel consumed. If, for the sake of argument, we assume the existence of a homogeneous stock of capital whose physical volume, $K$, cannot be measured, we might write,

$$F = a(KU) \tag{1}$$

where $F$ denotes the fuel consumed in powering the capital actually used in production, $KU$. This variable is formed by weighting the physical stock of capital, $K$, by the degree to which it is utilised, $U$. $Y$ denotes the output produced during the period and the technically fixed link between fuel consumption and the utilised part of the capital stock is summarised by the constant $a$. Hence, the functional relationship,

$$Y = f(K,L) \tag{2}$$

can be written,

$$Y = f(a,F,L) = g(F,L) \tag{3}$$

and wherever $f(\ )$ has neoclassical properties, so too will $g(\ )$. A fixed, 'technical' relationship such as equation (1), however, is only one of a number of alternatives. Later in this paper we turn to the question of technical changes in the fuel-capital link and also the possibility that fuel and capital are themselves substitutes in the production process.

The problem has more serious aspects which are not quite so easily resolved. Today few economists would claim that the traditional assumptions that underlie the neoclassical model are realistic. It is more widely claimed that the real world behaves 'as if' it is consistent with a neoclassical technology, but the approach has foundered on the difficulties of explaining why the real world behaves in this way.

The concept of the surrogate production function is the principle theoretical justification for the neoclassical production function. Samuelson (1962) attempted to demonstrate that a world characterised by heterogeneous capital goods would re-arrange itself under forces of competition to look 'as if' it was neoclassical when in long-run equilibrium. Other authors, including Garegnani (1970) and Robinson (1970), have since proved that the Samuelson case is a special one. Only where the measure of capital is independent of prices and distribution does the Samuelson approach work, and even the dynamics of the adjustment to long-run equilibrium have been overlooked. Until recently, capital has invariably been measured in value terms. The potentially diverse time patterns of inputs and outputs in a world of heterogeneous capital goods can result in the phenomena of reswitching and reversing, and the surrogate concept offers no rigorous theoretical justification for production functions whose capital is measured in value terms.

In a more recent article, Sato (1974) has claimed that the 'neoclassical postulate' (i.e., that higher wage/rental ratios are associated with higher capital to labour ratios) can be saved even in a world of heterogeneous capital goods. This variation on the surrogate theme assumed that: (a) capital is measured in units independent of prices and distribution; (b) technologies are chosen from a book of 'blue prints' whose surface is well behaved for some sub-set of technologies. On the basis of these assumptions, the 'neoclassical postulate' could be shown to be valid whenever the elasticity of substitution of the 'blue print' surface was not greater than unity. Removal of the assumption that capital is measured in units independent of prices and distribution causes the explanation to collapse (because the technology frontier and iso-*r* surface are then no longer independent of one another) and the problems of reversing and reswitching return. For this reason the Sato approach is also incapable of providing a rigorous theoretical under-pinning for the empirical estimates of neoclassical production functions that measure capital in value terms.

Proponents of fuel consumption proxies might argue that, because fuel can be measured in its own physical units (i.e., therms), then we may be more confident in the results obtained when using a fuel consumption proxy than those obtained when using the value of capital as long as the relationship between fuel consumption and capital utilisation is fully understood. Fuel consumption measures obviously comply with the requirement – see Solow (1956, p. 101) – that identical plants, used at the same level of intensity, should have the same capital rating. On the other hand, it is also true that quite different plants, (i.e., with different mixes of heterogeneous captial goods) might have the same thermal consumptions. In so far as the capital stock of the real world is heterogeneous and there are a great variety of fuel-capital links, the fuel consumption proxy may further complicate matters without really improving our understanding of the technical production relationship.

## 3 THE CAPITAL-FUEL LINK

Even if we assume a homogeneous stock of capital and a simple link between fuel and capital, the use of fuel based proxy for the capital input raises several important theoretical and practical problems even where the underlying technology of production is of the simple Cobb-Douglas form. It is fairly easy to demonstate that the coefficients from the production function and the capital-fuel relationship become inextricably interwined in a reduced form which is under-identified. This raises important questions of interpretation of any empirical results.

### TECHNICAL FUEL CAPITAL RELATIONSHIP

Economists who have advocated the use of fuel proxies have tended to treat the fuel-capital link as a purely technical relationship. There are practical reasons for doing so. We follow through the implications of a purely technical link firstly, in the case of a simple Cobb-Douglas function and secondly, for a vintage Cobb-Douglas form. The final part of this section treats fuel as a substitute for capital and labour and analyses the resulting form to be estimated.

(i) *Cobb-Douglas* It is assumed that underlying technology of production can be written as,

$$Y_t = A_o e^{gt} K_t^{\alpha} L_t^{\beta} \tag{4}$$

where $A$, $g$ $\alpha$ and $\beta$ are technically determined constants, $t$ is a time trend and $Y$ denotes value added. Technical progress is assumed to fall like 'manna from heaven' over time at a constant rate, $g$, on all production units. The analogous fuel-capital link might take the form,

$$F_t = F_o e^{-ht} K_t \tag{5}$$

Substituting for $K$ in the Cobb-Douglas function, yields,

$$Y_t = \frac{A_o e^{(g+h\alpha)t}}{F_o^\alpha} F_t^\alpha L_t^\beta \tag{6}$$

$$= B e^{qt} F_t^\alpha L_t^\beta \tag{7}$$

where, $B = (A_o/F_o^\alpha)$ and $q = g + h\alpha$. In trying to estimate this function on the basis of time series information, Moody (1974) found both the constant and time coefficient difficult to interpret. In cross-sectional studies only $C$, $(C = Be^{qt})$, can be distinguished and not $A_o$ $F_o$, $g$ or $h$.

If autonomously given information about the values of $F_o$ and $h$ were available, it would obviously be possible to separate $A$ and $g$. The time trend $g$, is probably the more important of these two. Where pooled time series and cross-sectional information are available, it may be possible to separate the parameters of the production function from those of the fuel-capital link on the assumption that $g$ and $h$ are constant across firms and over time. Estimating the function cross-sectionally for a number of years in turn, we can obtain a time series of observations of $B_t$ and $\alpha_t$. Hence, from

$$B_t = \frac{A_o e^{(g+\alpha h)t}}{F_o^\alpha} \tag{8}$$

we can obtain,

$$\log D_t = g + d\ (\alpha_{t-1} - \alpha_t) + h(\alpha_t t - \alpha_{t-1}(t-1)) \tag{9}$$

where, $\log D_t = \log\ (B_t/B_{t-1})$ and $d = \log F_o$. If, as equation (4) implies, $\alpha_t = \alpha_{t-1}$ for all $t$, then $\log D_t = g + \alpha h$ and the two growth rates cannot be separated. Given a sufficient number of cross-sectional estimates and a sufficient variation in $\alpha$ over time, $g$, $h$ and $F_o$ could be estimated using this two-stage procedure, on the basis of the rate of change information. There is no possibility of knowing whether econometric problems (e.g. multi-collinearity) will allow the coefficient to be estimated.

(ii) *Vintage Cobb-Douglas* Once we move into a vintage world, even of the simple Solow (1961) – Phelps (1962) kind, the possibility of estimating $g$ and $h$ as well as the normal production coefficients $\alpha$ and $\beta$ become even more remote. Allen (1968, pp. 281–304) has shown that we can form an aggregate Cobb-Doublas function of the form,

$$Y_t = A_o e^{g'\alpha t} K_t^{\alpha} L_t^{1-\alpha} \tag{10}$$

where $g' = g\{(1-\alpha)/\alpha\}$, on the assumption of a cost minimising allocation of labour to fixed stocks of capital according to the following technology of production,

$$Y_{vt} = Ae^{gv} K_v^{\alpha} L_{vt}^{1-\alpha} \tag{11}$$

where $v$ denotes the $v$th vintage of capital. To obtain this function, capital is assumed to be extremely long-lived with no depreciation and measured as,

$$K_t = \int_{-\infty}^{t} e^{-g'(t-v)} K_v dv \tag{12}$$

If we adopt the fuel proxy:

$$F_t = F_o e^{-hv} K_v \tag{13}$$

then substitution into equation (12) yields,

$$K_t = \frac{1}{F_o} e^{-g't} \int_{-\infty}^{t} e^{(g'-h)v} F_v dv \tag{14}$$

Except for the constant $F_o$, the production function to be estimated remains as before. If an 'errors in measurement' problem is to be avoided when aggregating, the two rates of technical change, (or some knowledge of their combined size), must be available before the function can be estimated.

## NEOCLASSICAL SUBSTITUTION AND THE FUEL-CAPITAL RELATIONSHIP

The neoclassical technology with its implied substitution between capital and labour in the generation of value added, appears intuitively inconsistent with a purely technical link between capital and fuel. It might be more consistent with traditions of a neoclassical theory to write,

$$Y' = Ae^{gt} K^{\alpha} L^{\beta} F^{\delta} R^{\theta} \tag{15}$$

where $Y'$ denotes the gross value of output; $R$ denotes the input of raw materials; $A$, $g$, $\alpha$, $\beta$, $\delta$ and $\theta$ are technically determined constants. Time subscripts are omitted for simplicity in exposition. On the basis of the cost function:

$$C = rK + WL + xF + zR \tag{16}$$

where $r$, $w$, $x$ and $z$ denote cost per unit of the associated factor, cost minimisation yields the following link between capital and fuel,

$$K = \frac{\alpha}{\delta}\frac{x}{r}F \tag{17}$$

Assuming that the raw material and fuel inputs can be appropriately purged from $Y'$, we have

$$Y = A_o e^{gt} K^{\alpha} L^{\beta} \tag{18}$$

and substitution of the fuel proxy for $K$ in (18) yields,

$$Y = A_o e^{gt} \left(\frac{\alpha}{\delta}\right)\left(\frac{x}{r}\right)^{\alpha} F^{\alpha} L^{\beta} \tag{19}$$

$x$ and $r$ may vary across industries and over time. Hence, the use of a simple fuel proxy, $F$, for the capital input, $K$, will be associated with an omitted variable problem.

It can be shown that Moody (1974) quite unintentionally goes some way to removing this problem. So long as the fuel-capital relationship, equation (17), applies at all levels of capital usage (in particular, full capacity $K = \tilde{K}$, where $\tilde{K}$ denotes the maximum input of capital services which are available), then the adjustment of $F$ by $(\tilde{K}/\tilde{F})$ goes some way towards accounting for the omitted variable $x/r$. From equation (17) we can write,

$$\frac{\tilde{K}}{\tilde{F}} = \frac{\alpha}{\delta}\frac{x}{r} \tag{20}$$

and hence, weighting $F$ by $(\tilde{K}/\tilde{F})$ to give $F'$ is equivalent to allowing for variations in the factor price ratio. Hence, estimating

$$Y = A_o e^{gt} F'^{\alpha} L^{\beta} \tag{21}$$

should enable $A_o$ and $g$ to be separately identified and equation (21) to be free from the omitted variable problem. If, as is more usual, there is only a limited number of observations of $(\tilde{K}/\tilde{F})$ available, the adjustment is incomplete and we replace an omitted variable problem by an 'errors of measurement' problem.

## 4 SOME OTHER PROBLEMS

This section looks at a number of problems of measurement and specification found in the literature on the fuel-capital relationship. The discussion centres on the use of different types of fuel to represent different types of capital stock. In more realistic (but generally less elegant) production functions than, for example, the two factor input Cobb-Douglas case, more than one type of capital may be separately distinguished. It may be even more important to distinguish different types of capital where fuel proxies for the capital input are used, because different types of capital may – as Adams and Miovic (1968) point out – differ in the efficiency with which they utilise the calorific content of fuels. Hence, unweighted aggregation of thermal consumption may lead to an 'error of measurement' problem.

This is fairly closely related to a problem faced by Heathfield (1972) and Moody (1974). They use electricity consumption as a proxy for capital usage and capital services respectively. Electricity consumption data is both readily available and not faced by problems of measurement caused by changing fuel inventories. However, electricity represents only a part of the total thermal consumption of fuels used in powering the capital stock. Moody ignored the possible consequences of this mismatch between electricity and the total stock of capital. In an attempt to avoid the problem, Heathfield chose to match electricity consumption with the stock of plant and machinery.

Tables 10.1 and 10.2 give some insights about the problems of matching capital types with the different fuels. Although it is not ideal, the only information we have about the stocks of various types of capital is in 1963 constant replacement prices. It is fairly obvious from the tables that there

TABLE 10.1 Thermal consumptions by fuel type within engineering

| *in £m.* | *1958* | *1963* | *1968* | *1973* |
|---|---|---|---|---|
| Coal | 999 | 825 | 602 | 510 |
| Coke | 322 | 250 | 124 | 95 |
| Gas | 403 | 440 | 512 | 1077 |
| Electricity | 382 | 513 | 622 | 782 |
| Petroleum | 677 | 1213 | 1781 | 1769 |
| Other liquids | 20 | 21 | 6 | 2 |
| *All fuels* | 2803 | 3262 | 3647 | 4235 |

*Source*: Power Digest

TABLE 10.2 Value of the capital stock by type (1963 constant replacement cost).

| *in £m.* | *1958* | *1963* | *1968* | *1973* |
|---|---|---|---|---|
| Plant and machinery | 4.96 | 5.83 | 6.87 | 7.74 |
| Vehicles | 0.15 | 0.12 | 0.16 | 0.23 |
| Buildings | 2.59 | 3.05 | 3.53 | 3.96 |
| *Total* | 7.70 | 9.00 | 10.56 | 11.93 |

*Source*: National Income and Expenditure Accounts

is no simple aggregation of fuel types that match the different stocks of capital that are distinguished. Electricity represents 18.46 per cent of total thermal consumption in 1973, but plant and machinery form 64.87 per cent of total capital stock. The discrepancy between these two proportions is partly explained by the fact that different types of capital have a different fuel-capital link. There is the additional problem that electricity is not the only fuel consumed in powering plant and machinery; for example, several other types of fuel might be used in heating furnaces.

## 5 SOME PRELIMINARY RESULTS

Problems of mismatching fuels with types of plant must be borne in mind. Nevertheless, it may still be realistic to expect electricity consumption to move more closely with the usage of plant and machinery than, say, total fuel consumption. In a similar way, we might expect petroleum (which includes motor vehicle fuels and derv consumption) to be more closely related to the usage of vehicles than are other types of fuels. A rigorous test of this hypothesis must wait until a later date. At this stage we simply begin by investigating some of the alternative relationships between the various types of fuels consumed and the different types of capital in use.

The results of estimating simple linear and log-linear relationships between fuel consumption and the stocks of machine tools are shown in Table 10.3. Information about the numbers of machine tools held by various MLHs is taken from *Production Engineering's* 'Survey of Machine Tools'. Results are given for 1961, 1966 and 1971, which are the years for which machine tool data are available. In addition, the regressions are repeated: first, relating total thermal consumption of all fuels, $F$, to the stocks of machine tools; and second, relating the thermal consumption of electricity to the stocks of machine tools. As we might expect, MLHs

TABLE 10.3 Regression results for the fuel consumption – machine tool relationships.

| *Year* | *Functional form* | $f_0$ | $f_1$ | $\bar{R}^2$ | *F* |
|---|---|---|---|---|---|
| 1961 | $F = f_0 + f_1 K$ | 16.9604 | 0.0016** | 0.80 | 75.72** |
| | $\log F = f_0 + f_1 \log K$ | –3.4570* | 0.7417** | 0.66 | 38.28** |
| | $E = f_0 + f_1 K$ | 1.7159 | 0.0003** | 0.82 | 89.87** |
| | $\log E = f_0 + f_1 \log K$ | –6.1525** | 0.8169** | 0.67 | 40.35** |
| 1966 | $F = f_0 + f_1 K$ | 16.5556 | 0.0021** | 0.69 | 43.87** |
| | $\log F = f_0 + f_1 \log K$ | –2.7793† | 0.6955** | 0.62 | 27.68** |
| | $E = f_0 + f_1 K$ | 1.6804 | 0.0004** | 0.72 | 53.11** |
| | $\log E = f_0 + f_1 \log K$ | –5.6669** | 0.7963** | 0.54 | 24.50** |
| 1971 | $F = f_0 + f_1 K$ | 0.1419 | 0.0031** | 0.72 | 72.33** |
| | $\log F = f_0 + f_1 \log K$ | –3.0828* | 0.7327** | 0.53 | 32.84** |
| | $E = f_0 + f_1 K$ | –1.6842 | 0.0006** | 0.74 | 79.91** |
| | $\log E = f_0 + f_1 \log K$ | –6.1924** | 0.8664** | 0.63 | 47.13** |

*Note*: In this table, and those that follow, the 1 per cent level of statistical significance is denoted**, the 5 per cent level by * and the 10 per cent level is indicated by †.

employing greater numbers of machine tools consume greater quantities of fuel. The slope coefficients are significant in all of the regressions and indicate that a 1 per cent increase in the number of machine tools is associated with a 0.70 – 0.75 per cent increase in total fuel consumption, but a 0.80 – 0.85 per cent rise in electricity consumption.

Numbers of machine tools relate to a specific category that forms only a small part of the total capital stock and numbers of machines are only a crude measure of the physical stocks of capital. The only other data that distinguishes different types of capital in the engineering sector is that reported by Armstrong and Stone (1974). Their information is for six industry groups within the engineering and allied trades sector (mechanical engineering and shipbuilding; electrical engineering, vehicles; aircraft; other vehicles; and metal goods not elsewhere specified) for eight years (1961–8). Information is given about the gross values of all capital, plant and machinery and vehicles in constant prices.

Table 10.4 reports the results of estimating the fuel-capital relationship on the basis of the cross-sectional data for 1961 and 1966. The regressions are again estimated in linear and log-linear forms. In the case of the total capital stock, only the results obtained where 'all fuels', *F*, appears as the dependent variable are reported. In the second case, the results obtained from regressing 'all fuels', *F*, and 'electricity' consumption, *E*, on the

TABLE 10.4 Regression results for the fuel consumption – capital stock relationship: 1961 and 1966

| *Year* | *Type of capital* | *Functional form* | $f_0$ | $f_1$ | $\bar{R}^2$ | $F$ |
|---|---|---|---|---|---|---|
| 1961 | Total capital | $F = f_0 + f_1 K$ | –15.7183 | 0.3922** | 0.96 | 135.16** |
| | | $\log F = f_0 + f_1 \log K$ | –2.0079 | 1.1403** | 0.88 | 37.35** |
| 1966 | | $F = f_0 + f_1 K$ | –0.1805 | 0.3672** | 0.96 | 121.80** |
| | | $\log F = f_0 + f_1 \log K$ | –2.3119† | 1.1744** | 0.89 | 41.96** |
| 1961 | Plant and machinery | $F = f_0 + f_1 K$ | –1.6272 | 0.5909** | 0.97 | 152.30** |
| | | $\log F = f_0 + f_1 \log K$ | –0.9331 | 1.0564** | 0.91 | 49.93** |
| | | $E = f_0 + f_1 K$ | 4.1897 | 0.0892** | 0.92 | 56.83** |
| | | $\log E = f_0 + f_1 \log K$ | –3.5442** | 1.1760** | 0.90 | 46.50** |
| 1966 | | $F = f_0 + f_1 K$ | 17.3892 | 0.5531** | 0.97 | 159.64** |
| | | $\log F = f_0 + f_1 \log K$ | –1.0207 | 1.0581** | 0.92 | 57.20** |
| | | $E = f_0 + f_1 K$ | 9.6978 | 0.0895** | 0.93 | 64.40** |
| | | $\log E = f_0 + f_1 \log K$ | –3.4539** | 1.1695 | 0.92 | 57.22** |
| 1961 | Vehicles | $F = f_0 + f_1 K$ | 127.4570 | 16.8099** | 0.96 | 122.20** |
| | | $\log F = f_0 + f_1 \log K$ | 4.2255** | 0.6793** | 0.94 | 80.99** |
| | | $V = f_0 + f_1 K$ | 2.0572 | 0.3566** | 0.86 | 32.10** |
| | | $\log V = f_0 + f_1 \log K$ | –0.5473 | 0.9373** | 0.81 | 21.74** |
| 1966 | | $F = f_0 + f_1 K$ | 168.703* | 16.7845** | 0.92 | 58.88** |
| | | $\log F = f_0 + f_1 \log K$ | 4.6019** | 0.5955** | 0.92 | 55.65** |
| | | $V = f_0 + f_1 K$ | 2.3254 | 0.3602** | 0.91 | 50.73** |
| | | $\log V = f_0 + f_1 \log K$ | 0.1467 | 0.7298** | 0.85 | 30.30** |

stocks of plant and machinery are reported. In the final case, 'all fuels' and 'motor vehicle fuels', $V$, are regressed on the stocks of vehicles.

There are strong relationships between the amounts of fuels consumed and the stocks of capital held by the various industries. Although they are not reported here, similar results were obtained for all of the sample period (1961, 1962, . . . , 1968). The small sample sizes (six observations for each year) make the results extremely tentative. Given the small size of the sample in each year, it seemed natural to pool the data (giving 48 observations) and to re-estimate the regressions. The results obtained are reported in Table 10.5. They again show a very strong relationship between fuel consumption and capital stock. The coefficient on capital is significant at the 1 per cent level in all of the cases. The $\bar{R}^2$ are all high and the $F$ statistics are all significant at the 1 per cent level. The inclusion of a time trend had little effect on the overall explanatory power and was itself significant only in the case where 'motor vehicle fuels' were regressed on the stocks of vehicles. In addition, its inclusion had little or no effect on

TABLE 10.5 Regression results for the fuel consumption – capital relationship: pooled data

| *Functional form* | $f_0$ | $f_1$ | $f_2$ | $\bar{R}^2$ | $F$ |
|---|---|---|---|---|---|
| *Total capital* | | | | | |
| $F = f_0 + f_1 K$ | 2.8410 | 0.3672** | – | 0.96 | 1208.50** |
| $F = f_0 + f_1 K + f_2 t$ | 13.7602 | 0.3672** | –0.4487 | 0.96 | 594.45** |
| $\log F = f_0 + f_1 \log K$ | –2.2197 | 1.1638 | – | 0.90 | 444.74** |
| $\log F = f_0 + f_1 \log K + f_2 t$ | –2.1920 | 1.1638** | –0.0011 | 0.90 | 218.27** |
| *Plant and machinery* | | | | | |
| $F = f_0 + f_1 K$ | 18.1487 | 0.5525** | – | 0.97 | 1528.93** |
| $F = f_0 + f_1 K + f_2 t$ | 27.4311 | 0.5526** | –0.3809 | 0.97 | 751.63** |
| $\log F = f_0 + f_1 \log K$ | –1.0954** | 1.0763** | – | 0.93 | 646.28** |
| $\log F = f_0 + f_1 \log K + f_2 t$ | –1.0828** | 1.0762** | –0.0005 | 0.93 | 316.39** |
| $E = f_0 + f_1 K$ | 8.1497** | 0.0882** | – | 0.93 | 655.33** |
| $E = f_0 + f_1 K + f_2 t$ | 4.0158 | 0.0882** | 0.1696 | 0.93 | 326.22** |
| $\log E = f_0 + f_1 \log K$ | –3.6132** | 1.1889** | – | 0.92 | 562.28** |
| $\log E = f_0 + f_1 \log K + f_2 t$ | –3.6412** | 1.1891** | 0.0011 | 0.92 | 275.88** |
| *Vehicles* | | | | | |
| $F = f_0 + f_1 K$ | 165.6580** | 16.1515** | – | 0.93 | 648.40** |
| $F = f_0 + f_1 K + f_2 t$ | 159.4640** | 16.1530** | 0.2516 | 0.93 | 317.47** |
| $\log F = f_0 + f_1 \log K$ | 4.5731** | 0.5920** | – | 0.93 | 588.17** |
| $\log F = f_0 + f_1 \log K + f_2 t$ | 4.5288** | 0.5927** | 0.0018 | 0.92 | 290.60** |
| $V = f_0 + f_1 K$ | 1.2808 | 0.2943** | – | 0.59 | 68.55** |
| $V = f_0 + f_1 K + f_2 t$ | –3.6469 | 0.2955** | 0.2002** | 0.66 | 46.63** |
| $\log V = f_0 + f_1 \log K$ | –0.5433* | 0.7750** | – | 0.62 | 76.87** |
| $\log V = f_0 + f_1 \log K + f_2 t$ | –1.4839** | 0.7897** | 0.0372** | 0.73 | 65.84** |

the size of the coefficient on capital. An alternative formulation, which was estimated but is not reported here, included a dummy for each year in the place of the time trend. This did not produce any real improvement in the results and, again with the exception of vehicles, the dummy for 1968 was not significantly different from its value in 1961 at the 10 per cent level or better. The results again reinforce those reported in Table 10.4.

Although information about the stock of capital is scarce, it is possible to construct investment data by type (total; plant and machinery; vehicles) at the MLH level (33 observations in each year) for at least twelve years (1961–72). There are no estimates of the capital stock at this level of detail and hence the investment data cannot be used to construct either a time series of capital stock or the percentage change in the capital stock. Therefore only a linear function in first difference form could be estimated. If the linear equations for periods $t$ and $t-1$ are written,

$$F_t = f_{ot} + f_1 K_t \tag{22}$$

and

$$F_{t-1} = f_{ot-1} + f_1 K_{t-1} \tag{23}$$

where $f_{ot}$ and $f_{ot-1}$ are constants in period $t$ and $t-1$ respectively. It is then possible to calculate

$$F_t - F_{t-1} = f_o + f_1(K_t - K_{t-1})$$

or

$$\Delta F = f_o + f_1 \Delta K = f_o + f_1 \sum_{t-1}^{t} I \tag{24}$$

where the change in capital is equal to the sum of net investment, $\Sigma I$, between periods $t$ and $t-1$. The results of estimating equation (24) using a five-year lag between $t$ and $t-1$ are reported in Table 10.6. The performance of the function is not as good as before: $\bar{R}^2$ is generally lower and the $F$ statistic is not always significant at a 5 per cent level or better. In addition the coefficient on investment varies considerably over time.

The results obtained to date are preliminary and extremely naïve in nature. At this stage, they do little more than confirm that there are strong

TABLE 10.6 Regression results for the relationship between the change in fuel consumption and the change in capital stock

| *Year* | *Functional form* | $f_0$ | $f_1$ | $\bar{R}^2$ | $F$ |
|---|---|---|---|---|---|
| *Total investment* | | | | | |
| 1961–66 | $\Delta F = f_0 + f_1 \Sigma I$ | −8.0494* | 0.2973** | 0.799 | 124.12** |
| 1966–71 | $\Delta F = f_0 + f_1 \Sigma I$ | −3.3919 | 0.0916** | 0.202 | 8.82** |
| *Plant and machinery* | | | | | |
| 1961–66 | $\Delta F = f_0 + f_1 \Sigma I$ | −7.8080* | 0.4257** | 0.82 | 145.08** |
| | $\Delta E = f_0 + f_1 \Sigma I$ | −7.4026 | 0.0857** | 0.88 | 236.95** |
| 1966–71 | $\Delta F = f_0 + f_1 \Sigma I$ | −3.9679 | 0.1162** | 0.19 | 7.60* |
| | $\Delta E = f_0 + f_1 \Sigma I$ | −1.2398 | 0.0507** | 0.62 | 46.83** |
| *Vehicles* | | | | | |
| 1961–66 | $\Delta F = f_0 + f_1 \Sigma I$ | 4.1034 | 2.6326 | 0.04 | 2.49 |
| | $\Delta Y = f_0 + f_1 \Sigma I$ | −0.0424 | 0.0657** | 0.29 | 13.80** |
| 1966–71 | $\Delta F = f_0 + f_1 \Sigma I$ | −4.6447 | 1.7988** | 0.12 | 5.33 |
| | $\Delta V = f_0 + f_1 \Sigma I$ | −0.0510 | 0.4833** | 0.68 | 65.72** |

relationships between the various types of fuel and the corresponding capital stocks. In addition, working with the data does give the user an intuitive feeling that the disaggregation by type of fuel and the attempt to match the different fuels with their corresponding types of capital are worthwhile activities. Playing around with the available data has also made it clear that a great deal more research is necessary. First, all of the results to date are associated with an omitted variable problem: the amount of fuel consumed depends not only on the stock of capital, but also the degree to which it is utilised. The quarterly CBI *Survey of Economic Trends* might, for example, be used to provide an independent measure of capital utilisation with which to weight the capital stock in each industry. Second, some of the more interesting specifications of the model, for example involving the influence of relative factor prices, have not yet been estimated. Third, by nesting the various specifications, it should for example, be possible to establish whether electricity consumption is more closely related to plant and machinery than is the consumption of all fuels in total. The work of earlier authors and the empirical work in this study have all assumed that the value of capital (in constant prices) forms a reliable and useful measure of the physical stock of capital. As far as fuel consumption is concerned, every unit of capital is assumed to have exactly the same energy requirement. The importance of this assumption is perhaps most obvious in the last empirical case considered. In using net investment as the measure of the change in capital stock, it has been assumed that the fuel consumption characteristics of capital being sold or scrapped are the same as the new capital being introduced. In later work it may be possible to separate out the influences of gross investment in new capital and the scrapping of old capital on the change in fuel consumption.

## 6. CONCLUSION

Fuel proxies for the input of capital services raise new questions that will require solutions before they can be used on anything like a regular basis. To take just one example, the problems of adding together different types of fuels involve questions about the weights that should be applied to them before aggregating. In principle, the weights should reflect both the marginal productivity of the particular type of capital and the technical link between the capital and the fuel consumed. Where capital of various types are distinguished separately in the production function, it may not be necessary to know these weightings – the technical links may be adequately subsumed in the constant term or time trend and the marginal products can then be calculated directly. However, certain problems still remain that are extremely difficult to overcome: first, a certain amount of aggregation is almost always inherent in published data; second, there remains the question of how to match capital types with the various fuels consumed.

## REFERENCES


Adams, F. G. and Miovic, P. (1968), 'On Relative Fuel Efficiency and the Output Elasticity of Energy Consumption in Western Europe', *Journal of Industrial Economics* vol. 17.

Allen, R. G. D. (1968), *Macro-Economic Theory* (London: Macmillan).

Armstrong, A. (1974), *Structural Change in the British Economy: 1948–68*, vol. 12 of Stone, R. (ed.) *A Programme for Growth* (Chapman and Hall).

Bosworth, D. (1974), 'Production Functions and Skill Requirements', in J. S. Wabe (ed.), *Problems in Manpower Forecasting* (Saxon House).

Bosworth, D. (1976), *Production Functions : A Theoretical and Empirical Study* (Saxon House).

Garegnani, P. (1970), 'Heterogeneous Capital, the Production Function and the Theory of Distribution', *Review of Economic Studies*, vol. 37.

Heathfield, D. (1972), 'The Measurement of Capital Usage Using Electricity Consumption Data for the U.K., *Journal of the Royal Statistical Society*, vol. 132.

Moody, C. E. (1974), 'The Measurement of Capital Services by Electrical Energy', *Oxford Bulletin of Economics and Statistics*, vol. 36.

Phelps, E. S. (1962), 'The New View of Investment', *Quarterly Journal of Economics*, vol. 76.

Robinson, J. (1970), 'Capital Theory up to Date', *Canadian Journal of Economics*, vol. 13.

Samuelson, P. A. (1962), 'Parable and Realism in Capital Theory : The Surrogate Production Function', *Review of Economic Studies*, vol. 39.

Sato, K. (1974), 'The Neoclassical Postulate and the Technology Frontier in Capital Theory', *Quarterly Journal of Economics*, vol. 88.

Solow, R. M. (1956), 'The Production Function and the Theory of Capital', *Review of Economic Studies*, vol. 23.

Solow, R. M. (1960), 'Investment and Technical Progress', in Arrow *et al.* (eds.) *Mathematical Methods in the Social Sciences* (Stanford University Press).

Taylor, J. (1967), 'A Surrogate for Regional Estimates of Capital Stock', *Bulletin of Economic Research*, vol.29.

# 11 Factor Demand Functions

WILLIAM PETERSON

*Cambridge University*

## INTRODUCTION

This paper sets out the theoretical derivation of a system of demand equations for productive inputs using the hypothesis of cost minimisation by producers, and tests the validity of this hypothesis using disaggregated data for two important UK manufacturing industries. The paper makes use of the methodology and results of consumer demand analysis to establish the restrictions which are implied for the demand functions by the cost minimisation hypothesis, and the additional restrictions which can be imposed if it is assumed that the production function is homothetic. These additional restrictions can often be imposed unintentionally by an inappropriate parameterisation of the demand functions or choice of functional form. In view of this problem, and of the limited range of production functions for which the demand functions can be expressed in explicit form, the system of demand functions used in this paper is derived by direct differentiation of a cost function, and the production function is not used in estimation. The system of demand functions is estimated under a variety of assumptions about substitution possibilities and the embodiment of technical progress. The results show that there is no need to adopt a vintage model of technology, but also that the evidence does not support the basic hypothesis of cost-minimisation.

## I

Throughout this paper I assume that the firm produces a single output $q$. Many of the results presented can be extended to multi-product firms without difficulty, providing it is assumed that the firm has no control over the relative prices it receives for different products. I also assume the firm has no control over the prices it pays for productive inputs. This means that the problem which is assumed to face the firm, the production of a given output at minimum cost, is well defined: it may be unrealistic to assume that firms behave in this way, but it is undeniably possible for them to do so. Output is defined as gross duplicated output, in accordance with the input-output framework within which the model of production is designed to fit. This means that the relationship between output and intermediate inputs must be specified explicitly, rather than being implicitly determined by the methods used to construct a suitable net output measure.

Within this framework the feature which distinguishes, at a theoretical level, between capital goods and intermediate inputs such as steel or motor components is that capital goods yield services for more than one period of production. In practice the important distinction is that we have data on the annual flow of intermediate inputs, but not on the services yielded by the currently available stock of capital goods. In addition, the difficulty of estimating retirements means that published estimates of the stock are less reliable than, for example, statistics for labour input. In the empirical work to be presented in this paper the factor demand functions are specified in terms of first differences, so that there is no need to make use of data on the level of the capital stock in the estimation procedure.

Since both capital goods and intermediate inputs are produced within the economic system, the assumption that a firm is a price-taker in the factor market must be supplemented by assuming that it behaves myopically. The simplest way to see what is meant by this is to consider the impact of an invention in industry *i* on the economy as a whole. Initially good *i* will become cheaper, and as a result of this other industries using good *i* as an intermediate input will experience reduced costs of production and, under competitive conditions, lower prices. This will result in a further reduction in the costs of producing good *i*, and so on.

In the case where all inputs are single-use intermediates (i.e. there is no fixed capital) it has been shown by Morishima (1964) that the industry experiencing the greatest reduction in costs will be that in which the original invention occurs. Thus if the firm's myopic response to a fall in price for a particular input is to increase its use of that input, its equilibrium response will be in the same direction. The same argument can be applied to changes in the rental price of capital services, and the demand for these services: however it cannot be used to analyse the effect of changes in the interest rate on the demand for capital stock. However, if the firm is assumed to behave myopically then we can assume that a fall in the interest rate will lower the rental of all capital goods in the short run (in which the price of capital goods is assumed to be unaffected). In the final equilibrium the price of capital goods (relative to output) may be higher and hence the optimal technique of production may be less capital-intensive: the assumption of myopic behaviour implies that firms do not perceive this in advance.

For theoretical purposes problems concerned with the meaning or measurement of capital can be evaded by specifying that the vector of productive inputs employed by the firm may include the services of machines of various types, and that the price of such services is the rental of the machine for the relevant period. This vector of productive inputs will be denoted by $v$, and the corresponding price vector by $w$: both $v$ and $w$ are assumed to have $n$ components. The production function is then specified as a relationship

$$q = f(v) \tag{1}$$

between inputs and output. It is shown by Shephard (1970) that such a function exists under comparatively mild assumptions about the nature of the underlying technology. However two additional assumptions on the production function itself are necessary if the resulting demand functions are to be suitable for econometric study.

A1 The production function is everywhere continuous, with continuous first and second order derivatives.

A2 The matrix $F_{vv}$ of second derivatives is negative definite under constraint: specifically

$$z'F_{vv}z < 0 \text{ for all } z \neq 0 \text{ such that } f_v'z = 0.$$

The effect of these assumptions is to exclude several types of technology of economic interest. A1 rules out the case where a fixed quantity of a particular input is always required in production: A2 rules out the possibility that an isoquant has a flat segment along which the marginal rate of substitution between two inputs is constant. In both cases there are analogous restrictions in higher dimensions. Thus the 'spectrum of techniques' model of production developed by Mrs Robinson and many others is incompatible with these two assumptions.

Under these assumptions, and using the notation set out above, the problem of the cost-minimising firm can be written as

$$\min_{v} w'v \quad \text{subject to} \quad f(v) = q.$$

Total differentiation of the first order conditions

$$\lambda f_v = w \tag{2}$$

gives

$$\lambda F_{vv} dv + f_v d\lambda = dw \tag{3(a)}$$

$$f_v' dv = dq \tag{3(b)}$$

It has been shown by Barten, Kloek and Lempers (1969) that A2 is sufficient to ensure that this set of equations has a unique solution, even if $F_{vv}$ is singular (as it will be if $f(v)$ displays constant returns to scale). Here we first derive the explicit form of the solution to (3) assuming $F_{vv}$ to be non-singular, and then show that, in the singular case, the explicit solution of the equations can always be derived by an appropriate transformation.

From 3(a) and assuming $F^{-1}$ exists,

$$dv = \lambda^{-1} F_{vv}^{-1} (dw - f_v d\lambda) \tag{4}$$

and from 3(b) and (4)

$$dq = \lambda^{-1} f_v' F_{vv}^{-1} dw - \lambda^{-1} f_v' F_{vv}^{-1} f_v d\lambda \tag{5}$$

Denoting the scalar $(f_v' F_{vv}^{-1} f_v)^{-1}$ by $\gamma$, and substituting the resulting expression for $d\lambda$ in equation (4)

$$d\lambda = \gamma f_v' F_{vv}^{-1} dw - \lambda \gamma dq \tag{6(a)}$$

$$dv = \lambda^{-1} (F_{vv}^{-1} - \gamma F_{vv}^{-1} f_v f_v' F_{vv}^{-1}) dw + \gamma F_{vv}^{-1} f_v dq \tag{6(b)}$$

We can now write down the restrictions on the output and price responses implied by cost minimisation

R1 $\quad \dfrac{\partial \lambda}{\partial w} = \dfrac{\partial v}{\partial q} = \gamma F_{vv}^{-1} f_v$

R2 $\quad w' \dfrac{\partial \lambda}{\partial w} = w' \dfrac{\partial v}{\partial q} = \gamma \lambda f_v' F_{vv}^{-1} f_v = \lambda$

R3 $\quad w' \dfrac{\partial v}{\partial w} = f_v' F_{vv}^{-1} - \gamma f_v' F_{vv}^{-1} f_v f_v' F_{vv}^{-1} = 0'$

R4 $\quad \dfrac{\partial v}{\partial w} = \dfrac{\partial v'}{\partial w}$

R5 $\quad \dfrac{\partial v}{\partial w}$ is negative semi-definite

R4 is an obvious result of the symmetry of $F_{vv}$: a proof of R5 is given in the paper by Barten *et al.*

Consider now the case where the production function displays constant returns to scale: then as direct consequences of Euler's theorem

$$f_v'v = f(v) \tag{7(a)}$$

$$F_{vv}v = 0 \tag{7(b)}$$

However in this case it is possible to assert that, providing A2 is satisfied, there exists a scalar $\mu$ such that

$$F_{vv} = F_{vv}^* + \mu f_v f_v' \tag{8}$$

and $F_{vv}^*$ is non-singular: this result is due to Greub (1963). Then

$$\lambda F_{vv}^* dv = dw - f_v d\lambda - \mu\lambda f_v dq. \tag{9}$$

Writing $(f_v' F_{vv}^{*-1} f_v)^{-1}$ as $\gamma^*$ and solving,

$$d\lambda = \gamma^* f_v' F_{vv}^{*-1} dw - \lambda\gamma^* dq - \lambda\mu dq \tag{10(a)}$$

$$dv = \lambda^{-1}(F_{vv}^{*-1} - \gamma^* F_{vv}^{*-1} f_v f_v' F_{vv}^{*-1})dw - \gamma^* F_{vv}^{*-1} f_v dq \tag{10(b)}$$

Clearly 10(b) is identical in form to 6(b) so that the input demand equations under constant returns to scale satisfy the restrictions R1 – R5 derived above. Additional restrictions can be derived by post-multiplying (8) by $v$ and using (7)

$$v = -\mu F_{vv}^{*-1} f_v q \tag{11}$$

$$\mu = -(f_v' F_{vv}^{*-1} f_v)^{-1} = -\gamma^*. \tag{12}$$

Substituting in 10(a)

$$d\lambda = \gamma^* f_v' F_{vv}^{*-1} dw \tag{13}$$

i.e. marginal cost is independent of output. Finally by comparing 10(a) and (11) we see that

$$q^{-1} v = \frac{\partial v}{\partial q} \tag{14}$$

i.e. all output elasticities are equal to 1.

Instead of assuming that the production function displays constant returns to scale it is frequently assumed to be homothetic. This implies that it can be expressed in the following form

$$q = f(v) = g(h(v)) \tag{15}$$

where $h(v)$ is a function which is homogeneous of degree $l$ and $g$ is a monotonic increasing function: thus constant returns to scale is clearly a special case of homotheticity. The first and second derivatives of a homothetic production function can be written as

$$f_v = g_h h_v \tag{16}$$

$$F_{vv} = g_h H_{vv} + g_{hh} h_v h_v' \tag{17}$$

where $h_v' v = h(v)$, $H_{vv} v = 0$. Provided that $g_{hh} \neq 0$ the matrix $F_{vv}$ is non-singular, so that the relevant differential demand functions are given by (6). Postmultiplying (17) by $v$ and simplifying

$$F_{vv} v = g_{hh} h_v q \tag{18}$$

$$v = g_h^{-1} g_{hh} F_{vv}^{-1} f_v q \tag{19}$$

so that the output elasticities are all equal

$$\hat{v}^{-1} q \frac{\partial v}{\partial q} = \gamma g_h g_{hh}^{-1} \tag{20}$$

To see how the assumption of homotheticity implies restrictions on the output elasticities additional to those implied by the hypothesis of cost minimisation, equation (6) can be transformed using the relation $\hat{x}\, d\log x = dx$, (where $\hat{x}$ is a diagonal matrix, with the elements of $x$ on the main diagonal)

$$\lambda\, d\log\lambda = \gamma f_v' F_{vv}^{-1} \hat{w}\, d\log w - \lambda\gamma q\, d\log q \tag{21(a)}$$

$$\hat{v}\, d\log v = \lambda^{-1}(F_{vv}^{-1} - \gamma F_{vv}^{-1} f_v f_v' F_{vv}^{-1})\hat{w}\, d\log w + \gamma F_{vv}^{-1} f_v q\, d\log q \tag{21(b)}$$

From the first order conditions $\hat{w} = \lambda \hat{f}_v$, and hence

$$d\log\lambda = \gamma f_v' F_{vv}^{-1} \hat{f}_v d\log w - \gamma q\, d\log q \tag{22(a)}$$

$$d\log v = \hat{v}^{-1}(F_{vv}^{-1} - \gamma F_{vv}^{-1} f_v f_v' F_{vv}^{-1})\hat{f}_v\, d\log w + \gamma \hat{v}^{-1} F_{vv}^{-1} f_v q\, d\log q. \tag{22(b)}$$

Define $\xi = \partial \log\lambda/\partial \log w$, $\psi = \partial\log\lambda/\partial\log q$, $\mathrm{H} = \partial\log v/\partial\log w$ and $\eta = \partial\log v/\partial\log q$. In addition define the vector

$$\alpha = \lambda^{-1} q^{-1} \hat{w} v \tag{23}$$

which is related to the vector $a$, which gives the share of each input as a proportion of the value of total output, by the equation

$$\mu a = \alpha \tag{24}$$

where $\mu$ is the markup of price on marginal cost (i.e. $p = \mu\lambda$). Then the restrictions R1 to R5 can be rewritten as

R′1 $\xi = \hat{\alpha}\eta = \gamma \hat{f}_v F_{vv}^{-1} f_v$

R′2 $\iota'\xi = \alpha'\eta = 1$

R′3 $\alpha' H = q^{-1} f_v'(F_{vv}^{-1} - \gamma F_{vv}^{-1} f_v f_v' F_{vv}^{-1})\hat{f}_v = 0'$

R′4 $\hat{\alpha} H = q^{-1} \hat{f}_v(F_{vv}^{-1} - \gamma F_{vv}^{-1} f_v f_v' F_{vv}^{-1})\hat{f}_v = [\hat{\alpha} H]'$

R′5 $\hat{\alpha} H$ is negative semi definite

R′5 follows from R5 and the fact that all components of $\hat{f}_v$ are positive.

In view of the popularity of the C.E.S. production function it is helpful to rewrite equation (23) in terms of partial elasticities of substitution (Allen (1938), Uzawa (1962)). Suppose we define the partial elasticity of production between two factors $i$ and $j$ as

$$S_{ij} = \sum_k \frac{\lambda f_k v_k}{v_i v_j} \frac{\partial v_i}{\partial w_j}. \tag{25}$$

Then 22(b) can be rewritten as

$$\begin{aligned} d \log v &= \hat{v}^{-1} (F_{vv}^{-1} - \gamma F_{vv}^{-1} f_v f_v' F_{vv}^{-1}) \hat{v}^{-1} (f_v' v) \hat{v} \hat{f}_v (f_v' v)^{-1}\, d \log w \\ &+ \gamma \hat{v}^{-1} F_{vv}^{-1} f_v q\, d \log q. \end{aligned} \tag{26}$$

For a production function displaying constant returns to scale

$$\hat{v} \hat{f}_v (f_v' v)^{-1} = \hat{\alpha} \tag{27}$$

$$d \log v = S\, \hat{\alpha}\, d \log w + \eta \log q \tag{28}$$

The restrictions on the price responses R3 to R5 can now be expressed as restrictions on $S$

R″3 $\alpha' S = f_v'(F_{vv}{}^{-1} - \gamma F_{vv}{}^{-1} f_v f_v' F_{vv}{}^{-1})\hat{v}^{-1} = 0'$

R″4 $S = (f_v' v)\hat{v}^{-1}(F_{vv}{}^{-1} - \gamma F_{vv}{}^{-1} f_v f_v' F_{vv}{}^{-1})\hat{v}^{-1} = S'$

R″5 $S$ is negative semi definite

where R″5 follows from R5 and the fact that all components of $\hat{v}$ are positive.

The three alternative formulations of the differential demand functions which have been presented above indicate the restrictions which must hold locally for any set of input demand functions which is derived from the hypothesis of cost minimisation. However an estimation process which involved the parameterisation of equations 6(b), 22(b) or (28) would imply that the associated restrictions were valid for all points in the input space. Thus a system of equations derived from 6(b)

$$dv = A\, dw + b\, dq \tag{29}$$

will only satisfy the homogeneity restriction R4 if $A$ is identically zero, i.e. if input demands are independent of relative prices. Similarly the only production function which possesses constant elasticities and therefore satisfies 22(b) everywhere is the multifactor Cobb-Douglas, and Uzawa (1962) has shown that the most general function possessing constant elasticities of substitution and therefore satisfying (28) has the form

$$f(v) = \prod_{s} \left[ \left( \sum_{j \in s} \beta_j v_j \rho^s \right)^{1/e^s} \right]^{\alpha_s} \tag{30}$$

This function is clearly a generalisation of the multi-factor Cobb-Douglas: however since the function is strongly separable, with the sub-production functions being additive in the inputs, it imposes powerful and unwanted restrictions on the relationships between output, own-price and cross-price responses. The unintended imposition of these restrictions on a system of demand equations for a large number of disparate inputs could lead to an unwarranted rejection of the basic hypothesis of cost minimisation.

The basic assumption needed for strong separability of the production function is that inputs can be classified into disjoint groups in such a way that the ratio of the marginal products of any two inputs is independent of the quantity of those inputs which are in different groups: if the production function is additive then each group contains precisely one input. A full analysis of the comparative statics of separability is given by Geary and Morishima (1973); here we concentrate on the implications of separability for the input demand functions, and on the relationships between separability, and constancy and equality of the partial elasticities of substitution (Berndt and Christensen (1973)).

A production function is strongly separable with respect to a partition of the inputs into non-intersecting groups ($N \ldots . N_s$) if and only if the following conditions are satisfied

$$\frac{\partial}{\partial v_k}(f_i/f_j) = 0 \qquad (i \in N_s, j \in N_t, k \notin N_s v N_t) \tag{31}$$

Expanding (31) we derive

$$\frac{f_{ik}}{f_i} = \frac{f_{jk}}{f_j} = \alpha(v) f_k \tag{32}$$

where $\alpha(v)$ is independent of $i, j$ and $k$. Hence strong separability implies

$$F_{vv} = G_{vv} + \alpha f_v f_v' \tag{33}$$

where $G_{vv}$ is a block-diagonal matrix. Furthermore we can express the inverse of $F_{vv}$ as

$$F_{vv}^{-1} = G_{vv}^{-1} - \alpha(1 + \alpha\beta)^{-1} G_{vv}^{-1} f_v f_v' G_{vv}^{-1} \tag{34}$$

where $\beta = (f_v' G_{vv}^{-1} f_v)$ and $G_{vv}^{-1}$ is block diagonal. By substituting (34) in 6(b), simplifying, and introducing scalars $\phi$ and $\psi$, we obtain

$$dv = \lambda^{-1} [G_{vv}^{-1} - \phi G_{vv}^{-1} f_v f_v' G_{vv}^{-1}] dw + \psi G_{vv}^{-1} f_v dq \tag{35}$$

Consider now $\partial v_i/\partial w_j$ where $i \in N_s$, $j \in N_t$ and $s \neq t$. Since $G_{vv}^{-1}$ is block diagonal we can write this as

$$\frac{\partial v_i}{\partial w_j} = -\lambda^{-1} \phi [G_{vv}^{-1} f_v f_v']_{ij} = -\lambda^{-1} \phi \psi^{-2} \frac{\partial v_i}{\partial q} \frac{\partial v_j}{\partial q} \tag{36}$$

Since $\lambda^{-1}$, $\phi$ and $\psi^{-2}$ are all independent of $i$ and $j$ this shows that strong separability implies that 'off-diagonal' price responses are proportional to the product of the output responses.

The two parameters $\phi$ and $\psi$ are related to the decomposition of $F_{vv}$ which was made in equation (33), since

$$\phi = [\gamma + \alpha(1 + \alpha\beta)^{-1}(1 - 2\gamma\beta) + \gamma\alpha^2\beta^2(1 + \alpha\beta)^{-2}] \tag{37}$$

$$\psi = [\gamma - \alpha\beta\gamma(1 + \alpha\beta)^{-1}] \tag{38}$$

where $\lambda = (f_v' F_{vv}^{-1} f_v)^{-1}$. These equations can be simplified by noting that

$$\begin{aligned} \gamma^{-1} &= f_v' F_{vv}^{-1} f_v = f_v' G_{vv}^{-1} f_v - \alpha(1 + \alpha\beta)^{-1} f_v' G_{vv}^{-1} f_v f_v' G_{vv}^{-1} f_v) \\ &= \beta(1 + \alpha\beta)^{-1} \end{aligned} \tag{39}$$

Hence

$$\phi = \beta^{-1} \tag{40}$$

$$\psi = \beta^{-1} \tag{41}$$

Consider now the formula for the partial elasticity of substitution, equation (25). Combining this with equation (36) we obtain

$$S_{ij} = -\beta \, \Sigma f_k v_k v_i^{-1} \frac{\partial v_i}{\partial q} v_j^{-1} \frac{\partial v_j}{\partial q} \tag{42}$$

and this expression is independent of $i$ and $j$ for any homothetic production function. Hence strong separability implies that all partial elasticities of substitution for inputs in different groups are equal. If we consider the special case of constant returns to scale, then we can express this common elasticity $\sigma$ as

$$\sigma = -\beta \, [f(v)]^{-1} \tag{43}$$

Since additivity is merely a special case of strong separability with one input in each group, it is clear that additivity implies the equality of all off-diagonal partial elasticities of substitution. In addition the homogeneity condition (previously stated as R″5) imposes significant restrictions on the diagonal terms: for

$$\alpha_i S_{ii} = - \sum_{j \neq i} \alpha_j S_{ij} \tag{44}$$

$$S_{ii} = \frac{(\alpha_i - 1)}{\alpha_i} \sigma \tag{45}$$

If we express this result in terms of conventional elasticities, using the relation $H_{ii} = S_{ii}\alpha_i$, then

$$H_{ii} = \alpha_i \sigma - \sigma \tag{46}$$

which implies the approximate (to order $1/n$) equality of all own-price elasticities. This is the analogue in the theory of production to Pigou's Law (Deaton (1974)): it is an even more restrictive result because we have assumed that all output elasticities are equal. It is clear from (44) that strong separability imposes a similar though weaker relationship, since

$$\sum_{j \in s} \alpha_j S_{ij} = - \sum_{k \in s} \alpha_k S_{ik}$$

$$= \Big(\sum_{j \in s} \alpha_j - 1\Big)\sigma \tag{47}$$

where $\sigma$ is defined by equation (43). The left hand side of this expression is the sum of the own-price elasticity for input $i$ and the cross price elasticities for other inputs in the same group: since the right hand side is independent of $i$ this sum must be the same for all inputs in the group. In addition strong separability imposes the restriction that the sums of the elasticities for each group are themselves approximately equal (to order $1/k$, where $k$ is the number of groups).

The preceding analysis has shown that systems embodying strong separability, although attractive because of the small number of parameters to be estimated, are unlikely to be able to model the wide range of substitution possibilities and price responses which we would wish to allow for in a model designed to explain choices between a large number of inputs.

However a possible approach is to assume that the underlying production function is weakly separable. This implies that the inputs can be partitioned into non-intersecting groups ($N_1 \ldots N_s$) such that

$$\frac{\partial}{\partial v_k}\left(\frac{f_i}{f_j}\right) = 0 \quad i, j \in N_s \quad k \notin N_s \tag{48}$$

so that the ratio of marginal products for two inputs in the same group is independent of the quantity of any input outside the group.

Equation (48) implies a corresponding restriction on the input demand functions

$$\frac{\partial v_i}{\partial w_j} = -\beta^{st} \frac{\partial v_i}{\partial q} \frac{\partial v_j}{\partial q} \qquad i \in N_s, j \in N_t \; s \neq t \tag{49}$$

The proof of (46), which is complex and not given here, is due to Goldman and Uzawa (1964). Clearly for a homothetic production function it will be possible to express the restriction implied by (49) in terms of substitution elasticities

$$S_{ij} = -\beta_{st}[f(v)]^{-1} \qquad (i \in N_s, j \in N_t) \tag{50}$$

However equation (50), even combined with homogeneity, does not impose particularly stringent restrictions on the own-price elasticities or on the cross-price elasticities for any two inputs which are in the same group. In addition it has been shown by Gorman (1959) that, if the production function is homothetic, weak separability is a sufficient condition for the feasibility of a two-level budgeting procedure in which, for example, the firm initially allocates expenditure between labour, investment goods, fuels and other inputs, and then decides on the optimal pattern of expenditure within each group. Elsewhere (Peterson (1974)) this hierarchic approach has been extended to the estimation procedure.

The analysis so far indicates the nature of the restrictions which can consciously or unconsciously be imposed on a set of input demand functions by choosing a specific functional form or parameterisation of the equations. However the choice of functional form is further complicated by the obvious fact that, for any but the most simple functions, the first order conditions are unlikely to be analytically solvable: in other words it is only when $f(v)$ has a particularly simple (and usually additive) form that we can proceed from the set of $(n + 1)$ equations

$$\begin{aligned} w_i &= \lambda f_i \qquad (i = 1 \ldots n) \\ q &= f(v) \end{aligned} \tag{51}$$

to the dual set of equations

$$v_i = g_i(q, w)$$
$$\lambda = \lambda(q, w) \tag{52}$$

which are the appropriate estimating equations for an individual cost-minimising producer facing fixed input prices. The obvious case where this transformation is possible is the C.E.S. production function: however since this function is additive it imposes all the restrictions demonstrated above.

Furthermore this problem of solving the first order conditions to derive a system of demand functions cannot be eliminated by estimating the differential demand equations derived from a general production function (the approach taken by Theil (1975) and the 'Rotterdam school' in consumer demand theory) because, as this paper has shown, parameterisation of the differential demand functions is equivalent to the choice of a highly restrictive (and additive) functional form for the production function. However a more satisfactory solution is to define the technology in terms of the cost function rather than in terms of the production function. It has been shown by Shephard (1970) that the two approaches are equivalent, in that to any production function there corresponds a dual factor-minimal cost function which gives the minimum cost of producing a given output at a given set of input prices. Furthermore, from a result due to Hotelling (1932), the first order conditions for a minimum of this function are the input demand functions. Thus we can select a suitable functional form for the cost function and derive the appropriate demand functions directly.

Two alternative forms for such a function have been suggested. The first of these is the generalised Leontief cost function suggested by Diewert (1971)

$$C(q, w) = h(q) \sum_i \sum_j w_i^{1/2} b_{ij} w_j^{1/2} \; (b_{ij} = b_{ji} \; i \neq j)$$
$$v_i = h(q)\, w_i^{-1/2} \sum_j \beta_{ij} w_j^{1/2} \tag{55}$$

where

$$\beta_{ij} = \tfrac{1}{2}(b_{ij} + b_{ji}).$$

This reduces to a conventional Leontief fixed-coeffients production function if the off-diagonal terms are zero and $h(q) = q$. The second form is the translog cost function developed by Christensen, Jorgenson and Lau (1973)

$$\ln C(q, w) = \ln a_o + \sum_i a_i \ln w_i + \tfrac{1}{2} \sum_i \sum_j b_{ij} \ln w_i \ln w_j$$

$$\frac{\partial \ln C}{\partial \ln w_i} = \frac{w_i v_i}{C} = a_i + \sum_j \beta_{ij} \ln w_j \tag{56}$$

This reduces to the additive Cobb-Douglas case if all the second-order $b_{ij}$ terms are zero. Since both cost functions are quadratic forms there is no loss of generality in assuming that $b_{ij} = b_{ji}$ for $i \neq j$: however the symmetry hypothesis can be tested by imposing the constraint $\beta_{ij} = \beta_{ji}$ on the estimating equations. Both functions can be considered as second-order Taylor series approximations to any cost function in the neighbourhood of a particular point in price space: clearly the fit to any particular body of data reflects partly the appropriateness of the chosen approximation over a wider region. It has been shown by Denny (1974) and Kiefer (1975) that both functions can be considered as special cases of a more general function

$$C(q, w) = h(q) \left(\sum_i \sum_j b_{ij} w_i^{\beta/2} w_j^{\beta/2}\right)^{1/\beta} \tag{57}$$

If all off-diagonal terms in this function are zero, it reduces to the C.E.S. function (and hence to Cobb-Douglas as $\beta \to 0$). If the off-diagonal terms are non-zero, then the form can encompass both generalised Leontief ($\beta = 1$) and translog ($\beta \to 0$) forms.

The disadvantage of deriving demand functions from a cost function is that the production function will now take a mathematically intractable form. Formally the production function is still defined by duality as

$$q(v) = \max \{ q \mid \sum_i w_i v_i \geqslant C(q, w) \} \tag{58}$$

since if the producer is minimising the cost of producing a given output he must also be producing the largest output level attainable at that cost. Thus, given a set of estimated input demand equations and of actual inputs, a series of calculated output can be generated by solving (58), since this requires only a one-dimensional search over $q$. However Diewert (1971) has shown that for the function (55) the equation (58) is analytically soluble and that the resulting production function is

$$q = h^{-1}(\bar{\mu}^{-1}) \tag{59}$$

where $\bar{\mu}$ is the largest eigenvalue of the matrix $\hat{v}^{-1/2} B \hat{v}^{-1/2}$. This result provides a justification for the use of (55) as the functional form for the cost function in the empirical section of this paper.

II

The empirical work to be presented in this section was undertaken to test two important hypotheses about the production process. The first aim was to study how much scope exists for substitution between alternative inputs, and whether such behaviour can be explained at least in part by the assumption that producers are attempting to minimise costs. It is of course possible that effective substitution is prohibited either by physical laws governing the productive process or by the fact that the past uneven development of knowledge has made certain techniques unambiguously superior (Atkinson and Stiglitz (1969)). However the functional form of the cost function (55) which we have chosen to represent the technology is sufficiently general to permit testing of this hypothesis.

A second problem to be considered concerns the extent to which technical progress and technical choice are embodied in capital equipment at the moment of its construction. Thus two alternative models, representing the two possible extremes, were specified and estimated. In the non-vintage model it is assumed that the producer can decide his optimal input proportions in each period without being in any way constrained by his past decisions: thus the appropriate demand functions (in first differences) are

$$\begin{aligned} v_i(t) - v_i(t-1) = {} & h(q(t))\, w_i(t)^{-\frac{1}{2}} \sum_j b_{ij}\, w_j(t)^{\frac{1}{2}} \\ & - h(q(t-1))\, w_i(t-1)^{-\frac{1}{2}} \sum_j b_{ij} w_j(t-1)^{\frac{1}{2}} \end{aligned} \tag{60}$$

To allow for the depreciation of capital goods the following replacement equation is added to (60)

$$I(t) = v_n(t) - v_n(t-1) + (d_O + d_1 t)\, q(t-1) \tag{61}$$

In contrast the vintage model assumes that input proportions can be freely chosen only when new equipment is installed: for the remainder of its working life operation of the machine requires current inputs in fixed proportions. Thus any change in aggregate inputs can occur only as a result either of new investment or of the scrapping of obsolete equipment (neglecting the possibility of changes in utilisation rates). Given our assumptions about technology and entrepreneurial motivation, the vector of inputs used with new equipment is explained as

$$v_{it} = h(q_t)\, w_i(t)^{-\frac{1}{2}} \sum_j b_{ij} w_j(t)^{\frac{1}{2}} \tag{62}$$

Furthermore, assume that equipment to be scrapped in year $t$ differs from that newly installed as a result of long-term improvements in technology rather than short-run movements in relative prices: then we can write

$$v_{it-T} = \beta_i(T) v_{it} \left(h(q_{t-T})/h(q_t)\right) \tag{63}$$

where $\beta_i(T)$ is a function of the rate at which technical progress is changing the need for input $i$ and of the age of equipment currently being scrapped, but is independent of relative prices. Thus combining (62) and (63) we obtain the following set of equations in first difference form

$$\begin{aligned} v_i(t) - v_i(t-1) = {} & (1 - \beta_i(T)\, h(q_{t-T})/h(q_t)) \\ & h(q_t)\, w_i(t)^{-\frac{1}{2}} \sum_j b_{ij}\, w_j(t)^{\frac{1}{2}} \end{aligned} \tag{64}$$

Finally note that the assumption that capacity scrapped in year $t$ is proportional to total output in the previous year (an assumption very similar to that made in (61)) is sufficient to determine both $q_{t-T}$ and $q_t$ since

$$q_t = q(t) - q(t-1) + q_{t-T} = q(t) - (1 - \delta) q(t-1). \tag{65}$$

Technical change can be incorporated into equations (60) and (64) in two ways. It is possible to argue that the effect of technical progress is to allow one man to do what two did before. Using this approach it is possible to define a set of efficiency units in which inputs can be measured and in terms of which technology does not change: however as time proceeds the number of efficiency units supplied per unit of measured input changes.

$$\begin{aligned} v_i^*(t) &= v_i(t)\, e^{g_i t} \\ w_i^*(t) &= w_i(t)\, e^{-g_i t} \end{aligned} \tag{66}$$

Equations (66) can be substituted into (60) or (64): however the resulting equations are cumbersome and expensive to estimate. An alternative approach is to assume that technical progress acts directly to change the parameters of the cost function. A particularly simple way to do this is to specify that

$$b_{ii}(t) = b_{ii}(0) + c_i t \quad (i = 1 \ldots n). \tag{67}$$

This technique is due to Parks (1971). Since only the diagonal terms of the substitution matrix change over time the symmetry constraint is not affected by this modification: however it is possible that the use of (67) might lead to violations of the concavity conditions on the cost function.

Equations (60) and (64) were estimated by Full Information Maximum Likelihood methods for two major UK manufacturing industries, engineering and motor vehicles, and for the time period 1954–68. The inputs were divided into five groups: labour, fuels, materials, services and capital goods. The data on labour input, gross investment and output is published in Armstrong (1974): data on other inputs was taken from the time series of social accounting matrices described by Barker (1972). Since the main aim of this paper was to focus on the choice between vintage and non-vintage models, no attempt was made to repeat earlier work (Peterson (1974)) and study the process of substitution within the broad groups. To give some idea about the scope for input substitution three alternative formulations were estimated for each model: the first of these, A, imposes only constant returns, while specification B restricts this by imposing the symmetry constraint on the substitution terms. Finally, specification C does not allow for any input substitution except between labour and investment goods.

Table 11.1 gives the resulting values, multiplied by two, of the log-likelihood function. Although it is not possible to make a clear choice between vintage and non-vintage models on the basis of these figures, since the two are not nested, they provide some evidence in favour of the non-vintage model. This is strengthened by noting that in every case the vector of single-equation R-squareds for the non-vintage model is uniformly greater than for the vintage model (these results are not presented in detail for reasons of space). The choice between alternative specifications of the substitution matrix can be based on the likelihood-ratio test. If this choice is made using the asymptotic distribution of the likelihood-ratio, the result is the rejection of the symmetry restrictions in both cases. If we proceed, conditionally on symmetry, to test the hypothesis that substitution is possible only between labour and investment goods, then

TABLE 11.1 Log-likelihood values

| | *Engineering* | | *Motor vehicles* | |
|---|---|---|---|---|
| | *Non-vintage* | *Vintage* | *Non-vintage* | *Vintage* |
| A (43) | –532.3527 | –544.1037† | 440.7758 | * |
| B (53) | –566.8167 | –621.7894† | –476.1934 | –507.3314 |
| C (62) | –584.2795 | –638.1000 | –496.9636 | –538.6376 |

$\chi^2_{.05}(10) = 18.3070$ $\chi^2_{.05}(9) = 16.9190$

*Model could not be estimated because of collinearity.
†Model did not converge fully.

TABLE 11.2 Coefficients and single-equation $R^2$ for engineering Model B (non-vintage)

| | Time | Relative prices | | | | | R-squared |
|---|---|---|---|---|---|---|---|
| Labour | −0.00174 | 0.07337 | −0.00512 | 0.07884 | 0.08092 | 0.11289* | 0.63526 |
| Fuels | 0.00065* | 0.00512 | −0.01775* | 0.00035 | 0.02532* | −0.00368 | 0.15974 |
| Materials | −0.00124 | 0.07884 | 0.00035 | 0.46002* | 0.00236 | −0.01315 | 0.71617 |
| Services | 0.00201 | 0.08092 | 0.02532* | 0.00236 | −0.01725 | −0.05757* | −0.08557 |
| Investment | 0.00032 | 0.11289* | −0.00368 | −0.01315 | −0.05757* | 0.01930 | 0.83546 |

Implied replacement equation: $I_t = K_t - K_{t-1} + (0.04253 - 0.00015t)Q_{t-1}$

*Partial elasticities of substitution*

| | | | | |
|---|---|---|---|---|
| −1.1425 | −117.5544 | 0.2215 | 2.4820 | 3.1971 |
| −117.5544 | * | 4.6585 | 3718.4692 | −499.2770 |
| 0.2215 | 4.6585 | −0.1182 | 0.0425 | −0.2182 |
| 2.4820 | 3718.4692 | 0.0425 | −12.9414 | −10.285 |
| 3.1971 | −499.2770 | −0.2182 | −10.4285 | −8.6916 |

TABLE 11.3 Coefficients and single-equation $R^2$ for motor vehicles Model B (non-vintage)

| | *Time* | *Relative prices* | | | | | *R-squared* |
|---|---|---|---|---|---|---|---|
| Employment | 0.00299 | −0.17098 | 0.11981 | 0.14393 | 0.08367* | 0.07585 | 0.7541 |
| Fuels | −0.00030 | 0.11981 | −0.01238 | −0.01409 | −0.00133 | −0.00480 | 0.7151 |
| Materials | −0.00494 | 0.14393 | 0.01409 | 0.38095* | 0.10208* | −0.02203 | 0.8946 |
| Services | −0.00177 | 0.08367* | −0.00133 | 0.10208* | −0.08451 | −0.04287 | 0.8325 |
| Investment | 0.00399 | 0.07585 | −0.00480 | −0.02203 | −0.04287 | −0.03323 | 0.5650 |

Implied replacement equation: $I_t = K_t - K_{t-1} + (0.03755^* - 0.00177^* t)Q_{t-1}$

*Partial elasticities of substitution*

| | | | | |
|---|---|---|---|---|
| −7.6237 | 4.4194 | 0.7446 | 3.9969 | −12.9840 |
| 4.4194 | −111.9408 | 1.0471 | −0.9094 | 11.7931 |
| 0.7446 | 1.0471 | −0.2536 | 0.9819 | 0.7591 |
| 3.9969 | −0.9094 | 0.9819 | −13.5129 | 13.6433 |
| −12.9840 | 11.7931 | 0.7591 | 13.6433 | −9.3236 |

this restriction is also rejected. However these results should not be interpreted as an outright refutation of the hypothesis of cost minimisation. The use of asymptotic test criteria leads to a bias in favour of rejection, since it is known (Anderson (1958)) that in linear models the use of approximations to the small sample distribution of the likelihood ratio test is less likely to lead to rejection, and it is plausible that analogous results will hold for non-linear models. Secondly it is of course impossible to distinguish between a rejection of the underlying hypothesis of cost-minimisation, and a rejection of the specific functional form selected for the cost function and input demand functions.

Tables 11.2 and 11.3 give coefficient values, single equation R-squareds and partial elasticities of substitution for 1963 for the non-vintage models (subject to the symmetry constraint). Coefficients which are significantly different from zero at the 5 per cent level are marked with an asterisk. The existence of negative values for some of the relative price coefficients indicates that the concavity conditions on the underlying cost function may be violated for some input price vectors. Since the necessary conditions for $C(q,w)$ to be increasing and concave in the components of $w$ are

$$\frac{\partial c}{\partial w_i} = v_i = h(q)\, w_i^{-1/2} \sum_j b_{ij} w_j^{1/2} > 0 \qquad (68)$$

$$\frac{\partial^2 C}{\partial w_i \partial w_j} \text{ negative semi-definite}$$

it is necessary to check the inequalities in (68) for each observation. The results of this check showed that both the estimated cost functions are not concave within the sample period: in addition the cost function for motor vehicles is decreasing in the price of investment goods. This latter result arises partly from the *ad hoc* way in which the replacement component of gross investment has been specified: since if calculated replacement demand is large relative to gross investment, and in some years exceeds it, the estimated expansion of the capital stock will be small or negative. Hence, given the imposition of constant returns on all the input demand equations, the resulting cost function will be unsatisfactory. However this reasoning cannot be applied to explain the fact that the cost function for engineering is decreasing in fuel prices for the period 1954–62: this result is due to the operation of the time trend and may reflect the change in fuel inputs from coal towards oil and electricity.

The implicit production function for the technology implied by the estimated set of input demand functions can be calculated using equation (59). The results of these calculations are shown in Tables 11.4 and 11.5.

TABLE 11.4 Implicit production function: Engineering

| *Year* | *Actual* | *Predicted* | *Error* |
|---|---|---|---|
| 1954 | 3,195.42 | 2,804.40 | 391.02 |
| 1955 | 3,432.98 | 3,041.01 | 391.97 |
| 1956 | 3,422.73 | 3,052.12 | 370.61 |
| 1957 | 3,557.38 | 3,294.46 | 262.92 |
| 1958 | 3,574.85 | 3,167.06 | 407.79 |
| 1959 | 3,775.73 | 3,342.68 | 433.05 |
| 1960 | 4,078.03 | 3,619.72 | 458.31 |
| 1961 | 4,351.35 | 3,919.06 | 432.29 |
| 1962 | 4,413.93 | 3,989.41 | 424.52 |
| 1963 | 4,531.00 | 3,918.98 | 612.02 |
| 1964 | 4,925.78 | 4,394.53 | 531.25 |
| 1965 | 5,135.75 | 4,678.29 | 457.46 |
| 1966 | 5,403.41 | 5,073.12 | 330.29 |
| 1967 | 5,458.09 | 5,126.67 | 331.43 |
| 1968 | 5,609.24 | 5,372.57 | 236.67 |

This was done for both industries, and the resulting charts of actual and potential output are given as Figs. 11.1 and 11.2. These show that the model is capable of following most of the important fluctuations in output. Thus it appears that nothing has been lost by using a model in which the explicit production function cannot be directly represented, and in which the system of demand functions is derived directly from the cost function. Since in this case the cost function chosen leads to demand

TABLE 11.5 Implicit production function: Motor vehicles

| *Year* | *Actual* | *Predicted* | *Error* |
|---|---|---|---|
| 1954 | 1,004.67 | 1,094.89 | −90.22 |
| 1955 | 1,164.23 | 1,290.68 | −126.46 |
| 1956 | 1,011.03 | 1,150.26 | −139.23 |
| 1957 | 1,113.20 | 1,210.87 | −97.68 |
| 1958 | 1,239.02 | 1,435.94 | −196.92 |
| 1959 | 1,468.03 | 1,678.51 | −210.48 |
| 1960 | 1,718.20 | 1,925.99 | −207.78 |
| 1961 | 1,544.12 | 1,698.51 | −154.39 |
| 1962 | 1,649.07 | 1,773.22 | −124.15 |
| 1963 | 1,931.00 | 1,976.18 | −45.18 |
| 1964 | 2,139.55 | 2,213.93 | −74.38 |
| 1965 | 2,155.37 | 2,244.50 | −89.13 |
| 1966 | 2,157.44 | 2,262.50 | −105.11 |
| 1967 | 2,022.41 | 2,149.69 | −127.28 |
| 1968 | 2,243.80 | 2,419.30 | −175.50 |

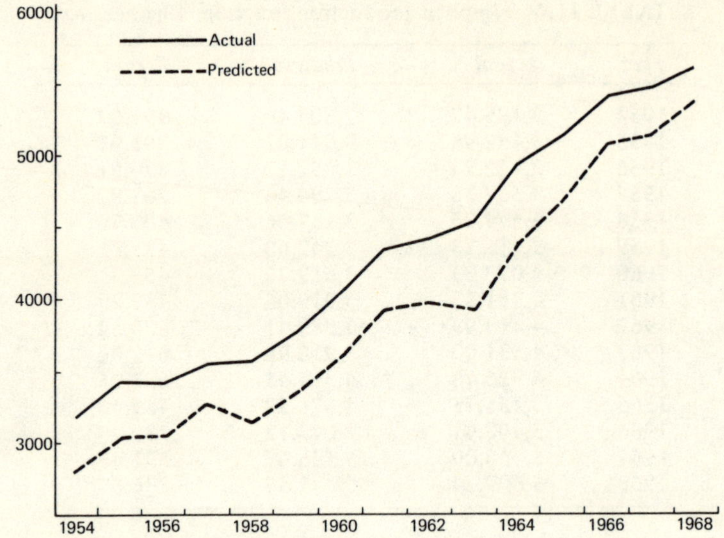


FIG. 11.1 Actual and potential output: Engineering

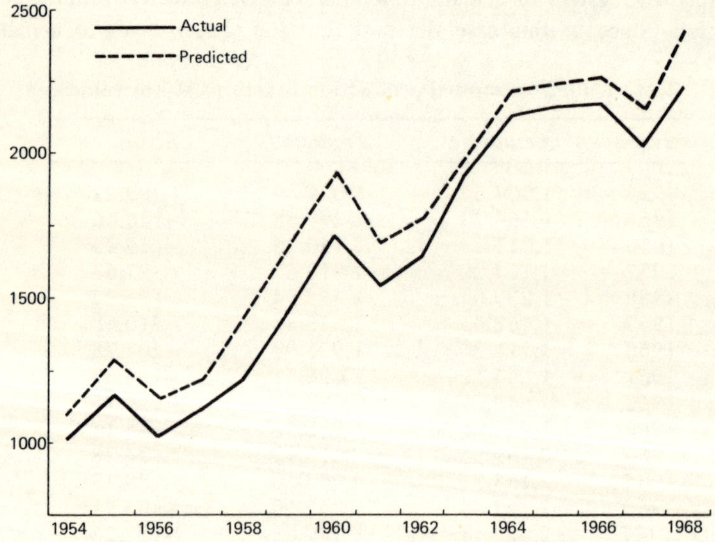


FIG. 11.2 Actual and potential output: Motor vehicles

functions which are linear and which allow for the testing of a wide range of hypotheses about substitution possibilities and the separability of technology, it is clear that the approach can have substantial benefits.

## NOTES

I am grateful to members of the Cambridge Growth Project, and the participants at the Southampton Conference on the Measurement of Capital, for their helpful comments.

## REFERENCES

Allen, R. G. D. (1938), *Mathematical Analysis for Economists* (London: Macmillan).

Anderson, T. W. (1958), *An Introduction to Multivariate Statistical Analysis* (New York: John Wiley & Sons).

Armstrong, A.G. (1974), *Structural Change in the British Economy 1948–68*, Vol. 12 of Stone, R. (ed.), *A Programme for Growth*, (London: Chapman and Hall).

Atkinson, A.B. and Stiglitz, J. E. (1969), 'A New View of Technological Change', *Economic Journal*, September, pp. 573–8.

Barker, T. S. (1972), *Updated Social Accounting Matrices: U.K. Commodity Accounts 1954–68*, Growth Project Paper 363, Department of Applied Economics, University of Cambridge.

Barten, A. P., Kloek, T. and Lempers, F. B. (1969), 'A Note on a Class of Utility and Production Functions Yielding Everywhere Differentiable Demand Functions', *Review of Economic Studies*, January, pp. 109–11.

Berndt, E. R. and Christensen L. R. (1973), 'The Internal Structure of Functional Relationships: Separability, Substitution and Aggregation', *Review of Economic Studies*, July, pp. 403–10.

Christensen, L. R., Jorgenson D. W. and Lau, L. J. (1973), 'Transcendental Logarithmic Production Frontiers', *Review of Economics and Statistics*, February, pp. 28–45.

Deaton, A. S. (1974), 'A Reconsideration of the Empirical Implications of Additive Preferences', *Economic Journal*, June, pp. 338–49.

Denny, M. (1974), 'The Relationship between Functional Forms for the Production System', *Canadian Journal of Economics*, February, pp. 21–31.

Diewert, W. E. (1971), 'An Application of the Shephard Duality Theorem: a Generalised Leontief Production Function', *Journal of Political Economy*, pp. 481–507.

Geary, P. T. and M. Morishima (1973), 'Demand and Supply under Separability' in Morishima, M. (ed.) Theory of Demand, (Oxford University Press).

Goldman, S. M. and Uzawa, H. (1964), 'A Note on Separability in Demand Analysis, *Econometrica*, July, pp. 387–98.

Gorman, W. M. (1959), 'Separable Utility and Aggregation', *Econometrica*, July, pp. 469–81.

Greub, W. H. (1963), *Linear Algebra* (Berlin: Springer-Verlag).

Hotelling, H. (1932), 'Edgeworth's Taxation Paradox and the Nature of Demand and Supply Functions', *Journals of Political Economy*, October, pp. 577–616.

Kiefer, N. H. (1975), *Quadratic Utility, Labor Supply and Commodity Demand*, Paper presented to 3rd World Congress of the Econometric Society, Toronto.

Morishima, M. (1964), *Equilibrium, Stability and Growth*, (Oxford University Press).

Parks, R. W. (1971), 'Price Responsiveness of Factor Utilisation in Swedish Manufacturing, 1870–1950'. *Review of Economics and Statistics*, May, pp. 129–39.

Peterson, A. W. A. (1974), *Factor Demand Equations and Input-Output Analysis*, Paper presented to Sixth International Conference on Input-Output Techniques, Vienna, April.

Sato, K. (1967), 'A Two-Level Constant Elasticity of Substitution Production Function', *Review of Economic Studies*, April, pp. 201–18.

Shephard, R. W. (1970), *Theory of Cost and Production Functions*, Princeton Studies in Mathematical Economics 4 (Princeton University Press).

Theil, H. (1975), *Theory and Measurement of Consumer Demand* (Amsterdam: North Holland).

Uzawa, H. (1962), 'Production Functions with Constant Elasticities of Substitution', *Review of Economic Studies*, October, pp. 291–9.

# Index